One (Un)Like the Other

SUNY series in Theology and Continental Thought
―――――――
Douglas L. Donkel, editor

One (Un)Like the Other

Rethinking Ethics, Empathy, and
Transcendence from Husserl to Derrida

MICHAEL F. ANDREWS

Cover Credit: Michelangelo, *The Creation of Adam* [detail]. c. 1512.

Published by State University of New York Press, Albany

© 2024 State University of New York

All rights reserved

Printed in the United States of America

No part of this book may be used or reproduced in any manner whatsoever without written permission. No part of this book may be stored in a retrieval system or transmitted in any form or by any means including electronic, electrostatic, magnetic tape, mechanical, photocopying, recording, or otherwise without the prior permission in writing of the publisher.

Links to third-party websites are provided as a convenience and for informational purposes only. They do not constitute an endorsement or an approval of any of the products, services, or opinions of the organization, companies, or individuals. SUNY Press bears no responsibility for the accuracy, legality, or content of a URL, the external website, or for that of subsequent websites.

For information, contact State University of New York Press, Albany, NY
www.sunypress.edu

Library of Congress Cataloging-in-Publication Data

Name: Andrews, Michael F., author.
Title: One (un)like the other : rethinking ethics, empathy, and transcendence from Husserl to Derrida / Michael F. Andrews.
Description: Albany : State University of New York Press, [2024] | Series: SUNY series in Theology and Continental Thought | Includes bibliographical references and index.
Identifiers: ISBN 9781438499291 (hardcover : alk. paper) | ISBN 9781438499314 (ebook) | ISBN 9781438499307 (pbk. : alk. paper)
Further information is available at the Library of Congress.

For Monica
. . . incipit la vita nuova . . .

You never really understand a person until you consider things from his point of view . . . until you climb inside of his skin and walk around in it.

—Harper Lee, *To Kill a Mockingbird*

Recognize what is before your eyes, and what is hidden will be revealed to you.

—*The Gospel of Thomas*

Contents

List of Abbreviations — ix

Acknowledgments — xi

Introduction — 1

Part One:
Empathy and the Theory of Transcendental Constitution

Introduction — 15

Chapter One
Husserl's Transcendental Turn: Empathy and the Task of the
Phenomenological Reduction — 19

Chapter Two
The Fifth Cartesian Meditation — 37

Chapter Three
The Significance of Empathy as Developed in *Ideas II*, with
Reference to Husserl's Later Works on Intersubjectivity — 65

Part Two:
Empathy as Reciprocity

Introduction — 101

Chapter Four
Max Scheler and the Phenomenology of Human Community   107

Chapter Five
Edith Stein and the Problem of Empathy   133

Chapter Six
Embodiment, Temporality, and Emotions in Acts of Empathy   149

Part Three:
A Reversal of the Law of Empathy

Introduction   169

Chapter Seven
Martin Heidegger's Critique of Empathy   173

Chapter Eight
Emmanuel Levinas and the Face of the Other   189

Chapter Nine
Jacques Derrida and the Possibility of an Empathic Antipathy   217

Part Four:
Ethics, Empathy, and Transcendence

Introduction   239

Chapter Ten
Gender and Reciprocity   247

Chapter Eleven
Empathy and an Ethics of (In)Finite Respect   263

Notes   279

Selected Bibliography   319

Index   337

Abbreviations

The following is a list of abbreviations for frequently cited works in this text. Full bibliographical information for all works appears in the endnotes and bibliography.

Works by Jacques Derrida

VM: *Violence and Metaphysics*

Works by Martin Heidegger

BT: *Being and Time*

Works by Edmund Husserl

CM: *Cartesian Meditations*
Ideas I: *Ideas Pertaining to a Pure Phenomenology and to a Phenomenological Philosophy, Book 1*
Ideas II: *Ideas Pertaining to a Pure Phenomenology and to a Phenomenological Philosophy, Book 2: Studies in the Phenomenology of Constitution*
IoP: *The Idea of Phenomenology*

Works by Emmanuel Levinas

EE: *Existence and Existents*
TI: *Totality and Infinity*
T&O: *Time and the Other*

Works by Max Scheler

FE: *Formalism in Ethics and Non-Formal Ethics of Values*
FKV: *On Feeling, Knowing, and Valuing*
Sympathy: *On Sympathy*

Works by Edith Stein

LJF: *Life in a Jewish Family: An Unfinished Autobiography*
Empathy: *On the Problem of Empathy*
PPH: *Philosophy of Psychology and the Humanities*
Letters: *Self-Portrait in Letters: 1916–1942*

Acknowledgments

This text, through its many forms and edits, originated from a basic philosophical question that concealed a vast and dangerous array of hidden perplexity. One evening during dinner and following a graduate seminar at Yale, "The Sacred and the Beautiful," professor Louis Dupré refilled my glass of wine and asked me, with a nonchalant wink of his eye, "What do you think are the conditions of possibility that make genuine knowledge of other persons—and, therefore, love—possible?" This study is my circuitous and hesitatingly deficient response to that question. We had been talking about mystical trends in modern thought, and moments earlier Dupré recommended I become familiar with Edith Stein's writings on Husserl, Thomas Aquinas, and John of the Cross. The question, of course, has been asked and re-asked in various ways and in infinite contexts for millennia by philosophers and lovers alike. From Plato's *Symposium* to Nietzsche's *Zarathustra*, "love" and its proper ordering—to quote the likes of St. Augustine (from his Easter Homily in 407 CE) as well as philosophers as diverse as Kierkegaard, Spinoza, Kant, and Blondel—remains restless and incomplete until it "does what it wills."

Alas, such "willing" can be complicated stuff, especially when the rigors of time and responsibility take hold. Over the years, a question posed to me during a playful dinner conversation concerning Hegel and Heidegger on the meaning of the work of art unfolded into myriad opportunities that have spanned years of reflection and research. This book, then, has been long in coming; it is a result of ideas gathered from unwritten thoughts, published essays and book chapters, conference presentations, dissertation and research drafts, journal entries, and countless discussions with colleagues and critics alike. It especially draws from my own teaching experiences at the undergraduate and graduate levels, including lectures and seminars given at universities that I have called "home" and that have nurtured and challenged my intellectual and spiritual journey along life's way: Georgetown and Yale; the Pontifical Gregorian University in Rome; Fairfield, Villanova, and Seattle universities; the University of Portland; and Loyola University Chicago. Of course, whatever insights I've been able to gather, from collaborative and professional publications, conference presentations, scholarly lectures, and senior-level administrative experiences, point to one conclusion—namely, that nothing herein is original in the sense that all our thoughts and insights are co-constituted in a web of mutuality and reciprocity. Empathy is a kind of *revelation* that posits we are part and parcel of a multiplicity of horizons and "lifeworlds" that shape, challenge, and inspire us, as Husserl might say.

And so, it is with immense gratitude that I warmly acknowledge my late mentors—Michael J. Buckley, SJ; Louis Dupré; Jitendra Mohanty; Peter Henrici, SJ; Hans Frei; and Monica Hellwig—under whose guidance I had the pleasure of studying and whose fingerprints, mentorship, and subtle observations over the course of many years can be found everywhere on these pages. I am grateful to professors John D. Caputo, Thomas Busch, and Barbara Wall, whose early insights and mature prodding both challenged and sustained my original foray into exploring the phenomenology of empathy in general and the theme of "empathy as ethics" in particular. I am grateful to my professional colleagues, especially from the International Association for the Study of the Philosophy of Edith Stein (the "Edith Stein Circle") and the Society for Phenomenology and the Human Sciences, who have listened, agreed, and argued with me through various social gatherings, conferences, and professional publications. While I hope they will take credit for what I "get right," they hold no responsibility for my own intellectual failings and shortfalls. I am especially indebted to the anonymous external reviewers who read and commented on various stages of this manuscript. Their brilliant and careful attention to issues and details that I missed along the way is deeply appreciated and most gratefully noted. I hope my responses to their generous comments and reflections meet their justifiable expectations. Also a special and most sincere note of thanks to Douglas L. Donkel and James Peltz, gifted editors at SUNY Press, and their remarkable and helpful editorial team.

Finally, to my parents, who passed away far too many years ago, and to my wife, Monica, and my daughter, Elisa—and to our "other kids" Bacio and Luna, who kept me company through many ups and downs over long hours of writing, researching, editing, and rewriting—I share a profound and heartfelt "grazie per tutto ciò che avete reso possible."

My cup runneth over.

December 21, 2023
East Matunuck, Rhode Island

Introduction

What are the conditions of possibility that make genuine knowledge of other persons—and, therefore, love—possible?

The Task of Rethinking Ethics

My aim in this book is to rethink ethics and transcendence in light of the phenomenology of empathy and social ontology. In everyday speech, the word "empathy" is often used in an overly simplified manner that may lead to naive assumptions and even misunderstandings about its complex social and ethical implications. Generally speaking, empathy is the capacity to understand or feel what another person is experiencing from their own reference or standpoint. Empathy is intrinsically tied to emotive, cognitive, social, and psychological processes of understanding and interpretation, and not merely about substitutional or vicarious transference of feelings. It is toward an analysis of these complex processes of understanding, including the origin of psycho-spiritual values, intersubjectivity, and the genesis of authentic community, that we are interested in exploring. To what extent can I "know" or "see" the world from an Other's perspective? How can I be certain if the world that I see is the same world that you see? To what extent can I experience the world in its objective concreteness apart from the certainty of my own existence? Is genuine relationship with others possible if by "Other" is meant precisely that-which-is-not-me? Or, perhaps better stated, If "I" and "Other" share similar feelings, understandings, and values, in what way can it be said that I am different from the Other, from all others, and vice versa? Upon even a cursory exploration, we note that empathy announces both sameness and difference. Consequently, what is meant by the "Other" manifests the horizon of our inquiry. What I want to explore by way of phenomenology, then, is the givenness of person-in-the-world, living always and everywhere with Others.[1] It may be thus noted that we stand at an abyss of complexities, including ethical and metaphysical, concerning human freedom and transcendence.

A focus of this study is the theme of social ontology, a branch of philosophy that examines how phenomena, including the world itself, arise through social interaction. In particular, we are interested in exploring the origin of values and the genesis of authentic community through phenomenological inquiry, especially as developed early on by Edmund Husserl and his students and colleagues in the 1910s and 1920s.[2] Generally speaking, we will explore the givenness of the Other in terms of embodiment, alterity, and transcendence. Our starting point is that empathy describes the awareness *sui generis* of a primordial experience of a non-primordial experience. It is a condition of my being-in-the-world, a way of interpreting the meaning of personal and social experience. In terms of ethics and objectivity, empathy describes how consciousness apprehends the world as a "we-world" of shared, lived experiences.[3] Consequently, by "Other" is designated everything *not*-me, whether defined as objects, thoughts, a singular "Thou," or a plurality of things and individuals. We call the total collection of real and possible objects "phenomena." Hence, by "the phenomenology of empathy" is meant the study by which consciousness grasps objects in the real or imagined world as phenomena of human experience, *including itself*. Largely relegated by Edmund Husserl in the first half of the twentieth century to epistemologically based descriptions of monadic constitution, later theorists of the phenomenology of empathy began to explore additional analyses that gave priority to the order of experience in describing the constitution of the world in terms of intersubjectivity and the emotions. These more robust accounts of the constitutive nature of consciousness in general are included in what I will explore in terms of social ontology. By conceiving of the emotions as equi-primordial centers of value along with cognition, many of Husserl's earliest students and colleagues—including Max Scheler, Edith Stein, Adolf Reinach, and Roman Ingarden—began to explore the growing role that emotions and embodiment play in describing the constitution of the objective world. What was for Husserl a rather strict and formal model of cognitive constitution erupts in the second half of the twentieth century through critical analyses of a number of Husserl's philosophical assumptions by several of his former students, most notably Emmanuel Levinas and Jacques Derrida, in terms of more radical descriptions of ethics and alterity, including deconstruction.

Phenomenologically speaking, empathy describes how the Other is constituted or grasped or experienced as something like me, only different. Such grasping of what is *not*-me implies the givenness of the Other in terms of alterity. Even as I grasp the Other as other, the Other, *precisely as other*, slips from my fingers. A constitutive relationship between alterity and transcendence is essential in every act of genuine understanding. As we shall explore at length, empathy describes how the Other is constituted in terms of alterity and transcendence, how the Other is given (so to speak) as a phenomenon of encounter in the world. Without the Other, the "I" remains elusive, inadequate, fictive, and unattainable, a specter or ghostly presence. Empathy describes how the Other gets embodied or constituted in a sea of intersubjectivity. Empathy is therefore Other-directed; it reveals the givenness of phenomena and at the same time distinguishes "my" experience from experiences of every Other.

The Historical Emergence of Empathy

The phenomenology of empathy entails an investigation into the relationship between epistemology and ethics according to a single thematic of "alterity" that runs from Husserl to Derrida and includes Max Scheler, Edith Stein, Martin Heidegger, and Emmanuel Levinas, among others. Broadly speaking, empathy emerged as an issue of philosophical concern in the early 1900s, when a growing number of philosophers and social scientists began to explore empathy as a way of responding to developments in the newly emerging fields of psychology, sociology, and political science. Whereas Theodor Lipps had initially adhered the theory of empathy or *Einfühlung* ("in-feeling") as an unconscious "fusion" between the self and its object of perception, this faulty understanding of empathy led to a common misunderstanding that empathy was a trait of inner imitation or "sympathy" that all people share. Such naive optimism soon ran amuck amidst the devastating human and cultural losses that ravaged Europe during the Great War that began with an assassin's bullet in 1914.[4]

Shortly after November 11, 1919, a false optimism engendered by the League of Nations dominated talk of empathy theory in diplomatic conversations and academic institutions from London to New York, Berlin to Rome, Paris to Moscow. Discussions concerning social and economic restructuring of a new world order hinged on a Wilsonian vision that future wars could be avoided by developing a sense of "cultural empathy" based on historic and international cooperation between nations and cultures. Following the signing of the Armistice Treaty at Versailles, however, German academic discussions that had previously focused on empathy theory in the early 1910s began to give way in the 1920s to more pressing concerns in Freiburg and München.

As the economically depressed early 1930s gave way to a rising militant tide of ideological extremism, there resulted in Germany a coordinated attack against nonracial empathy theories under the propagandist machine fueled by the National Socialist Party. Infamous Nazi ideologues such as Hans F. K. Günther, Alfred Rosenberg, and Joseph Goebbels developed institutionalized systems of propaganda in order to disseminate mounting racial laws that began classifying all non-Aryans as more or less *Untermenschen* ("subhuman"). Based on the Nazi idealization of *Blut und Boten* ("blood and soil"), Rosenberg's *The Myth of the Twentieth Century*, published in 1930, ushered in a bestial attempt to denigrate nascent empathy theories that had been able to reject racially based government policies.[5] In their place, Nazi literature sought to legitimize National Socialist racial policy as the singular antidote to all social and economic ills. Almost overnight, official Nazi propagandists began to denounce as degenerate and *anti-Volk* any philosophical or artistic theory that did not expound the virtue of racial distinction. Ideologically organized attacks against empathy theory as a way of organizing the state were clearly underway.

The carnage and destruction of innumerable lives, including those of European Jews between the years 1939 and 1944, remains a disturbing legacy that continues to haunt us to this day.[6] Even now, in light of increasing racial tensions, ideologically inspired acts of terrorism, the rising tide and reemergence of nationalism and populism, and increasing exposure of environmental degradation—along with the perceived dehumanization of vast populations of people due to economic, religious, cultural, and gender exploitation—the *lack* of a proper understanding of cultural empathy threatens to tear at the very fabric of human society. A comprehensive phenomenological description of empathy is therefore both timely and relevant. By "phenomenology of empathy" is meant a critical examination of the intellectual and ethical capacities by which human beings recognize and appreciate cultural differences and diverse perspectives concerning the nature of human reality. A proper understanding of empathy is essential for responding to complex ethical issues facing human communities, especially the needs of those who suffer from the effects of war, poverty, resource deprivation, and both blatant and hidden forms of discrimination based on gender, sexual identity, religion, and cultural and racial profiling. Turning to its philosophical origin, empathy describes the phenomenality of foreign experience. Epistemologically formulated, empathy describes how the body of the other is primordially given whereas the other's conscious life is analogically apperceived. In terms of ethics, what is at stake is a revaluation of vast expanses of populations and historically conditioned systems of legal and economic assumptions, religious beliefs, and social artifacts.

What empathy makes manifest is that the Other is never given without some kind of accompanying ethical orientation. Every act of givenness entails a genealogy or precognitive stream or flow of nonconscious life by which the Other *as other* is both perceived and valued. A primary ethical analysis concerning the phenomenology of empathy, then, requires stepping outside merely binary-based ways of seeing and defining reality. The phenomenology of empathy explores ethics as first a philosophy and not a derivative of cultural ideology or the artificial construction of social values writ large in terms of grand historical narratives. The emergence of a nonbinary relationship between ethics, ontology, and epistemology is therefore an underlying theme of the investigation of the phenomenology of empathy. How does the data of foreign experience point to differing structures of value-acts from which foreign experience is comprehended *as such*? The problem of empathy—that is, the phenomenological description of the givenness of other persons—must be recast in terms of intersubjectivity and the emergent ethical relationship between epistemology, ontology, and metaphysics. The question "How can I have knowledge of other persons?" poses an incomplete articulation of the problem unless two other questions are posed alongside it: (1) "What is the *origin* of such knowledge?" and (2) "How is experience of the Other gained and warranted in terms of ethical actions?" It is with these questions that we begin our exploration.

The Scope of Inquiry

Our method of inquiry will be primarily thematic rather than merely historical. We will investigate three different models or approaches to the phenomenology of empathy based on three different accounts of alterity given by Edmund Husserl and two of his most distinguished students: Edith Stein, who received her PhD under Husserl summa cum laude in 1916 and served as his research assistant from 1916 to 1918, and Emmanuel Levinas, who studied at Freiburg in the final months of Husserl's distinguished career and translated *Cartesian Meditations* into French in 1931. There is no indication that Stein and Levinas ever met or read one another's work, though both authors drank from the same Husserlian spring, so to speak. In order to accentuate the different orientations of each formalized theory, I will focus my investigation on a few exemplary texts from each author. Because a lengthy introduction to each of the three parts explains the historical and thematic settings for what is included in those chapters, I shall now provide a brief overview of the project in its most general scope and methodology.

Turning to tensions drawn from ethical dimensions of constitution, we will compare and contrast three different thematic approaches to the phenomenology of empathy, based mainly on Husserl's written and public texts that were published and therefore widely known by his students and colleagues in the 1910s and 1920s. Some additional reflections involving later posthumous texts, notes, and lectures published after Husserl's death will also be referenced, though these texts were never formally approved by Husserl during his lifetime (such as *Ideas II* and works centered on intersubjectivity later published in *Husserliana* volumes XIII, XIV, and XV). The first approach involves an egocentric model of rational apperception, by which the self has no direct grasp of what is presumed to be shared by the Other and so operates mainly by analogy. The second model holds that human reality is essentially constituted by intersubjective reciprocity, that human beings are primordially part of an interconnected network of social relationships, and that knowledge of other persons is built into this social network. The third model approaches the philosophical problem of the givenness of other persons by reversing the direction of intentionality and denying any positive role to empathy whatsoever. It describes the Other as an event that comes from outside every horizon of expectability by laying an ethical (and hence unconditional) claim upon me. Two underlying themes we shall follow throughout this study concern the role that empathy plays in establishing an epistemological foundation for the self, along with the relationship of that epistemology to ethics.

In part one, "Empathy and the Theory of Transcendental Constitution," we will explore how Husserl represents the conceptual approach of modern transcendental philosophy. Husserl argues that the question of the Other is always posed in connection with the problem of world constitution. Because transcendental phenomenology encounters the Other as an alien I, as *alter ego*, the Other is said to be constituted by pairing and analogical apperception. This means that the alien I—the Other—is an object of intentionality, not its origin in the order of experience; similarly, in the order of knowledge, upon lifting the reduction to the sphere of ownness it is the embodied encounter of the other person into my sphere of perception that inaugurates a transfer of sense from me to the Other. In chapter one we will investigate the first four of Husserl's *Cartesian Meditations*, followed by a comprehensive analysis of the transcendental constitution of the Objective world in chapter two, drawn from Husserl's famous Fifth Cartesian meditation. Husserl's account of the reduction to the sphere of ownness remains a classic articulation of empathy in terms of transcendental phenomenology. Hence, it is indispensable for introducing the founding sense of empathy or *Einfühlung* into our discussion.

By offering a detailed exegesis of *Ideas II* in chapter three, we will investigate the structure of intentionality, especially the role that empathy plays in the constitution of the common and material world, the animate world, and the spiritual and cultural world. Although the cultural world is the shared (objective) world of intersubjectively constituted values, for Husserl the origin of reciprocity remains monadological. Without empathy, there can be no objective world of common objects or shared values. This means that empathy is necessary for intersubjective experienceability. Empathic constitution is based upon an intersubjectively experienceable Body (*Leib*) that can be understood by the person who enacts the *act* of empathy as the Body of the corresponding psychic being. By making a distinction between the body as *Leib*, the living body, and *Körper*, the body as inanimate physical matter, Husserl concludes that the living body (*Leib*) makes empathy possible, since it is the other's living body that draws me into pairing. Bodies, of course, can be multiple and social; hence, the living body of the Other is for Husserl a requirement for constitution. I cannot constitute my own participation in pairing just as I cannot by myself constitute the origin of the transcendental Ego or the lived stream of internal time consciousness. This means I am motivated to an immediate yet peripheral pairing of bodies. The living body of the Other draws from me an imaginative capacity to transfer my *here* to the Other's *there*.

In part two, "Empathy and Reciprocity," we turn our attention to the wider scope of the empathy debate popular in Göttingen in the early

1910s. In chapter four, we shall turn to an investigation concerning the influence of Max Scheler and his profound effect on the fledgling phenomenological community, including Edith Stein. We will examine Scheler's argument regarding the genesis of community that the givenness of the Other concerns (a) the meaning and intelligibility of human emotions and (b) the way in which community is constituted by the sharing of feelings and thoughts among individual persons. In sharp contrast to Husserlian constitution, Scheler holds that a primordial "psychic stream" exists prior to constitution into which everyone is swept at birth before the emergence of experiential differentiation. This rejection of Husserl's reduction to the sphere of ownness means that Scheler's task was not so much to describe how the Other gets constituted as it was to explain the process by which the "I" differentiates itself *from* the Other.

One implication of Scheler's thesis is that values are not solely constituted monadologically or merely cognitively. Rather, we feel-into things (*Einfühlen*). Such feeling-into provides the basis from which conscious activity emerges. Because every experience is constituted by the primacy of the givenness of human emotions, Scheler concludes that cognitive activity is a secondary, derivative phenomenon. What he means is that emotions, along with cognition, discern the essences of values. Since emotions inform the will, Scheler argues *contra* Husserl that the constitution of other human beings implies a pre-conscious, *pre-*egoic activity.

Next, we shall turn to a formal analysis of Edith Stein's philosophical contributions to the phenomenology of the givenness of other persons in chapter five. Stein in effect offers a Schelerian modification of Husserl's strict epistemological description of constitution by emphasizing how embodiment, affectivity, and the emotions are drawn from Husserl's description of constitution of the person in terms of reciprocity, including through the encounter of *emotional* experience. Stein's early philosophical work on empathy offers a profound contribution to the early phenomenological circle gathered around Husserl. Although she worked alongside fellow phenomenologists such as Max Scheler, Martin Heidegger, Roman Ingarden, Adolf Reinach, and Edmund Husserl, I submit that the notoriety afforded to her male colleagues was largely eclipsed due to Stein's gender and later to her being Jewish. Her feminine voice was overshadowed by the intellectual milieu of early 1900 Germany, which made it virtually impossible for her to hold a teaching position at the university level as a woman, let alone a Jewish woman in pre-1930s Germany. A critical assessment of Stein's work on empathy may offer important critical insights about how *Einfühlung* discloses constitution from the psychological realm to the spiritual or cultural lifeworld.

Edith Stein studied under both Husserl and Scheler, and so her dissertation, *On the Problem of Empathy*, can be read as a theory of interpretation (hermeneutic) of the human person that explores some of the tensions that existed between Scheler and Husserl.[7] Edith Stein describes *Einfühlung* primarily in terms of the question of the givenness of others, yet modifies Husserl's strict epistemological project in order to co-privilege the emotions and affective life. Indebted to Husserl's epistemological description of constitution, Stein emphasizes the unitive structure of embodied consciousness and the unambiguous role that the body plays in every act of perception. Stein offers a phenomenological account of how foreign subjects and their experiences are given through what she describes as the "current of community," though in a way different from Scheler's notion of an "undifferentiated stream." For Stein, the Other announces a foreign experience that disrupts the strictly monadological origin that Husserlian epistemology took for granted. Reciprocity and the constitution of social community, investigated in chapter six, explores the process by which I and Other co-constitute the shared life of a particular community by way of social ontology. According to Edith Stein, empathy describes the genesis of community in terms of reciprocal dependencies between individuals and cultural phenomena.

Part three, "A Reversal of the Law of Empathy," presents a response to the problem of empathy that is perhaps best represented by Martin Heidegger's rejection of empathy and Levinas's even more radical reversal of Husserlian constitution. In chapter seven, we will explore Martin Heidegger's existential critique of Husserl's transcendental phenomenology in his discussion of "the *they*" in *Being and Time*. Heidegger's rejection of Husserl's phenomenology of empathy sets the stage for Levinas's fundamental critique of Husserl's theory of constitution, discussed in chapter eight. In *Totality and Infinity*, Levinas rejects Husserl's transcendental description of intentionality out of hand. Levinas raises a critique against Husserl's phenomenological method by arguing that empathy has no moral signification whatsoever. In effect, Levinas reverses Husserl's arrow of intentionality. As we will discuss in depth, Levinas argues that Husserl's account concerning the ego's constitution of the Other ultimately compromises the alterity of the Other, thereby leading to a sort of ethical (and hence metaphysical) solipsism. On account of this radical reversal of Husserl's description of intentionality, Levinas argues that the face of the Other *founds* ethics in that the face of the other comes from outside every horizon of expectation. The face speaks, and its voice betrays an infinity that I can neither comprehend nor constitute. Hence, whereas for Husserl the Other is given through eidetic laws of perception, and for Stein the Other is co-constitutive in every act of reciprocal value making, for Levinas the Other lies structurally outside every realm of expectation, outside the structure of intentionality—that is, outside every condition of possibility of rationality and foreseeability. Levinas's reversal of Husserl's arrow of intentionality means that the Other remains irreducibly and *wholly other*. The radical alterity of the Other reveals a totality and infinity that allows neither access nor compromise. For Levinas, this means that ethics is first philosophy, prior to ontology and irreducible to empathy.

Although the critical work of Levinas in effect reverses the arrow of Husserl's model of intentionality, Levinas's dis-privileging of the role that Husserl assigns to cognition in favor of ethics contains the seeds of its own undoing. For example, in a critique of Levinas in his essay "Violence and Metaphysics," Jacques Derrida argues that Levinas's wholly Other cannot be "wholly" *other*. Otherwise, the wholly Other would be wholly unrecognizable. Instead, as we will discuss in chapter nine, Derrida claims that Levinas's ethical asymmetry presupposes a transcendental symmetry in the order of knowledge. What Derrida shows is that, for Levinas, some form of analogy must exist between the same and the Other. In calling such analogical symmetry an *antipathy*, I mean to imply that the wholly Other requires as a condition of possibility that it not be *wholly* other. For the Other to be recognized *as* Other—that is, like me, only different—the Other requires a trace of the same; it requires an experience of empathy.

Finally, in part four, "Empathy, Ethics and Transcendence," we will draw on the phenomenology of empathy as a lens to explore the givenness of transcendence and alterity in terms of ethics. I am interested in pursuing a conversation between Stein and Derrida regarding the limited nature of human discourse inherent in speaking about God (i.e., the name that announces Infinity). This is not merely a theoretical problem but in fact raises serious ethical and metaphysical concerns. In light of Edith Stein's description of empathy as foreign experience and her reservations concerning Husserl's strict epistemological model of transcendental constitution on the one hand and Derrida's critique of Levinas's position on the other hand, the question must be asked: Are Husserl's notions of apperception and analogical variation ultimately vindicated in Stein's description of empathy as "foreign experience?" Or is Levinas justified in fearing that Husserl's emphasis on cognition implies the privileging of epistemology over ethics and the reduction of transcendence to the sphere of the same? Might Edith Stein's notion of "reciprocal solidarity" offer a new way of encountering ethics that bridges Husserl's transcendental phenomenology with Levinas's description of *il y a* and "the face beyond the face"? I submit that the description of such an ethics of infinite respect would be more compatible with Husserl's transcendental position than is generally acknowledged by his critics. How might Stein's analysis of the constitution of foreign experience offer a more practical response to both Husserl's monadological account of ego constitution and Levinas's reversal of intentionality in terms of ethics? Finally, if, as both Stein and Levinas claim, the Other is the *to whom* I must address every act, what sorts of ethical and epistemological implications can be drawn from Edith Stein's social ontology and her understanding that the Other appears as an addressee of transcendence from outside the sphere of expectation? How might empathy make possible a subject who demands from me an infinite capacity of welcome, hospitality, and responsibility? Does Edith Stein's definition of empathy anticipate Derrida's critique of Levinas and lead to a kind of impossible ethics, a "quasi-transcendental," an apophatic specter of transcendence regarding the Other that contains its own undoing?

Turning to contemporary critical and feminist theory, as well as a reworking of St. Thomas Aquinas's notion of *adequatio*, I will explore in chapters ten and eleven a phenomenological description of empathy, now in terms of transcendence and an ethics of (infinite) respect. Properly understood, the phenomenology of empathy both supplies the conditions of possibility that give the Other to me and, at the same time, withholds the Other from me. The epistemological event by which the givenness of the Other apophatically appears as foreign experience is structurally similar to the nonappearance of transcendence. Empathy is a sign of the deconstructability of the givenness of transcendence by which sameness and alterity are constituted by cognition as binary poles of meaning. Empathy both gives and withdraws transcendence. Consequently, the appearance of transcendence is grasped not merely cognitively but also ethically, intuitively, and emotively as a nonappearance, that is, outside the principle of sufficient reason. The structural non-phenomenality of transcendence anticipates both alterity and sameness, a similar structure of givenness described by the phenomenology of empathy. Might a deconstructive element persist in St. Thomas's apophatic description of transcendence similar to how the phenomenology of empathy describes alterity? This could mean, among other things, that empathy is a constitut*ing* phenomenon, and not merely constitut*ed*. Empathy renders and retains the conditions of possibility by which "I" and "Other" are constituted by the givenness of transcendence through emotive and cognitive life. Empathy both constructs and deconstructs every attempt to justify the givenness of transcendence as an event of ethical encounter. Every I-Thou relationship marks an ethical rupture in what can be given. In encountering genuine transcendence, I come to recognize every self as one (un)like the other.

Part One

Empathy and the Theory of Transcendental Constitution

Part One

Introduction

Discussions concerning an emotive component of constitution were largely vacant from early phenomenological analyses concerning empathy. Beginning with Franz Brentano, emotions were considered subjective, qualitative, or irrational bodily states and as intentional mental acts built on mental cognitions and directed toward the world. Described in terms of affective intentionality, early phenomenologists (following Brentano and Husserl) largely assigned empathy a mainly cognitive role that included affectivity as one particular mental function among others. At the same time, limitations associated with Husserl's transcendental description of constitution soon created great misgivings amongst many of Husserl's colleagues who had championed his earlier realist position. A large part of this study will explore why Husserl's so-called transcendental turn was originally met with grave misgivings as a regression into idealism, and how this rejection of Husserl's transcendental project in turn planted seeds for more radical phenomenological and even postmodern approaches to issues of alterity and transcendence that even today remain largely unresolved. For example, early phenomenologists like Martin Heidegger, who broke from Husserl in large part due to his so-called transcendental turn, began to explore new models and approaches of inquiry by rejecting empathy outright. Maurice Merleau-Ponty and Emmanuel Levinas, in particular, explored intentionality as a multilayered phenomenon in its own right. Paving paths of inquiry that include the whole world of values, contemporary social ontology sometimes describes embodied dimensions of givenness principally in terms of ethics, perception, and emotional acts. Intrinsic in every epistemic analysis, this complex relationship between ethics and empathy—particularly by way of describing the phenomenology of empathy through affective, emotional, and embodied givenness—has not yet been fully or thematically explored.

What is empathy and what makes empathy possible? To what extent can the phenomenology of empathy reveal the interior life of other persons? Are motivations and intentions of social groups accessible to and impacted by individual thoughts and feelings? How are the inner lives of individuals influenced by social contagions, movements, and policies, whether in terms of family, the state, race, or culture? How is empathy related to ethics and transcendence? Can the Other be known, or is the experience of alterity so radically transcendent that limitations imposed by language and principles of sufficient reason render genuine empathy impossible? How might empathy open up new paradigms of knowing that were previously thought inaccessible, especially in terms of social phenomena and political life? What are some of the implications to engaging empathy beyond purely epistemological systems of discourse and rational ethical principles?

These are some of the questions we are needing to address concerning the phenomenology of empathy—generally speaking, from Husserl to Derrida—over the course of this study. Consequently, providing a general road map of several key themes will help set the stage for further discussion. Thematically speaking, we are exploring the theme of empathy as expounded by Edmund Husserl and his students and colleagues principally from the 1910s and 1920s, and thus focusing on the written, published works approved by Husserl during his lifetime of which Husserl's students and colleagues would have had access. Additional reference to some works published posthumously will also be included, notably *Ideas II* as well as occasional references to lectures, notes, and materials on intersubjectivity drawn, for example, from *Husserliana* volumes XIII, XIV, and XV. Several important themes—empathy, ethics, alterity, difference, transcendence, freedom, the Other—may appear ambiguous at the start but assuredly will be expanded throughout this study. We begin an exploration of empathy in part one through engaging the phenomenological *epoché*. By bracketing consciousness as a phenomenon, we are able to examine the genesis of conscious life in light of Husserl's transcendental reduction. In particular, we will explore the phenomenology of empathy by way of the construction of various life-forms of social reality on the one hand and the disintegration of contemporary cultural, political, and community cohesion on the other hand. Let us start, then, with a deceptively simple question: What is empathy? As has already been noted, there are many layers of meaning required to answer even this question in an adequate philosophical manner. And so, let us begin by trying to explain what empathy is *not*. Empathy is not merely "feeling-with" or "entering into" the inner life or shared primordial experiences of other persons. Empathy is not about formulating mental processes of abstraction in order to present a faultless epistemological argument concerning the extent to which I can know other minds. My argument is that empathy cannot be adequately understood through merely cognitive or rational descriptions, but it also contains a unique bodily and hence emotional or affective element that transcends experiences based solely on mental cognition. Constitutively speaking, empathy includes emotional experiences as well that can be "felt" across the spectrum of human existence and examined in terms of givenness. I submit that these emotive and affective acts of intentionality play an increasingly central role in the givenness of the world, including personal, social, and cultural values given through embodied encounters with other persons.

In the following chapters, empathy will be explored as a constitutive phenomenon. By bracketing or separating appearances of empathy from other natural experiences, we are able to explore the phenomenology of empathy on its own terms and in a more thematic, intentional, and ethical capacity. Empathy involves an ethical component because empathy does not merely engage aspects of perceptions of other persons toward whom I am drawn or repelled. As well, empathy describes or explores how I constitute myself as a distinct and singular human person living in a public world always with and amongst others. For Martin Heidegger, such condition of fallenness is a rejoinder that empathy is merely a constituted phenomenon worthy of rejection; whereas for Stein, the "I" of self-reflection is never given to itself *solus ipse*. On the contrary, the "I" or ego is both a constitut*ed* and constitut*ing* phenomenon, living always amidst experiences of givenness of radical alterity that appear as other persons as well as social movements, political events, national and economic systems, religious and secular forces, and phenomena that remain far outside my capacity to control them and the human ability to comprehend or withstand. That is to say: empathy is other-directed, it is constitutive, its being is grounded or constituted through appearances of difference and transcendence.

The phenomenology of empathy points to the givenness of alterity. As noted by Edith Stein, empathy describes the emergent primordial experience of a non-primordial experience. Following the descriptive analysis of Jacque Derrida, we shall call the experience of givenness of such a nonappearance an "event" in the transcendental sense that empathy ushers something new into the field of phenomena that can be grasped only in its non-phenomenality, as a trace. What is new is what appears by not appearing alongside what is given structurally in every act of perception. In empathy, what is given primordially must at the same time remain non-primordial or there would be no distinction between "I" and "Other." Alterity in effect grasps the Other as foreign experience—precisely in order to preserve the inaccessibility and hiddenness of the otherness of the Other qua other. In this sense, every appearance of givenness contains a residue or trace of what is foreign and so cannot appear, regardless of whether it is thematized. The felt awareness of foreign experience is thus constituted emotively as well as cognitively and thematized as "wholly other" through every encounter with the face or appearance of the Other. For Emmanuel Levinas, the face of the Other entails an eruption of transcendence. Alterity lays claim upon me and demands from me a response of infinite concern. Phenomenologically speaking, empathy describes how consciousness constitutes alterity as an event of experience of the nonappearance of transcendence. In terms of givenness of the lifeworld, empathy raises ethical insights through encountering foreign experience *as such*. Intersubjectivity thus describes how meaning gets raised through a socially constituted web of interrelated values and systems of coherence between individual existential experience on the one hand and the public world of shared values and social expectations on the other hand.

Phenomenologically speaking, empathy posits a felt recognition that every experience of the other qua other "lies absolutely beyond my comprehension and should be preserved in all its irreducible strangeness."[1] Hence, empathy constitutes both sameness and difference; it describes how foreign experience is given and, at the same time, acknowledges the impossibility of comprehending foreign experience in its infinite and radical otherness. How can the Other's infinity be preserved without sacrificing the Other to my own stream of conscious experience? How might ethics constitute horizons of meaning without lending primordial status to ideological dependency? Can infinity appear outside totality, that is, exterior to what is known cognitively? These questions ground the context of our study.

Chapter One

Husserl's Transcendental Turn

Empathy and the Task of the Phenomenological Reduction

Introduction

One of Husserl's dreams was that phenomenology would make of philosophy a rigorous science of infinite tasks, an indispensable element in discerning how the world gets constituted by consciousness.[1] Of course, such longing for apodicticity betrays a desire to return to the Greek hegemony of science (*episteme*), of theory (*theoria*), of the infinite as *eidos*. This quest for apodicticity holds more than a fleeting interest in Husserl's genetic and static descriptions of how knowledge, and especially knowledge of other persons, is constituted.[2] It marks Husserl's great discovery that what we mean by the world is always constituted: the world has a genealogy. Husserl's transcendental reduction, then, does not merely describe how consciousness of objects (whether real or imagined) is built up over time. The reduction describes how consciousness is *itself* constituted.[3] There are several important themes behind Husserl's doctrine of the transcendental reduction that are imperative for understanding how the thematic of empathy eventually took on such important considerations for Husserl and the early phenomenologists gathered around him.

Husserl's theory of transcendental reduction has been classified in terms of "idealism," though he remained adamant of his rejection of empiricist idealism. Husserl holds that consciousness alone is absolute being, in the sense that consciousness is absolutely given, whereas the world is relative being, in the sense that the world is given relative to consciousness. In principle, the transcendental reduction does not admit complete adequation between the *noetic* and the *noematic* realms. It is important to note that Husserl's doctrine of the transcendental reduction characterizes every attempt to define "infinity" in terms of Greek metaphysics as a false infinity. Like all phenomena, the phenomenon of infinity can be explained only *via* the apparatus of phenomenality, that is, through acts of protention and retention.[4] Since what alone subsists primordially is transcendental consciousness, it is toward a description of the founding mode of constitution that Husserl was primarily concerned.

§1. The Task of Husserlian Phenomenology

A review of the fundamental significance of the transcendental reduction remains indispensable for understanding what Husserl hoped to achieve by way of the phenomenological method and in light of his later emphasis on empathy. The development of Husserl's understanding of transcendental constitution as explicated in his approved published works, and its influence on Husserl's students and colleagues in the 1910s and 1920s, is therefore indispensable for investigating the phenomenology of empathy in terms of ethics and transcendence. Of course, various descriptive analyses of the transcendental reduction were formulated, abandoned, and reformulated by Husserl at both Göttingen and Freiburg between the years 1901 and 1933.[5] According to Edith Stein, Husserl's prized doctoral student and personal research assistant from 1916 to 1918, the essential task of phenomenology entails nothing less than clarifying and ascertaining the ultimate basis for all knowledge.[6] The goal of Husserl's entire transcendental project thus includes providing philosophy with its most absolute and radical starting point.[7] Consequently, Husserl begins by distinguishing the natural sciences from the philosophical sciences. *Naturwissenschaften* originate in the "natural attitude," whereas *Geisteswissenschaften* take their point of departure from the "philosophical attitude."[8] In the natural attitude, the world is given as unquestionably and obviously existing. Depending upon where we stand at any particular point in time, the world appears to us this way or that.

In the natural attitude, all conclusions and presuppositions are based on a mundane experience of the world, regardless of whether such judgments are singular or universal. All such judgments from experience are classified by Husserl as being naive in the sense that they are based on inductive or deductive reasoning. But insofar as philosophy is never merely natural science, its aim implies a reduction to the most originary form of radical presuppositionlessness that no natural science can attain. Whereas the starting point for natural scientists is the presupposed foundation of our experience of the world as something obvious and pre-given, Husserl asserts that the essential foundation of the philosophical attitude proceeds from an immediate vision or an original intuition of the essence (*eidos*) of things themselves.[9]

Phenomenology requires that the most radical and absolute starting point of philosophy cannot be assigned in any single principle, concept, or *cogito*. Rather, the origin of philosophy rests in the entire field of original experience by which the world is given as infinite. Husserl calls this the "principle of all principles," by which he asserts that neither induction nor deduction but only intuition can offer the precise analyses and exact descriptions that are necessary for all acts of rational discourse.[10] The presuppositions and methods used by the natural, physical, and social sciences are described by Husserl as being necessarily derivative from what is purely intuited. Every harmonious sequence of events is built up by consciousness in terms of a coherent synthesis of meanings that is neither absolute nor unmediated.

As an essential correlation between *appearance* on one hand and *that which appears* on the other hand, Husserl holds that consciousness alone is *absolute*. Conversely, the transcendent world is something that exists intentionally and is thereby relative to consciousness. In effect, Husserl clarifies the principle of constitution on the basis of pure consciousness. As a realm purged of all beliefs in transcendent existence, Marvin Farber insists that what Husserl introduced to philosophy was nothing less than its most radical articulation of presuppositionlessness.[11] Iso Kern as well concludes that the whole field of absolute consciousness remains intact regardless of whether actual existence is grasped by consciousness.[12] Noting the radical nature of the discovery of the correlation between consciousness and the world, Husserl comments that "it is this which remains as the phenomenological residuum we were in quest of"(*Ideas I* 154). The discovery of this residuum, which is a misleading expression, includes worldly transcendence *itself* as an intentional correlate.

§2. Intuition and Intentionality

In light of the discovery of this residuum, Husserl held that the goal of phenomenology was to gather data from every conceivable source so that essential and incontestable conclusions regarding Nature and the Objective world can be described impartially and accurately. This spirit characterizes the task of philosophy as infinite: what is meant by "the world" is always already an intentional product. It falls to phenomenology to describe the process "through which the intentional world is constituted in transcendental consciousness and to do so in a manner which grounds all description and analysis in originary intuition."[13]

In spite of any apparent shortcomings, even the most contemporary phenomenological analysis continues to carry out what Husserl called "descriptive eidetics" as its modus operandi. These critical analyses of essential structures of phenomena describe the constitution of different categories of objects for pure consciousness, that is to say, these analyses describe the way objects get constituted *as such*. What makes phenomenology a "science" of phenomena, then, is not so much a stringent, unified set of Husserlian doctrines that all orthodox phenomenologists follow but rather a shared spirit of inquiry, a common way of proceeding, a recourse to take "intuition" as an overall governing principle of "seeing."[14] Husserl's theory of philosophical method—with its fundamental appeal to intuition—ultimately relies on intuiting the essence of this or that entity. But whereas intuition itself is *not* contingent, Husserl argues that all objects of intuition *are* contingent.[15] Walter Fuchs concurs with Husserl's observation and contends that it falls to the task of intentional analysis to trace everything that is founded back to the original founding intuition.[16] Knowledge is ultimately derived from, and consists of, objects given through intuition. Accordingly, for Husserl, it will not do to draw conclusions from existences of which one knows but cannot see. "Seeing" does not lend itself to demonstration or deduction. It is patently absurd to try to explain possibilities (and unmediated possibilities at that) by drawing logical conclusions from nonintuitive knowledge (*IoP* 2).

All knowledge consists of, or derives from, the presence of an object (whether real or imagined) before consciousness. Hence, every true statement about the world arises from the givenness of the world itself; that is, it is founded on the basis of my experience of the world as given.[17] The matter of truth and falsity is constituted in an infinite horizon of perspectives rather than as a Kantian *Ding-an-sich* or an Aristotelean theory of correspondences. Irreducible to a theory of analogical correspondences, Husserl's rich conception of the truth of the world might be likened more to what Derrida describes as an infinite series of play and signification rather than a Cartesian mind/body dualism or a Kantian in-itself/for-itself distinction.[18]

The inexhaustibility of the task of disclosing reality marks for Husserl the infinite yet contingent nature of objective reality. This is one feature of Husserl's meaning of the term *intentionality*. According to Maurice Natanson, "[T]o say 'real world' is to say 'world-meant-as-real.'" In intentional terms, phenomenology is predicated on the distinction between the real and the meant-as-real, a distinction that is itself constituted by the lived experience of the privileged position of consciousness.[19] Husserl's description involves a noetic-noematic correlation that describes consciousness in terms of temporal flows of unities of intentional life. The transcendental reduction is the sine qua non by which the intelligibility of the world is constituted qua world. Consequently, the transcendental reduction allows phenomena to give themselves to consciousness. For Husserl, the reduction is a condition of possibility of meaning and sense; it allows the Earth to be an earth; it describes how the world is constituted *as a world* by an infinite series of profiles and adumbrations.[20]

§3. The Cartesian Project: Objectivity and the Science of Phenomena

J. N. Mohanty offers a telling glimpse into the pivotal role that objectivity plays in Husserl's theory of transcendental constitution. Mohanty argues that meanings of experiences, perceptions, beliefs, hopes and desires, *in fine*, of all intentional acts, are necessarily and infinitely given.[21] Toward this end, Husserl's description of the transcendental reduction purports to expose the processes of cognition itself. Husserl called this attempt to offer an objective analysis of the emergence of cognition the "science of all phenomena." By using the term "transcendental," Husserl wanted to include every condition of possibility by which the whole of reality is infinitely and variably given.

Husserl conceived the transcendental reduction as a science of essences, as opposed to sciences of facts. The reduction thus makes possible phenomenology as an infinite task of disclosing reality. In *Ideen I*, for example, Husserl argues that phenomenology is a foundational science. As a science concerned with what gets disclosed to consciousness in intuition, reduced to pure *eidos*, its results must be necessary truths and not merely contingent ones. Husserl defines "essence" in terms of the principle "that which in the intimate self-being of an individual discloses to us '*what*' it is" (*Ideas I* 22). Pure intuition can never be limited to ideality; on the contrary, it must derive from experience and eidetic variation. Emmanuel Levinas's comments on this point deserve reflection:

> In characterizing the essence of the object, Husserl does not limit himself to talking about its ideality, he does not exclusively oppose it to the individual, the "this-here"; in his view it is not sufficient to raise the individual object, with all its determinations, to generality, to the realm of the ideal in order to make an essence out of it. In the determinations of the object there is a hierarchy, and the first ones are required in order for the others to be possible. The essence of the object thus is its necessary structure: what makes it into what it is, that which before each empirical characteristic trait of the object makes it possible and understandable, in short—its principle.[22]

Taken sui generis, "essence" signifies a condition of possibility of knowledge qua knowledge. By "essence" Husserl implies that which makes possible the actuality of an existing world over and above any actual or possible instantiations.

Husserl's attempt to relate the concept of essence to the concept of meaning remained for him a lifelong task. This is what Husserlian "givenness" means in all its complexity. Initially, Husserl examined the laws of logic and mathematics and established that, in general, it is impossible to reduce ideas to facts or to reduce essences to concrete individual things. Later in *Ideas I* and also in *The Idea of Phenomenology*, Husserl turned to examine the Cartesian origin of modern science. In the introduction to Husserl's 1907 Göttingen lecture series, George Nakhnikian argues that what Husserl discovered in Descartes's method of doubt was in fact the prototype for the cognitive project that came to characterize his later and more mature transcendental epistemology.[23] Cartesian methodological doubt offers a certain model of the right *attitude* toward locating the presuppositionless objects of phenomenological inquiry, viz. the element of "withholding" belief, but not actually doubting. Husserl applies the Cartesian model of doubt as a partial model only, and then only in terms of withholding judgment. Consequently, Husserl's self-appointed task of razing historicism began by radicalizing Cartesian doubt in terms of *epoché*.

In *The Idea of Phenomenology*, for instance, Husserl intuits essences in a manner of presuppositionlessness reminiscent of Descartes: "The problem for the critique of knowledge is to locate the absolutely bare, presuppositionless data on which to build the whole of knowledge; more precisely, the problem is to intuit the essence of knowledge, and thereby to 'see' how valid cognition is an unquestionable fact. . . . The Cartesian method of doubt, Husserl suggests, requires that we locate pure data, themselves independent of all presuppositions and logically adequate for the critical reconstruction of knowledge" (*IoP* xv).

§4. The Ego as Monad: Revisiting *Cartesian Meditations I–IV*

Husserl explores the relationship between consciousness and the world with rigorous precision in *Cartesian Meditations I–IV*.[24] He rejects the notion that "world" and "consciousness" are two distinct things or units that co-constitute each other. World and consciousness are constituted realities. This is why Husserl describes the task of phenomenology as the "systematic disclosure of constituting intentionality" (*CM* 119:86). Constitution, in a manner of speaking, is always rather pregnant (*CM* 56). It originates from the realm of privacy and then moves ek-statically outward, toward the public. As a field of latencies, potencies, and limited horizons, consciousness transcendentally builds up meaning, knowledge, and the world of sense.

Accordingly, all meaning—whether real or imagined, empirical, or pure—becomes constituted within the life of what Husserl calls the ego.[25] Phenomenological reflection creates neither the world nor the ego; rather, it *unfolds* or makes manifest what lies anonymous and potential and implicit in every conscious belief. It brings into the light the modes of givenness that verify every intention. Every synthesis constitutes a noetic-noematic correlation in which the world gives itself to me at the same time that consciousness constitutes the world as given. The given always appears as the correlate of a conscious act, as a *noema* corresponding to a *noesis*.

> Objects exist for me, and are for me what they are, only as objects of actual and possible consciousness. If this is not to be an empty statement and a theme for empty speculations, it must be shown what makes up concretely this existence and being-thus for me, or what sort of actual and possible consciousness

is concerned, what the structure of this consciousness is, what "possibility" signifies here, and so forth. This can be done solely by constitutional investigation. (*CM* 65)

In the sphere of solitary verification, I interpret the world in terms of what may be called "self-evidence," that is, as what is meant *for me*. In a broad sense, Husserl's notion of *Evidenz* denotes a "universal primal phenomenon of intentional life, namely . . . the preeminent mode of consciousness that consists in the *self-appearance*, the *self-giving* . . . of a value . . . *given originaliter*" (*CM* 57). Yet, because every piece of evidence (*Evidenz*) originates by my making it manifest *to myself*, Husserl's theory of givenness appears to lead, at first glance at least, to a kind of solipsism.[26] The most important precondition toward fulfilling any intention is that "the subjectivity that is made the object of philosophical reflection should be my own."[27] We are thus faced with a perplexing problem: How can a theory of monadological constitution that takes *the ego as originary* adequately account for the constitution of an infinitely existing world that includes other egos?[28] Let us take a closer look at what Husserl means by describing the ego as a monad.[29]

The Ego,[30] Husserl claims, is not a pure flow of consciousness, an empty pole, but rather the "fully concrete" Ego now experienced transcendentally. It is an "I"—*das Ich*—constituted *as the same I* through the primordial givenness of its own acts and habits. As such, it lives this and that subjective process and lives through this and that *cogito* (*CM* 66). Husserl explains the discovery of the transcendental ego in terms of a kind of synthesis that unites the multiplicities of *cogitationes* into an identical Ego. In a manner of speaking, the Ego fills itself in, or "builds itself up," by acquiring abiding properties in the form of procured judgments to which it may return. These "havings" are described as *habitualities*, and the Ego is the substrate of these habitualities. According to a law of transcendental generation, every *act* emanates from the Ego and thus acquires a *new* objective sense, what Husserl calls "a new abiding property" (*CM* 66).

Constituted by a kind of temporal unity or temporal enduring, Husserl notes that the Ego is neither a *res cogitans* nor a *res substantia* any more than it is a process or continuity of processes. The Ego is that which underlies all processes and possibilities. The transcendental ego is what it is "solely in relation to intentional objectivities" and the harmoniousness of these experiences (*CM* 65). Hence, the monad in full concreteness does not merely "have" a history: the concrete Ego *is* its history. This "flow," which the Ego *is*, is described by Husserl in terms of protentions and retentions. As a unitary *cogito-cogitationes-cogitatum*, the Ego has/is a "personal character" (*CM* 67).

Together, the Ego as "identity pole" and the substratum of habitualities constitute what Husserl calls the *concrete monad* or the ego as monad.[31] The transcendental ego becomes concrete only in the flowing manifold of its intentional life, along with the objects meant in its concrete acts. Such abiding acquisitions constitute the entirety of the surrounding world, and thereby constitute all anticipatory horizons and all formal and objective structures of knowledge. This means that the monadic concrete ego includes the whole of actual and potential conscious life: I exist for myself and am continuously given to myself in experiential evidence as "I myself." In other words, the ego grasps itself not only as a flow of life but, more importantly, as an "I" who lives through the cogitations of this flow as the self-same "I myself." Every analysis concerning the self-constitution of the transcendental ego must be engaged for Husserl through constitutional analyses (*CM* 99–100). As an identical substratum of ego properties, the concrete monad constitutes itself as a fixed and abiding *presence*, that is, a *personal* ego (*CM* 66–67).

In its essential monadological structure, the centering Ego is complete. Nevertheless, the monad is not an empty pole of identity. Rather, it acquires a new abiding property every time an act emanates from it. What appears from Husserl's analysis is a development in Husserl's own thought that may be observed by noting the following: (a) In the *Logical Investigations* there is no mention of an ego; (b) while in *Ideas*, the ego appears only in terms of its being an identity pole; whereas now, (c) in the *Cartesian Meditations*, the ego is a monad or *concrete*.[32] Hence, the Ego includes its meant objects, the world that exists for me, the world that surrounds the Ego *as meant*: "As ego, I have a surrounding world, which is continually 'existing for me'; and, in it, objects as 'existing for me'—already with the abiding distinction between those with which I am acquainted and those only anticipated as objects with which I may become acquainted. . . . This, my activity of positing and explicating being, sets up a habituality of my Ego, by virtue of which the object, as having its manifold determinations, is mine abidingly" (*CM* 68).

The totality of the centering ego as a field of consciousness is reflected in Husserl's description of the concrete Ego as monad. This means that the Ego can be considered concrete only in the flowing multiformity of its intentional life, along with the objects meant, and in some cases constituted as existent for the Ego, in that life (*CM* 68). Hence, Husserl's phenomenological description of the ego as monad includes all constitutional problems. And this, precisely, is Husserl's Leibnizian moment. The monad *is* the totality of the Ego as a field of intentional consciousness. In its concreteness, the monad constitutes the point of view of the ego of the whole world (*CM* 68).

According to Husserl, the Ego as monad is constituted in terms of three distinct elements: (1) the ego as identity pole, (2) the substratum of habitualities (what Husserl calls "immanent transcendencies"), and (3) the fleeting acts. Founded as a field of consciousness, these three elements co-constitute the monad insofar as the Ego is directed toward an object as meant. The Ego taken by Husserl as fully concrete becomes designated by its Leibnizian name ("monad") and defined in terms of intentional objects—what Husserl calls "position-taking" (*CM* 68). This constitutive correlation between *noema* and *noemata*, of the Ego as pole of its acts and substrate of habitualities, marks the phenomenological genesis of genetic phenomenology (*CM* 69).[33]

The whole range of phenomenological givenness lies for Husserl in the exploration of the concrete ego as monad. As a unitary perspective of the whole, each concrete monad constitutes the whole field of conscious activity for itself. This means that the concrete ego is the whole world of intentional life taken from its own perspective: "The Ego can be concrete only in the flowing multiformity of his intentional life, along with the objects meant—and in some cases constituted as existent for him—in that life. Manifestly, in the case of an object so constituted, its abiding existence and being-thus are a correlate of the habituality constituted in the Ego-pole himself by virtue of his position-taking" (*CM* 68). This unitary, flowing, harmonious life of the Cartesian ego and its constitution of the world as meant *engenders* the monad. According to Husserl, the ego as yet remains within the realm of the monadological but *transcendental* attitude.[34] The question of how I can get outside my own "island of consciousness" has not yet been raised phenomenologically. The question as to *how* phenomena manifest themselves in consciousness acquires objective significance that needs to be raised anew.[35]

§5. The Transcendental Reduction

Husserl's attempt to resolve the confusion over what he called "the first question in the theory of knowledge" is entirely taken up with how transcendence is given. First articulated in *The Idea of Phenomenology*, the concept was altered and enriched several times over in subsequent writings, by which Husserl argued that the theory of transcendental reduction is purely methodological or, better yet, epistemological. Husserl's own varied usage of the term "reduction," however, often led to great confusion, especially since he sometimes applied the expressions "reduction" and *epoché* interchangeably. Consequently, he was forced to add to the term "reduction" several qualifiers in order to distinguish one sense from another: philosophical, psychological, eidetic, phenomenological, and transcendental.[36]

Husserl speaks in quite general terms of a phenomenological reduction, by which he means the process by which we are led to believe something that is made evident beyond normal, intramundane experience. In terms of the distinction described earlier between the natural attitude and the phenomenological attitude, reduction in this most general sense refers to how consciousness arrives at that kind of (transcendental) knowledge of which everyday thinking has mostly lost sight. In more precise settings, Husserl distinguishes three distinct aspects of the phenomenological reduction: (1) The *epoché* brackets our belief in existence. It is derived from the Greek verb *epechein*, which means a temporary cessation of movement. *Epoché* refers to a suspension of judgment in such a way that the Ego no longer inhabits or participates in the belief, but without casting any doubt *on* the belief. (2) The *transcendental reduction* describes the reduction of object to subject, that is, in terms of the *noematic-noetic* correlation. Generally speaking, Husserl understands by the transcendental reduction that procedure by means of which objects are shown to be effects of the anonymous acts of constitution by transcendental subjectivity. Through the transcendental reduction, I discover or encounter myself as a pure ego living in the pure stream of my cogitation. Hence, the field of transcendental self-experience opened up by the transcendental reduction is rightly called by Husserl "transcendental subjectivity"; it is the ultimate condition of possibility or source of the meaning of everything that exists. (3) In the *eidetic reduction* we imaginatively vary the variable aspects of any object in order to isolate its invariant structure. This means that the eidetic reduction eliminates all references to anything particular and individual in any given phenomenon.[37]

Concerned primarily with the way knowledge of the world is constituted, Husserl took it as absurd to ask whether or not we can have knowledge of things-in-themselves. The *epoché* puts the existence of "reality" in brackets. Insofar as philosophical analyses of phenomena lie outside the realm of the natural attitude, phenomenology—which Husserl defines as the study of such phenomena—can be classified as neither metaphysical nor psychologistic. What alone can be made use of, then, is what alone is adequately self-given, that is, what is genuinely immanent (*reell Immanentes*). Everything else, Husserl contends, lies beyond the grasp of what I can know or trust in any pure or apodictic sense. The transcendental reduction excludes anything that is transcendently posited.[38] It classifies everything that is not immanent in my experience as epistemologically derivative.[39]

The transcendental reduction opens up the meaning of the world: it describes the noetic-noematic correlation; it moves within the field of a transcendentally reduced ego by making possible eidetic abstraction in the field of consciousness.[40] Husserl contends that such correlation between *noema* and *noemata* makes accessible every domain of meaning. Without this correlation, meaning does not exist. This is what Henry Pietersma asserts when he argues that, for Husserl, "the scope of the mind defines reality."[41] Taken in its complexity, Husserl's transcendental reduction signifies not that the world does not exist independently of consciousness but rather that the meaning of the world cannot be found without consciousness' constitution of it. The meaning of things in the world, whether physical, mental, or metaphysical, is unfolded by and for consciousness. By a method of transcendental reduction, Husserl argues that "each of us, as Cartesian mediator . . . [is led] back to his transcendental ego—naturally with its concrete-monadic contents as this *de facto* ego, the one and only absolute ego" (*CM* 69).[42]

§6. Transcendental Idealism

Husserl called his epistemological position transcendental idealism, which he argued is not to be confused with metaphysical idealism. But as the years went by, the suspicion grew that Husserl's transcendental view was not merely epistemological but metaphysical and that he was not describing how knowledge is constituted but rather giving a metaphysical account of reality in-itself.[43] I submit that this reading of Husserl offers a gross misrepresentation of Husserl's position. The *epoché* neither doubts nor denies the existence of the world. Rather, the *epoché* merely suspends my belief in the existence of the natural world. By placing the question of the reality of the world in abeyance, Husserl in effect rescued the *epoché* from radical Cartesian skepticism. For Husserl, doubt is an attitude dependent upon the transcendental reduction. The suspension of belief necessitated by the transcendental reduction has nothing to do with the obliteration of the world or its contents. In effect, the world does not change when it is placed in *epoché*. Rather, what changes is my conscious attitude to the world that has undergone transformation: "Everything specifiable in the ordinary attitude is retained in the new, but retained *as* an object of perceptual experience.... What remains after suspension is everything seen in the philosophically neutralized perspective of consciousness in direct touch with its world."[44] The suspicion that Husserl had struck some sort of "metaphysical deal" with the position held by German Idealists needs to be firmly resisted. Husserl never makes reality an issue for consciousness. For Husserl the transcendental reduction seeks to explain how knowledge—and *not* being—is constituted, or given, by consciousness.

Transcendental idealism, therefore, offers an epistemology, a theory of knowledge that describes how objects are constituted by consciousness (*CM* 73). In this sense, Husserl is a decidedly original and rather un-Greek thinker. Unlike Parmenides, Husserl does not think he is thinking Being. Contrary to Heidegger, Husserl does not claim that the transcendental reduction answers the question of the meaning of the being of Being. In effect, Husserl claims to offer neither an ontological description of being qua being nor a theo-onto-metaphysical justification for asking the question of the meaning of Being. On the contrary, Husserl stresses that knowledge of things is constituted in terms of laws of active and passive genesis, similar to the laws of association, and given in terms of synthesis. This means that either we come to understand how knowledge of things is constituted or we remain trapped in the natural attitude by naive presuppositions.[45]

Herein lies precisely what Husserl designated as "the great problem." For Husserl, it is quite well understandable that I can attain certainties, even compelling evidences, in the domain of my own consciousness.[46] But how can that which is constituted within the immanency of my own subjective conscious life acquire Objective significance? By introducing the theory of transcendental idealism, Husserl hoped to describe once and for all how the ego "constitutes himself for himself in, so to speak, the unity of a 'history'" (*CM* 75). Husserl sets out to render a general theory of how knowledge of objects and the world is attained. Consequently, Husserl's theory of transcendental idealism offers an eidetic and transcendental account of how consciousness constitutes meanings, how things are formed by consciousness, how the world is made possible as an object of knowledge.

Nevertheless, inasmuch as every phenomenological analysis begins with the transcendental ego, transcendental idealism is wrought with grave methodological ambiguities, especially concerning problems of solipsism. Although Husserl himself resisted placing the individual ego in a self-enclosed Cartesian box, his appropriation of idealism was nevertheless met with severe criticism especially by "realist" phenomenologists who rejected out of hand his controversial appropriation of transcendental idealism.[47]

§7. Husserl's Hermeneutic Turn

Insofar as the world is reduced to my own perspective, to what extent does monadological egology remain vulnerable to the charge of solipsism? To a very real extent, such a charge of solipsism betrays a fundamental misunderstanding of Husserl's overall project.[48] In effect, what Husserl is describing by way of the transcendental reduction is not a self-enclosed, self-sufficient solipsistic entity but an underlying principle of interpretive hermeneutics.[49] What the transcendental reduction points to is the unfinished task of disclosing reality, namely, that the very *meaning* of meaning is constituted by the necessary fact that I always already have my own unique perspective. For Husserl, this means that there is always an anticipatory hermeneutic at work in every noetic-noematic correlation. What Husserl proposes in order to refute the charge of solipsism is a static analysis of the transcendental ego, an epistemological description of originary givenness in terms of how every ego comes to see the whole world from its own unique perspective. Husserl uses the terms "passivity" and "activity" in order to describe how the experience of givenness is constituted by the transcendental reduction.

In describing the transcendental reduction, Husserl discovered that a "history" unfolds within the constraints of certain types, analogous, in a sense, to Leibniz's own theory of compossible possibilities. Such possibilities are possible only in a certain order and at certain *loci*. Husserl means by this that the Ego's history is essentially an a priori history, not a history of chronological dates but a history of how things must have unfolded. Consequently, what is a priori does not at all concern causal necessity. Rather, the ego's history is constituted from a law of motivation whereby the ego is moved—motivated—to form certain unities that are neither coerced nor arbitrarily free. This means that the ego constitutes a sui generis feature of intentionality: "The ego constitutes himself for himself in, so to speak, the unity of a 'history'" (*CM* 75). Tracing the unity of this history is what Husserl proposes by *genetic* phenomenology; whereas the *static* phenomenology of the Fifth Meditation examines only a-historical stratifications and structures.⁵⁰

There are, essentially, two kinds of constitutive genesis: active and passive, the latter preceding the former. *Passive* genesis is the means by which physical objects are given to perception. Although it is in a sense involuntary and does not require conscious active intervention, passive genesis is a synthesis with a history. Given "beforehand," passive genesis establishes the ground upon which higher-order active genesis is constituted. Essential to the being of the concrete ego, passive genesis describes how the Ego comes to itself in relation to a particular environment. "Thanks to the aforesaid passive synthesis (into which the performances of active synthesis also enter), the Ego always has an environment of 'objects'" (*CM* 79).

The process of passive genesis is grounded principally by the law of *association*. For Husserl, association designates a phenomenological axiom of meaning rather than any sort of naturalistic or empiricist causation. Consequently, Husserl distinguished his notion of association from the definition given by the popular naturalistic psychologisms of the day, particularly those derived from Mead and Hume. As a matter of intentionality, Husserl contends that association is not a naturalistic process. Rather, association is the innate a priori conformity of consciousness to eidetic laws, without which an ego as such is unthinkable. In effect, the ego can be understood only from the basis of genetic phenomenology's principle of passive genesis, which affirms that the ego is constituted ("built up") as an infinite nexus in time. Only through passive genesis can temporality and meaning be constituted as structural concepts (*CM* 81).⁵¹

Husserl's notion of a priori association stands in stark contrast to Hume's psychologistic and Mead's naturalistic understanding of association. However, if we were to eliminate those prejudices from Hume's theory, we would in fact discover the precursor to genetic phenomenology:

> Association is a fundamental concept belonging to transcendental phenomenology (and, in the psychological parallel, a fundamental concept belonging to a purely intentional psychology). The old concepts of association and of laws of association . . . are only naturalistic distortions of the corresponding genuine, intentional concepts. (*CM* 80)

§8. Concluding Reflections

For Husserl, neither the empirical ego nor the transcendental ego functions as a premise from which we eventually make our way over to transcendence. Rather, Husserl sees in the transcendental reduction a condition of possibility of describing how to open up a whole new field of experience, namely, the infinite realm of the objective world. The transcendental reduction marks the limit by which an infinite and unexplored region of reflection is given; it discloses its unfinished task of describing reality far beyond the natural attitude's capacity to describe it. Through the transcendental reduction, nothing is lost. Rather, the world as infinite emerges and, with it, its transcendental structure as a temporal stream or flow (*Erlebnisse*) of intentionalities.

Such transcendental structure does not presume an implicit representationalism that doubts the existence of the world. On the contrary, the transcendental reduction stipulates that the givenness of the world to consciousness is relative, whereas the givenness of consciousness to itself is absolute. Even if the world was no longer constituted as a harmonious unit, consciousness would nevertheless remain unspoiled in the residuum of its own stream. Hence, for Husserl intentionality is not a mere act of will. In contradistinction to the medieval philosophers, Husserl in effect defines consciousness not as *il quod* (that in which) but *id quo* (that *by* which).

The transcendental reduction brackets natural assumptions. Whereas the empirical and psychological ego is naive and interested in the world, the transcendental ego is disinterested and critical.[52] In the flow of temporal multiplicities, a unity emerges into view by which the constituting subject (Ego) synthesizes what is being given to it. This constituting subject does not produce the world. Rather, the world is constituted as a harmonious unity of perspectives gathered and ordered from a particular egological viewpoint. There are fore-structures, predelineations, "as"-structures, habitualities, and so on by which the transcendental ego makes explicit the work that is going on anonymously in the natural world. The "work" of the transcendental reduction, then, is the work of *Ausleben*; that is, its work is to lay out, to unfold, to interpret, to explicate, to lay bare the world that appears always as fact. Consequently, for Husserl, consciousness does not infer Kant's formal a priori synthetic "I," nor is consciousness a substance, a thing, a Nietzschean fiction of grammar, or even a Humean collection of ideas. Although the world is a presumptive unity and consciousness is a presumptive unity, according to Husserl the transcendental reduction reveals that all such unity is merely contingent: it could be otherwise.

In effect, Husserl separates the phenomenological notion that the world's harmony is contingent from Descartes's radical skepticism. Cartesian doubt withholds assent as to whether or not the world actually exists. Husserl holds no such doubt. Reason is what is given, it is not merely produced by rules of deductive inference. Consequently, Husserl's doctrine of transcendental idealism describes not simply how objects of consciousness are constituted but how the world *must* be constituted if world-making is to be phenomenology's unique and infinite task. The transcendental reduction does not disclose the secret metaphysical origin of Being. Rather, it describes how meaning is constituted as an infinite task. Consequently, for Husserl the alternative to transcendental idealism is either pure non-sense on the one hand or a magic formula on the other hand. Either the transcendental reduction offers us a phenomenological description of how the world qua world gets constituted in terms of infinite meaning or we must rely on a purely psychologistic or Kantian formula to give some sort of idealist explanation that accounts for the categorical being of the world.

What Husserl discovers by way of the transcendental reduction is that consciousness alone is absolute being: it is absolutely given, whereas the world is relative being: it is given relatively, that is to say, it is given in relation to consciousness. In principle, Husserl never allows a full adequation to be established between *noema* and *noemata*. Every "infinity" is always a false infinity in the sense that, Husserlianly speaking, even the phenomenon of infinity must be explained via the apparatus of phenomenality, that is, through protention and retention.[53] In other words, infinity is itself meaningful only in so far as "infinity" is grasped as an idea or experience constituted by consciousness. In this sense we must say, along with Husserl, that the transcendental reduction is the condition of possibility by which the world is given in its infinite phenomenality. Such an act of infinite givenness is characteristic of higher-order ego acts, for example, those pertaining to culture (*Geist*), spiritual activities, the constitution of higher-order products, and even reason-itself (*CM* 78).[54] The methodology of inquiry of the transcendental reduction is therefore founded upon a static analysis of the transcendental ego; it clearly adheres to the roots of its Cartesian inheritance while also planting the seeds for its betrayal.

Chapter Two

The Fifth Cartesian Meditation

Introduction

How—and to what extent—can we say that the *objective* world that I experience is the same world that you experience? In what sense does my ego, which always constitutes the world as meant *for me*, constitute, under the heading "experience of something other," the world as meant *for you*? In general terms, this is what is often called "the problem of the Other." If the other is truly other, how can the other be known at all? In the Fifth Cartesian Meditation, Husserl explores the problem of the Other by recasting objectivity in terms of the constitution of the intersubjective community of egos. He tries to show how the transcendental ego constitutes other egos as equal partners that, in turn, form the foundation for the objective, that is, the intersubjective, world. Husserl designates by "transcendental intersubjectivity" the notion of an objective world that is valid for everyone.

Such a task must take into consideration three important factors. First, an experience of other egos must be real and not merely possible. Second, such experience must be grounded in some sort of reciprocal relationship between egos or "monads," to use Liebniz's designation. Others must experience me in the same way that I experience them; otherwise, objectivity remains merely possible but not actual. And third, any knowledge of the world must be founded on the experience of its not being my own private world. By "objectivity" Husserl means a shared and intersubjective world that is constituted *as the same world* by others. For Husserl, the act of empathy plays a founding role in the pursuit of Objectivity and in helping explain the constitution of the alter ego. The term "Other" describes the principle of alterity without which Objectivity remains purely illusive. The Other implies *alter ego*, and the ego referred to by this relation is "I myself," the subject of a concrete intentional life. Husserlian intentionality is thus not primarily concerned with thingly transcendence in its more generalized sense. Rather, Husserl posits empathy as a way of describing how the alter ego is constituted as a for-itself in the sphere of my own conscious experience.[1]

According to Husserl's strict, cognitive analysis, the world is invariably grasped intentionally. This means that consciousness is always consciousness *of* something *as meant*. Hence, the world and the objects in it appear to emerge—at first glance, at least—as constituted intentional acts of the individual ego. The other as alter ego is taken by consciousness as *the-other-as-meant-for-me*.[2] But if what is meant by other (i.e., everything that is-not-me) appears always in the mode *meant-for-me*, then in what sense can the other ever be said to be radically and authentically *other*? Does Husserl's transcendental egology lead to a solipsistic affirmation that embraces Kantian idealism? Does Berkley's classic formulation (*esse est percipi*) have the final say, after all (*CM* 86)? Is Husserl's transcendental description of the intentional object ultimately reducible to a sort of shadowy appearance of a phenomenon that remains distinct from the thing-in-itself? And what about the existence of the alter Ego, namely, the Other as a self-conscious subject? Is the Other merely an object constituted by the transcendental ego as an object *for me*? Or is the alter ego genuinely *other*, a for-itself in the genuine sense that *I* am a for-itself? In this chapter the following questions will be raised: (1) What does Husserl mean by Objectivity? (2) To what extent does Husserl succeed in finding in empathy the key to a constituted world that is objectively valid for everyone? (3) How can an explication of intentionality lay the foundation for a transcendental theory of experiencing someone else, that is to say, a transcendental theory of empathy? In effect, Husserl accounts for the givenness of genuine alterity in light of his insistence that the Other is always experienced as an alter ego, an analogous image of myself, another *I*. The question with which our investigation is mainly concerned may be expressed thus: Can we find in empathy a more originary experience of intersubjectivity that is not *itself* constituted by my ego?

§1. The Problem of the Other

At the end of the Fourth Cartesian Meditation, Husserl says that I always see the world from my own unique perspective.[3] Conversely, in the Fifth

Cartesian Meditation he suggests that there is one thing that exists not merely for me but *for itself*. The Other's ego is constituted as a being-for-itself. Husserl wonders: How can I constitute a being such as *that*? Whereas on the one hand in the natural attitude the transcendence of both objects and other egos is assumed, on the other hand the transcendental attitude raises a rather opaque question: How does the alter ego get constituted by the concrete Ego? Husserl in effect designates *this* problem as the problem of empathy. "But what about other egos," Husserl writes, "who surely are not a mere intending and intended *in me*, but, according to their sense, precisely [transcendent] *others*?"[4] (*CM* 89–90). By recasting the question posed by the Other's presence in the transcendental attitude, Husserl brackets *epoché*, the issue of factual existence. Hence, the (Cartesian) formulation of the question of knowledge as an inside/outside problem of consciousness is eliminated.

Husserl underscores in no uncertain terms the central challenge posed by the performance of the transcendental-phenomenological reduction. "When I, the meditating I, reduce myself to my absolute transcendental ego by phenomenological *epoché*, do I not become *solus ipse*," he asks, "and do I not remain that, as long as I carry on a consistent self-explication under the name phenomenology?" (*CM* 89). Husserl notes the difficulty of his position: "Should not a phenomenology that proposed to solve the problems of Objective being, and to present itself actually as philosophy, be branded therefore as transcendental solipsism?" (*CM* 89). At this point, we need to be clear in understanding that Husserl's question is not whether or not a world or another ego exists independent from any conscious constitution of it. That question was already affirmed by him in the distinction made between the natural and phenomenological attitudes. Here, the question becomes more nuanced. How does the abiding Ego account for an experience of genuine alterity when the subjectivity of a for-itself is constituted by the abiding Ego in the living stream of its own experience? This is the issue.[5]

Maurice Natanson suggests that this more creative version of the problem of solipsism need not be confined to epistemological concerns alone. Even *if* the ego-predicament resulted in some sort of enclosed solipsistic circle, Natanson muses, nevertheless it would *not* be necessary for Husserl to deny existence to Others, but it would mean that each individual would be an island cut off from every other island of consciousness, a metaphysics without a mainland.[6] It seems to me that Natanson shares Husserl's dilemma but not his remedy. In effect, Natanson asserts that solipsism is a logically coherent theory: the real problem posed by the transcendental reduction is not whether I can account for myself, but how do I account for others?[7]

Consequently, even when the argument is put forward that all mundane experience is intersubjectively experienced by a plurality of egos (and this, in effect, is the argument proposed by Husserl in the Fifth Mediation), the solipsist is able to reply that "it is only through the self—himself—that this can even be asserted."[8] Natanson notes that every effort to refute solipsism is thus craftily rejected by the solipsist himself: "Charge and countercharge are nothing but presentations to consciousness, givens to the experiencing self—*my* self." Natanson's comments on this topic are worth noting in their entirety:

> Brilliantly consistent as this position is, its very insularity points to its cardinal limitation: solipsism is essentially a denying philosophy. Even its affirmations prove to be negations, for it begins with a deprivation of mundane existence and ends with the hubris inevitable to any thinker who denies the works of Others under the guise of original authorship. The one commandment the solipsist cannot follow without self-contradiction is: Honor thy father and mother. If it is true that the solipsist has no trouble handling the problem of other selves, it is because solipsism defines itself through a denial of sociality.[9]

According to Natanson, the only viable way to refute solipsism is through an affirmation of sociality.[10] For this reason, Husserl insists that the alter ego is given in experience; that is, he begins with this experience and his only task is to explicate its phenomenological intelligibility.[11] Husserl calls this the "transcendental clue" and stipulates that the "experienced Other" is "given to me in straightforward consciousness" (*CM* 90). Husserl continues: "In changeable harmonious multiplicities of experience I experience others as actually existing and, on the one hand, as world Objects—not as mere physical things belonging to Nature. . . . They are in fact experienced also as governing psychically in their respective natural organisms" (*CM* 91). The Other is always already there, a for-itself that I encounter in the natural attitude as what is most evident in the field of everything that is given.[12] But how can an *object* that I constitute *for me* also be, at the same time, a *subject* that exists *for-itself*? Does the Other constitute *me* in precisely the same way that I constitute *it*?[13]

Husserl's analysis of the constitution of the Other consequentially needs to include two seemingly contradictory components: (1) a reduction to the purely private sphere of experience that the ego has within the sphere of ownness and (2) an account of the intersubjective constitution of the Objective world that preserves the Other's quintessential mode of difference as being-for-itself. Because Husserl does not present an empirical description but rather offers an eidetic account of experiencing other persons, we need to raise his theory of constitution in a more radical and robust sense: Is it possible for me to have a primordial experience of the Other if what is in fact meant by alter ego is precisely what is given to me non-primordially? How can I know another ego if only *my* ego is given absolutely in my conscious stream of lived experience? Or, as Anthony Steinbeck asks, "How can phenomenology account for the originality of the other subjectivity that transcends my own experience and yet whose sense as other is constituted in and from my intentional life? How can another ego (transcendence in the true sense) that is not merely intended as an object in my experience be constituted as precisely other?"[14]

§2. The Givenness of Experience

Husserl acknowledges that neither the existence of objects nor the world is ever in doubt. "The world exists in itself," Husserl contends, "over against all experiencing subjects and their world-phenomena" (*CM* 91). But the (human) Other is not an object like other objects. Constituted in the phenomenological attitude, human others appear or present themselves from beyond the reach of my own transcendental experience, that is, in terms of what Husserl calls the "*noematic-ontic* mode of givenness of the Other" (*CM* 90). Somehow, I recognize in my field of objects some objects that are not like any of the others that I encounter. They present themselves to me not only as objects that are known but as subjects who *know me*.[15] For Husserl, the experiences of these peculiar Others form part of my intentional life, though without at the same time ever being my own experience. This is what Husserl means by an experience of empathy.

What is at stake is not merely the question of the "otherness-for-me" of others, a transcendental theory of experiencing someone else. The problem of empathy appears "much greater than at first it seems" (*CM* 92) and precipitates for Husserl the founding stratum of a transcendental theory of the Objective world. Only through an analysis of empathy can "Objective actuality" include the whole of reality in its full, intersubjective manifestness in terms of givenness of the natural, cultural, and spiritual worlds (*CM* 92). Consequently, it is for this reason that Maurice Natanson ponders Husserl's definition of empathy in terms of sociality and discourse and Rudolf Makkreel explores the problem of empathy as quintessentially involving questions of interpretation and understanding [*Verstehen*], that is, of hermeneutics and the origin of transcendental knowledge.[16] In describing how the problem of other selves involves methodological conceptions of communication, Natanson holds that empathy in fact constitutes the formative conditions by which intersubjective communication is rendered possible.

§3. Reduction to the Sphere of Ownness

Either the Other "appears" by magic or Husserl must give an account for how the Other gets constituted in its alterity as an equi-primordial subject, a for-itself in the proper sense, without reducing the alterity of the Other to a mere representation of myself. For this, Husserl insists, we need to make a second reduction within the phenomenological attitude. This second reduction is made to the sphere of ownness (*Eigenheitssphäre*), to the transcendental sphere of I-myself. Husserl introduces the sphere of ownness in order to explain the evident fact that we know other persons.[17] In effecting a reduction to the sphere of radical privacy, I take my own psychophysical organism as the only living conscious thing in the world. Bracketing everything that is alien (*Fremde*) to me, I eliminate the results of all intersubjectively shared empathic life. I treat every psychophysical organism in the world as if it had no subjectivity or living consciousness apart from me. In effect, through a second bracketing of experience, everything is reduced to mere-physical-appearance-*for-me*.

This is the founding stratum of the experience of the Other. I alone become the living animal organism that gets uniquely singled out by disregarding everything that is non-alien, including all those objects of constitutional effects that relate to other subjectivities (*CM* 93). Husserl characterizes the bracketing of everything other-than-I-myself as the "thematic exclusion of the constitutional effects produced by experiencing something other, together with the effects of all further modes of consciousness relating to something other" (*CM* 95). By virtue of this second reduction, every cultural predicate—specifically everything characterized in the natural attitude as Objective, as accessible to and for everyone—is excluded. What alone remains is what is peculiarly my own, what is given to me absolutely and *originarily*, what is experienced by me as non-alien.

Because every possibility for shared empathy is eliminated through the enactment of this second reduction, everything not-me becomes reduced to mere physical appearance *for me*. All forms of life and activity that are not immediately intuited must be bracketed as well, including all conscious life as well as every cultural object. Things are only spatiotemporal material objects, with no sort of consciousness attached to them.[18] What I am reduced to is my own ego, my own egoic stream of consciousness, what is actually present to me and given *originaliter*. And it is this alone that I hold as the apodictic evidence of transcendental self-perception (*CM* 103).

Husserl's reduction to the sphere of ownness is methodologically essential for distinguishing between (a) what gets brought about in my transcendental ego and (b) the universe that is constituted therein. "On the one hand, there is the sphere of my ownness and the coherent stratum of meaning consisting in my own experience of a world reduced to what is included in my ownness. On the other hand, there is the sphere of what is 'other.'"[19] It could not be otherwise, Husserl asserts, lest *my* experience would belong to someone else, and vice versa. Hence, without a reduction to ownness, self-experience would remain allusive, at best. The distinction between my stream of conscious experience and someone else's *Erlebnis* marks the abyss that separates me from every possible Other.

§4. Appearances of Transcendence

Paul Ricoeur calls Husserl's reduction to the sphere of ownness an "audacious methodological decision even more paradoxical than the problem to be solved."[20] Essentially, Ricoeur argues that Husserl succeeds only in transforming the objection of solipsism into an argument. In the self-reflective experience of ownness, only "one" subject is "I," whereas all the rest are categorized in a derivative sense precisely in terms of their being *others*. Ricoeur notes that the I-Other relationship is born (here) as a philosophical problem. To constitute the Other as Other, in and through myself, is to show how the sense "ego," born with reflective coming to awareness of my existence as an entry way for all sense, is communicated to these Others and permits me to say that those Others over there are also selves, egos. But they are egos only in a derivative, secondary sense, because the sense "ego" is initially constituted in me and for me. This parentage is in no way chronological; rather, it follows the logical order of sense.[21]

Although the second reduction is a product of abstraction, Ricoeur nevertheless insists that it remains "methodologically necessary" because it places in correct order a primary sense of the word "me" and a secondary sense that attaches to whomever is an Other *for* me. Ricoeur grants Husserl's point that without the primary constitution of the sense "ego," it would prove methodologically impossible for me to then transfer the sense "alter ego" to the Other. From his analysis, Ricoeur demonstrates that the Husserlian experience of ego-constitution holds primary significance, at least in the order of knowledge. The Other is constituted as a necessary yet second-order experience, a derivative possibility drawn from the primordial sphere of ego-constitution. David Bell, on the other hand, does not share the same level of enthusiasm for Husserl's reduction to ownness as does Ricoeur. According to Bell, the exclusivity of the egocentric perspective denies outright any possibility for the givenness of genuine alterity. "There can only be one space, one ego, one living body, and one intentional world: *mine*."[22] What makes knowledge of others possible, Bell contends, is not the primary constitution of the ego, but rather its *abdication* or *negation*. The methodological significance of the reduction to ownness consists, then, not in the primary experience of what the ego *is*, but, rather, in what the ego *is not*: "It is only in so far as I can remove myself . . . from the geometrical centre of that perspective that there is created so much as the possibility of another ego."[23]

Of course, Bell's analysis simply does not go far enough for Husserl. In the Fifth Cartesian Meditation, for example, Husserl insists that I also have to transfer the sense of "living ego" *to* the other. We have followed Husserl into muddy waters indeed! Can we find some sort of a middle ground between Ricoeur's and Bell's interpretations of Husserl's reduction to the sphere of ownness that does not take the concept of the self either too narrowly or too broadly? Frederick Elliston, I submit, points toward such an approach by arguing that we need to place the second reduction in its proper perspective. In other words, we need to remember that the sphere of ownness (out of which the sense *alter ego* is constituted), always includes its world of meant, or intended, objects. The Other is not created ex nihilo. Rather, the Other is constituted by the transcendental field of immanent subjectivity. Husserl never encapsulates the self within its mental life so as to create an abyss it must mysteriously bridge in *getting* to know others. Husserl's doctrine of intentionality, which is operative in the noetic-noematic correlation, refutes this formulation of the problem. For Husserl, the problem is hermeneutical. How do I come to interpret something within the sphere of immediate experience as another self?[24]

What Elliston presents is a balanced reading of Husserl that, to my mind, raises a key issue concerning Husserl's analysis of the relationship between transcendence and immanence. For Husserl, the primordial world is a "bare nature" (*CM* 96), what Michael Theunissen characterizes as "a world of things that the act of abstraction has artificially reduced to its pure corporeality."[25] This intentional substratum in which a reduced world shows itself is designated by Husserl an "immanent transcendency" (*CM* 106). Husserl contrasts immanent transcendency with "the sought-for transcendence of the 'alien,' whereby we are to understand, as the immanence in question, that very ideal belonging of the egologically constituted world to myself" (*CM* 57). According to Husserl's static analysis, the alter ego is constituted within a horizon of a world of objects. This means that the founding stratum that gives to me the sense *alter ego* also makes possible the experience of the Objective world via a reduction to the sphere of ownness. The very meaning of Husserl's transcendental theory of the Objective world is thus founded on intersubjectivity. The world that is valid for everyone becomes phenomenologically manifest once the reduction to ownness is performed and the analogical transfer is carried out. Reduction is a preliminary methodological step. Objectivity requires a second step of analogical transference. Husserl argues this point vigorously: "This unitary stratum, furthermore, is distinguished by being essentially the founding stratum—that is to say: I obviously cannot have the 'alien' or 'other' as an experience, and therefore cannot have the sense 'Objective world' as an experiential sense, without having this stratum in actual experience; while the reverse is not the case" (*CM* 96). According to Elliston, Husserl's descriptive analysis of the sphere of ownness is logically prior to empathy and to all higher forms of social consciousness. In the order of knowledge, the ego constitutes our experience of *all others*—including any possible experience of the Other as alter ego, subject, alien, for-itself. This means that, in the order of knowledge, the transcendental-I comes before every alter ego and is indeed its epistemic condition of possibility. Insofar as the alter ego is constituted as an *object* within my sphere of ownness, the Other is constituted as an immanent, perceived entity. "Within and by means of this ownness, the transcendental ego constitutes . . . at the first level, the other in the mode: alter ego" (*CM* 100).

We will examine important implications of Husserl's position in detail in the following chapters of this book. For now, I wish only to alert the reader to the fact that Husserl has still not really answered Bell's (or, for that matter, Ricoeur's) objections. Elliston merely draws out the logical steps to Husserl's argument yet leaves the fundamental problem of the appearance of transcendence untouched. Of course, Husserl's second reduction to the sphere of ownness does not offer an adequate constitutional account of an alter ego that is not a mere intended in me but a fully intending subject for-itself. Husserl's notion of a reduction to the sphere of radical privacy is only a preliminary step. The other has the *content* "living self," though in a passive or genetic sense. Husserl is not saying that "I" as Ego transfer or isolate the other. What Husserl discovers is that I am always already isolated within an overarching relationship regardless of whether I and Other have explicitly perceived one another as isolated beings. Hence, to perceive the Other qua other means to be drawn into a relationship such that alterity is always already given. Husserl's description of the reduction to ownness is the first or preliminary step; the second step is the transfer itself and requires embodiment. Let us look more closely at Husserl's analysis.

§5. Embodiment

Within the sphere of ownness, I perceive bodies; yet, only *my* body is singled out as an *animate organism*. The subjectivities of all other bodies are bracketed in this reduction precisely because they are not—and cannot be—actually present to me as *my own consciousness* (*CM* 97).[26] Everything "other"—including other persons—appears to me as a material object. My body alone is taken as a presumptive unity in such a way that I perceive embodiment as the embodiment of myself. I experience myself as a unique subject incarnated, *acting*, or "holding sway" over my body. In other words, my body is co-given along with my ego. Or, as Husserl describes it, I become motivated to co-intuit my body in light of the "*ownness-essence* of the Objective phenomenon: '*I, as this man*' " (*CM* 97). What remains totally inaccessible to me, therefore, is the subjectivity of every other ego.

The consciousness of the Other is methodologically excluded from the sphere of ownness. While I can always walk a few feet in another direction in order to see my house from a different angle (spatial), or return later this afternoon to make a second withdrawal from my checking account at the local bank (temporal), the subjectivity of the other remains genuinely transcendent because it admits of no intuition or original presentation. The Other's intentional stream of conscious inner-lived experience (*Erlibnis*) cannot be experienced by me: it is *originaliter* to itself, but not *for me*. Thus, all that I perceive of the other ego is its *body*,[27] which, at this point in the meditation, appears only as a physical body (*Körper*), not as a lived-body (*Leib*), like my own.[28]

"Every consciousness of what is other," Husserl reminds us, "every mode of appearance of it, belongs in the [sphere of ownness]" (*CM* 100). This includes the Other as embodied. But if it is within and by means of my sphere of ownness that the alter ego is given, does the Other somehow become known, familiar, representational in my experience? Or does the Other's primordial sphere of conscious life remain differentiated and inaccessible from my own? How can I know an experience of alterity when, by definition, alterity means precisely what must remain foreign (*Fremde*) and non-primordial and distinct from me? To what degree can the Other be said to be a *for-itself*, if, in the order of knowledge, the alter ego must somehow first appear to me as a constituted reality?

The reduction to the sphere of ownness eliminates as given anything living or conscious that is not me or mine; I even have to engender experience of my own body. This means that only my ego is given absolutely, whereas my body is given apperceptively. Nevertheless, my ego is never given in a non-bodily way. Body-image is constituted according to tactile sensations that are always localized and embodied.[29] This means that embodiment is constituted by a series of localizations of conscious acts that occur in my body. Hence, my hand is not an object *for* consciousness; rather, it is a localization where consciousness finds itself as belonging to a primordial *Here*, as the place where I build up over time a sense of myself *as* embodied. Husserl introduces "mundanizing self-apperception" in order to describe the mutual sense in which (1) I apperceive my body from the primordial givenness of *Erlebnis* while, at the same time, (2) my psychic states never appear in the world except through the mediation of a body (*CM* 96–100).

As the seat of consciousness, my ego can never be constituted in a non-bodily way. In fact, what Husserl means by perception can be defined as the place wherein consciousness finds itself as belonging to a primordial *Here*. For example, I see/am conscious of my hands. My tactile sensations are localized, and it is by such localizations that I am then motivated to constitute a particular body-image. This means that I preside *Here* in my body, even though I have to engender, or constitute, this very experience. I build up a sense of what my hand is. The hand *is* where my conscious stream is embedded, insofar as I constitute the world by touching, by perceiving, by feeling, by encountering the world *with my hands* (*CM* 99–100).

Hence, what Husserl indicates by my body is that unique place constituted in nature in which *I* rule and hold sway. The body that I encounter in the reduction to the sphere of ownness is not a negative residue added *on to* pure consciousness. Rather, the reduction signifies a positive phenomenology of embodiment, of corporeality, of incarnation. For Husserl, consciousness is never pure, disembodied ego; my body is always a prominent, inseparable feature of every intentional act. Husserl calls my body the "first body"; it is a living body, constituted as an irreducible center, the heart and soul and source of monadology. This means that what is given in the sphere of ownness in terms of embodiment is not what is ours but what is mine: the living stream (*Erlebnis*) of another person's flow of conscious life remains beyond my grasp and comprehension. There is no possibility of culture, language, or communication in the sphere of ownness; the only things that exist are objects of various sizes and shapes. Still, it is important to note that for Husserl the reduction to privacy is not the negation of the public; it is that upon which the public is founded (*CM* 100).

§6. Analogical Apperception of the Other

Husserl's description of the constitution of the alter ego is not accomplished merely genealogically but also statically, in terms of its component strata:

> Here it is not a matter of uncovering a genesis going on in time, but a matter of "*static analysis*." The Objective world is constantly there before me as already finished. . . . It is a matter of examining this experience itself and uncovering intentionally the manner in which it [the Objective world] bestows sense, the manner in which it can occur as experience and become verified as evidence relating to an actual existent with an explicatable essence of *its* own, which is not *my* own

essence and has no place as a constituent part thereof, though it nevertheless can acquire sense and verification only in my essence. (*CM* 106)

Up to now, Husserl has argued, the Other is presupposed in its corporeal unity as being present, felt, embodied, before me. Hence, neither the primordial essence of the Other nor the Other's lived experience can be said to be given to me in any sense *originaliter*. Otherwise, I would be that person and not myself. (Consequently, the very notion of experiencing the experiences of another person makes no sense.) What gets constituted as the intrinsically *first other* is the first non-primordial Ego, the *other*, or alien, ego. We may now characterize Husserl's theory of ego-constitution as a movement from the sphere of ownness toward the first other, that is, toward what gets constituted as an embodied alter ego. According to Husserl, the discovery of this other Ego "makes constitutionally possible a new infinite domain of what is other: an *Objective Nature* and a whole Objective world, to which all other Egos and I myself belong" (*CM* 107). Husserl describes the substratum of this infinite domain as Nature, and he places *this* substratum in contrast to the Objective nature investigated by the natural sciences.

How does the "first other" come to be if all that I can know primordially is my own *Erlebnis*, from which I apperceive my body? Husserl explains the constitution of alter ego in three steps, each of which we will now follow in some detail: analogical apperception, harmonious verification, and imaginative variation. According to Husserl, the way perceptual objects are built up over time is through the process of apperception and analogy. When I see the front of a building, for instance, I instinctively and imaginatively apperceive its various sides that are not open to my immediate visual perception. Likewise, since the mind is motivated by laws of association and analogy, pairing one object with another is a primal form of passive synthesis, which Husserl designates as association. Whenever the side of a physical object is present, I am motivated to apperceive those other sides that remain hidden from view. In an analogous sense, once my own body is apperceived, I am then motivated to constitute the bodies of other persons. Husserl writes: "Since my animate organism is the only body that is or can be constituted originally as an animate organism . . . the body over there, which is nevertheless apprehended as an animate organism, must have derived this sense by an apperceptive transfer from my animate organism, and done so in a manner that excludes an actually direct . . . showing of the predicates belonging to an animate organism specifically, a showing of them in perception proper" (*CM* 110–11). Whenever I see another person face-to-face, I apperceive his or her whole body. But when I hear someone's words, feel their presence, see them step into view, and so forth, I do not merely apperceive what remains physically hidden from view. Rather, I also apperceive *what is not given*, that is, the Other's flow of conscious, intentional life. If the Other were only a body constituted in my sphere of ownness, then the Other would merely be another material object but not another ego. Therefore, when Husserl describes how another ego comes to be present before me "in person"—in the flesh, so to speak—he does not mean that the *Erlebnis* of this alter ego or their stream of consciousness is present to me as my own. If that were the case, the Other would not be other but only the same as myself (*CM* 109). The Other is more than body and yet always appears in the flesh, that is, bodily, so to speak. In a manner of speaking, the Other appears by means of a mixture of presence and absence, a co-mingling of what *is* along with that which is *not*, the "co-perception of what does not appear with absolute originality."[30] In this co-perception of accessibility, transcendence is apperceived.

For Husserl, appresentation mediates the alter ego as a subject in the world, a "transcendent transcendence," as what appears to me without appearing, what is more than body and yet appears always *leiblich*. Michael Theunissen's comments cut to the bone of what Husserl is driving at:

> Inasmuch as the category of appresentation now, to a certain extent, delivers over the Other to the thing-world, it endangers the realization of the most essential task that the transcendental theory of alien experience is, according to Husserl, supposed to accomplish, namely, the certification of the character of the Other as transcendent transcendence. For, that the Others are given to me in transcendent transcendence means, negatively, that they are "not given to me in perspectival unities, not in ideal immanence like thing objects." Considered in this way, the task of the theory of experience of the alien therefore consists in bringing to light the distinction between the mode of being of the thing and that of the Other. However, the use made of the category of appresentation, which levels down the Other and the thing, stands in its way.[31]

For Husserl, there are two kinds of appresentation: (1) the appresentation of external perceptions of physical things (e.g., the back-side of a tree hidden from view) and (2) the appresentation of another subjectivity (which, Husserl argues, always exists in its originary sphere). The external appresentation of the back-side of a tree, for example, can be verified by walking around the tree on all its sides and looking at it, or by collecting data from other sources in order to describe what the back-side of a tree should look like. Husserl calls this kind of perception *fulfilling presentations* and contrasts it with external appresentation, which remains markedly different from analogical appresentation, since verification of the latter is excluded a priori. Whereas I can always (theoretically, at least) later verify through further inquiry the side of an object that is presently outside my perspectival grasp, another person's *Erlebnis* can *never* be given.[32] The alter ego remains a strange and essential mystery. It signifies a structural withholding of what cannot be intuitively grasped, namely what Johannes Climacus in *Fear and Trembling* calls "the secret," a non-comprehensible Truth that remains outside every primordial sphere of knowability. Transcendence remains essential in every act of empathy.

Alter ego is what gets constituted by me through an experience of the co-mingling of immanence and transcendence, absence and presence. Alter ego is thus an alien consciousness that always remains infinitely beyond my grasp. "What is *appresented*," Husserl says, "can never attain actual presence, never become an object of perception proper" (*CM* 12). How, then, does Husserl maintain his theory that another subjectivity is *given to me* as a non-originary "making present through analogical appresentation"? In other words, how does something alien and transcendent in its radical otherness become immanent in my own conscious experience?

Having made the reduction to the sphere of ownness—in which only *my* body is present as an animate organism—Husserl argues that the other body can now appear only as a material object, one among a multitude of others. (This is what was noted earlier in terms of "immanent transcendency.") The similarity of the alien body *over there* with my own body *over here* motivates me to constitute an awareness of the alien body as an animate, living organism similar, though different, from my own. Such analogical apperception, however, results neither from the product of an inference nor the culmination of a pensive act (*CM* 111). It is a kind of making co-present, a givenness constituted by a certain mediacy; it is what Husserl designates "analogical transference."

The analogical grasping of an alter ego marks the decisive theme of the Fifth Meditation. "Balanced in it are the two requirements of phenomenology: respect for the otherness of the Other and the rooting of this experience of transcendence 'in' primordial experience."[33] Every experience I have of the Other announces the Other as being-*there* (*Dasein*) "in flesh and blood," though without being given in the original. Paul Ricoeur comments that "the Other is not 'presented' directly, immediately, but 'appresented' through his body, which alone is 'presented,' since it appears in my primordial sphere just as other bodies do. Hence, the key to the problem is to be sought in connection with the body of the Other."[34] As such, only the body of the Other (i.e., *his* or *her* body as such) can be *given* to my perception while at the same time *giving* the Other. The task at hand, Ricoeur reminds us, is to somehow relate appresentation—or mediate grasping of the Other—to the Other's own body, and apperception—or reified consciousness—to myself.

What is given to me first is the other's body, from which I am then motivated to apperceive the other's ego.[35] For Husserl, this is the way that analogy works, namely, from body to body. What gets signified initially by me as ego moves from *my* body, apperceived in the world, to the body of the Other, which appresents the possibility of another life-force, a for-itself that is at the same time both similar and dissimilar to me. Hence, the sense ego is transferred from my body *Here* to the alien body perceived *over There*:

> Let us assume that another man enters our perceptual sphere. Primordially reduced that signifies: In the perceptual sphere pertaining to my primordial Nature, a body [*Körper*] is presented, which, as primordial, is of course only a determining part of myself: an "immanent transcendency." Since, in this Nature and this world, my animate organism [*Leib*] is the only body [*Körper*] that is or can be constituted originally as an animate organism [*Leib*] (a functioning organ), the body [*Körper*] over there, which is nevertheless apprehended as an animate organism [*Leib*], must have derived this sense by an *apperceptive transfer from my animate organism*, and done so in a manner that excludes an actually direct, and hence primordial, showing of the predicates belonging to an animate organism [*Leiblichkeit*] specifically, a showing of them in perception proper. It is clear from the very beginning that only a similarity connecting, within my primordial sphere,

> that other body [*Körper*] over there with my body can serve as the motivational basis for the *"analogizing"* apprehension of that body [*Leib*] as another animate organism. (*CM* 110–11)

Every motivation to apperceive the Other as having a body different from mine (rather than its being a mere extension of my own body) is based on my experience that the Other is irreducibly other *to me*. In a manner of speaking, the alterity of the alter ego is constitutive of my experience of what lies outside the givenness of my own experience: experience is original consciousness (*CM* 108). Constituted transcendentally in the sphere of ownness, I first encounter the Other's body as a material body (*Körper*). It is only via analogical transference that I am later motivated to apperceive the Other's body as *alive*; that is to say, I am motivated to constitute the Other as an alter ego, a living body (*Leib*) like me, only different. Husserl muses:

> The other is himself there before us "in person." But this being there in person does not keep us from admitting forthwith that, properly speaking, neither the other Ego himself nor his subjective processes or his appearances themselves, nor anything else belonging to his own essence, becomes given in us experience originally. If it were, if what belongs to the other's own essence were directly accessible, it would be merely a moment of my own essence, and ultimately he himself and I myself would be the same. . . . We have here a kind of making "co-present," a kind of "appresentation" (*CM* 109).

§7. Pairing

Through a reduction to ownness, I see diverse objects moving in the world. These objects are grasped analogically, namely, by comparison in which I apprehend commonalities and differences to various degrees. One of the things I apperceive is my own body. My consciousness, on the other hand, is what is given absolutely, what is peculiarly my own, what is alone apodictic (*CM* 95). Consequently, I enter pairing with the Other by being motivated to pair my live body with the live body of the Other. It is as wholes that we are initially paired, and because of that, we can pair organs and limbs, and so on. In other words, as I apperceive my body, I am drawn to other bodies in an analogical sense, first whole to whole and then part to part. Through "pairing" (or "twinning"), I match my own body with that of the Other, and then piece by piece with other bodily parts. I am motivated to constitute the alter ego in the manner of creative analogical transferences, first based on whole body to whole body and subsequently based upon a hand-to-hand and face-to-face relation. Although I am aware of my own consciousness first, my body is founded by apperception; whereas in the constitution of the Other, I am first aware of her body and then only later do I apperceive her consciousness. Thus, the other body given similarly to mine is paired with my own and appresented as an alter ego.[36] Because its conscious life is not accessible to me *originaliter*, the body of the Other is truly other; it cannot be *my* animate organism: "Insofar as the Other remains an analogue of my ego, the Other is only a modification of my ego; but, in showing himself as addressed toward me in concordant behavior, he truly becomes 'Other.'"[37] As acts motivated by the perceptual law of analogy, pairing is constituted in terms of neither a logical analogy nor an ego act, nor even active genesis. It is a passive genesis by which I am moved by a perceptual analogy to constitute another body as like mine, only different. The mind is in general motivated by the laws of association. One of the ways I associate is by *pairs*, which is a primal form of that passive synthesis that Husserl designates as association. Motivated by the law of association, pairing is a form of passive genesis based on analogy. In other words, although the Other is given to me as a body (*Körper*), I apperceive that it is living (*Lieb*). Hence, two distinct spheres of givenness are made evident through pairing: (1) the givenness of my own inner-lived experience and (2) that which is irreducibly alien to me, what gets constituted by me as being outside the givenness of my own primordial experience. What Husserl describes in terms of pairing is a rather formal structure that contains no content. The alter ego must be enriched by syntheses of verification; otherwise, it cannot be constituted by me as an alter *ego*. I am thus motivated to fill in the Other with the content *of* the Other. Alterity builds up content, and the space between ego and alter ego becomes filled in by me *analogically* (CM 113).

§8. Imagination

The role that Husserl affords imagination, whether through free variations or harmonious verification, becomes significant in his account of the progression from the "empty sense" of material body to the "fulfilled sense" of the analogical grasping of the Other as an embodied, expressive subjectivity. Imagination *opens up* the possibility for reflection. Whereas the whole preceding analysis takes place within the circle of perception—pairing is actually a perceptual experience—imagination serves to "'illustrate' or 'presentiate' the associative link which the first stage of the constitution of the Other provides."[38] It is only by imaginative variations of what is given that the alter ego becomes constituted as a living body. I am first motivated to form a pre-conscious attitude of the Other's body and only later posit a consciousness *into* that foreign body that is remarkably similar to my own. (Of course, the foreign body must be different in the sense that it is *not-mine*.) Every body-to-body meeting spontaneously motivates me to constitute the intersubjectivity of the Other.

Whereas the Other is never absolutely given to me but only analogically apperceived, so the constitution of the Other needs to be verified by what Husserl calls "harmonious units" of similarity. This means that the very idea of intersubjectivity contains a self-limiting notion, namely an understanding that verification can never be complete. As an infinite task composed of intersubjective units of verification and apperception, I never perceive the Other's consciousness wholly or directly. Quentin Lauer argues that if I could see the Other's stream of consciousness, then the Other would not be *alter* ego but merely an extension of my own ego: "The self is constituted in and with its experiences, but since I cannot constitute another's experiences, how can I constitute another's subjectivity? And, if I cannot do this, how can another *be for me*?"[39]

Husserl responds by saying that since my animate living organism is reflexively *Here*, whereas the Other's body is over *There*, I can, through imaginative variation, change my position and convert a *There* into a *Here*.[40] Through imaginative variations, I come to realize that the Other is not a duplicate carbon copy of myself. Reflexively, I become conscious that my experience revolves around my *Here*, not the *There* where I perceive the Other's body to be situated. Furthermore, because I experience the Other's body as distinct from my own, my being *Here* confirms the otherness of the Other's body insofar as the Other's body is always over *There*. What is interesting to note is that "here" and "there" are relational terms constituted within the horizon of my own temporal and spatial experience. Since *here* implies *there*—and vice versa—we may conclude that for Husserl the primary givenness of the alter ego is encountered through *imaginative* (i.e., cognitive) constitution. Ricoeur notes that imagination is a fiction that liberates me from absolutizing any and all particular perspectives. Imagination propels me to move into or engage another (i.e., the Other's) point of view: "I am 'here' (*hic*), the Other is 'there' (*illic*), but 'there' is where I could be if I were to move. From 'over there' I would see the same things but under another perspective. Hence, through imagination I can coordinate the *other places*, the *other* perspectives, to *my* place and to *my* perspective. *Illic*, that is where I can go. Hence, it is my potential *hic*."[41] Imaginative transference of my life into another life is never given to me in an originary or primordial sense. The appresentation of the Other is always given as a reproduction in the mode of "if I were over there." (Of course, in order for me to be "me"—that is, *this* I—means precisely for me not to be *there*, but to be *here*.) Given concretely in terms of imaginative experience, the life of the alter ego can never be for me equivalent to the one life of which I have originary experience. Although the alter ego is constituted through analogical appresentation in my sphere of ownness, the coexistence of the Other remains incompatible within the primordial sphere of my own conscious stream of lived experience. What gets constituted in terms of a non-originary experience is precisely the inner flow of the alter ego's subjective, conscious stream; this, in fact, is what constitutes the Other as *alter ego*. The bodily appearance of the Other motivates me to concomitantly constitute what is both given and withheld within the horizonality of those very conditions that make constitution possible. What gets regarded by me as *alter* ego is thus made manifest by a co-mingling of presence and absence, givenness and nonappearance, immanence and transcendence.

As we will see, for Levinas the Other is always a source of novelty. Language is the way we interact, and we go back and forth in conversation because we are never quite sure what either I or the Other will say next. For Husserl, the novelty occurs as the continuing verifications that fill in the alter ego become synthesized. The condition of possibility of novelty is associative constitution, the very stuff of verification and Objectivity. Analogy functions always in the mode of "as if." Tempered in the tension of the subjective mood, Husserl's "as if" finds its roots in Kant and demonstrates how phenomenology offers an account in perception and in language of the liminal. For Husserl, the "as if" functions as the softest kind of analogy, that is to say, "as if" is barely perceptible. My *Here* and the Other's *There* are "as if" the same, yet different. In effect, imagination posits the possibility "as if" there exists another "here." Experienced as a displacement from my primordial sphere of ownness, I begin to grasp the possible emergence of another perspective. Were I *There*, I might perceive the same world differently. But because I can never be both *Here* and *There* in the same instant, I can only imagine the possibility of alterity "as if." In discovering that there may exist other centers—other *Here*'s for other Others—Husserl does not prove the existence of other egos existing outside my sphere of ownness. Rather, he describes how the life of my Ego is constituted and layered by multiple strata of meanings and intentions.

§9. The Intersubjective Constitution of the World

If that which is absent is the *Erlebnis* of the Other and alterity is appresented on the basis of that which is primordially given (namely, my own lived experience), then it follows that the Other's subjectivity can never become present within my sphere of ownness. From the perspective of the constituting ego, this means that the subjectivity of alter ego is genuinely transcendent. Husserl in fact describes subjectivity in phenomenological terms as what is structurally absent. By this he means that the core of presentation, namely, what is presupposed by appresentation and made present in a non-originary sense, cannot be shared amongst a plurality of egos. Consequently, the transcendence of the Other rests on the basis of what is present, that is, the body of the Other (*Körper*) paired with my own animated body (*Leib*). My ego becomes motivated to posit what is absent as such. "Thus every perception of this type is transcending: it posits more as itself-there than it makes 'actually' present at anytime" (*CM* 122).

For Husserl, this means that the body of the other is the first intersubjective object. I see that what is "here" for the other ego is also "there" for me. The same perceptual object is given from two different perspectives and is intersubjectively constituted. The sphere of ownness is a methodological abstraction posed by Husserl in order to provide a point of departure or basis for the analogy between the self and the Other. Consequently, the Other is constituted *outside* the sphere of ownness. This is what Husserl means by other or alter Ego. Otherwise, the Other would merely be an extension of the same. The Other is constituted on the basis of an analogy with the sphere of ownness. This is why the first intersubjective object is the body of the other.

A third "body" is now brought into discussion, this being the body that we all perceive and is intersubjectively constituted (e.g., the world). Of course, this is the second intersubjective object: the natural world at large.

The first common object (structurally speaking, not temporally speaking) that is experienced from two different perspectives is the Other's body. The first common object is what is common "for us," what gets constituted as a material object. As we have seen, this in turn sets in motion multiple layers of meaning, common objects that different egos apprehend from their various points of view. By ego Husserl means that I see the whole world from my own perspective.[42] Accordingly, "the world" as given is what Husserl means by Objectivity, since it is the realm constituted by the public, by what is intersubjectively shared among different egos. Husserl in fact defines the Objective world as an immanent transcendency, an *idea*, the "ideal correlate of an intersubjective (intersubjectively communalized) experience which ideally can be and is carried on as constantly harmonious" (*CM* 107–8). As a harmony rising from the synthesis of transcendental monads, the world is what we all agree upon. Whereas in *Ideen* Husserl argued that objectivity means what the transcendental-*I* is motivated to see as a harmonious unity, in the Fifth Cartesian Meditation Husserl expands his definition of the objective world to mean what we, as an intersubjective community, are motivated to see as a harmonious and synthetic unity. The constitution of the Objective world essentially involves this "harmony" of monads (*CM* 108).

Husserl's sense of Objectivity is constituted by intersubjectivity, and the key to Objectivity is perspectivism. Husserl in fact argues that "the first thing constituted in the form of community, and the foundation for all intersubjectively common things, is the commonness of Nature, along with that of the Other's organism and his psychophysical Ego, as paired with my own psychophysical Ego" (*CM* 120). What Husserl means by this is that the recognition of the alter ego as Other provides the possibility for the constitution of Nature held in common by various perspectives, along with a cultural world where characteristic objects—books, values, laws—are correlatively shared among genuine communities of persons. Intersubjectivity thus involves an understanding of the constitution of a common Objectivity gleamed from an excess of perspectives. Let us take a look at this more closely.

The Other's body, along with my own body, belongs to the world of nature. By "Nature" Husserl designates not what is mine, or yours, but *ours*. Nature signifies the Objective world, the world that is intersubjectively shared and inter-monadologically constituted. Nature is the common object that constitutes Husserl's third perspective of embodiment: the shared, Objective world of the "we." Whereas my own primordial sense of *Here* founds my first perspective on the Other (i.e., the Other as object), and the Other's primordial sense of *Here* founds a second perspective, which is the Other's (i.e., the Other as subject), so the *intersubjective* perspectivity of "we" founds the third and most robust sense of Objectivity as commonly held Nature. This means that the Other's body is the first common, intersubjective, mundane thing.

The problem here, of course, is that the analogical grasping of the Other remains essentially asymmetrical and nonreciprocal. Husserl's theory of the reduction to ownness maintains that there is only one ego of which I can attain apodictic certainty, and this ego is multiplied associatively. Ricoeur traces the root of this predicament to Husserl's recognition of the Other "in a resolutely egological philosophy. . . . The apodicticity of the existence of the Other remains derivative from mine. Only one ego is presented; all Others are appresented."[43] Grounded upon this asymmetrical relation, Ricoeur concludes that "from this point forward we are assured that however real these 'communities' may be, they are never absolute in the sense that the ego alone is real in reflection."[44]

What Husserl intended to present was a theory of intersubjectivity that describes how each monad discovers for itself that the same world is grasped from different points of view, that each different perspective perceives the identical world *differently*. But what he in fact achieves is a theory of intersubjectivity that describes how other perspectives are mere appresentations of one originary perspective: *mine*. Consequently, although there may be an infinite number of egos that perceive the world each from their own unique perspective, nevertheless all other perspectives are cognitively constituted from *my* sphere of ownness. One stratum ("mine") lives through in the original, whereas all other strata are appresented by me as *not-mine*. Hence, the world that I perceive is the same world that the Other perceives, though in his or her own originary sphere. Here is the nexus of Husserl's descriptive account of the transcendental phenomenology of empathy. For Husserl, apperception ensures that the Other is like me, only different. The alter ego is both a constitut*ing* and a constitut*ed* phenomenon. For Husserl, such inter-active consciousnesses signify that I belong to a community, a socially constituted "we-world." Taken as a unitary experience, these analogically similar (yet distinct) egos that Husserl calls the inter-monadic community constitute a common, public world (*CM* 128).

Structurally speaking, reciprocity sets in for Husserl only *after* the Other is constituted.[45] Consequently, Husserl's theory of intersubjectivity does not contradict his fundamental theory of constitution. The phenomenology of empathy describes a theory of intersubjective constitution that explains intentionality in terms of the presence of other subjects in the cognitive sphere. Quentin Lauer notes that "intersubjective constitution is but an extension of the theory of objective constitution, concerned with an object which is constituted both as an object and as a subject."[46] Objectivity is what gets constituted by a plurality of egos; it is a cultural phenomenon toward which a multiplicity of perspectives converge.

§10. From "My" World to "Ours"

Constituted within my sphere of ownness, the Other is another *like me*, only different. Although Husserl does not know what the Other will say when she opens her mouth, that the Other says *something* is not at all shocking to him. The Other is one who shares the world with me. Hence, "the world" always has for Husserl a public sense. Further, because the Other sees the same world that I see—though differently—we may say that a structure of sociality now ensues between my ego and the alien ego. I see myself as one who is seen by the Other; I interact with the Other according to higher levels of inter-monadic communities.[47] A formal "philosophy of community" is thus built up on the founding stratum of empathic constitution. Such built up higher levels of meaning imply a mutual being-for-one-another (*CM* 129), in the sense that I come to experience myself as other *for an Other*, that is to say, as "one" among "others," as another *Other*. In this way, each Ego takes itself as a center of conscious and bodily meaning and grasps that every other Ego does the same. For Husserl, this symmetry or "equalization" of egos leads to the constitution of common, higher-order cultural objects of spiritual life.

According to Husserl's theory of apperception, there always exists some sort of analogical transference between what is mine and what is other. The strange is somehow made familiar, otherwise it would remain merely unknowable. Observe, however, that what gets recognized as "other" is no longer simply an alter ego, but now an alien lifeworld, what Husserl calls the *Umwelt* of the other. We noted earlier that what was originally designated as *Fremde* at the opening of the Fifth Meditation was the alter ego. Now, Husserl employs *Fremde* to designate other cultures and communities of egos that lie "outside" my own culture. The reclassification of what is alien gets redescribed in terms of the movement from our *Umwelt* to their *Umwelt*. What is experienced as foreign cannot be grasped fully and directly. Like the alter ego, foreign cultures can be constituted mediatively, analogically, apperceptively, through pairing and imaginative variation. For Husserl, this means that the law of empathy, which is based on analogical transference, can be extended from the individual ego to the community of egos. This grounds Husserl's understanding of cultural empathy: "To me and to those who share in my culture, an alien culture is accessible only by a kind of 'experience of someone else,' a kind of 'empathy,' by which we project ourselves into the alien cultural community and its culture" (*CM* 134–35).

According to Husserl's analysis, Nature and the Objective world are transcendentally constituted, first passively by the individual ego and consequently by a plurality of individual egos. This is what he means when he describes the social constitution of the lifeworld. Husserl's theory of sociality contends that every intentional act of consciousness originates "for me" in the sphere of ownness and then moves ek-statically toward the Other, toward the public. In like manner, what is constituted in terms of culture, that is, what gets constituted as *our* lifeworld, begins in the sphere of a shared lifeworld and then moves ek-statically toward what is culturally foreign, alien, unfamiliar. For Husserl, this means that empathy describes experiences of the givenness of the alter ego; it operates both on the level of the constitution of other egos and of other cultural communities, what we shall designate as *cultural empathy*. Without empathy, human communication is inconceivable:

> Everyone, as a matter of *a priori* necessity, lives in the same Nature, with the necessary communalization of his life and the lives of others, he has fashioned into a cultural world in his individual and communalized living and doing—a world having human significances. . . . Here I and my culture are primordial, over against every alien culture. To me and to those who share in my culture, an alien culture is accessible only by a kind of "experience of someone else," a kind of "empathy," by which we project ourselves into the alien cultural community and its culture. (*CM* 133–35)

§11. Cultural Empathy and a Return to the Same

Husserl means by empathy that the world of the other is given by pairing and analogy with the world of the same. By Objectivity, he means what is intersubjectively constituted. Hence, Husserl's theory of empathy encompasses the horizon of the entire world of transcendental objects given intersubjectively. In a word, cultural empathy describes the world given as potentially *infinite*: "As a further consequence, an 'empathizing' of definite contents belonging to the 'higher psychic sphere' arises. . . . In this sphere, every successful understanding of what occurs in others has the effect of opening up new associations and new possibilities of understanding" (*CM* 120). Consequently, the problem that plagued Husserl throughout the Fifth Meditation, that is, the problem of empathy, of trying to demonstrate that the ego is not alone in the world, is seemingly solved through higher-order levels of analogical variation and described in terms of cultural empathy. Husserl in effect concludes his experiment to the sphere of ownness by noting that "the illusion of solipsism is dissolved" (*CM* 150) only via a description of empathic constitution: "[T]he theory of experiencing someone else, the theory of so-called 'empathy,' belongs in the first story about our 'transcendental aesthetics.' There is need only to indicate that what we said about the psychological problems of origin in the lower story applies here as well: For the first time, the problem of empathy has been given its true sense, and the true method for its solution has been furnished, by constitutional phenomenology" (*CM* 147). Is Husserl justified in making such a bold claim? First, let us recall that Husserl's theory of empathic constitution is based on transcendental egological monadology. What he presents in the Fifth Meditation in terms of cultural empathy is a description of how other persons are constituted by the transcendental ego. Husserl remains adamant that no isolated self ever exists, not even for a single moment.[48] By way of a static analysis, he attempts to explain how I constitute Others precisely as embodied human persons who possess a sense of incarnate consciousness similar, yet different, to my own.

Second, every ontology must be traced back to the constituting, transcendental ego. My originary stream of consciousness and those structures by which the world and its objectivity are given grounds Husserl's description of the phenomenology of empathy. Because phenomenology excludes all speculative excess, Husserl remains confident that he is not establishing any sort of metaphysical doctrine. On the contrary, the transcendental ego is neither the first cause of Being nor the Unmoved Mover. Rather, transcendental ego is what is given first in the order of knowledge. Cultural objects become constituted later, as higher-order phenomena constitutively held in common by a community of egos. If the world is the world of all com-possible worlds, of all the worlds that can converge into one another, then transcendental phenomenology does not present metaphysical doctrines but instead describes the epistemic layers that describe how we go about constituting what we know about the world, ourselves, life, existence, God. Husserl's overall goal is to explicate or describe the sense of otherness that lies hidden yet implicit in everything we know, in everything *un*known that arises from what is *given*.

And finally, we should note that, whether implicit or explicit, real or ideal, all values and cultural artifacts are *public* and, therefore, built up via sedimentation over time. For Husserl, the "I" is not a self-sufficient creator of itself. The individually existing Ego is always and already part of a community, a member of many different communities that overlap and coexist. Especially here in terms of cultural empathy, Husserl notes that the I is never *naturally* reciprocal. Every sense of the Ego as "public nature" is theoretically derived from the genesis of ego-constitution. If I find myself always already in a public world, a "we"-world, a world of "us," a world constituted by art, tools, science, meaning, and especially language, this is only possible because what is "ours" must first be constituted by me *as* ours. In this sense, Husserl's cognitive approach to epistemology remains largely traditional, vulnerable to what Levinas calls "the history of ontology." For Husserl, a *purely* "private" world is theoretically conceivable though certainly not experientially possible.

§12. Descartes's Dream

As developed in the Fifth Meditation, Husserl's description of the constitution of the alter ego remains ultimately insufficient. Although Husserl succeeds in describing the constitution of cultural empathy in terms of monadological intersubjectivity, a weakness in Husserl's analysis appears in his inability to account for the givenness of foreign experience apart from my own conscious stream of lived experience with a sense of apodictic certainty. In cognitive terms, transcendental phenomenology reduces the Other—in principle, that is—to being a derivative foreign-*I*, an analogous *re*-presentation of what is given originarily to *I-myself* in terms of an embodied stream of inner-lived experience. Genuine alterity, however, must be both *genuine* (in the sense that the Other is not merely a representation of myself) and *alter* (in the sense that the Other must remain distinct throughout all processes of cognition). I submit that

Husserl's strict epistemological approach of describing the constitution of the Other in the Fifth Cartesian Meditation does not adequately describe the givenness of *genuine* alterity in light of his presuppositionless quest for epistemological purity:

> The immanent transcendence of the thing-world is only immanent because it does not overstep my "I-self." On the other hand, the specific transcendence of the Other is transcendent or "authentic" transcendence because the Other is entirely distinct from me. The attenuation of the distinction of transcendent and immanent transcendence disclosed in the application of the category of appresentation to the givenness of the Other therefore, at the same time, obscures the difference of the Other from me. This tendency comes into full operation in the theory of empathy.[49]

Through his theory of transcendental phenomenology, Edmund Husserl marks the fulfillment of Descartes's dream of presenting a thorough methodological project for describing all the de facto sciences, material and formal ontologies—even the egological roots—that account for all kinds of knowledge. But whereas Descartes's strictly cognitive project served as an inspiration for the Fifth Meditation, Husserl's search for apodicticity exposes the weaknesses inherent in his own cognitive experiment. What was initially regarded by Husserl as "derivative" may in fact play a far more radical and primordial role than originally envisioned. In terms of his phenomenological description of cultural empathy, Husserl's transcendental phenomenology contains an ethical element that needs to be explored further.

Chapter Three

The Significance of Empathy as Developed in *Ideas II*

With Reference to Husserl's Later Works on Intersubjectivity

Introduction

Husserl sketches a more robust description of the problem of empathy in *Ideas II* than he presented by way of the model outlined in the Fifth Cartesian Meditation. It is important, then, to examine Husserl's analysis of empathy in this different setting, that is, in light of a transcendental description of the intersubjective constitution of sociality, nature, and culture. Let us recall briefly what was Husserl's position during his famous Paris lectures by invitation from the Institut d'Études Germaniques and the Société Française. On February 23-24, 1929, Husserl painstakingly described transcendental phenomenology in terms of strict, concrete monadology. The objective world was defined primarily in terms of shared objects built up over time by a nexus, or intersubjective community, of monads.[1] Most clearly articulated in the famous Fifth Cartesian Meditation, Husserl sought to demonstrate that "the world is commonly constituted [as] a common world with different modalities, so that one world is for different subjects both the same and different."[2]

A closer analysis of the similarities and differences by which *Einfühlung* is treated in *Cartesian Meditations* and *Ideas II* suggests there is more to the development of Husserl's description of empathy than meets the eye. We know that Husserl's 1905 *Lectures on Internal Time Consciousness* was not published until 1928, and then under the (mistaken) editorial heading of Martin Heidegger.[3] The text was drawn from Husserl's lectures given at Göttingen on internal time consciousness and originally tasked to Edith Stein to transcribe and place into order.[4] Likewise, it is Edith Stein who was tasked with organizing the text that we now know as *Ideas II* from hundreds of random and handwritten notes, as well as Husserl's formal lectures and unpublished papers on social constitution theory. The text published as *Ideas II* was in fact written far earlier than Husserl's Paris lectures on Descartes, though it was never formally approved by Husserl for publication during his lifetime. Although the book was published in 1955, the genesis of *Ideas II* concerns a set of lectures given by Husserl at Göttingen from the early 1910s. Consequently, the focus of descriptive analysis is remarkably different from *Ideas II* than it is in *Cartesian Meditations*. In *Ideas II*, Husserl takes into account a description of higher-order cultural objects and the role that empathy plays in the constitution of social reality.

In this chapter I shall offer an analysis of givenness of the lifeworld in light of Husserl's description of cultural empathy specifically in terms of the constitution of (a) the common material world, (b) the animate world, and (c) the cultural and spiritual world. I will follow the constitution of each stratum, especially (c) the cultural and spiritual world. In *Ideas II*, Husserl designates empathy as a dominant theme for understanding culture and sociality, one that cannot be explained statically (i.e., in terms of its component strata) but must be examined genetically. To what extent did Husserl's formerly strict monadological and egologically cognitive approach from the Fifth Meditation diminish the role of sociality in the constitution of the cultural world? How might empathy, subsequently redescribed by Husserl in terms of reciprocity in *Ideas II*, constitute a found*ing* mode of experience in terms of culture and transcendence?

Finally, I will conclude this chapter by bringing into focus some of Husserl's later works, particularly his writings on intersubjectivity, including his Freiburg lectures and unfinished notes and manuscripts mainly between 1916 and 1938. As we will see, significant portions of Husserl's later thinking on intersubjectivity remained largely unpublished during his lifetime, in large part due to his own ongoing intellectual development concerning the critical role played by the lifeworld in terms of constitution. The focus of this study, then, is primarily Husserl's earlier work from the 1910s and 1920s, including *Ideas*, *Ideas II*, and *Cartesian Meditations*, alongside reactions from his early students and collaborators in phenomenology, mainly during his profoundly productive "teaching years" at Göttingen until his retirement from the University of Freiburg on July 25, 1928, rather than Husserl's later thinking on social ontology, including essays and manuscripts left unpublished (and unfinished) during his lifetime. Of course, Husserl's posthumously published writings, including those still currently in unpublished manuscript form, will likewise continue to provide significant and fruitful recourse for later phenomenologists interested in exploring the ongoing development of Husserl's progressive thinking regarding social ontology. For example, Husserl's personal lecture notes and draft essays on the phenomenology of intersubjectivity, published in 1973 as volumes XIII, XIV, and XV of *Husserliana*, were not formally approved for publication by Husserl himself, as he considered these manuscripts unfinished and in need of substantive editing and organization. While it is important to address some of the contributions that Husserl offered by way of these later lectures and writings, for the purpose of this study our primary concern revolves around the formal, published texts that Husserl and his students and colleagues—most notably, Heidegger, Stein, Scheler, Levinas, and Derrida, amongst others—would all have had great familiarity in terms of content and explication. Consequently, after turning our attention to *Ideas II*, we will conclude this chapter with a brief overview of how several themes drawn from Husserl's Freiburg lectures and notes, though unpublished during his lifetime, nevertheless lay significant groundwork for appreciating how Husserl's later ruminations on intersubjectivity remain a sine qua non for future variations and approaches to social constitution, including critical phenomenology.

§1. Background of *Ideas II*

Cartesian Meditations is a much later work than the *Ideen* project,[5] although in many ways the Fifth Meditation lays the philosophical groundwork without which *Ideas II* remains confused and misdirected.[6] For this reason we must now venture backward from Husserl's 1929 Paris lectures and return to Göttingen in the spring of the early 1910s. *Ideas II* is a complicated text. Its origin dates as early as 1912 when, in a series of pencil notes and paragraph revisions, Husserl first proposed to undertake a comprehensive study of social constitution theory (*Ideas II* xi). Initially, *Ideas II* was planned by Husserl to have been part of a single, grand project called

Ideas. But after the first volume of that project was published in 1913, Husserl left the remaining notes and essays in disarray. The book that we today call *Ideas II* was neither completed by Husserl nor definitively accepted by him as a finished work. Marly Biemel is responsible for the final arrangement of the edition published by *Husserliana*, in which she provides essential information about the work of two previous editors.[7] And it was Ludwig Landgrebe who brought together the final redaction of texts and supplements that Husserl reviewed concerning this particular project. Richard Rojcewicz points out that *Ideas II* underwent revision after revision, spanning almost twenty years. The book owes its form to the work of many hands, and its unity is one that has been imposed upon it. Yet there is nothing here that cannot be traced back, at least in terms of inspiration, to Husserl himself (*Ideas II* xi–xvi). Husserl last amended a final redaction of the text in 1928. It was then "set aside until posthumously edited and published by the Husserl-Archives in 1952" (*Ideas II* xi–xvi).

As a result of its complicated editorial history, a critical evaluation of the development of the "empathy texts" from *Ideas II* is indispensable to our task. What was finally published in 1952 were books two and three of *Ideas*, the former, 446 pages, and the latter totaling another 171 pages. *Ideas II* is divided into three unequal sections. Section one is the shortest of the three and deals primarily with the constitution of material nature. It is followed by an analysis of the constitution of animal nature in the second section. The third section, "The Constitution of the Spiritual World," contains the longest analysis in the book. It describes how "empathy towards other persons" constitutes the psychical world of culture and value. What is perhaps most intriguing is the fact that empathy—which received scant attention in book one of *Ideas* published in 1913—now takes on primal significance in book two. We might recall that only in the concluding notes at the end of the first book of *Ideas* does Husserl first hint at the important role that he had already assigned to social constitution theory. Cultural empathy or empathy of other peoples' experiences is essential for understanding how objectivity makes intersubjectivity and a shared "with-world" possible.

The transcendental description of "empathizing a feeling that originally was someone else's" was not a major concern for Husserl in book one of *Ideas*.[8] In *Ideas II*, however, the problem of empathy gets recast. Husserl understands *Einfühlung* as a condition of possibility of objective experience. Empathy makes possible the natural world as "the *object of natural science*" (*Ideas II* 3). Without the availability of a multiplicity of viewpoints that can be coordinated and shared, every experience of Objectivity remains at a merely theoretical level:

> [The] constitution [of the Objective world] is related to an open plurality in relation to subjects "understanding one another." The intersubjective world is the correlate of intersubjective experience, i.e., "experience" mediated by "*empathy*." We are, as a consequence, referred to the multiple unities of things pertaining to the senses which are already individually constituted by the many subjects; in further course we are referred to the corresponding perceptual multiplicities thus belonging to different Ego-subjects and streams of consciousness; above all, however, we are referred to the novel factor of empathy and to the question of how it plays a constitutive role in "Objective" experience and bestows unity on those separated multiplicities. (*Ideas II* 372–73)

In order to appreciate the importance of cultural empathy for Husserl, let us take a few pages to review the theme of the intersubjective constitution of the Objective world as developed by Husserl in the *Ideas II* texts.

§2. The Constitution of Material Nature

According to Husserl, every object is given always as a physical entity. What he describes in terms of *Körper* is the object composed of material nature: every object has a body. By material nature Husserl means the lowest and most basic sense of the totality of "real" things. Husserl thus acknowledges that "the entire world of things, the 'universe,' nature, which in its forms of space and time, encompasses all factual realities but also includes, obviously on essential grounds, all *a priori* possible realities as well" (*Ideas II* 30). What Husserl means by "Nature" concerns all the objects of natural science, including the total spatiotemporal universe, whether real or imagined. As the total domain of every possible experience, Nature is constituted as a field of transcendent realities. This does not mean that Nature is predetermined or that events in Nature are causally necessary. On the contrary, Husserl designates by Nature the total com-possibility of all intentional objects of possible knowledge. Nature, therefore, must first be constituted by a theoretical or cognitive subject. "*Nature, as mere nature, contains no values, no works of art*, etc., though these are indeed objects of possible knowledge and science" (*Ideas II* 4).

For Husserl, this means that there are two different kinds of attitudes that constitute the com-possibility of all possible objects: (1) the natural (or "practical") attitude of consciously lived, mundane experiences, composed of representing, judging, and thinking acts and (2) a theoretical attitude in which the subject *lives in* these acts and does so in a phenomenologically preeminent way. These secondary, cognitive acts are classified as subject-acts, predicate acts of a higher-order intensity. To paraphrase Husserl, perception needs to be distinguished from judgment and reflection. Perception involves living in the world, whereas Husserl designates judgment and reflection as "living in the seeing." Husserl argues that

> [i]t is one thing to see, i.e., to live through it all, to experience, to have something in the perceptual field, and it is another thing altogether to perform attentively an act of seeing in the specific sense, to "live" in the seeing in a pre-eminent way, to take an active part oneself in a "believing" and a judging, as an Ego in the specific sense, to perform an act of judging as a *cogito*, to be directed with an active focus to what is objective, to be directed in a specifically *intentional* way. (*Ideas II* 5)

Husserl's account of material constitution is founded upon "the reflecting of an intentional ray upon its synthetic 'results'" (*Ideas II* 8). He begins by expanding the notion of the *noetic-noematic* correlation described in the first book of *Ideas*. There, Husserl argued that theoretical acts—namely, the performance of which makes the subject the *theoretical subject*—belong to the peculiar character of the theoretical attitude. In them, objects that for the first time will become theoretical are already, in a certain derivative sense, laid out in advance. Husserl does not deny that the world, objects, things, others, and so on exist independently from my knowing them. Rather, Husserl insists that common, non-theoretical objects are *already* constituted pre-thematically since they are not "objects intended in the pre-eminent sense, and much less are they objects of theoretically determining acts" (*Ideas II* 8).

Pre-given or pre-thematic objectivities do not "spring" from theoretical acts. They are constituted in intentional, lived experiences. This is true for affective acts as well, such as "losing oneself" in the blueness of the sky or the pounding surf at the ocean's edge or "forgetting oneself" while becoming enraptured in music or a much-loved hobby or a deeply meditative experience. Beauty, desire, delight, joy—even their opposites—do not presuppose the existence of universal categories of value.[9] On the contrary, every value-object includes *already* "that feeling in which the ego lives with the consciousness of being in the presence of the Object 'itself' in the manner of feelings" (*Ideas II* 11). In other words, the constitution of material nature is characterized primordially by consciousness according to the basic intentional dispositions of the conscious act itself, which includes objects of judgment, objects of value, and objects of will.[10] Intentionality implies for Husserl the a priori possibility that the subject's attitude or perspective can change. Hence, what Husserl means by the constitution of material nature includes *the theoretical attitude itself*. For Husserl, the constitution of material nature does not designate a metaphysical or psychologistic description of reality. Rather, the theoretical attitude offers a phenomenological account of the way that consciousness must learn to take the world that is given.

§3. The Constitution of Animate Nature

Some objects are not *merely* material; there is movement, sway, intentionality, activity, animation. In particular, human beings are singled out by Husserl as what are also always given in terms of "animate nature." By "animate" Husserl implies "nature in a second, broadened sense, i.e., things that have a soul, in the genuine sense of 'living'" (*Ideas II* 30). Husserl contrasts the term *Leib* to infer an animated, en-souled, living Body (*Lieb*) as opposed to the merely material body designated by *Körper*. Concerning the constitution of animal nature, Husserl holds the position that things—whether concrete or imaginary—have essences and that the truths about these realities are apodictic. He further notes that the field of study that includes definitions of material essences never remains wholly restricted to material nature alone. On the contrary, there is a nonempirical science that defines essences according to particular "regional ontologies." Husserl sets for the constitution of animal constitution the task of examining, in eidetic intuition, the essences of these regional ontologies. *Leib* refers to the "living experience" in general and as such, precisely as it is made explicit in *every* experience (*Ideas II* 96–97).

According to Husserl's analysis, regional ontologies are first grasped in ordinary, prescientific experience. He calls these areas of investigation "regions" because they constitute the scientific domains of the natural sciences within which particular communities of scientists carry out their investigations, and he calls them "ontologies" because the methodology used to produce the unfolding of a universal essence in thought leads to the systematic development of a particular ontology. Through the doctrine of the constitution of animate nature, Husserl not only formulates the principles that ground the eidetic doctrine of essences. He also describes "the unfolding of the intentions essentially involved in such experience . . . in a rigorous analysis and description" (*Ideas II* 97).[11]

By use of the word *Leib* Husserl indicates that the human Body (*Leib*) constitutes the experience of spatio-thingly perception through a series of touch-sensations that are localized and synthesized through a series of retentions and protentions.[12] I am inclined, Husserl says, to speak of a physical object (my "left hand," for instance) whenever I attempt to describe the particular sensation of "feeling" or "touching" an object physically distinct from me. What I am in fact doing is *abstracting* from these sensations a spatial position vis-à-vis my Body in relation to the Object being touched. These abstractions are then synthesized, or organized, or constituted into a coherency. My hand, now resting quietly on the table, appears as a thing. It is not that my hand suddenly *becomes* something from nothing, a creation ex nihilo. On the contrary, I become conscious of my hand to the very degree that I am able to constitute *it* (my hand) as a center of localizations and touch-sensations. My hand is constituted as Body precisely *by* and *at* those places on its corporeal surface where it touches (or is touched by) another object that is *not* my hand. The physical thing—my left hand—becomes constituted *as hand* through sensations of tactile contact:

> All the sensations thus produced have their *localization*, i.e., they are distinguished by means of their place on the appearing Corporeality, and they belong phenomenally to it. Hence the Body is originally constituted in a double way: first, it is a physical thing, *matter*; it has its extension, in which are included its real properties, its color, smoothness, hardness, warmth, and whatever other material qualities of that kind there are. Secondly, I find on it, and I *sense* "on" it and "in" it: warmth on the back of the hand, coldness in the feet, sensations of touch in the fingertips. I sense, extended over larger

Bodily areas, the pressure and pull of my clothes. Moving my fingers, I have motion sensations, whereby a sensation in an ever changing way extends itself over and traverses the surface of the fingers. (*Ideas II* 153)

These localized sensations are not properties of the body as a physical thing, but rather properties of the animate Body that arise only *when* the Body is touched and only *where* it is touched at the time when it is touched. Husserl notes that "even two lifeless things can touch one another, but the touching of the Body provides sensations on it or in it" (*Ideas II* 154). This means that every perception of my Body is necessarily founded upon perceptual apprehension, along with its concomitant sensation of touch. The distinctive feature of the Body as a field of localizations summarily indicates that it (my Body or *Lieb*) is distinct from every other material thing (*Körper*) in the world. As the thing that has a stratum of localized sensations, I take my Body as an organ of the will, the "one and only Object which, for the will of my pure Ego, is *moveable immediately and spontaneously* and is a means for producing a mediate spontaneous movement in other things" (*Ideas II* 159).[13]

The Ego possesses a faculty—what Husserl terms the "I can" (*fiat*)—to freely move its Body and thereby perceive an external world of transcendent reality precisely by means of such movement (*Ideas II* 159). At the same time, Husserl is equally clear that "sensuous" feelings—such as sensations of pleasure and pain, well-being, joy, and despair, feelings that can permeate and fill the whole Body—are given in immediate intuition. Not only spatial Objects but also acts of valuing are constituted by the Body in terms of intentional lived experiences. These "higher-order" Objectivities are constituted as *values* in an analogous way that material objects are constituted as sense-things. For Husserl, all kinds of sensations—even those that he claims are difficult to analyze and discuss—belong here as well, for example, sensations that form the material substrate for the life of desire and will, sensations of energetic tension and relaxation, sensations of anxiety, paralysis, tiredness, excitement, doubt, fear, hope, and so forth: "All these groups of sensations, as *sensings*, have an immediate Bodily localization. Thus, for every human being, they *belong, in a way that is immediately intuitable, to the Body as to his particular Body*, i.e., as a subjective objectivity distinguished from the Body as a mere material thing by means of this whole stratum of localized sensations" (*Ideas II* 160).

§4. Constitution of the Cultural and Spiritual World

For Husserl, immediate sensings constitute the sphere of psychic, or spiritual, activity. As functions of intentionality, these immediate Bodily localizations are bound to both the material and animate strata. The valuing of such intentional lived experiences, however, is never directly or properly localized. The primary sensations "undergo apprehension, are taken up in perceptions, upon which, then, perceptual judgments are built" (*Ideas II* 160). Consciousness is not localized in the Body in the same way that the touch-sensation is localized in the touching finger. Rather, consciousness *is* the Body (*Leib*) insofar as consciousness constitutes the entire field of intuited apprehensions. Or, as Husserl describes it, "soul and psychic Ego *have* a Body" (*Ideas II* 165).

What marks the distinction between *material* reality on the one hand and *psychic* or *spiritual* reality on the other? For one thing, Husserl makes clear that material reality is not opposed to psychic reality. He reminds us that "material" and "psyche" are not two distinct *things* that can be placed beside one another. Nor is psyche something that goes beyond material nature. Although Husserl draws an important distinction between body (*Körper*), inanimate physical matter, and Body (*Leib*), the animated flesh of an animal or human being, this distinction does not signify a real separation but rather a description. In effect, the spiritual *penetrates* the physical whole in the same way that a book *animates* not "each word taken for itself, but rather the word-nexus, which [is] bound together by the sense into meaningful forms, and these later bound into higher formations, etc." (*Ideas II* 250–51). The human person is *Leib*. This means that the spiritual sense *fuses* the physical body (*Körper*) in such a way that they are not merely "bound together" as two distinct yet complimentary halves of a higher identity. The living Body (*Leib*) is a psycho-spiritual integration. Consequently, the living Body is already pre-constituted, pre-thematized, pre-given. The Body is what I discover about myself when I discover myself *as* "I"-myself.

What is physical is not opposed to what is spiritual. Consequently, the spiritual sphere does not exist in contradistinction to the physical. Husserl maintains that these two strata are united in the *Leib*. The physical and the spiritual reflect or describe two distinct *attitudes*, two different ways of seeing, two variant apprehensions. Taken together, these two attitudes express the totality that constitutes the integrated human personality.[14]

For Husserl, "an ideal harmony" therefore exists between physical and spiritual being:

> I see the man, and in seeing him I also see his Body (*Leib*). . . . In a certain way, the apprehension of a man as such goes through the appearance of the body, which here is a Body. In a certain sense, the apprehension does not stop at the body, its dart is not aimed at that, but it goes through it. . . . And the apprehension of the human, the apprehension of that person there, who dances, laughs when amused, and chatters or who discusses something with me in science, etc., is not the apprehension of a spirit fastened to a Body: it has a Corporeality, it has a body which is a physical thing with such and such qualities, and it has lived experiences and lived dispositions. . . . Man, in his movements, in his action, in his speaking and writing, etc., is not a mere connection or linking up of one thing, called a soul, with another thing, the Body. The Body is, as Body, filled with the soul through and through. Each movement of the Body is full of soul. (*Ideas II* 252)

For Husserl, every physical seeing implies also a spiritual seeing, whether or not the spiritual is recognized as such. This means that the constitution of animate nature—especially in terms of the psycho-physical constitution of the Body—involves not only the founding stratum of a surrounding world but my very participation in it. My Body is never given statically as a merely spatial or material object. Rather, every apprehension of my Body as *Leib* constitutes for me the condition of possibility of every sense of my having intentional lived experiences at all. Accordingly, "the spiritual is not a second something, is not an appendix, but is precisely animating; and the unity is not a connection of two, but, on the contrary, one and only one is there" (*Ideas II* 250–52).

Husserl's description of the constitution of the spiritual world suggests that every analysis of the Ego as a subject of sensual faculties must always include corporeality as a condition of givenness. These faculties, or drives, are not determined by instincts, inclinations, or causality. Higher-order values are instead driven by "a higher, autonomous, freely acting Ego, in particular one guided by rational motives, and not one that is merely dragged along and unfree" (*Ideas II* 267). In proposing that the physical and the spiritual are neither existentially nor mutually exclusive from one another, Husserl affirms that they form a coherent, singular identity: "[W]hat we have here is not a surplus which would be posited on top of the physical, but rather this is spiritual being which essentially includes the sensuous but which does not include it as a part, the way one physical thing is part of another" (*Ideas II* 251). In other words, the spiritual world encompasses the realm of what is possible, it constitutes the field of the "I can" (*fiat*) in a way that transcends the limitations imposed by physical nature alone. Husserl says that "the Ego, as unity, is a system of the 'I can.'"[15] Given now in terms of motivation, the question of the effects of the soul (*Seele*) on the Body (*Leib*) can never be said to be reduced to mere relations of either sentient or physical causality. The spiritual does not display any concern for the factual (physical) act of doing, but rather for my *being able* to do (*fiat*). This is an important characteristic of what Husserl means by motivation.[16]

The complex co-constitutive relationship between Body (*Leib*) and soul (*Seele*) reflects a distinction drawn earlier by Husserl in *Philosophy as Rigorous Science*. This distinction gets reinforced in *Ideas II* as a tension between phenomenology and psychology. In both these works Husserl underscores the autonomy of philosophical inquiry in respect to the social and natural sciences. He also deems it essential that there should be a critical (and therefore philosophical) examination of the structures that characterize them. Husserl offers a vigorous attempt to separate natural sciences (*Naturwissenschaften*) from human sciences (*Geisteswissenschaften*). He holds that the basic concepts of the newly emerging science of psychology must first be reconfigured according to a phenomenological account. Only by virtue of its subordination to the rigors of phenomenological inquiry can the foundations of psychology—like every other science open to scrutiny—be analyzed critically, scientifically, and objectively.[17]

In *Ideas II* Husserl expands his analysis of constitution from concrete monadology (as described in *Cartesian Meditations*) toward emphasizing how every psycho-physical thing "is given and is to be given only through appearances . . . which do not belong to an individual consciousness *but to a societal consciousness* as a total group of possible appearances that is constructed out of individual groups" (*Ideas II* 93).[18] Husserl ceases describing the givenness of the spiritual and cultural world primarily in terms of the concrete individual ego. Instead, he turns to describing the world in terms of a nexus of social relationships that exist between individual egos and groups of egos.[19] Especially higher-order values such as culture, art, language, ethics, and religion are products of social constitution. Husserl notes that the task of phenomenology is to "gather up into unity all the social Objectivities . . . that are in communication with one another. It should be noted that the *idea of communication* obviously extends from the single personal subject even to the *social* associations of subjects, which, for their part, present personal unities of a higher level" (*Ideas II* 206).

For Husserl, the spiritual or cultural world denotes the shared (Objective) world of intersubjective constitution, that is, the world of co-constituted objects and values, the emergence of cultural empathy. These unities, however, do not merely suppose "a collection of social subjectivities, but instead they coalesce into a social subjectivity inwardly organized to a greater or lesser degree, which has its common opposite pole in a surrounding world, or an external world, i.e., in a world which is *for* it" (*Ideas II* 206). Such an associated plurality of subjects, of individual spirits and spiritual communities, constitutes ever higher-order levels of meanings and significations.[20] Husserl holds that "it is characteristic of empathy that it refers to an originary Body-spirit-consciousness, but one I cannot myself accomplish originarily, I who am not the other and who only function, in regard to him, as a comprehending analogon" (*Ideas II* 208). In terms of strict epistemology, Husserl argues that empathy is a founding mode of social constitution.[21]

§5. Experiences of Empathy

Husserl next raises the problem of empathy according to a more complex notion of what he calls *pre-social subjectivity* (*Ideas II* 209). "I can have a 'direct' experience of myself," he claims, "and it is *only my intersubjective form of reality* that I cannot, in principle, experience. For that I need the mediation of empathy. I can experience others, but only through empathy" (*Ideas II* 210). For Husserl, empathy (*Einfühlung*) makes possible the transcendental experience of alterity. In fact, without the experience of alien subjectivity, I would not be able to constitute the world, society, nature or culture with any sense of Objectivity. This is what Husserl means when he says that pre-social subjectivity "does not yet presuppose empathy" (*Ideas II* 209). In effect, Husserl argues that the experience of empathy makes possible the manifestation of two different types of givenness: (a) *inner experience*, which is absolute, originary, and contains no elements of presentification and (b) *external experience*, which is a mediated experience of co-presentation, an experience of appresentation. "Here," Husserl notes, "we have experience of other subjects as well as of their inner life, an experience in which their character and their properties come to givenness for us, an experience of forms of community, community affairs, Objects of the spirit. Everywhere in this kind of experience, a moment of presentification through empathy is involved which can never be converted into immediate presentation" (*Ideas II* 209).

For Husserl, inner experience and external experience together constitute what is meant by empathy. Every genuinely intersubjective experience, therefore, must consist of two distinct yet related elements: (1) that which the personal subject can experience immediately and originarily as a member of the communicative world and (2) that which the personal subject experiences only mediately. Husserl describes this second group as the experience of empathy, as "experiences of a *co*-presence on the basis of what is actually perceptively experienced or what may be perceived in the course of experience, a co-presence that is not perceptible itself and which cannot be converted into the subject's perceptions, i.e., in terms of his own content of being" (*Ideas II* 210). Empathy thus implies the reciprocity of egos in the binding of a community, that is to say, the positing of the Other as a *co*-presence, a co-constituting subject who shares the same world as me but who nevertheless cannot share my originary experiences because they are mine and mine alone. In *Ideas II*, Husserl holds that the origin of the experience of empathy remains necessarily monadological: what I experience through empathy is an analogical re-presentation of the Other's primordial experience, now constituted in my own sphere of primordial givenness. At the same time, Husserl posits that, without empathy, there can be no cultural world or objective world of common objects or shared values. By its primary emergence in the cultural world, communication is a social—and therefore, empathic—phenomenon.

In effect, Husserl concludes that *Geist* and culture are accessible only through *Einfühlung*. The Objectivity of meanings and judgments cannot be constituted apart from the experience of empathy.[22] Hence, empathy must be both (a) constitut*ed* by acts of cultural constitution always given in "social experiences"[23] while, at the same time, (b) constitut*ive* of higher-order values. This means there must be both difference and similarity in every act of empathy. Otherwise, empathy would merely constitute an economy of sameness, the dissolving of my sphere of ownness into that of the Other.[24]

§6. The Significance of the Body in Husserl's Notion of Empathy

Empathic constitution is founded on an intersubjectively experienceable Body (*Leib*) that can be understood by the person who just enacted the *act* of empathy as the Body of the corresponding psychic being. Constituted as an irreducible center, my living body (*Leib*) becomes the empathic source of the constitution of the alter ego and vice versa. In terms of culture, this means that what I recognize as belonging to the Other is a lifeworld similar to mine, yet different. For Husserl, the law of empathy is founded on analogical transference. Culture therefore designates precisely what is held in common by an intersubjective community of egos. Objectivity is empathically constituted insofar as material and cultural values are shared and intersubjectively constituted at all.

In an analogous way that I experience my-self as a living Body, so too the Other's living Body is given to me in terms of an intentional center of orientation that is not my own. The Other is a co-subject who exists in the same world *with* me: "In the *comprehensive experience of the existence of the other*, we thus understand him, without further ado, as a personal subject and thereby as related to Objectivities, ones to which we too are related: the earth and sky, the fields and the woods, the room in which we dwell communally, the picture we see, etc." (*Ideas II* 201). For Husserl, my ego and the Other ego do not merely cohabit a singular world made up of an infinite number of possible lifeworlds. Ego and alter ego are primordially related to each other through the emergent possibility of cultural empathy. In fact, the communalization of social reality means that what is given in terms of Objectivity implies what is intersubjectively shared by experiences of empathic constitution. The primordial subjectivity of I and Thou co-constitute the Objective or intersubjective common world:

> We are in a relation to a common surrounding world—we are in a personal association: these belong together. We could not be persons for others if a common surrounding world did not stand there for us in a community, in an intentional linkage of our lives. Correlatively spoken, the one is constituted essentially with the other. Each Ego can, for himself and for the others, become a person in the normal sense, a person in a personal

> association, only if comprehension brings about the relation to a common surrounding world. (*Ideas II* 201)

Through the perspective of my own inner lived experience, I am motivated to constitute the Other as a spiritual being in whose life I can participate, and *at the same time* I assume that the Other is motivated to constitute me as a spiritual being in an analogous way. Persons influence persons not only by way of physical stimuli (i.e., through repulsion and attraction) but in their spiritual activity as well. Husserl states that persons "direct themselves toward one another (the Ego toward the other and vice versa), they perform acts with the intention of being understood by the other and of determining the other, in his understanding grasp of these acts (insofar as they are externalized in this intention), to certain personal modes of behavior" (*Ideas II* 202). A common, surrounding world is constituted through acts of empathy. For Husserl, cultural empathy founds the communicative world, the world in which

> *relations of mutual understanding* are formed: speaking elicits response; the theoretical, valuing, or practical appeal, addressed by the one to the other, elicits, as it were, a response coming back, assent (agreement) or refusal (disagreement) and perhaps a counter-proposal, etc. In these relations of mutual understanding, there is produced a conscious *mutual relation* of persons and at the same time a unitary relation of them to a common surrounding world. Furthermore, this might be not merely a physical and animal (or personal) surrounding world but also an ideal one, e.g., the "world" of mathematics. (*Ideas II* 202–3)

It is important to note, however, that by "mutual relations of understanding" Husserl does not mean that I and Other share a single, unified stream of lived experience. By "mutual" Husserl means the world that is mutually agreed upon. Such mutuality does not imply that I have direct access to knowing the Other's inner lived experience in the same way I know my own. In principle, I can apprehend an Other's spiritual life in the same way that I can read the words on this page: "[N]ot even each of my lived experiences, as components of the 'world' (of the Objective spatio-temporal sphere of reality) is experienceable directly, for the form of reality (that of intersubjective Objectivity) is not an immanent form" (*Ideas II* 210).

The Other is always experienced bodily.[25] Husserl argues that the body (*Körper*) of the Other is as essential to empathic apperception as is my own.[26] As noted previously, the constitution of *Leib* is founded on the primal tactile experience of my own body as a play of surfaces that interacts with other bodies already existing in the world. The elemental founding sense of the *Here* and *There* of my own living body already implies the real possibility of other concrete centers of orientation. This sense of the "relativity of the near and the far" is taken by Husserl to permeate all experience.[27] "Sociality is constituted by *specifically social, communicative acts*," Husserl says, "acts in which the Ego turns to others and in which the Ego is conscious of these others as ones toward which it is turning, and ones which, furthermore, understand this turning, perhaps adjust their behavior to it and reciprocate by turning toward that Ego in acts of agreement or disagreement" (*Ideas II* 204).

According to Husserl, empathic reciprocity is structural and describes how the alter ego is constituted as a live body within my own conscious stream through pairing and analogical apperception. Reciprocity may therefore be considered a founding mode of constitution, since constitution always entails passive synthesis and embodied, emotional engagement amongst mutually animate, live bodies. I am motivated to "see" the Other, but I "see" her seeing me. My body and the body of the Other are constituted as animate objects founded upon a reciprocity of pairing my body with the whole body of the Other. As Dermot Moran notes in his interpretation of *Husserlian XIII*, Husserl begins from the recognition of the other's body as sensitive and as possessing a sensory field of its own.[28] According to Moran's analysis of Husserl's project, "[B]odily expressions are thus already mediated by the primary apprehension of the foreign body as *Leib*."[29] It is thus experiences of localizations of physical and psychic processes of the other's body that get reciprocally constituted in a "seeing" of mutual recognition. For Husserl, the sphere of ownness is constituted according to such processes of retention and protention, in a similar way that my body and the body of the Other are reciprocally constituted by apperception and the coordination of sensory data. In chapter four of "The Constitution of Psychic Reality in Empathy," Husserl notes the following:

> In my physical surrounding world I encounter Bodies, i.e., material things of the same type as the material thing constituted in solipsistic experience, "my Body," and I apprehend them as Bodies, that is, I feel by empathy that in them there

is an Ego-subject, along with everything that pertains to it and with the particular content demanded from case to case. Transferred over to the other Bodies thereby is first of all that "localization" I accomplish in various sense-fields (field of touch, warmth, coldness, smell, taste, pain, sensuous pleasure) and sense-regions (sensations of movement), and then in a similar way there is a transfer of my indirect localization of spiritual activities. (*Ideas II* 172)

In the order of experience, the concrete monad is a founded phenomenon. Even the experience of my own body must first be constituted apperceptively. It is only on account of my own corporeal zero-point center of orientation that objects and other bodies like mine can be apperceived at all and, along with them, alter egos and their corresponding gestures and expressions. As Moran notes, in empathy "to see something as a gesture or expressions is already to recognize the presence of another intentional consciousness."[30] Husserl observes:

[I]n the case of touching an object, there belongs to every position of my hand and finger a corresponding touch-aspect of the object, just as, on the other side, there is a touch-sensation in the finger, etc., and obviously there is visually a certain image of my touching hand and its touching movements. All this is given to me myself as belonging together in co-presence and is then transferred over in empathy: the other's touching hand, which I see, appresents to me his solipsistic view of this hand and then also everything that must belong to it in presentified co-presence. (*Ideas II* 174)

Without pairing and analogical transference, neither the constitution of alter ego nor the Objective or cultural world held in common by a community of alter egos could ever be possible. Empathy is not merely significant but essential for the constitution of the reality "I as man." Husserl argues that "it would not occur to me at all in the attitude of 'self-experience' to take all that is psychic in me, my Ego, my acts, my appearances as well, with their sense data, etc. and seriously place, i.e., 'introject,' all this into my Body" (*Ideas II* 175). Husserl concludes: "It is only with empathy and the constant orientation of empirical reflection onto the psychic life which is appresented along with the other's Body and which is continually taken

Objectively, together with the Body, that the closed unity, man, is constituted, and I transfer this unity subsequently to myself" (*Ideas II* 175).

Cultural empathy makes possible the shared (Objective) world of intersubjectively constituted values. The intertwining of egos implies my positing the Other as a co-constituting subject who shares the same world as me, the world of culture, the world that Husserl calls the transcendental spiritual community:

> [T]here is constituted the idea of a world as *world of spirit* in the form of a sum total of social subjects of lower or higher levels (and we include here the isolated person as zero limit-case of social subjectivity) which are in communication with each other, actually or in part actually in part potentially, together with the sum total of the social Objectivities pertaining to it. For every subject that in this way is a member of a social association as a totality, there is constituted one and the same world of spirit, although from the "standpoint" of this or that subject it is apprehended and posited with a corresponding (hence different from subject to subject) apprehended sense. An associated plurality of subjects, of individual spirits and spiritual communities, related to a world of things, a world of "objects," i.e., an actuality which is not spirit but which is actuality *for* the spirit. (*Ideas II* 207)

Structurally speaking, for Husserl the epistemological foundation of knowledge of alter ego remains monadological. The presence of the Other is neither disclosed outside the terms of a transcendental ego nor understood apart from them. This epistemological interpretation of a transcendental origin of the social and cultural world dominates Husserl's thinking, even in *Ideas II*. Alfred Schutz expresses Husserl's point clearly and succinctly: "It should be stressed that this transcendental intersubjectivity exists purely in me, the meditating ego. It is constituted purely from the sources of my intentionality, but in such a manner that it is the *same* transcendental intersubjectivity in every single human being . . . in his intentional experiences."[31] Empathy is a necessary condition of intersubjectivity, an experience without which alterity—and, therefore, Objectivity, culture, values, communication, and reciprocity—cannot be constituted.[32]

For Husserl, there must always be both difference and similarity in every analogical transfer, or, as Walter Fuchs puts it, "the absent is given as co-primordial with the present. Presence and absence are co-constitutive of the real, of being, and the intuition of the living presence is not given without the intuition of absence at the same moment."[33] Cognitively speaking, the Other's *Erlebnis* remains absent, whereas the Body (*Leib*) of the Other is given to me through pairing and analogical transfer of my own Body as *Leib*. What Husserl argues in *Ideas II* is that empathy is a found*ing* mode of Objectivity. Through cultural empathy, the givenness of other human persons is necessary in order to account for the constitution of higher-order cultural and spiritual objects. Conversely, the law of empathy is found*ed* on analogical transference. Because the Other is intended from the standpoint of the self, so Husserl argues, the cultural world is intersubjectively constituted through social acts of empathy. Individually embodied human persons remain *epistemologically* derivative. For Husserl, the priority of the transcendental ego determines the condition of possibility of all knowledge, even so-called Objective knowledge, including the social, physical, cultural, human, and natural sciences. Empathy is an epistemological structure that first becomes constituted in my sphere of ownness through analogical apperception:

> I place myself at the standpoint of the other, any other whatever, and I acknowledge that each encounters every other as the natural being, man, and that I then have to identify myself with the man seen from the standpoint of external intuition. Man as Object is thus a transcendent external Object, an Object of an external intuition; that is, we have here an experience of two strata: interwoven with external primally presenting perception is appresenting (or introjecting into the exterior) empathy, in an apperception, specifically, which *realizes* the entire psychic life and psychic being in a sort of unity of appearance. (*Ideas II* 178)

Husserl seemingly solves the problem of empathy through epistemological abstraction. Yet it is precisely on account of Husserl's dry, strict, cognitive analysis of cultural empathy that several of his students and contemporaries, including Martin Heidegger, Max Scheler, Edith Stein, Emanuel Levinas, and Jacques Derrida, make fundamental (and contradictory) modifications to Husserl's transcendental position regarding the structural and existential importance of the phenomenology of empathy.[34]

§7. Husserl: Reflections on Analogy, Pairing, and Constitution

As we have seen, for Husserl phenomenology does not merely describe how the world is constituted by perception; it also offers, I submit, a critical and penetrating analysis of the experience of consciousness-itself in terms of the intersubjective constitution of the world. In effect, consciousness brings us de facto in touch with our own mortality and the lack of comprehension of immanent transcendence that surrounds us. For Husserl, every apperception enacts a kind of seeing that itself constitutes a conscious apprehension of alterity. What is encountered, then, through analogy and pairing is not merely a one-to-one object correlation but rather a particular world being encountered intersubjectively.[35] In an important way, this means that what gets constituted via analogy and pairing is the embodied Other *as such*, and not merely individual aspects of bodily appendages. Whereas Husserl offers a robust schematic description of analogical pairing in *Cartesian Meditations*, he also presents a rich and fleshed out analysis of empathy as defined by alterity,[36] for example, as noted in his posthumously published lectures on intersubjectivity, such as found in *Husserliana* volumes XIII, XIV, and XV as well as the preparatory notes to Husserl's 1910–1911 lectures centered upon "The Intersubjective Reduction as Reduction to the Psychologically Pure Intersubjectivity." Husserl notes:

> Every I finds in its surrounding, and more often in its surrounding of immediate interest, things which it regards as lived bodies but which it sharply contrasts to its "own" lived body as other lived bodies. It does this in such a way that to each such lived body there belongs again an I, but a different, other I. . . . All I's apprehend themselves as relative middle points of one and the same spatial-temporal world that in its indeterminate infinity is the total surrounding of each I. . . . For example, the I changes bodily its place in space, and while it continues to say "here" it knows that "here" in each case is spatially different. . . . [B]y way of empathy all that which we have here discussed can be attributed to other I's; that under normal conditions the perspectives, which vary from one I to another I, stand in a certain correspondence, being in accordance with the necessarily different spatial spots, which the different I's find as their respective places.[37]

Of course, the lectures of 1910–1911 remained incomplete, or at least inconclusive, to Husserl's satisfaction. Janet Donohoe notes, "What Husserl lays out in these lectures from 1910–1911 was not entirely satisfactory to him. He continued working on the project until roughly 1921, when it was put aside so that he could dedicate himself to a comprehensive systematic work, which, in typical Husserlian fashion, never got published in such a form. The project of intersubjectivity seriously takes center stage again only when he begins work on the *Cartesian Meditations*."[38] In the Fifth Cartesian Meditation, Edmund Husserl again returns his attention to the genesis of apperception and the analogical structure of phenomenological seeing that entails transcendental structures of consciousness, including pairing and imaginative variation. Drawing on critical discussions concerning Husserl's notion of value-apprehension (*Wertnehmung*) as well as Husserl's "Nature and Spirit" lectures, it is important to note that ethical dimensions of empathy influenced the entirety of Husserl's project and his understanding of the important implications of the phenomenological reduction, though as noted throughout this study, an important contextual focus of Husserl's investigations, including ethics, was mainly epistemological.

One of the prominent issues raised by Husserl in the Fifth Meditation is the question of origin, namely, the contextual manifestation of a meaning-horizon from which and into which emerges the idealizing primal establishment of a teleological structure (i.e., the meaning-structure of "empathy"). For Husserl, the point of origin—whether of geometry or religion or language or community—is not a particular chronologically primary moment in the philological-historical development of an individual or community identity. In fact, what is meant by Husserl concerning "origin" has no bearing whatsoever in any strict, time-bound ontic sense.[39] Origin, for Husserl, can never be grasped phenomenologically as a merely historical event if it is to have any sort of eternal (objective) validity. Otherwise, structure and meaning would be culturally subjective, "understandable only by those men who shared the same merely factual presuppositions of understanding."[40]

I submit that Husserl's search for the origin of the constitution of the world, though contextualized as an egological investigation, is not primarily an ego-centric or monadological interrogation of Being-itself. Rather, Husserl engages egology to describe an historical search for the emergence of "first" consciousness as the founding ego-act in the world qua phenomena. The question of origin is oriented toward the way in which differences in consciousness of time (temporality) are "constituted intuitively and authentically as the originary . . . sources of all certainties relative to time."[41] The question of origin, therefore, contains something of an ethical component and is not primarily constricted by epistemology or metaphysics. Consequently, for Husserl, origin is constituted intersubjectively and not limited to egology alone.[42] For Husserl, the question of "origin" pertains to the constitution of the lifeworld. Maurice Natanson comments, "Since the activity of consciousness involves its own temporal dimension, the structure of the world as the correlate of intentional acts is necessarily related to and affected by the order of its constitutive history. Phenomena, for Husserl, are historical in essence because they are products of a genesis of intentional meaning. Turning to the constitution of phenomena is searching for their origin in consciousness. Phenomenology concerns itself with the becoming of the world in transcendental subjectivity."[43]

What emerges from Husserl's transcendental reduction is his belief that empathy is the locus—the ongoing possibility—an occasion, if you will, by which every manner of constitution emerges as a founding of an intersubjective ethical relationship. Regarded in this way, "the source of objective states of affairs as bearers of meaning is to be found in the intentional ground of intentional consciousness."[44] Phenomenology is not concerned with the gathering of historical facts about empathy but with describing empathy as a condition of possibility of alterity in which knowledge of the world becomes possible at all. Empathy describes "how are things, persons and events there for us in the first place?"[45]

The operative phrase for Husserl, of course, is "for us." At the heart of the transcendental reduction is not simply the thesis that empathy can make the world appear *there* in its objective reality (which it does, unless there is some sort of breakdown on the noetic side). Even more importantly, empathy must be involved if there is to be a world at all.[46] Through empathy, what is given or grasped in its fulfilled manifestation in the natural attitude is traced back intentionally to its sources in transcendental subjectivity.[47] In effect, this means that the world that is given as *there* is never *solus ipse*, as mine alone. It is always and already a shared world, an intersubjectively constituted we-world of culture and values.[48] What gets constituted through analogy and pairing is the Other as an embodied for-itself. Through empathy, it is not only that the Other is given in the Other's own unique spatial-temporal there/their-ness. Even more: what is given in empathy for Husserl is a kind of apperception of "self-alterity"[49] by which I experience myself as other than myself; that is to say, I experience the Here of my own perspectival experience as both Here *and* There, a point that constitutes time and space inasmuch as the condition of possibility of my own being is traversed by a kind of radical alterity that constitutes *me* as a self.

It is important therefore not only to pose the question of how knowledge of the other is possible for Husserl; we must also ask, What is the origin of such knowledge and what is the relation of such knowledge to ethics? While our focus on Husserl has so far largely centered on epistemological descriptions of monadic constitution in terms of empathy, it is important to note that Husserl's use of analogy is both limited and limiting. For Husserl, analogy, including analogical apperception, needs to be balanced with an emphasis on reciprocity of pairing, as articulated in the Fifth Cartesian Meditation, as well as descriptions of social constitution of the lifeworld as addressed in *Ideas II*. For example, I submit that there is an "as-if" analogy in the Fifth Cartesian Meditation by which Husserl's description of "original pairing" manifests itself as a kind of limited or working analogy, what Husserl calls an "analogizing apprehension." Peter Costello concurs: "[F]or Husserl, empathy, as the foundation of community, presents itself as immediately, though 'analogically,' engaging my awareness of my own temporal self-relation. I feel empathy with other persons, I sense their experience as they live it, because what it means to unify two I's, two lived experiences, is not foreign to me."[50] In effect, Husserl argues that "ego and alter ego are always and necessarily given in an original pairing." Furthermore, such pairing occurs "in configuration as a pair and then as a group, a plurality," thereby constituting a universal phenomenon of the transcendental sphere.[51] Leonard Lawson argues that, in her conclusion, Natalie Depraz similarly follows closely Eugen Fink's ontologization of phenomenology as depicted in the Sixth Meditation. There, Lawson notes, "Fink speaks of 'transcendental being,' which would be fundamentally plural, 'the originary pluralization of being.' "[52] For Husserl, too, empathy constitutes a kind of pluralization of being, it describes how my live body is always there and sensually prominent, how my live body always and already encounters an animate organism with a body "similar" to mine. Such experience of another animate organism, "as-if" similar to my own yet different, is experienced as having a physical side that indicates something psychic appresentatively. Husserl notes that the character of the existent Other has its basis in this kind of verifiable accessibility of what is not originally accessible (i.e., its psychic life). Through intentional modification, another monad becomes constituted appresentively in a similar way that "my seeing the other as seeing me" constitutes a kind of ipseic flux by which I grasp my being as a for-itself *for the Other*.

Significantly, what has so far been described as Husserl's strict epistemological description of constitution in part one begins to break down a bit at this point. Husserl's descriptive account of the emotions presents an important thread for Edith Stein and Max Scheler in their respective descriptions of the constitution of authentic community and values, as we will see in part two. Following recent publications involving Husserl's later texts on social ontology, Husserl scholars have notably turned their attention to filling in this important lacuna. Principally drawn to Husserl's notes and lectures published posthumously in *Husserliana* volumes XIII, XIV, and XV, scholars have shown great interest in critically exploring early phenomenological discussions on intersubjectivity that revolved around aspects of Husserl's own developing thought.[53] Angela Ales Bello, for example, emphasizes "the intimate connection between" Stein's earliest works, *On the Problem of Empathy* and *Philosophy of Psychology and the Humanities*, with Husserl's unpublished second volume of his *Ideas* project (to which Stein served as first editor). Ales Bello notes that this "strict relation" between Husserl's and Stein's works on empathy "is indispensable in order to understand the development of Husserlian phenomenology, especially regarding the ethical and teleological questions that ultimately culminate in *The Crisis of the European Sciences and Transcendental Phenomenology*."[54] A number of contemporary Stein-Husserl scholars concur.[55]

Peter Costello persuasively argues that what Husserl means by intuition is the overlapping and overlaying of variations that allows the essence to shine through on its own, in a sense utilizing the same logic of pairing and intersubjectivity by which the overlaying of self and other allows the givenness of community to shine through. Empathy "enlarges itself toward third persons and thus into community."[56] While Husserl largely provides an epistemological description of how pairing and analogy "must" work in terms of empathy in the order of understanding in *Cartesian Meditations*—phenomenologically speaking, that is—the implications for ethics and social ontology in terms of the constitution of community and shared values is also evident. For Husserl, the "involvement of consciousness with any and all of its 'objects' (in the sense of 'object' that would include other subjects), is a matter of correlations of meaning."[57] In effect, Husserl's notion of pairing prioritizes neither oneself nor the Other but rather emphasizes a mutuality or reciprocity by which I and Thou begin to distinguish one from the other. Although we are exploring the Husserlian theme of pairing as central to the givenness of the Other as a live, animate body similar to me yet different, we will return to this theme in greater detail in part two, notably by drawing out Edith Stein's understanding of reciprocity in terms of ethics and solidarity. For now, however, what seems important to note is that, for Husserl, pairing and analogy describe how we see essences by means of and on behalf of others who make possible the givenness of apprehensions of perspectives, values, and variations of meanings not fully evident except as foreign experience. For Husserl, pairing does not give the Other to me "as-if" the Other is merely "another I." Rather, pairing constitutes the Other qua other. Through empathy, we distinguish between what *the object seems like* to the perceiver on the one hand and what *perceiving feels like* to the perceiver on the other hand. This is similar to what Dan Zahavi describes as "modes of givenness." Following Husserl's analysis of the constitution of the "we-world," Zahavi notes that various modes of givenness share a common feature:

> [T]he quality of mineness, that is, the fact that the experiences are characterized by a first-personal givenness that immediately reveals them as one's own. . . . If I feel hunger or see a sunrise, I cannot be in doubt or be mistaken about who the subject of the experience is. . . . If the experience is given in a first-personal mode of presentation, it is experienced as my experience, otherwise not. . . . The mineness is not something attended to; it simply figures as a subtle background presence. Nevertheless, the particular first-person givenness of the experience makes it mine and distinguishes it for me from whatever experiences others might have.[58]

Phenomenologically speaking, for Husserl consciousness constitutes the world through common sense and interpretive (and pre-interpretive) acts of meaning and value. Thus "something is seen as a mountain, not as a patchwork of related masses; a street scene is comprehended as a conflux of people purposefully going about their business, not a conglomeration of bodies occupying different and shifting segments of space."[59] Consciousness does not discover meaning already present in objects, nor does consciousness ontologically create the world ex nihilo. What is given is the world as phenomenon, always already there. Without pairing, however, both *here* and *there* are completely meaningless, since if there is no *here* in terms of a seeing and valuing Ego, then there can be no judgment for an alter ego to be *there*. In a similar way, Roman Ingarden comments that, in transcendental idealism, "what is real is nothing but a constituted noematic unity of a special kind of sense which in its being and quality results from a set of experiences of a special kind and is quite impossible without them."[60] This means that to exclude pure consciousness means to exclude the world, since the existence of what is perceived is nothing in-itself, but only something for the experiencing ego.[61] Hence, constitution for Husserl is less cognition and creation and more like reception and recognition. For Husserl, constitution includes as little interpretation and as pure an intuition as possible.[62] Of course, as we saw earlier in *Ideas*, constitution requires a parallelism or agency between *noesis* and *noema*. The call and response of *noesis* and *noema* with a notion of experience situates subject and object in a correlation of reciprocity. Consequently, constitution is not static and performed in my ego only, but rather it emerges through a flowing between *noesis* and *noema*. In this way, I become motivated to draw rays of meaning that move from the object (or from the Other) toward me in a complementary and yet different way than how rays move from me to the object. Of course, the world seen by the Other is apprehended only empathetically, and in this way "social subjectivity" cannot be a first or last reality; it is only a sort of derived consciousness, as opposed to a unique, originary consciousness that is my own. Paul Ricoeur notes:

> Here is a difficulty which is presented in the opposite way in the Fifth Cartesian Meditation. In *Ideas II* Husserl goes directly to those "communities of persons" which elaborate primitively, so it seems, the sense of things, values, and persons as cultural objects. . . . In just the opposite manner, the Fifth Cartesian Meditation immediately opens out from the impasse of transcendental solipsism. It raises the paradoxical question of constituting the Other as "outsider" and yet "in" me. The experience of the Other is only represented to me by transfer on the basis of a "pairing" between the ways in which the body of the Other and my own appear within my sphere of ownness. This is why the Other is "presentiated by sympathetic imagination." Only my mental life is "presented originarily." The intersubjective relations of the ego with the Other who is always "in" me, yet is always escaping from my originary experience, are instituted on this basis.[63]

For Husserl, the Ego is thus motivated to give "free rein to the seeing eye and to bracket the references which go beyond the 'seeing' and are entangled with the seeing, along with the entities which are supposedly given and thought along with the 'seeing,' and, finally, to bracket what is read into them through the accompanying reflections."[64] In this way, all objects—whether perceptual, imaginary, intuited, wishful, universal—are constituted by the noesis-noema correlation, which acts in an analogical "as-if" capacity through pairing and perception, along with retention of what is perceived. The world is constituted by consciousness, though not by the Ego only since the Other is neither given to nor found in consciousness. For Husserl, there is no "inside" and "outside" of consciousness; consciousness is not the Ego but rather the correlation of *noesis* and *noema*. Phenomenologically speaking, what is meant by "consciousness" is not that the Ego alone constitutes the world but that a community of egos intends the world as meant: "[T]he one who is knowing directly experiences his own mental life and that of others by way of analogy to it in 'empathy.' "[65] Husserl's phenomenological description of the meaning of constitution takes into account not merely my reality but social or objective reality, what Husserl calls empathy, and not as something extrinsic "added to" the ego but as a condition of possibility. In describing Husserl's social ontology, Maurice Natanson notes:

> Man finds himself in a world which existed before his birth, born of parents who are unique to him, the inheritor of a natural language, the scion of a history and a culture, and a participant in a life which includes fellow men, work, love, and the recognition of human finitude. The social world is not only an interpreted but a preinterpreted reality. Family, language, history, culture, intersubjectivity in all of its modes, and the comprehension of death are aspects of the frame of life within which the individual makes his choices. Unlike inert objects which are simply in the world, human beings have a world.[66]

What Husserl seems to be saying is that constitution entails the language of passive synthesis and embodied, emotional engagement as much as it entails the language of the single Ego "constituting" the world. In either description, what is required is a sense of reciprocity. In other words, it is not my Ego alone that constitutes the world, including the givenness of the Other qua other. On the contrary, Husserl's profound fecundity is that *noesis* and *noema*, self and other, are given as "mutual beings" prior to their distinction—though, as we shall see in part two, in a way that differs substantively from Scheler's "undifferentiated stream" of consciousness life. For Husserl, I am always already given with the pairing with the Other, and this on account that mutuality and analogy allows for the imaginative elaboration. In Husserl's account of empathy, I do not merely see the Other. I see him seeing me,[67] I recognize him as a subject, a for-itself, a member of a community of other persons with a commitment to values and sensory and emotive perceptions that entails a reciprocal or "mutual" being-for-one-another. The other's body is no longer given as an object but "as a counter-subject that co-exists with me and whose spiritual life I can understand as directly as I can read the words in a book for their meaning,"[68] by which Husserl infers an open community of monads and designates as transcendental intersubjectivity:

> If, with my understanding of someone else, I penetrate more deeply into him, into his horizon of ownness, I shall soon run into the fact that, just as his animate bodily organism lies in my field of perception, so my animate organism lies in his field of perception and that, in general, he experiences me forthwith as an Other for him, just as I experience him as my Other. . . . Likewise, I shall find that, in the case of a plurality of Others, they are experienced also by one another as Others.[69]

§8. Later Developments (1929–1938) in Husserl's Understanding of Intersubjectivity

A primary focus of this study is to explore the development of the phenomenology of empathy in conversation with Husserl and the early texts, lectures, notes, and resources published by Husserl during his lifetime and available to his contemporary students and colleagues, most notably Max Scheler, Edith Stein, Martin Heidegger, and Emmanuel Levinas. Following Husserl's death in 1938 and during the subsequent destruction wrought by the Second World War, nearly 40,000 pages of Husserl's handwritten notes, along with his entire research library, were secretly smuggled to the Catholic University Louvain in Belgium. Over the next decades, significant portions of Husserl's typed texts and handwritten notes in his unique Gabelsberger shorthand have been published in the *Husserliana* critical edition series. Of course, many of Husserl's former students and colleagues, including those highlighted in this study, did not have direct access to redactions and notes from these critical texts. Then, beginning in the late 1950s and with easier access to the archival materials, new insights into Husserlian scholarship were explored, including perhaps most notably by Jacques Derrida. As we shall see in part three of this study, Derrida addressed significant issues related to the phenomenology of empathy and had recourse to the same published materials that were also explored decades earlier by Edith Stein, Max Scheler, Martin Heidegger, Emmanuel Levinas, and others, including Merleau-Ponty, Sartre, and so on. Because Derrida largely drew from many of the same sources accessed by the phenomenologists highlighted in this study, an important part of Derrida's work is included in the last section of this study.

Subsequent and important secondary literature and ongoing interest in Husserl's theory of transcendental intersubjectivity and constitution, particularly in light of contemporary French phenomenology, has grown exponentially, especially in the last few decades. Several important aspects of investigations centered around social ontology, critical phenomenology, and other issues are central to the focus of this study, and so their historical and thematic scopes will be explored, to some extent, in my final reflections in part four. For now, it will be helpful to explore a few recent primary Husserl texts, contemporary philosophers, and related themes that draw upon later developments in Husserl's complex understanding of intersubjectivity. While this brief overview of recently published primary and secondary texts is meant to be neither exhaustive nor conclusive, I hope it provides additional directions and resources to engage the thematic of transcendental intersubjectivity in light of Husserl's developing theory of constitution, especially as presented in his unpublished lectures, critical notes, and essays.

As discussed earlier in this chapter, volumes XIII, XIV, and XV of the *Husserliana* edition of Husserl's work contain significant sources of critically edited material concerning Husserl's unpublished notes, unfinished essays, and posthumously completed manuscripts on intersubjectivity. Some of these resources have not been translated and so are accessible only in German. Significant texts are based on paper manuscripts, handwritten notes (in Gabelsberger), and microfilm of assorted texts. In summer 2000, I received a grant to explore some of these texts at the Husserl Archive in Cologne, in particular the assortment of notes and texts used as a basis for compiling the final text of *Ideen II*, published posthumously by the

Husserl Archive in Leuven in 1952 following many unsatisfactory revisions ultimately discarded by Husserl, as previously noted. The collection of primary materials written by Husserl and edited by his research assistants and later redactors, including Edith Stein and also Fink, Landgrebe, Kern, Bliemel, Bernet, and others, range as early as 1905 through 1935. An overview of these documents was published by professor Natalie Depraz in 1992 by the Jesuit Faculty of Philosophy at Centre Sèvres, Paris. In her short and important compendium, *Les Figures de L'Intersubjectivité Étude des Husserlaiana XIII-XIV-XV zur Intersubjektivität* (Archives de Philosophie), Depraz outlines a comprehensive overview of many of the developments, twists, and turns in Husserl's later thought concerning transcendental intersubjectivity, the doctrine of constitution, and an analysis of the lifeworld. Husserl himself, of course, remained largely ambivalent and even unsatisfied with the unfinished drafts of these manuscripts. Posthumous publications are based on years of editing, redrafting, and revising notes, lectures, and essays from many different sources, including providing introductions, editing new alignments of material, and mixing and restructuring different source documents. In particular, Depraz highlights three different configurations in Husserl's approach in explicating the theme of Husserlian intersubjectivity. The "plurality of forms" or "three ways" involved in the historical reconstruction of Husserl's notes presented through the multiplicity of the groups of manuscripts put together, along with their dissemination among the three volumes of *Husserliana* XIII, XIV, and XV, include (1) *Einfühlung* (or "empathy" as it is referred as the "Cartesian way"); (2) intersubjective reduction (by way of psychology); and (3) the spiritual common lifeworld (Husserl's notion of *Lebenswelt*).[70] Each of these three Husserlian approaches responding to the "problem of empathy" is explored in detail in part one of this study.

Consequently, several important complications regarding the assimilation of various parcels of texts into a comprehensive thematization of Husserl's position on intersubjectivity are noted by Depraz. For one, Husserl himself never definitively approved any of these posthumously attributed texts for publication. They were considered "unfinished," and therefore it is problematical if they are presented as a "finished task" of a singular Husserlian perspective. Depraz notes, "[C]orresponding to the phenomenology of intersubjectivity, we were faced with problems that had not yet arisen in this way for the previous volumes of the *Husserliana*. These problems resulted from the particular character of the manuscripts . . . with texts that Husserl did not write for the public (nor for a group of readers, not for listeners, but for itself as 'Monological Meditations' (*Husserliana* XIII, Preface, xviii). Iso Kern therefore raises the important question of 'how to publish such Meditations.' "[71]

A second complication raised by incorporating Husserl's unpublished manuscripts into the current study concerns the accessibility of key developments in Husserl's account of constitution beyond what was historically known at the time when early descriptions of transcendental intersubjectivity were initially explored and finalized by Husserl. The focus of this study relies on the lively interpretation of key concepts and published texts drawn from the common pool of Husserlian sources, though of course significant posthumous publications of Husserl's notes are also included, with the caveat that Husserl himself had worked tirelessly on some of these manuscripts (e.g., *Ideas II*) without approving them for publication. While aware of the development of Husserl's thought on varying levels based on familiarity of lectures and discussions, many of Husserl's students and colleagues did not have firsthand access to manuscripts and documents subsequently published in the *Husserliana* critical editions of volumes XIII, XIV, and XV. Consequently, for our purposes in this study, we need to draw principally on those historical and thematic primary sources that Husserl himself approved, that were readily available to all Husserl's students and colleagues, and that were published under Husserl's tacit approval.

It is important to note that, given the extent of material from Husserl on intersubjectivity, what becomes "readily apparent from Husserl's later manuscripts, and especially his late writings on intersubjectivity, is that he begins to recognize that one cannot understand the self without having a conception of what is other."[72] The implications to Husserl's description of social ontology offer a profound impact on the course of phenomenological research in general and on the direction of critical phenomenology in particular, including themes of ethics, alterity, and transcendence. We shall return to these themes later in the study. For now, however, it is important to note that, for Husserl, the Other is, constitutionally speaking, the "intrinsically first" human being.[73] Janet Donohoe notes that

> without the Other, the ego cannot constitute itself as human. . . . This means that the position of the ego in a human community requires the priority of the other, since the ego can only truly be a person within the community of Others.[74]

There is much material that subsequently needs to be published and explored in future studies and based on the focus years of this project, namely the 1910s and 1920s. As Rudolf Makkreel notes, "Husserl wrote so much on the topic of empathy that the above account of it on the basis of *Ideen II* needs to be supplemented somewhat," notably by "the three volumes entitled *Zur Phänomenologie der Intersubjektivität* (XIII, XIV, XV)."[75] Significant issues rooted in Husserl's engagement with ethics and intersubjectivity, based in no small part on tensions highlighted by Husserl's descriptive analysis of constitution from static to genetic phenomenology, are clearly rooted in his early understanding of the importance of empathy in matters of constitution and his incorporation of the transcendental ego as a substantive element in the constitution of other persons. Rudolf Makkreel concurs and notes that "it is sometimes argued that Husserl's empathy is not concerned to provide empirical understanding, but represents a transcendental condition for intersubjectivity, as established in the fifth of the *Cartesian Meditations*."[76]

According to Makkreel, "Michael Theunissen claims that ordinary empathy involves feeling *into* an *alter ego*, whereas Husserl's transcendental empathy is constitutive *of* the *alter ego* as such."[77] A comprehensive guide to the development of key themes central to Husserl's later description of constitution, including from his post-1928 retirement at Freiburg, is offered in J. N. Mohanty's *Edmund Husserl's Freiberg Years 1916–1938*. As expected, Mohanty deftly incorporates significant aspects of Husserl's posthumously published notes and manuscripts from lectures over the last decade of Husserl's life. These unpublished manuscripts and key writing projects are presented in a chronological and thematic compendium that traces many issues raised in Husserl's final years. For Husserl, empathy engages an intuitive understanding of identity of the kind of descriptive account "involved in the original community of a lifeworld or a local *Umwelt*."[78] Mohanty's analyses and thematic foci offer a helpful conversation with the historic scope of the current study, including the relationship between empathy and reciprocity, as will be outlined in part two.

Part Two

Empathy and Reciprocity

Part Two

Introduction

Edith Stein was well aware of Husserl's position that empathy is a form of transcendental constitution, especially after having worked through the problem of empathy with him in her own dissertation.[1] But soon after, she began to voice serious misgivings concerning Husserl's transcendental project.[2] On February 3, 1917, Stein wrote a cryptic note to Roman Ingarden from Freiburg, in which she confessed, "I now imagine I know pretty well what 'constitution' is—but with a break from Idealism. An absolutely existing physical nature on the one hand, a distinctly structured subjectivity on the other, seem to me to be *prerequisites* before an intuiting nature can constitute itself. I have not yet had the chance to confess my heresy to the Master."[3] What was Edith Stein's self-confessed "heresy" concerning Husserl's theory of transcendental constitution? A follow-up letter written to Ingarden on March 20, 1917, gives us a clue: "I have begun to examine more closely one of the points on which the Master and I differ: the necessity of a body for empathy" (*Letters* 13).

Husserl's turn to transcendental Idealism echoed a deep methodological rift that ensued between Husserl and other members of the Göttingen circle (notably Max Scheler, Edith Stein, and Roman Ingarden), shortly after the publication of *Ideas I*. Whereas Husserl intended to describe empathy as a form of transcendental constitution in terms of the structure of cognition, Edith Stein, following Max Scheler, argues that experiences of empathy are also experienced or given *emotively*.[4] Stein's distinction in emphasis concerning emotive and cognitive characteristics of empathy reflects a modification or specification from Husserl's more strictly epistemological model of constitution, though of course Husserl too was concerned with exploring processes of social givenness in terms of emotions, gestures, and sensual life.[5] In the following chapters, I shall present evidence of a growing chorus of criticism raised against Husserl's transcendental project[6] in terms of its Idealist implications, as noted by several of Husserl's most notable students and colleagues, for example Scheler, Stein, Heidegger, and Levinas.[7]

Edith Stein casts her phenomenological investigation of empathy by including an analysis of emotional sharing and feelings alongside cognition,[8] in what I describe as a reciprocal model of constitution.[9] Consequently, what distinguishes Stein's position from Husserl's entails a difference of orientation, a modification (though not a reversal) of the genesis and motivation of constitution. By stressing a strict cognitive description of empathy, Husserl tended to subsume what I shall later describe as a co-primordial role that emotions and affectivity play alongside cognition in every encounter between persons.[10] My contention is that Edith Stein did not so much reject Husserl's monadological position as she attempted to modify his strict cognitive approach by granting priority to the sharing of emotional life and feelings by which individual egos are constituted. In effect, Stein proposes that social and cultural environments are as equi-primordial as cognition in terms of the changing paradigm of empathy theory amongst early phenomenologists. One of my arguments in part two is that Stein's 1917 description of empathy largely anticipated Husserl's socially founded descriptions of constitution (such as depicted in *Cartesian Meditations* and *Ideas II*) and, at the same time, stretched Husserl's transcendental Idealism to its breaking point.

In calling Edith Stein's analysis of empathy a "reciprocal model" of constitution, I do not mean to imply that she dismisses Husserl's monadological theory of constitution out of hand, as is the case, for example, with Levinas. On the contrary, her intention is to *modify* Husserl's phenomenological description of the ordinary flow of mutual sharing that is involved in every empathic experience. Stein's model of empathy entails an examination of the constitution of the human person that includes emotional experiences, feelings, and relationships based on mutuality, care, and interdependence.[11] In Husserl's case, the predominant focus of the constitution of human persons is mainly cognitive and thus tends toward greater autonomy; for Stein, empathy involves a coequal emotive capacity as well, and so it leads to the preservation of social bonds and emotional integration.[12] Likewise, whereas for Husserl the individual monad precedes the community in the order of knowledge, for Stein the community precedes the ego in the order of experience. Although, in either case, the body (*Leib*) remains the condition of possibility of empathic constitution, nevertheless it is my contention that Stein's model of "emotive" constitution offers a modified and rich analysis of social description and the constitution of the alter ego than Husserl's more strict, cognitive theory may allow.

Of course, Stein's emotive model of empathy must account for an experience of alterity that comes from *outside* the self, just as is true of the theory of apperception proposed by Edmund Husserl.[13] Either the Other comes from outside the economy of sameness or the Other must somehow help constitute it.[14] Accordingly, Stein includes in her account of empathy a description of emotive experience as a non-primordial feeling that announces a primordial one, a "feeling" of something foreign (*fremdes*) and alien. In Stein's analysis, empathy entails a primordial experience with non-primordial content.[15] Hence, for Stein empathy must include an account of the *felt* experience of alterity, cognized as the non-primordial content of the Other qua other, in order to be grasped equi-primordially in my conscious stream of inner-lived experience (*Erlebnis*).

Let me be clear here. My argument is that appreciating Edith Stein's contributions to the phenomenology of empathy requires that intersubjectivity be encountered as an *ethical* issue and not just described in terms of epistemology. This means that Stein's questions related to the phenomenology of empathy concerning its ethical implications must be raised anew, apart from Husserl's strict cognitive analysis. Specifically, I argue that the issue of Edith Stein's gender eclipsed the philosophical recognition that would have been afforded her had she, in fact, been a male student of philosophy working under Husserl's direction. Much of what Stein wrote in her 1916 dissertation and 1922 *Jahrbuch* essays is creative, thoughtful, and culturally observant. I submit, however, that there was a privileging of Husserl's cognitive account of empathy in the 1910s and 1920s that silenced Edith Stein's feminine voice and thereby weakened her contribution to the empathy debate, in part likely on account of her gender.[16]

For too long, Edith Stein has been relegated as a sort of "appendage" to Husserl, her thought merely a faded reflection of its originating source. This uncritical interpretation of Stein's early phenomenological work needs serious reexamination. Edith Stein's contributions to the phenomenology of empathy pose nothing less than an ethical challenge for us to remember the dead, to allow ourselves to remain open and vulnerable to the call from those whom history has marginalized and designated as expendable, surplus, refuse, nonessential, foreign, alien, *other*.[17] Empathy, according to Stein's model, urges us to listen to what goes *un*heard, to care for that which is not clearly perceptible, visible, permissible. The historical silencing of Edith Stein's voice demonstrates how a "canon of discourse" becomes constituted within a particular social and contemporary environment; it describes how the "keepers" of such a canon in turn arbitrate the value and accessibility of those voices raised even in its own defense.

In the following chapters, I shall support the thesis of Edith Stein's equal standing with Husserl. I do not claim that she is wholly independent from Husserl's influence, nor that her work is untouched by the time and locale in which she wrote. Rather, I shall demonstrate that the ideas that she presents in her doctoral dissertation both modify and, to a certain extent, anticipate Husserl's subsequent and more famous cognitive description of the constitution of the alter ego as outlined earlier in part one. Husserl's celebrated texts on intersubjective constitution (*Cartesian Meditations* in 1929 and *Ideas II*, posthumously published in 1950) were de facto issued many years following Stein's original published drafts. My contention is that Husserl's investigations concerning the phenomenological data of intersubjective constitution were inspired to a large extent by Stein's influence as Husserl's research assistant in the late 1910s[18] *in much the same way* that Stein's research was inspired by Husserl's lectures and the German intellectual and political environment in which both she and Husserl found themselves at the turn of the twentieth century.[19]

Although Husserl largely focused his examination on the significance of transcendental intersubjectivity according to his own epistemological concerns, Stein's indebtedness to Husserl (and Husserl's indebtedness to Stein) remains apparent throughout their respective expositions concerning the problem of empathy. What I want to explore is a modified account of the constitution of the human person in emotional experiences than Husserl's more benign model of cognition ostensibly permits. I submit that a more expansive analysis of empathy in terms of Stein's emotive emphasis on constitution hints at the possibility that (1) emotions are as equi-primordial as cognition in the order of knowledge, and (2) the Other is emotively, rather than merely cognitively, given in the order of experience.

Part two is divided into three chapters. First, "Max Scheler and the Phenomenology of Human Community" presents certain aspects of Scheler's phenomenological ethics, particularly in terms of its influence on Edith Stein. A systematic study of Scheler's work, however desirable, is not possible within the limits of this study.[20] Hence, in this chapter I will principally focus on (1) Scheler's rejection of Husserl's transcendental Idealism; (2) Scheler's rejection of the claim that the Other is given in terms of associations, assimilations, analogical inferences, or empathic transfers from one's own ego "into" that of others; and (3) Scheler's notion that an "undifferentiated psychic stream" exists *prior to* any distinction between ego and alter.

The following chapter, "Edith Stein and the Problem of Empathy," offers a detailed exegesis of the givenness of others, as this theory was first elaborated by Stein in her 1916 dissertation written under Husserl. Empathy as the understanding of spiritual persons explores Stein's claim that what is given to me first in the order of experience is the Other's felt presence, whereas what is given to me first in the order of knowledge is what is theoretically derived from this experience. Specifically, I shall demonstrate the significance of Edith Stein's emotive modification of Husserl's strict cognitive description of transcendental constitution regarding future discourse concerning the phenomenology of empathy. My analysis will focus on Stein's contention that the human person is constituted in emotional experiences. What does Edith Stein mean when she says that the "I" is constituted in emotions? Following Scheler, Edith Stein argues *contra* Husserl that the felt experience of the existence of other human beings is as equally co-given as is the cognitive constitution *of* this experience. Yet at the same time, Stein agrees with Husserl in saying that the Other is always given first as embodied, that is, given in bodily perception. What Stein argues is that although the body of the Other is the basis for the constitution of the Other, the way in which I experience how the Other is first given to me always includes an *emotive* rather than a merely cognitive encounter of the embodied Other.

The following chapter, "Edith Stein and the Significance of Embodiment, Temporality, and Emotions in Acts of Empathy," draws in part on Stein's analysis of social constitution theory as developed in her 1919 habilitation treatise, later published in 1922 as *Philosophy of Psychology and the Humanities*. Does Stein's notion of reciprocal empathy allow a more radical view of alterity than Husserl's strictly monadological model permits? Specifically, I shall reexamine the concept of reciprocity, now in terms of what she calls "solidarity." For Stein, solidarity means that I am a priori motivated to extend my concern to unknown others. Care, then, is a command of solidarity that comes from outside the closed circle of reciprocity yet founds the intersubjective relationships constituted within that circle. Whenever individuals are "open" to one another, a communal life subsists in that two individuals have become members of one community. Is this openness to solidarity an "infinite-open" that extends even beyond my own community, tribe, and state? What happens to "other others" who do not appear to share anything in common with me, not even the same language or customs? In what sense am I responsible for people who live outside my community or who may even be antithetical to the laws and customs of my state? Does Stein's notion of solidarity offer an account of how I am able to transcend cultural differences?

My goal in part two is to describe the richness of phenomenological descriptions of empathy depicted by Max Scheler and Edith Stein in terms of reciprocity, social contagion, and emotive constitution, as opposed to a more strict, cognitive model of transcendental constitution that remains vulnerable to charges of solipsism and monadism. Although Husserl repeatedly rejected the charge of "solipsism" in connection with his work, neither his critics nor his supporters ever definitively embraced a strict, cognitive paradigm. Even Husserl himself, sometimes caricatured by his own transcendental description of constitution, remained ultimately dissatisfied by the claims and limitations of Idealism. For Husserl, reflection can be described as either natural or transcendental or pure, but such descriptions do not mean that the transcendental ego is a different ego from the pure ego or natural attitude. Such reflections posit merely different ways of describing how perception "gets done" in the world of perception, which is really the only world there is. Transcendental constitution is neither absolute nor exclusive. For Husserl, the task of phenomenology describes how the other person is constituted as a for-itself within my own stream of lived experience. Hence, contrary to solipsism, the existence of Others is never in doubt. Nevertheless, Husserl's emphasis on a strict cognitive model implies the certainty that everything is reducible to what is ultimately cognizable *for me*, including the alter ego. What a significant number of Husserl's colleagues sought to explore—including Edith Stein, Max Scheler, and Emmanuel Levinas, who form the nexus for the remainder of this study—is that a more robust phenomenological description of constitution is needed beyond a purely cognitive approach. In addition to cognitive elements, the constitution of the person in emotional experiences is necessary in order to understand empathy as an originary, reciprocal, co-constitutive relationship between I and Other, ego and alter, care and obligation.[21]

Chapter Four

Max Scheler and the Phenomenology of Human Community

Introduction

Max Scheler, like Edmund Husserl and Edith Stein, was born in a Jewish family and later converted to Christianity.[1] Born in Munich on August 22, 1874, Scheler received his doctorate from Jena University under Rudolf Eucken, who was himself later awarded a Nobel Prize in 1908 for trying to achieve "a unity of mankind in order to prevent the destructive forces that worked in modern society."[2] In 1899, Scheler completed his habilitation thesis and began a long and controversial career teaching moral theory immediately thereafter. According to extant records, Scheler's lectures provided a riveting source of inspiration to his students. Edith Stein offers a colorful description of Scheler, both in terms of his personality and stature as a philosopher:

> Scheler's practice of scattering about ingenious suggestions without pursuing them systematically had something dazzling and seductive about it. Moreover, he chose topics of vital personal importance to his young listeners, who, consequently, were easily affected by them. Husserl, on the other hand, addressed sober, abstract matters. . . . One's first impression of Scheler was fascination. In no other person have I ever encountered the "phenomenon of genius" as clearly. The light of a more exalted world shone from his large blue eyes. His features were

handsome and noble; still, life had left some devastating traces in his face. Betty Heymann said he reminded her of the picture of Dorian Gray: that mysterious portrait on which the dissolute life of the original painted its distorting lines, while the person preserved the handsome features of his youth. Scheler spoke with great insistence, indeed with dramatic liveliness. Words he was particularly fond of (for example, "*pure Washeit*" [pure whatness]) were spoken with devotion and tenderness. When expressing disagreement with presumed opponents, he used a contemptuous tone. . . . In real life situations, Scheler was as helpless as a child. . . . At such times it was impossible to be angry with him, not even when he did things one would condemn in other persons. Even the victims of his aberrations tended to come to his defense. (*LJF* 258–60)

In 1906 Scheler moved to the Catholic University of Munich, but he lost his position in 1910, as a result of personal scandal,[3] and his vocal support of leftist political parties not favorable to the Bavarian diocese of the Catholic Church.[4] Subsequently he earned his living by giving private lectures—often in hotel rooms rented by his friend Dietrich von Hildebrand—and by writing.[5]

It was during this time (between 1911 and 1922) that Scheler entered a most productive period of publishing and lecturing. Within a few years after having met Husserl, Scheler was invited to lecture to the newly founded Göttingen Philosophical Circle. These lectures were presented over the course of several weeks each semester.[6] Edith Stein paints a vivid portrait of the intellectual excitement that surrounded Scheler's regular visits to this small band of phenomenologists:

> For several weeks of each semester, the Philosophical Society invited him [Scheler] to Göttingen to give lectures. He was not permitted to hold lectures at the university; nor were we permitted to announce them on the bulletin board. We could only call attention to them by word of mouth. We had to meet in the social rooms of some hotel or café. At the end of this semester Scheler came once again. At first, the lectures were scheduled for several nights a week; but, as he did not know how to allocate his time properly, there was so much material left to be crammed in that, finally, we had to meet daily. After

the formal presentation was over, he would stay on for hours in the café with a smaller group. (*LJF* 258)

The list of names of various members of the Göttingen Phenomenological Circle who gathered around Scheler in the summer of 1913 is impressive, especially in terms of the intimate friendships they shared and the collective impact they made on twentieth-century philosophy: Adolf Reinach (who was *privatdocent* in philosophy at Göttingen and served as Husserl's "student tutor"[7]), Hans Lipps, Fritz Kaufmann, Conrad and Hedwig Martius, Dietrich von Hildebrand, Alexander Koyre, Jean Hering, Roman Ingarden, and Edith Stein.[8]

Scheler was an especially formidable presence to the early phenomenological community. His descriptions of social constitution, ethics, and the emotions are foundational. Edith Stein notes that "it was Max Scheler's *Formalism in Ethics and Non-formal Ethics of Values* which has probably affected the entire intellectual world of recent decades even more than Husserl's *Ideas*. The young phenomenologists"—and we should include Stein herself in this list—"were greatly influenced by Scheler; some, like Hildebrand and Clemens, depended more on him than on Husserl" (*LJF* 258). For example, in his major work, *The Nature of Sympathy*, Scheler focused on giving a phenomenological description of human emotions and love, rather than cognition. Scheler offered a significant contribution to early phenomenological studies regarding the constitution of the human person by describing how the ego, reason, and consciousness *presuppose* the sphere of the person.[9] Contrary to Husserl, Scheler denied outright the theoretical need for a pure, transcendental ego. According to Scheler, Husserl's account of a pure stream of conscious life merely offers an idealistic description of what really happens in common, corporeal, intersubjective experience. The notion of a transcendental ego is thereby necessarily derivative of a more primordial, emotive experience. Scheler openly criticized Husserl's well-known account of transcendental Idealism—so much so that he "availed himself of every opportunity to insist he was not one of Husserl's disciples but that, instead, he had discovered the phenomenological method for himself."[10] For Scheler it is the human heart as the seat of love, rather than a transcendental ego or a pure stream of conscious life, that accounts for the emergence of human existence.[11]

Throughout his writings, Scheler categorized various types and intensities of emotions, though he believed that most feelings remain hidden and personal. Primordial among the totality of emotions is that of love, which is central to all human activity.¹² By love Scheler means that the human person is first and foremost a loving being (*ens amans*) rather than a rational animal. He argues that feelings possess their own sense of logic, a type of logic quite different from the logic of reason. Of course, by "emotions" Scheler does not mean mere sentimentality. Rather, Scheler designates the emotive as a noncognitive faculty that obtains knowledge of principal truths that are themselves the basis for reasoning and judgment.¹³

§1. Scheler's Distinction between the Emotive and the Rational

In a manner reminiscent of Pascal, Scheler held that the *ordre du coeur*, or *logique du coeur*, is not reducible to a simple unification between the categories of Greek rationality on the one hand and sensibility (*Sinnlichkeit*) on the other hand. "The emotive elements of spirit, such as feeling, preferring, loving, hating, and willing, also possess original *a priori* contents which are not borrowed from 'thinking,' and which ethics must show to be independent of logic" (*FE* 63). In arguing that emotional experience is not subsumed by the intellect, Scheler rejects Kant's identification of the *a priori* to strict, cognitive rationalism. According to Scheler, Kant is the philosopher *par excellence* who mistakenly "connected *a priori* knowledge with the formal, the spontaneity of reason, universality, and necessity."¹⁴ Scheler, contrarily, holds that reason is subject to historical change and that "only its ability to have forms of thinking, intuition [*Anschauung*], and valuation, is constant. In this, he [Scheler] is in agreement with Spengler: 'Kant's table of categories is only the table of categories of European thinking.' "¹⁵

Scheler attempts to distinguish the "*a priori* contents independent of inductive experience and pure laws of thought" from "emotive ethics." He argues that "moral values" can no longer be said to derive "from observation and induction. Feeling, preferring and rejecting, loving and hating, which belong to the totality of spirit [*des Geistes*], possess their own *a priori* contents independent of inductive experience and pure laws of thought" (*FE* 65). Hence, the task now falls to phenomenologists to "find the peculiar essence of moral values through feeling," since "feeling is found *with* man, as are all laws pertaining to acts of value-feeling, preferring, loving, hating, etc." (*FE* 271). Accordingly, pure autonomous acts of the emotional life are designated *a priori* manifestations of pure intuition

(*Anschauung*). Values and their interconnections do not differ in principle "from the way in which we find propositions and laws of arithmetic, mechanics, physics, and chemistry. These, as well as propositions valid for all life, are found 'with' man" (*FE* 271). In other words, it is precisely the emotional world *as a whole* that reveals itself in Scheler's phenomenological analysis. Emotional capacity, like man's rational capacity, lies *a priori* apart from historical and social development and change.[16] According to Manfred Frings, this means that for Scheler "genuine understanding of an individual or any social unity (family, people, nation, race, etc.), or any historical epoch, can only be obtained by way of cognition about their feeling and conceiving values as well as the respective structure of their value-order, as it appears in acts of preferring or rejecting."[17]

The issue that Scheler raises cuts to the heart of his critique against Husserl's theory of transcendental constitution. In effect, Scheler argues that essences never simply appear to the human person outside of how they are intuited, and intuition is never given in just a logical or merely cognitive capacity. Rather, intuition is always co-constituted *emotively* as well as rationally. Essences, therefore, are intuited according to emotive capacities determined, in part, by the constituting agent, whether that agent is an individual person or a nexus of social organizations. Intuition is always *more than* merely cognitive. It is "subjective" and "relative" to human organization. "Cognition is doomed to become bare of content—in the final analysis, to become mere relations that are relations of nothing—to the degree that it is reduced to purely logical factors" (*FE* 63). Scheler concludes that intuition implies "original *thing*-interconnections, not laws of objects just because they are laws of acts apprehending objects." Intuitive interconnections are *a priori* because "they are grounded in essences, not in objects and goods. They are *a priori*, but not because "'understanding' or 'reason' 'produces' them" (*FE* 68). According to Scheler,

> The *phenomenology of values* and the *phenomenology of emotive life* are completely independent of logic, having an autonomous area of objects and research. . . . Hence, contrary to Kant, we recognize an emotive apriorism as a definite necessity, and we demand a new division of the false unity of apriorism and rationalism that hitherto has existed. . . . [By] *a priori* we designate those ideal units of meaning [*Bedeutungseinheiten*] and propositions which become self-evident [*zur Selbstgegebenheit kommen*] by the content [*Gehalt*] of an immediate intuition

[*Anschauung*], in the absence of any kind of positing [*Setzung*] of their thinking subjects and their natural constitution, and in the absence of any kind of positing an object to which they would be applicable. (*FE* 64–68ff)

By distinguishing the true *a priori* from Kant's notion of the "formal," Scheler exposes what he calls the "erroneous" and "groundless assumption" held by many philosophers (and Scheler includes Husserl among them) who attempt to make what is *a priori* understandable, logical, purely cognitive. Scheler charges that Kantian ethics render "all love for the other [as] reducible to self-love, and even that all love is reducible to egoism." Scheler characterizes every attempt to prioritize the absolute autonomy of reason over feelings and emotions as "an attitude of 'hostility' toward or 'distrust' of the given *as* such, a fear of the given as 'chaos,' an anxiety—an attitude that can be expressed as 'the world outside me, nature within me'" (*FE* 67).

§2. The Human Person as *Ordo Amoris*

Scheler defines the human person as "act-being," a pre-conscious nexus of acts of feelings and preferences.[18] The phenomenon of act-being implies that one and the same individual person remains unitively integrated throughout all possible variations of specific actions. Living human beings not only possess connections with objects outside themselves but also possess a state of "having" themselves, a state of being *to* themselves, a psychic inner-manifestness of being-*self*, what Scheler calls innerliness, *Innesein*. Of course, what Scheler calls "person" exists in and through the execution of particular, individuated acts: this is what is meant by identity in variation. Manfred Frings notes that "it is of utmost phenomenological importance to keep in mind that while the person exists 'in' executing any act or acts, the person 'varies' in and through the differences acts have among them."[19] Scheler thus defines "person" phenomenologically, in terms of intentionalities, urges and actions, experiences of consciousness, drives and resistances.

A "person" is a unified act of consciousness that unifies all human acts of different qualities into an integrated whole.[20] Acts of consciousness may include, for example, thinking, hoping, wishing, doubting, loving, hating, remembering, expecting, dreaming, hallucinating, lying, paying attention, understanding, believing, thanking, praying, willing, denying, and so on. Scheler observes that different acts often overlap and anticipate other acts, such as, for example, an act of loving someone that is also an act of remembering them and as such may elicit a still different act, such as giving thanks to God for that person's presence. In each act of consciousness, what is significant is that love and knowledge are brought together in an inseparable union or blending. A "person" permeates every act with his or her own uniquely distinctive identity, and, in turn, every act is saturated by an individual person. In other words, an act of love is not derivative from an act of knowledge: to love something (or someone) means to know them in the deepest sense.[21] Person, therefore, constitutes a unity-of-different-acts of love, insofar as these acts are realized, performed, and integrated.

In Schelerian terms, love is "a bridge, or better, a movement from poorer to richer knowledge. Love is an ontic agent . . . and grows as it presses more deeply into its object" (*FKV* 152–53). This is what Scheler means by "personalism." The world and its objects are constituted emotively according to various degrees of attraction and repulsion. Hence, constitution is not merely passive or cognitive or logical. Every object is constituted in terms of value by an emotive, rather than the merely cognitive, sphere. What is known in the order of knowledge is representational and derivative from what is first felt emotively, primordially. Scheler at one point comments that the epistemological tradition in effect gives precedence to cognitive experience precisely because it has remained beholden to Plato's unfortunate mistrust of the role played by eros: "In the ontic stipulation of eros as a power, however, in which Plato may have seemed to approach the idea of a world-creating love, 'creation' also became completely modified. What Plato called 'creating' is actually a mere *image* of a 'creation for us,' the sphere of 'representation' [*doxa*]. For knowledge in the strong sense [*episteme*], apparent creation is *not* creation, not production, but only *re*production of form" (*FKV* 153). The epistemological tradition of which Husserl is an heir needs to be inverted. According to Scheler, the order of experience *precedes* the order of logic; hence, cognition is dependent upon the primacy of emotive experience.

Scheler in effect transforms the Augustinian notion of *volo ergo sum*[22] to mean that representation and perception *follow from* the direction and intensity of our original interest toward objects in the world.[23] Like Husserl, Scheler insists that objects give themselves to us. But what distinguishes Scheler's account of givenness from Husserl's version is Scheler's insistence that we first learn to "take" objects according to the varying degrees of our personal interest *in* those objects. Further, because the emotional has its own *a priori* content, it follows that the emotional cognition of values is specifically different from acts of perception and thinking. Hence, the seat of the value *a priori* of all acts of feeling is exhibited in ethics (where cognition of values and value intuition take place) and not in logic. Scheler calls this interest "love" and "hate," respectively, and argues that "an increase of intuition or meaning in which an object stands before our consciousness depends upon an increase of our interest in the object, at bottom our love (or hate) of it. . . . [T]he content, structure, and connection of the elements of our worldview are determined already in the process of *becoming* every *possible* worldview by the forming and directing acts of taking an interest and love. All deepening and widening of our worldview is connected to a *preceding* deepening and widening of our spheres of interest and love" (*FKV* 163).

Love, therefore, is always a movement from lower to higher values, whereas hatred is a movement in the opposite direction.[24] But what is particularly important to note is that, for Scheler, neither love nor hatred are actual feelings at all. As fundamental orientations or attitudes or movements of intentionality in the world, love and hate "govern" my appreciation of objects in a way that remains autonomous and not susceptible to rational judgment. Before an object is constituted cognitively, I am always and already primordially drawn or repulsed by feelings of hatred or love toward all objects. Accordingly "it is in such acts of preferring, rejecting, loving, hating, as intentional functions, where values become apparent, i.e., during the *pursuance* of emotional acts the *a priori* value-content is given. This value-evidence, as such, is absolutely independent of judgments or propositions about them."[25] Love and hatred, Scheler notes, "are not feelings about or of something, rather one can only love and hate something, because a thing can be felt to have positive values in the absence of love. They are unique attitudes towards objects of value in that they comprehend values and their grades and they refer to objects themselves inasmuch as they have values."[26]

In a significant sense, Scheler agrees wholeheartedly with Husserl that every foreign object "gives itself" to consciousness. Whereas Husserl believes that one goal of phenomenology is to describe cognitively how the alter ego becomes constituted as a for-itself within my sphere of ownness, Scheler argues that the phenomenological reduction reveals instead the level of interest of the person who is intuiting the world toward other egos *who are already given* in that person's originary experience. He calls this the "self-revealing" of the object: "An image is a consequence of a 'question' asked with 'love' that the world answers and in so doing reveals itself. In this revelation the world *comes to its full existence and value*" (*FKV* 164). According to Scheler, Husserl's cognitive description of a non-personal transcendental ego must be utterly and definitively rejected. What is primordial is not the transcendental ego, but rather my own variations of attitudes, the differing degrees of love and hate that make knowledge (whether of an alter ego or any other object in the world) possible as such. Manfred Frings notes that this Schelerian position rests in sharp contrast to Husserl, for whom the transcendental ego does not allow of personal variations. For Husserl, the transcendental ego is a condition of possibility of the Objective world. It alone precedes what can be objectively constituted in the order of knowledge as a "person."[27]

Arguments concerning the meaning of the transcendental ego and Husserl's turn toward Idealism severely strained the otherwise fairly amicable relationship between Husserl and Scheler. Edith Stein comments that "Scheler was also one who keenly opposed reverting to idealism; and his comments were almost condescending; thereupon some of the young men allowed themselves a note of irony which infuriated me since it smacked of disrespect and ingratitude. Relations between Husserl and Scheler were not entirely placid . . . they often met for a lively exchange of ideas" (*LJF* 259). But why did Scheler (and Edith Stein, among others), find Husserl's notion of a transcendental ego so disturbing? Although we have alluded to this question before, let us now take a closer look at the problem that Husserl's phenomenological description of the transcendental ego poses in sharper detail.

§3. Scheler's Rejection of Husserl's Transcendental Idealism

According to Walter Fuchs, an unresolved problematic regarding Husserl's doctrine of transcendental Idealism began to emerge as early as 1901.[28] In the fifth and sixth *Logical Investigations*, Husserl introduced a theory of signification that began "not from what is most silent in the operation of consciousness, but from its relationship to things mediated by signs as these are elaborated in a spoken culture."[29] In fact, in the later *Investigations* Husserl appears to make no real distinction between the psychology of perception and the content of perception: what distinguishes one from the other is merely a change of *signs*. Fuchs argues that, for Husserl, a sign merely functions as a structure of substitution, as what points toward, or stands in for, something else: "Here meaning is constituted in the act of meaning which refers to the object intended. This second act of consciousness functions so as to represent the object, making the object present through the intention as what is meant. This second type of act of consciousness we shall call representational; meaning is constituted by means of representational consciousness of the intended object."[30] There is no usefulness to a sign, then, except insofar as its meaning is merely intentional: a sign never announces itself but rather makes present something else, what is referred to by the sign. Consequently, the theory of signification that was developed in the second volume of the *Investigations* began to look so much like the psychologism it was attempting to undermine that a certain amount of confusion became attached to it, including a certain amount of confusion provoked by Husserl himself concerning just what the theory of "psychologism" meant.[31]

In effect, Husserl argues in the second volume of the *Investigations* that psychology can never found logical meaning. It is insufficient to speak about the things-themselves. In addition to the things-themselves, Husserl notes, there must be someone who speaks about the things. Of course, Husserl is not denying that a logical entity *is* what it is. Rather, he is saying that the concept of a logical meaning is itself meaningless unless there already exists someone who operates with this meaning intention.[32] Husserl in effect moves from the thing-itself *back to* the subject that is the giving-thing *of* intentionality. The objects of logical intentions are objects for the subject that constitutes them. We may thus note that by 1913, Husserl had definitively abandoned his enthusiasm for ontological realism, an enthusiasm which he first presented in *Investigations I-IV*. The publication of *Ideas* completed the transformation begun in *Investigations V* and *VI*. According to his critics, the early and uncompromising proponent of a "new scholastic realism" had committed nothing short of phenomenological apostasy. Husserl was publicly castigated for embracing transcendental Idealism as a way of describing the phenomenon of objective givenness—a charge that Husserl himself was never quite able to dispel to the satisfaction of his critics no matter what his effort.[33]

Husserl posited the doctrine of the transcendental ego in order to describe the condition of possibility of the constitution of objective meaning (*Bedeutung*).[34] He argues that, within the sphere of ownness, what is most alien of all—the alter ego, the Other—becomes knowable only on account of the constitution of a foreign subjectivity by virtue of analogical variation. For Husserl, every experience of the Other is derivatively and cognitively constituted. Hence, the subjectivity of foreign consciousness is always mediated through apperception; what is alter is never given to my *Erlebnis* on the Other's own terms: "[T]he mediacy that is already at work from the beginning is the (in itself multiform) mediatedness of the Other through the world. And only because Husserl, with reference *to* the world, at the same time thinks the Other *out* of the world, is mediacy for him the essential trait of *all* alien experience."[35] This means that Husserl's transcendental-*I* is conceptually pure and functional: it is a non-substantial, impersonal condition of possibility that makes the phenomenological reduction possible. Consequently, the significance of the transcendental ego remains essential for Husserl's account of *Wissenschaft*, a philosophy of social and cultural sciences. Transcendental constitution theory needs a pure (transcendental) ego; without it, Objectivity remains elusive. Hence, there is only *one* ego, regarded either empirically or transcendentally. The empirical ego is the product or *sign* of a method—namely, the method of reduction (*epoché*).[36]

Maurice Natanson concurs with Fuchs and notes that the most telling feature of Husserl's theory of transcendental Idealism rests on the notion of the primacy of consciousness. What Husserl argues is that the constitutive grounding of the Objective world by transcendental intersubjectivity is essentially posited by the universality of the (non-personal) transcendental ego: "It is possible, in reading Husserl, to speak of *the* transcendental ego or of transcendental egos. Though a kind of monadology emerges, the meaning of 'my' and 'your' transcendental ego proves to be the meaning of *the* transcendental ego. Referred to in the singular or plural, 'transcendental ego' signifies the primacy of consciousness."[37] The transcendental ego about which Husserl speaks is thus not equivalent to the sense of "I" that is classically designated in terms of an embodied human being, an en-fleshed subject of act and will.[38] Nor by "transcendental ego" does Husserl mean *person* in the Schelerian sense of *ordo amoris*.[39] The transcendental ego merely postulates for Husserl a logical condition of possibility. It is a condition of possibility of cognition and, therefore, a transcendental condition of Objectivity.

Husserl describes the universality of the transcendental ego in terms of Idealism.[40] His doctrine of the "pure transcendental-*I* of empathic constitution," however, initially caused much confusion for Max Scheler and the precocious band of European phenomenologists attracted to Husserl's early radical realist position.[41] In an attempt to distance himself from psychologism, Husserl was initially taken to be a realist, especially insofar as the first volume of *Logical Investigations* appeared to indulge a rendering of Platonic realism.[42] Beginning with *The Idea of Phenomenology* in 1907, however, and reaching mature expression with the publication of *Ideas* in 1913, Husserl's theory of transcendental Idealism became so controversial that many phenomenologists believed Husserl had decidedly abandoned his prior realist position altogether. Although Scheler and Ingarden remained deeply skeptical, Husserl testified repeatedly that the Idealism that he was espousing was merely methodological or, better yet, epistemological.

Walter Biemel argues that Husserl himself in point of fact never quite called his own position one of "realism"—even in his *Logical Investigations*—though, of course, he was primarily interested in presenting an ontological eidetic phenomenology that goes to the things-themselves: *zu den Sachen Selbst*.[43] In critiquing psychologism, Husserl held that the data of the understanding, concepts, and judgments should not be studied merely as psychological facts. Rather, as Paul Ricoeur notes, for Husserl they must "be considered as general elements of representation, elements independent of the consciousness we can have of them."[44] (For example, in his early phenomenological writings, Husserl attributed an *ideal being* to mathematical and logical objects.) Insofar as Husserl's "Platonic theory is right to emphasize the identity, objectivity, and communicability of meanings," so also the "psychological theories are right not to want to sever meanings from the mental life of persons; but not having a concept of the mental as intentional, they locate meanings in real parts of the flow of mental life."[45] Jitendranath Mohanty notes that Husserl's increasing reference to the transcendental Ego in lectures and essays from 1912 onward did little to appease the growing consternation from Scheler and others that Husserl was, in spirit if not in fact, a Kantian.[46]

§4. Scheler's Rejection of Analogical Apperception

Dismissing Husserl's transcendental ego as an Idealist conception, Max Scheler went on to argue that ethics must give a realist account of how human beings are interrelated with other persons and to their surrounding social and cultural worlds. In *The Nature of Sympathy*, Scheler offers a phenomenological analysis that describes how Others are given to the self in terms of social acts. In effect, Scheler argues that Husserl's doctrine of analogical apperception—by which alterity is constituted on the basis of the sphere of ownness—rests on a more originary and primordial experience of *social* constitution than transcendental monadology can allow. According to Scheler, Husserl's theory of cognitive apperception *presupposes* a co-given emotive experience that deems necessary the existence of other selves. In modifying Husserl's theory of analogical apperception, Scheler argues that apperception proceeds affectively and not merely cognitively, that I am motivated to apperceptively "fill in" other bodies on the basis of a primary and originary *feeling*. The cognitive content of this non-thematic encounter is then added on in terms of color, size, depth, location, and so forth. Hence, I am cognitively motivated to apperceive the Other according to an apperceptive, *a priori* emotive (and, hence, not merely cognitive) experience. For Scheler, the felt experience of otherness is a founding mode, whereas every cognitive content *of* that experience presupposes a subject-of-encounter upon which all acts of cognition are cofounded. The Other is constituted apperceptively in feeling, not cognition. Hence, the Other as foreign experience is always and already *there*: "But it should be clear (before we even begin to consider the class of acts [of projective empathy]), that any kind of rejoicing or pity *presupposes*, in principle some sort of knowledge of the act, nature and quality of experience in other people, *just as the possibility of such knowledge presupposes, as its condition, the existence of other conscious beings*" (Sympathy 8).

For Scheler, the problem of empathy—or "fellow-feeling"—does not pose merely epistemological questions for us, but serious ethical concerns as well: "[T]he problem of individual and society, and of self and other as conscious subjects, is also, in its most fundamental sense, a problem of *value*, an ethical as well as a juristic problem" (Sympathy 227). Scheler thus distinguishes "fellow-feeling" (*Mitfühlen*) from "all such attitudes as merely contribute to our *apprehending, understanding*, and, in general, *reproducing* (emotionally) the experience of others, including their states of feeling" (Sympathy 8). In so arguing, Scheler rejects Husserl's strict cognitive model that conceives the human person as a purely rational ego. According to Manfred Frings, Max Scheler gives "primacy of the givenness of contents of values over any other acts of consciousness." Values are constituted by us only "in" the feeling of them, not through any cognitive representation. "Without 'seeing' there are no colors. Without 'feeling' there are no values. The priority of feelings over thinking and willing, for that matter, is one of order [i.e., the order of experience], not one of sequence [i.e., the order of knowledge]."[47]

Clearly, for Scheler, the ego is not a pure *cogitans*, a rational entity, a *res*. "Feelings" imply values, and values are oftentimes at odds with rational speculation. (Some "values" may even be said to be irrational or non-rational or even supra-rational.) As a result, Scheler believed that the essences of values are first given emotively via experience and feeling.[48] For this reason, Scheler notes that even the lowest sensible feelings are said to possess an *inner pre-rational preference* toward higher values and feelings:

> It is impossible, for example, that a sensible feeling could by itself prefer the uncomfortable to the comfortable. Our lived bodies do not simply "prefer" pain over pleasure. This subliminal, quasi-automatic emotive preferring is already "in" the feeling; that is, the preference is essential to value feeling in that it is stretched, as it were, always between at least two values. Feeling of values has its foundation . . . in the preferring and not in choosing. . . . Already, therefore, the lowest feelings of sensation possess an *inherent* drift of their own toward preferring of what is comfortable.[49]

Scheler makes a further distinction between vertical and horizontal preferences, the latter concerning pre-rational activities that "tend toward" positive values over negative ones (such as the desire for bodily comfort). He opposes such transient values as ease and comfort with what he calls vertical preferences; that is, the order of *personal* or transcendent values. These "indivisible values," such as justice, beauty, knowledge, and the holy, are not weathered by time like those values fulfilled by pleasure and comfort, regardless of the degree and intensity of such impressions. Whereas horizontal values are fleeting and sensual, vertical values indicate nonquantifiable feelings that are pure and absolute, in a sense "detached" from sensibility. The absolute values of love, justice, holiness, beauty, knowledge, and so on become accessible only in Scheler's *personalistic* sense. For Scheler, such "pure values" constitute the distinct sphere of value-feelings; they are, therefore, primordially given in terms of *personal feelings* rather than rational analyses. Accordingly, Husserl's doctrine of an originary sphere of ownness (and, along with it, his cognitive account of how knowledge of other persons is analogically apperceived), is criticized by Scheler as being "merely derivative." If it were otherwise, Scheler notes, "an idealist or strictly monistic parallelism would seem to require telepathy both real and apparent" (*Sympathy* 227). In light of his critique of the cognitive primacy of analogical apperception, Scheler argues that Husserl's theory of the transcendental Ego succeeds only in muddying the clear waters of phenomenological description. In effect, Husserl confuses what should be the proper subject of phenomenological reflection (i.e., the genuine foreign experience of non-thematic *feeling*), with the description of a merely cognitive event:

> The (traditional) argument from analogy is merely an epistemological tailpiece tacked on to *one particular system of metaphysics*, namely the Cartesian and Lotzean dualism of interacting substances, which does *not* postulate a supra-individual mind. It is the same with the epistemological idealists (such as Husserl and others); either they accept an unaccountable miracle, in assuming the reality of other selves at all (granted, that is, that the self is admitted to be intrinsically individuated, and not merely by virtue of its empirical content or relationship to the body; for the latter, combined with an idealist theory of consciousness would inevitably lead to solipsism); or else we have another unaccountable miracle, namely that within the total content of 'consciousness in general' (which is supposed to contain each individual self as part of its objective content), there should still be individual centres of consciousness which are obliged to take special cognizance of their own existence. (*Sympathy* 226)

"Ownness," for Scheler, is always a constitut*ed* phenomenon. It is not an originary sphere, but rather an ontic realm, constituted from a more primordial and hence purely *emotive* experience.

§5. Scheler on Intentional Reference

In phenomenological terms, Scheler holds that all fellow-feeling involves *intentional reference* of the feeling of love (attraction/joy) or hate (repulsion/sorrow) toward an other person.[50] By granting recourse to such distinction, Scheler proposes that the constitution of other persons is not only cognitive but entails an emotive element as well. He distinguishes between *Einfühlung* ("in-feeling" or "empathy") on the one hand and *Mitfühlung* ("fellow-feeling" or "sympathy") on the other hand, and he argues that any such visualized feeling that "remains within the cognitive sphere . . . is not a morally relevant act" (*Sympathy* 9). "The reproduction of feeling or experience must therefore be sharply distinguished from fellow-feeling. It is indeed a case of feeling the other's feeling, not just knowing of it, nor judging that the other has it; but it is not the same as going through the experience itself. In reproduced feeling we sense the *quality* of the other's feeling, without it being transmitted to us, or evoking a similar real emotion in us" (*Sympathy* 9).

Thought, in a manner of speaking, follows from a more primitive sense of attraction and repulsion. According to Scheler, empathy—in distinction to sympathy—has no need to attain any logical grounds for justification or rational legitimation, whether by analogy, prior judgment, or intimation: A's suffering is first presented *as* A's in an act of understanding or "vicarious" feeling experienced as such, and it is to this material that B's primary commiseration is directed. That is, *my* commiseration and *his* suffering are, phenomenologically speaking, *two different facts*, not *one* fact. Scheler notes that any distinctions made between "understanding" and "vicarious feeling" remain manifest "even *while* [I am] experiencing them." He says: "Fellow-feeling proper, actual 'participation,' presents itself in the very phenomenon as a *re-action* to the state and value of the other's feelings—as these are 'visualized' in vicarious feeling. Thus in this case the two functions of *vicariously visualized* feeling, and *participation* in feeling are separately given and must be sharply distinguished. Very many descriptions of fellow-feeling suffer from failure to make this distinction" (*Sympathy* 8). Consequently, what Scheler proposes is a rejection of Husserl's theory of cognition in that there can be no such thing as feeling *apart from* value: all experience implies an intentional reference to other human persons, though of course without having to imply that such persons "must already have been encountered in some sort of experience, and above all without warranting the assumption that these intrinsically social acts can only have occurred and originated in the actual commerce of men with one another" (*Sympathy* 229). We can "feel" the quality of the other's sorrow without having to suffer with him, Scheler notes, or feel the quality of his joy without ourselves rejoicing with him.[51] Understanding another person "does not come about as the conclusion to an 'argument from analogy,' nor by any projective 'empathy' or 'mimetic impulse' [as with] Lipps" (*Sympathy* 9). It is intrinsically impossible for value to be given in advance of experience. Scheler notes that "this applies still more once the further error is committed of attempting to base this givenness of value upon acts of recognition and appreciation [i.e., analogy and apperception], when all ideal obligation and all recognition of such obligation imply that such value is already given. This act of 'recognition and appreciation' would be a complete shot in the dark if the personal existence of something (X), and the value of this, were not already *given in advance*" (*Sympathy*, 228–29).

According to Max Scheler, Husserl's theory of constitution remains ultimately inadequate, not because Scheler does not think that the world is a constituted phenomenon but because he does not believe "constitution" is primarily a cognitive function. Rather, Husserl's cognitive description of constitution offers little more than a conceptual framework that distinguishes "primary" from "derivative" phenomena. Scheler's argument is that Husserl fails to take into account an underlying, emotive experience that makes possible every cognitive experience *as such*. Husserl's failure lies not in his epistemological description of how I come to know the alter ego on the basis of an analogical transfer from my sphere of ownness. Rather, it results in his failure to grasp that the very condition of possibility that makes the experience of empathy possible is *emotive* rather than rational: "It is *in* the blush that we perceive shame, *in* the laughter joy" (*Sympathy* 10).

§6. The Rejection of Projective Empathy and "Fellow-Feeling"

As with Husserl, so too Scheler holds that the experience of empathy is primordial, *a priori*, given in terms of feeling, preference, and value-intention. Such experience "*presupposes*, in general, some sort of *knowledge* of the fact, nature, and quality of experience in other people, just as the possibility of such knowledge presupposes as its condition, the existence of other conscious beings" (*Sympathy* 8).[52] Although neither "arguments from analogy" nor "projective empathy" establish the apodicticity of other persons, apperception nevertheless *presupposes* what is already made present in the order of knowledge—namely, that the Other is always and already given originarily and emotively in the order of experience. Scheler notes that "the reproduction of feeling or experience must therefore be sharply distinguished from fellow-feeling" (*Sympathy*, 9).

But if foreign experience is first given emotively rather than cognitively, how can it be distinguished from my own experience without there being a cross-contamination between what is primordially mine and what is other? To answer this question, Scheler describes the experience of other persons as being given "exactly like a landscape which we 'see' subjectively in memory, or a melody which we 'hear' in similar fashion" (*Sympathy* 9). Although such experience is constituted as a real seeing or hearing, no object is perceived as "really present." Just as the past is "represented" without its object being present, so too the reproduction of the feeling or "sharing" of an other person's experience does not at all imply any sort of "participation" in the Other's inner psychic experience. Projective experiences of fellow-feeling are "always additional to an experience in the Other *which is already* grasped and understood" (*Sympathy* 9). In this sense, Scheler's position anticipates Husserl's own argument concerning the realm of absolute privacy, though without Scheler's falling into a transcendental or Idealist conclusion. "The other person has—like ourselves—a sphere of absolute privacy," Scheler writes, "which can never be given to us. But that 'experiences' occur there is given for us *in* expressive phenomena—again, not by inference, but directly, as a sort of primary 'perception'" (*Sympathy* 10).

Scheler designates the relationship between experience and perception as symbolic, rather than causal. A child, for example, involuntarily imitates a gesture of fear or joy after it has just seen its mother's expression. Such imitation, Scheler argues, "is never called forth simply by the visual image of the gesture; the impulse to imitate only arises when we have *already* apprehended the gesture *as* an expression of fear or joy" (*Sympathy* 10). Otherwise, apprehension would remain limited to mere imitation and reproduction, rather than genuine understanding. Scheler adds that the fact that we can understand the experience of animals further argues against Husserl's analogical theory of imitation. Although we cannot imitate their manner of expression (e.g., a dog expresses joy by wagging its tail, a bird expresses fear or excitement by twittering its feathers), nevertheless we can in fact understand the *experiences* and *feelings* of animals (e.g., of joy and fear), even if such feelings and experiences are not cognitively discernable.

The relationship between expression and experience contains for Scheler "a *fundamental* basis of connection, which is independent of our specifically human gestures of expression" (*Sympathy* 10). He notes: "We have here, as it were, a universal grammar, valid for all languages of expression, and the ultimate basis of understanding for all forms of mime and pantomime among living creatures. Only so are we able to perceive the inadequacy of a person's gesture to his experience, and even the contradiction between what the gesture expresses and what it is meant to express" (*Sympathy* 11). What does Scheler mean by "universal grammar"? For one thing, he proposes that an imitation of another person's expressive gestures does not mean that I necessarily fully comprehend his or her inner life (*Erlebnis*). I can "ape" or "mimic" in caricature someone else's expressions without ever understanding the Other's intentions or motivations. Consequently, my having an experience similar to someone else's has nothing *necessarily* whatsoever to do with understanding that individual or his or her experience. Neither analogy nor imitation adequately describe the phenomenon of genuine understanding. In terms of the givenness of other persons, Scheler in fact argues that the apprehension of the Other as alter ego *presupposes* that the Other's body is already a foreign field of latent expressions and meanings: "The only way of explaining imitation and the reproduction of a personal experience similar to that underlying a perceived expressive gesture, is that, through this, a genuine experience takes place in me, objectively similar to that which occurs in the other person whose expression I imitate" (*Sympathy* 11).

Max Scheler, of course, worked extensively in the field of child psychology and was therefore quite familiar with the work of William Stern, with whom Edith Stein studied before coming to Göttingen in 1913. Like Stein and Stern, Scheler too rejected the popular position held by Theodore Lipps—namely, that empathy is primarily imitative, a "feeling-into" other persons.[53] Anticipating Merleau-Ponty's now classic example of the infant imitating its mother's facial expressions, Scheler argues that an infant is motivated to show reactions to expressions much earlier than the cognitive occurrences of "associations" and "transfers" would allow.[54]

§7. The Primordial Givenness of the Community over the Individual

The being of the human person implies an essential relation between "Thou" and "I."[55] According to Scheler, "[E]ven the essential character of human consciousness is such that the community is in some sense implicit in every individual, and that man is not only part of society, but that society and the social bond are an essential part of himself; that not only is the 'I' a member of the 'We,' but also that the 'We' is a necessary member of the 'I'" (*Sympathy* 229–30). What he means here is that every human individual possesses an intuited *a priori* of communality, even if (hypothetically speaking, as in the case of Robinson Crusoe) that individual exists in the *absence* of a physical community: "Initially, humans find themselves ecstatically absorbed in a social world without having an ego experience of their own. Phenomenologically, the *a priori* of the 'thou' functions as a 'sphere' of consciousness. 'Sphere,' in this instance, is just another word for what can be irreducibly given as a meaning in consciousness: communality is a 'phenomenon' "(*Sympathy* 83). In effect, Scheler notes repeatedly that even Robinson Crusoe—a man who has never in any way perceived beings of his own kind, or any traces or signs of them, and has no other evidence for the existence of such beings—would nevertheless "not only possess the notion and idea of community, but would also think: 'I know that there is a community, and that I belong to one (or several such); but I am unacquainted with the individuals comprising them, and with the empirical groups of such individuals which constitute the community as it actually exists' " (*Sympathy* 234).

For Scheler, human consciousness innately experiences an *a priori* "lack of communality." There exists, Scheler says, an "intrinsic orientation of the particular individual towards a possible society . . . such that by a purely immanent scrutiny of the intrinsic activity of any given self, prior to and apart from any chance empirical acquaintance or actual intercourse among men, one might discover in it a further orientation towards a multiplicity of groups and communal interest of very different kinds." In other words, whether or not Crusoe's social intentions are fulfilled is merely of secondary concern. What is primary and given, Scheler argues, is what Frings calls "the intentional referent of otherness *as such*. His social acts, such as loving, promising, thanking, obeying, serving, answering, etc., refer to a sphere of communality even without members being physically present."[56] In fact, Scheler in no small way anticipates Heidegger's notion of Being-with-others, arguing that it is in the felt *absence* of Others that the social *a priori* of communality is first constituted.

Manfred Frings acknowledges that, for Scheler, "the thou is always fundamental and given prior to the I. There is no ego without 'we,' and experiencing the thou is an experience of a reality."[57] But if the "thou" is prior to the "I," then does it not follow that intersubjectivity between self and Other is thus at first *undifferentiated*, meaning that the root of intersubjectivity is experienced in a "psychic stream" into which all persons are swept at birth even prior to experiential differentiation? Scheler acknowledges such a possibility. "It is possible," Scheler states, "for the same experiences to be given both 'as our own' and 'as someone else's'. . . . What occurs, is an immediate flow of experiences, *undifferentiated as between mine and thine*, which actually contains both our own and other's experiences intermingled and without distinction from one another" (*Sympathy* 246). The contents of such an undifferentiated stream of intersubjectivity is what Scheler refers to as "the contents of a tradition. These contents come from others and the past even though we experience them as our own." Frings offers a commentary on Scheler's point, namely that "One lives more in a communal experience than in one's own individual self. Ideas and feelings that came to govern us when we were very young are initially those of the members of what is the basic form of the life-community into which we are born, namely, the family."[58] In terms of the infant-mother relationship mentioned earlier, it is the historical family—hence represented by the state; the church; social, political, economic, and educational institutions; and so on—that initially form the child's fate and give to the child his or her sense of moral tenor and model-consciousness:

> An infant who is swept up in this initial psychic stream in which thine and mine are still undifferentiated only very slowly raises his head, as it were, above this stream flooding over it. The infant finds himself as a being who also at times has feelings, ideas and tendencies of his own. And this, moreover, only occurs to the extent that the child *objectifies* the experiences of his environment in which he lives and partakes, and thereby gains *detachment* from them.[59]

In concrete terms, Scheler in fact (unknowingly) agrees with much that Husserl says, namely that it is impossible for the self (*das Ich*) to constitute the "world" transcendentally and independently apart from the thou.[60] (For Husserl, of course, the Objective world is an intersubjective, not a subjective, achievement, such that the sphere of ownness is regarded as a cognitive abstraction.) Of course, by "self" Scheler means the entire field, or network, of experiences of inner perceptions, values, and feelings. What distinguishes Scheler's analysis from Husserl's is Scheler's conviction that the self is primordially and intersubjectively communal. For Scheler, the sphere of the I is inseparably tied to the sphere of the thou, especially in terms of the felt experience of the absence of the members of a community. Husserl's cognitive appropriation of "projective empathy"—in which we begin with a natural belief in the existence of the other and then attempt to explain it—fails for Scheler precisely on the grounds that the argument from analogy begs the question of the existence of other persons. "When all is said, the theory of empathy offers no grounds for assuming the existence of other selves, let alone other individuals. For it can only serve to confirm the belief that it is my self which is present 'all over again,' and never that this self is other and different from my own" (*Sympathy* 242). Scheler is adamant that the problem of projective empathy is not so much that we impute our own experience onto others, "but the *opposite* tendency, in which we entertain the experiences of other people as if they were our own" (*Sympathy* 246).

§8. Some Critical Reflections Concerning Scheler's Position

In the end, Husserl's strict cognitive account of analogical apperception fails to respond to Scheler's more radical description of an undifferentiated stream of intersubjective communal experience and his more provocative analysis of the Thou-I phenomenon. Such an emotive, originary, noncognitive encounter with alterity would essentially be even more primordial than the cognitive constitution *of* such experience. According to Scheler's phenomenological analysis, the experience of alterity subsists prior to and is, therefore, constitutive of every cognitive assimilation *of* such experience. This principle, Scheler argues, holds true even for Husserl, who himself contended that "the Other" is constituted as a for-itself only mediatedly, conditionally, analogically. Hence, Scheler concludes that Husserl's transcendental theory of cognition in effect violates the very principle of constitution upon which analogy is based. And since no purely cognitive analysis fully describes the *eidos* of experience, Scheler's point is well taken. In light of Scheler's critique, we may now acknowledge that Husserl's strict cognitive account of the constitution of the alter ego in the order of knowledge does *not* describe the phenomenality of experiences of empathy. Rather, it gives a purely rational description of how the Other is transcendentally constituted in the order of knowledge.

Paradoxically, however, what is given phenomenologically in terms of transcendental constitution is precisely what cannot be given in the order of experience. Contradicting Husserl, Scheler contends that the transcendental ego is an epistemological abstraction. Rather than defining empathy as "fellow-feeling," Scheler describes empathy as a condition of possibility that makes possible *foreign* feeling as a constitutive phenomenon. Scheler argues that Husserl's cognitive model *presupposes* a more primordial, originary, noncognitive, emotive experience that is first experienced by the feeling of otherness *as such*. According to Scheler, foreign experience cannot, in principle, be constituted cognitively unless it is first and primordially felt *as* foreign, alien, other. What is given in terms of cognition is precisely the non-accessibility of the Other's primordial experience. Because empathy does not "give" the Other to me in any definitive or apodictic sense, my emotive experience of the non-accessibility of the Other must be co-given along with its being cognized in the order of knowledge. Alterity is thus primordially emotive and derivatively cognitive. Of course, on principle I could analogically transfer my sense of feeling to the other ego as a feeling being. If that were the case, Husserl's emotive analysis would hold, except that it would then take place on the level of affectivity and not cognition. Scheler feared that such a projective principle would render the constitution of the other as merely derivative and thereby relinquish the constitutive potency of empathy in favor of a mere "feeling-into" other persons.

What constitutes alterity in Scheler's analysis, then, is the Other's *difference*, not his or her analogical similarity. For Scheler, the Other is a condition of possibility of the phenomenality of my own experience. It is not that the Other is first constituted cognitively and apperceived analogically. Rather, the Other is first and foremost an uncanny affection of what is foreign and non-thematic, an experience of feeling rather than thought, a felt encounter with a Thou that makes possible all conditions of constitution. By rejecting Husserl's doctrine of the transcendental ego, Scheler argues that the "I" does not constitute the Other first in the order of cognition. In terms of the order of experience, I and Other are equally primordial, co-constitutive, reciprocal. Neither I nor Thou is more primary or derivative in any absolute or classically transcendental sense. In effect, the originary, reciprocal relationship between I and Other constitutes meaning, existence, and contingency. This notion of the co-primordiality of the Thou is pointedly placed alongside the givenness of the I (*das Ich*):

> [T]here is an "I" and a "Thou" in a general sense. But which individual self it may be, that owns a given experience, whether it is our own or another's, is something that is not necessarily apparent in the experience as immediately presented . . . in other words, a man tends, in the first instance, to live more in others than in himself; more in the community that in his own individual self. This is confirmed by the facts of child psychology, and also in the thought of all primitive peoples. The ideas, feelings and tendencies . . . are initially confined

> entirely to those of his immediate environment, his parents and relatives, his elder brothers and sisters, his teachers, his home, his people, and so on. Imbued as he is with "family feeling," his own life is at first almost completely hidden from him. Rapt, as it were, and hypnotized by the ideas and feelings of this concrete environment of his, the only experiences which succeed in crossing the threshold of his inner awareness are those which fit into the sociologically conditioned patterns which form a kind of channel for the stream of his mental environment. (*Sympathy* 247)

In effect, Scheler rejects every notion that ascribes to the individual ego an originary apperceptive role regarding the constitution of the Other as alter ego: "It is wholly by means of specific experiences . . . and by means of the positive sense of vacancy they engender, that Crusoe fashions these ideas of the 'Thou' and of the community generally" (*Sympathy* 235).

Alterity, for Scheler, does not constitute an "immediate apprehension of something that cannot be experienced" (*Sympathy*, 235), as is the case with Husserl. Inasmuch as the Other is not given in terms of associations, assimilations, analogical inferences, transfers or empathy of one's own ego "into" that of others, Scheler concludes that Thou-I constitutes all genuine experiences in which reality as a whole is lived and fashioned, namely biological, social, and psychic/spiritual. Hence, apart from cognition, the felt experience of alterity constitutes an "independent sphere of essential being" (*Sympathy* 236). In terms of the absolute irreducibility of the alter ego, the "very important *distinction between the givenness* of the unitary psycho-somatic *vital* centres in others and the givenness of their *spiritual centres* of personality" together raise the question "of the prior givenness *a priori* of the Thou in general" (*Sympathy* 237). For Scheler, a proper description of the phenomenality of empathy undermines Husserl's strict, rational model. In the order of experience, the Other is emotively experienced *prior to* the cognitive constitution of it *as* Other. Otherwise, the Other would never be able to attain for itself an *a priori* independent sphere of essential being. And if this were the case, then the alter ego could not possibly (i.e., logically) share with me a sense of primal being.

In effect, Scheler refutes Husserl's theory of the primordiality of the sphere of ownness more than fifteen years prior to Husserl's description of the alter ego as presented in the Fifth Cartesian Meditation.[61] Scheler adamantly rejects Husserl's notion of the primacy of the Ego over the alter ego in the order of experience by arguing that the I and the Thou are equally and reciprocally co-constituted in emotional experience. As conditions of possibility, *das Ich* and *der Andere* are emotively co-given as originary phenomena in the order of experience. Of course, for Husserl, too, the Other is given in the order of experience, but only analogically, apperceptively, imaginatively. In terms of Husserlian constitution, this means that the alter ego is derived principally from a strictly *cognitive* sense. According to Husserl, the Other remains always structurally absent; whereas for Scheler, analogical apperception in fact presupposes that the other, the *Thou*—regardless whether it is present *or* absent—is first and foremost, always and already *there*, given structurally and intuitively as an *apodictic* condition of possibility.

Chapter Five

Edith Stein and the Problem of Empathy

Introduction

In the opening paragraphs of the foreword to her 1916 dissertation written under Husserl's direction, Edith Stein observes that the basic problem of empathy concerns "the experiencing [*Erfahrung*] of foreign [*fremdes*] subjects and their experience [*Erleben*]" (*Empathy* 1).[1] Her articulation of the problem of empathy reflects the theme and context of the intellectual milieu in which she studied and wrote, namely, the German intellectual tradition of the 1910s, dominated by the touring influence of Edmund Husserl and Max Scheler. The first chapter of her dissertation, which treated the nature of empathy in a purely historical setting, was never published and has subsequently been lost. Although no known surviving copy exists, Stein herself writes that her doctoral exposition "began with a purely historical treatment of the problems emerging one by one in the literature on empathy: aesthetic empathy, empathy as the cognitive source of foreign [*fremdes*] experience, ethical empathy, etc." (*Empathy* 1). The three extant chapters of Stein's treatise, however, were published in 1917 at Halle[2] and were widely read at the time by many leading phenomenologists of the day.[3]

A careful reading of this work demonstrates a decidedly Schelerian flair to her dissertation in terms of Stein's subject matter and the overall spirit of the work. In investigating Edith Stein's detailed analysis of empathy in dialogue with Husserl's description of constitution, especially in terms of pairing and analogy, it is equally important to investigate the concealed influence that Scheler's rejection of Husserl's transcendental project exerted on Stein in light of her own phenomenological descriptions of these modifications.[4]

§1. The Problem of Empathy Revisited

According to Edith Stein, empathy is not a constituted sense, one among others. Rather, empathy is a "kind of act of perceiving [*eine Art erfahrender Akte*] *sui generis*" (*Empathy* 11). It is an act that is present in experience, though non-primordial in content. (For example, I may share the "content" of empathy by virtue of a non-primordial experience of memory, expectation, or fantasy.) Edith Stein notes that the subject of the empathized experience is not the subject empathizing, but an *other*. Empathy is distinct from memory, expectation, and fantasy in that the subject of empathy does not issue from *my* "I." The difference between primordial feelings and non-primordial feelings are the modes of experiencing them (originarily or mediated through an other). Properly speaking, then, the subject of empathy is the Other. The Other, Stein notes, is an other human primordial subject who "is primordial although I do not experience it as primordial. In my non-primordial experience I feel, as it were, led by a primordial one not experienced by me but still there, manifesting itself in my non-primordial experience" (*Empathy* 11).

Edith Stein describes empathy as the experience of foreign consciousness in general. Empathy differentiates I from Thou according to "the perception of psycho-physical individuals and their experience of personality" (*Empathy* 11). The experience that an individual "I" has of another "I" as a center of human subjectivity becomes cognized, or thematized, in terms of foreign psychic givenness. In contrast to Theodore Lipps and William Dilthey, Stein rejects the popular definition appropriated to *Einfühlung* by many German aesthetic theorists at the turn of the twentieth century. Lipps, for example, portrayed empathy as "an 'inner participation' in foreign experiences" (*Empathy* 12). By this, he argued that the primary significance of *Einfühlung* meant "in-feeling" in the sense that I "feel-into" the other, the way I find myself "feeling-within" the other's experiences.

The problem here, of course, is Lipps's confusion between non-primordial and primordial experiences. Early twentieth-century German aesthetic theorists were in fact notorious for misappropriating the term *Einfühlung* (literally "in-feeling") without making this necessary distinction.[5] In *The Cognition of the Literary Work of Art*, published in Polish in 1936,

Roman Ingarden independently concurs with Stein's analysis, although it should be noted that Stein wrote her analysis twenty years before Ingarden wrote his. In his pioneering work in the field of phenomenological aesthetics, Ingarden demonstrates how "the tendencies to psychologism in aesthetics . . . were still active in the beginning of the century (especially in Germany, for instance in the works of Theodor Lipps), and the aftereffects of the psychology and historicism of Dilthey."[6]

It is toward clarifying the problem of empathy apart from such confusions instigated by psychologism that Edith Stein was principally concerned. "Our position," she notes early in her dissertation, "is that there is the *phenomenon* of 'foreign experience' and correlatively the '*perception* of foreign experience.' The phenomenon in which all knowledge and certainty must finally be anchored is indubitable. . . . Thus the first task in this domain, as in all domains, is to comprehend the phenomenon in its pure essence, freed from all the accidents of appearance" (*Empathy* 21).

What is foreign experience in its pure, essential givenness? How does the perception of foreign experience look? These two questions, Stein tells us early on, guide her entire project. Yet these concerns also bear witness to an observation from Husserl's critics that Husserl's articulation of the problem of empathy in effect *presupposes* the being whose development it is seeking to ground. Concerning genetic psychology, Stein remains adamant that "a rigorous delineation of what phenomenology and psychology are to accomplish for the problem of empathy by no means proclaims their complete independence from one another." At the same time, Stein adheres to Husserl's clear methodological distinction between phenomenology and psychology. On the one hand, Stein notes that phenomenology is not tied to the results of psychologism, whereas on the other hand "psychology is entirely bound to the results of phenomenology. Phenomenology investigates the essence of empathy, and wherever empathy is realized this general essence must be retained. Genetic psychology, presupposing the phenomenon of empathy, investigates the process of this realization and must be led back to the phenomenon when its task is completed" (*Empathy* 22).

By foreign experience Stein denotes an encounter with alterity, with the unknown as such. How, then, can the perception of foreign experience be described in terms of essences and objectivity? Drawing on Edith Stein's preliminary observations, we need to note clearly that the phenomenology of empathy as portrayed by Stein primarily describes essences of phenomena of foreign givenness as such. In light of the ensuing debate between proponents of psychologism and phenomenology (something about which Husserl, too, was deeply concerned), it is important to note that Edith Stein was the first phenomenologist to publish on the theme of empathy.[7] Her contributions to the problem of empathy, inasmuch as they were inspired by Husserl and Scheler, must nevertheless be judged according to the weight of their own merits and in light of their own significance. Although Husserl certainly discussed the concept of empathy in his lectures on Spirit and Nature in 1910 and in subsequent lectures and notes on intersubjectivity posthumously published in *Husserliana* volumes XIII, XIV, and XIV, and which greatly influenced Edith Stein, he made only scant reference to it in the *Ideas* of 1913. Along with his lectures on intersubjectivity (published posthumously in 1952 as *Ideas II*), it was in his 1929 lectures on constitution and transcendental intersubjectivity (published as *Cartesian Meditations*) that Husserl assigned a primary status to empathy, thereby ensuring that the whole treatise leads up to his famous analysis of pairing and an analogical theory of apperception. Husserl thus designated empathy as a principal topic for phenomenological analysis. The theme of empathy as intersubjectivity was further enshrined in the Husserlian canon of scholarship with the posthumous publication of *Ideas II* in 1952, some thirty-five years following the date when Stein's painstaking inquiry was completed and published at Halle. In her *Autobiography*, Edith Stein describes how she first stumbled onto the idea of treating empathy as a phenomenon suitable for descriptive analysis:

> Now the question needed to be settled: what did I want to work on [for my dissertation]? I had no difficulty on this. In his course on nature and spirit, Husserl had said that an objective outer world could only be experienced intersubjectively, i.e., through a plurality of perceiving individuals who relate in a mutual exchange of information. Accordingly an experience of other individuals is a prerequisite. To the experience, an application of the work of Theodor Lipps, Husserl gave the name *Einfühlung* [empathy]. What it consists of, however, he nowhere detailed. Here was a lacuna to be filled; therefore, I wished to examine what empathy might be. The Master found this suggestion not bad at all. (*LJF* 269)

In order to appreciate Edith Stein's contributions to the problem of empathy, we initially need to investigate more fully what she was attempting to accomplish by refuting Lipps's position. It is Theodor Lipps, therefore, who sets the context for Stein's dissertation, and not Husserl.[8]

§2. The Essence of Acts of Empathy

At the very beginning of her essay, Stein notes Lipps's argument that empathy requires a "unity of our own and the foreign 'I'" such that "there is no distinction between our own and the foreign 'I,' that they are one" (*Empathy* 16). Watching a trapeze artist swinging from his rope, standing before Michelangelo's *Last Judgment*, even sharing in a friend's joy at the birth of his child for Lipps means that I lose myself, or "feel myself into," the artwork or performance or feeling with which I am engaged. In its classical formulation, Lipps characterized empathy as "a process of involuntary, inner imitation whereby a subject identifies through a feeling with the movement of another body. . . . Because empathy involves an involuntary projection into something else, the individual subject tends to lose itself."[9] Were Lipps's description correct, Stein surmises, then the real distinction between I and Thou, "the distinction between foreign and our own experiences, as well as that between the foreign and our own-'I,' would actually be suspended" (*Empathy* 16).

Stein correctly points out Lipps's misunderstanding of empathy. He reduces the Other to a merely vicarious "living-through" experience. For example, while watching an acrobat swing on his trapeze wire, Lipps incorrectly believes that I, too, undergo the motions *with* him. Through empathy, Lipps argues, I transfer my real self *into* a foreign object, such that my ideal self merges, or becomes absorbed, *in* it.[10] Lipps in effect mistakenly confuses what might be called "self-forgetfulness," that is, a cognitive process by which I can surrender myself to an object (such as what happens when I "lose myself" by living wholly in a memory, or fantasy, or an altered state of consciousness), with a "dissolution of the 'I' *in* the object" (*Empathy* 17).

An important contribution that Edith Stein offers in her analysis of empathy is the marked insistence that the *feeling* of my own primordial experience, for example, of happiness, grief, dizziness, arousal, joy, ecstasy, and so on, always contains its own distinctive sense content apart from any foreign manifestation of such content. Let us suppose, for example, that I share my brother's joy at the news of the birth of his daughter or that I am filled with grief as I weep alongside my friend who is suffering a painful loss. In each of these cases, the feeling of *my* joy or grief is essentially related to, yet absolutely distinct from, the primordial givenness of joy and grief as experienced by the *foreign* "I." Empathy is a non-primordial experience that announces the manifestness of primordial givenness. Hence, every act of genuine empathy requires (1) an experience originarily given by someone else who is not myself and (2) my own individual experience of another person's primordial experience. This distinction between an originary experience of givenness on the one hand and a non-originary experience of givenness on the other hand constitutes the sole criterion for what need properly be referred by the term *empathy*: "Empathy . . . is the experience of foreign consciousness in general, irrespective of the kind of the experiencing subject or of the subject whose consciousness is experienced" (*Empathy* 11). Edith Stein's phenomenological description of empathy is clear and precise on this point. "The experiences not coming from me appear to belong to 'the other' and to lie in his movements," she notes. Nevertheless, "I am not one with the acrobat but only 'at' him." In order to distance herself from the popular psychologism of the day, Stein counters Lipps's position by appropriating Husserl's rule that individualized, egoic streams of consciousness (*Erlebnis*) must remain absolutely distinct from one another: "I do not actually go through his motions but only *quasi*" (*Empathy* 16). Otherwise, Stein notes, what is given as my own primordial experience would rather be only an appropriated experience and not the experience of empathy itself. "Empathy in our strictly defined sense as the experience of foreign consciousness can only be the non-primordial experience which announces a primordial one. It is neither the primordial experience nor the 'assumed' one" (*Empathy* 14).

Clearly, the distinction between experiences that are originary or primordial and those that are non-originary or non-primordial needs further reflection. Edith Stein proposes that an experience is originary if it is first constituted as *my* experience, not someone else's; it is non-originary if the content of what I experience is initially given through someone else's experience. The same, of course, may be said in terms of the primordial givenness of the absolute Now of lived experience. In effect, Stein notes that a present non-primordiality may in fact point back to a past primordiality, such that an experience in the past has the character of a *former*-now.[11] Take the experience of joy, for instance. Empathy is concerned with grasping what is here and now (*Empathy* 8). An experience of joy, however, may be experienced either primordially or non-primordially, depending of course on whether the "I" as the subject of a remembered experience of joy is experiencing joy in the past or the present: "There are two possibilities: The 'I' as the subject of the act of remembering, in this act of representation, can look back at the past joy. Then the past joy is the intentional object of the 'I,' its subject being with and in the 'I' of the past. Thus the present 'I' and the past 'I' face each other as subject and object. . . . [T]he distinction between the primordially remembering 'I' and the 'I' non-primordially remembered persists" (*Empathy* 8). The differentiation between primordiality and non-primordiality exists similarly with experiences of fantasy and memory. In such cases, the "I" producing the memory or fantasized world is primordial, whereas the "I" living in it is non-primordial. Of course, Edith Stein acknowledges that fantasized experiences are different from memory in one very important sense; namely, fantasized experiences "are not given as a representation of actual experiences but as the non-primordial form of present experiences."[12] Nevertheless, her distinction between originary and non-originary experience clearly supports her thesis that empathy *tends toward* what is foreign, *fremde*, alter. Empathy essentially describes essences of acts that are primordial as present experience, though non-primordial in content (*Empathy* 8).

§3. The Distinction between Perception, Knowledge, and Reflection

The distinction between my primordial experience of personal perception on the one hand and my primordial experience of the non-primordiality of foreign experience on the other hand effectually constitutes the self-givenness of the Other as the foreign subject (*fremde Erlebnis*) in all acts of empathy. Drawing upon Scheler's distinction between essential differences of givenness, Stein distinguishes knowledge from acts of reflection and these from acts of perception. She defines reflection (*Reflexion*) as "the comprehension of an experience [*Erfassen eines Erlebnisses*]," whereas perception (*Wahrnehmung*) is limited to "the apperception of 'self'[*die Apperzeption des Selbst*] in the sense of the individual [*im Sinne des Individuums*] and his experiences [*Erlebnisse*] within the context of individual experience [*individuellen Erlebens*]" (*Empathy* 32, 30). Perception has its object before it in embodied givenness, whereas empathy does not. Similar to reflection, knowledge (*Wissen*) also reaches its object without ever having or possessing it. Knowledge "stands before its object," Stein tells us, "but does not see it. Knowledge is blind, empty, and restless, always pointing back to some kind of experienced, seen act [*erfahrenden, sehenden Akte*]. And the experience [*Erfahrung*] back to which knowledge of foreign experience [*fremdes Erleben*] points is called empathy [*Einfühlung*]" (*Empathy* 19).

In phenomenological terms, Edith Stein contrasts reflection, which designates the absolute givenness of experience, with inner perception. She makes careful note that in the latter experience, what I may assume to be "a feeling actually present" may, in point of fact, have been constituted by psychological delusion, the environment, a foreign contagion of feeling, a deception of value, or even mere prejudice. Turning again to Lipps, she even suggests that what he designates as "reflexive sympathy" might best be called "reiterated" empathy. For example, I can have a reflection on reflection, and so on, as an "ideal possibility *ad infinitum*. Similarly, there is a willing of willing, a liking of liking, etc. In fact, all representations can be reiterated" (*Empathy* 18).

Stein makes a careful distinction between *acts of reflection* and *acts of perception*. In terms of a feeling actually present, Stein acknowledges that such a feeling cannot be called a perception if it is not first perceived. Take, for example, a situation in which I am not aware that I am acting toward another person out of a feeling of love, or hatred, or resentment, and so forth. Insofar as I do not perceive that I am acting out of a particular feeling because nothing in my perceptual framework has made me aware of this reality, Stein argues that I am merely living in the natural attitude and, *ergo*, I cannot perceive that I am being deceived or, better yet, that I am "deceiving myself." I may be deceived in the object of my love, but not in my perception of what I am feeling. With further reflection, of course, I may eventually awaken to the fact that what I am feeling is itself a deception, a deception based on a misreading (or even a lack of comprehension) of events that have transpired within my environment, even under my very nose, without my notice.

In the same way, I cannot claim to be deceived in acts of perception when I do not hear a sound in my auditory environment or when I overlook an object in my visual field. My perception may be skewed or faulty, but it is always mine, and as such it establishes the environment of my natural attitude. Perception constitutes the world at the same time that it influences how I learn to take or interpret the world that I perceptually constitute. For this reason, I cannot assert that my perception is deceptive when I unknowingly take on foreign attitudes and values from an external source, such as a national or political or social or religious entity. Insofar as this foreign perspective is taken as *mine*, it must be classified as genuine:

> As we live in the feelings of our environment, we take them for our own, though they do not clarify our own feelings at all. . . . Suppose that I have taken over from my environment a hatred and contempt for the members of a particular race or party. For example, as the child of conservative parents, I may hate Jews and social democrats. . . . Then this would be an entirely genuine and sincere hatred save for the fact that it is based on an empathic valuing, rather than on a primordial one. This hatred may also be increased by contagion of feeling to such a degree that it is not legitimately related to the felt dis-value. . . . Feelings "acquired by reading" are not different. Should the enamored schoolboy think he feels Romeo's passion, this does not mean he believes he has a stronger feeling than is actually present. He actually feels passion because he has blown his spark into a flame by borrowed embers. This flame will go out of its own accord as soon as the embers die out. (*Empathy* 31–32)

Empathy points to another matter entirely when described in its essential structure within the phenomenological attitude. In order for the reflecting glance to be directed toward an experience, Stein insists that it must assume the form of a specific *cogito*. This means that the value of my feelings remains distinct from the actuality or non-actuality of a particular memory, experience, or expectation that gives rise to such feelings. In effect, what results when the natural attitude is left behind or when my belief in the world and the objects of perception are suspended (*epoché*) is that deception is no longer possible. Since what is given in ideational abstraction are essences of perception, what "perception is essentially as such" (*Empathy* 4), empathy points "back to the basic nature of acts in which foreign experience is comprehended." The "I" that performs the *epoché* is experienced as distinct from the personal-I taken as a psychic individual. Stein calls this the phenomenological or pure-I, the "indescribable, qualityless subject" of actual experience (*Empathy* 38).

Perception in the natural attitude is subject to deception on the part of the perceiver in the performance of a particular value-act. Yet, once perception-itself is constituted as a transcendental act in immanently given, pure consciousness, the pure-I is unable any longer to be deceived. Only in the natural attitude do the terms "own" and "foreign" mean "belonging to different individuals, i.e., different substantial, qualitatively elaborated, psychic subjects" (*Empathy* 29). When making a decision, I can in fact remain thoroughly unaware of the non-actual background experiences and secondary motivations that are operating on me unconsciously and that also play a role, such as social, ethnic, national, familial, and so on, images and assumptions that flood my senses at every moment. Since perception sees merely what is visible, it cannot expose what shelters and hides in the shadows.

This is true in terms of a contagion of feelings that get transferred through literature and multifarious forms of media, such as happens when we take feelings acquired by reading to be our own. Imagine, for instance, a young man who thinks he feels Romeo's passion, or a woman who imagines she can feel Anna Karenina's despair as Anna inches her way up to the train station platform, or Antigone's terror on the road outside of Thebes.[13] The potency of shared feelings transferred through literature demonstrates how acts of inner perception are primordially given, whereas in empathic acts there is a non-primordial, reflective givenness of the constituting experiences. Stein associates primordial givenness with genuine or originary experience: "Because a primordial valuing is lacking as a foundation, we also have 'non-genuineness' here. This results in a false relationship between the feeling, on the one hand, and its subject and object, on the other. And the youth's deception is that he attributes Romeo's passion to himself, not that he thinks he has a strong feeling" (*Empathy*, 31–32). Stein is not naive about the world she is investigating. "People are generally inclined to ascribe to themselves better motives than they actually have and are not conscious of many of their emotional impulses at all. . . . But this does not cause the feelings to cease enduring or functioning" (*Empathy* 33). Her point is well-taken that perception allows deception, whereas reflection is the comprehension of an actual experience: "[I]t is trivial to say that an experience I comprehend does not elude me" (*Empathy* 30). Perception can misperceive; it can confuse peripheral experiences with central experiences. In acts of phenomenological or pure reflection, however, *I cannot be deceived*. Such freedom from deception is possible, Stein argues, not because I can be absolutely clear about the failure of the basic primordial valuing but because I cannot reflect on an act *that is not present* to the pure-I, to what is absolutely given in intuition. It is precisely for this reason that Edith Stein objects to Husserl's inclusion of empathy under the term "inner perception."

§4. The Comprehension of Foreign Experience

The problem of empathy concerns the problem of the comprehension of foreign experience by my own constituting ego. Stein asks how it is that "in one psycho-physical individual the perception of another such individual occurs. This has led to the origination of theories of imitation, of inference by analogy, and of empathy by association" (*Empathy* 21). Whereas theories of imitation and association generally intend to give genetic explanations of foreign experience, inferences by analogy specify the form in which knowledge of foreign consciousness is possible. Consequently, we cannot deny that inferences by analogy do occur in knowledge of foreign experience. Stein notes, "It is easily possible for another's expression to remind me of one of my own so that I ascribe to his expression its usual meaning for me. Only then can we assume the comprehension of another 'I' with a bodily expression as a psychic expression. The inference by analogy replaces the empathy perhaps denied. It does not yield perception but a more or less probable knowledge of the foreign experience" (*Empathy* 27).

Phenomenology investigates the essence of empathy; it is not tied to the results of genetic psychology in the way that psychology is entirely bound to the results of phenomenology. Genetic psychology *presupposes* the phenomenon of empathy. Here, Stein distinguishes between the phenomenon of foreign experience on the one hand and the perception of foreign experience on the other hand. By leaving undecided whether there really is such a foreign experience or whether this perception is authentic, Stein in effect offers a reflective explication of foreign experience *as such*. She notes that a phenomenological description of the constitution of *der Andere* marks "the genuine object of *prima filosofia*" (*Empathy* 21). Accordingly, not only the investigation of the nature of the perception of foreign experiencing but also the justification of this perception must precede genetic psychology. For Stein, this means that the primary task of phenomenology is to describe the comprehension of foreign experience, to investigate "the origination of the knowledge that a real psycho-physical individual has of other such individuals" (*Empathy* 21–22).

In every genuine experience of empathy, an actual valuing is based on something that is non-actual. This means that I can in fact mistake the foreign-I for my living-I, or even misconstrue what is non-primordially given as foreign experience with what is primordially given as my own. For example, suppose that I plan to meet my friend for a walk in the park. As I approach our appointed meeting place, I notice that there are tears in her eyes. She is talking with someone and is apparently quite agitated. Since I do not want to interrupt their conversation, I remain at a distance, apprehensive, tense, unable to hear what she is saying. A few minutes later she beckons for me to come over, and I do so with a heavy heart, my shoulders slumped, the muscles in my face and neck tight and tense. But as I approach my friend, she reaches out in a playful embrace and invites me to share her joy at the happy news of her engagement. As she introduces me to her fiancé, I quickly become aware that the tears I initially took to be a sign of sadness are, in fact, tears of happiness. Suddenly, my whole demeanor changes on account of *her* joy: my body rests, the tightness in my neck gives way to relaxation, and I see that what I mistakenly perceived to be agitation was, in effect, a flirtatious display of affection. I too feel joy, but the origin of the joy that *I* feel does not come from myself but from *outside myself*. Or, rather, the non-primordial joy that *I* feel is based on a primordial experience that is announced but not accessed through the inner life of another person, that is, a joy that is not primordially my own.

This example illustrates two important aspects of Stein's theory of empathy. First, the other person is never given to me in an apodictic sense. Whether I constitute my knowledge of the other person cognitively or emotively, the essential fact remains that I cannot merely identify with the Other, as Lipps had argued. I must posit the other as *ganz anderes*. For example, there is nothing in empathy that prohibits me from being utterly mistaken about what I perceive by the non-primordial experience of the bodily appearance of another person. What I initially interpret to be tears of sorrow may, upon closer examination, turn out to be tears of joy, an allergic reaction to pollen, a small splinter in someone's eye, or merely a biochemical reaction to peeling an onion. Second, Stein acknowledges that what is announced in empathy is the primordiality of *foreign* experience, thereby ensuring that I can ever get "inside" the other's stream of conscious experience. Stein's schema is to unpack in transcendental reflection what happens when I intend the other person. She thus contends that a proper analysis of the perception of foreign experience is critical to understanding the genesis of acts of empathy. This means that a foreign individual is not so much perceived as *empathized*: "Just as our own individual is announced in our own perceived experiences, so the foreign individual is announced in empathized ones. But we also see that in one case there is a primordial, while in the other a non-primordial, givenness of the constituting experiences. If I experience a *feeling* as that of another, I have it given twice: once primordially as my own and once non-primordially in empathy as *originally foreign*" (*Empathy* 34).

§5. A Distinction between Primordial and Non-Primordial Experience

What is given twice in every genuine empathic experience, therefore, is not the redundancy of the same feeling but in fact *two different experiences*—one primordial and the other non-primordial—constituted from a singular foreign source. This important distinction between originary and non-originary experience leads Stein to reject the term "inner perception" for describing the comprehension of our own and foreign experience. Instead, she turns to "inner intuition" (*innere Anschauung*) to designate what is meant by the experience of non-primordial givenness: "The level where I am at the foreign 'I' and explain its experience by living it after the other seems to be much more parallel to the primordial experience itself than to its givenness in inner perception" (*Empathy* 34).

We may now define empathy as a primordial experience of foreign experience *as such*. This means that what is primordially given as mine, in this case, foreign experience, is essentially announced in my own stream of consciousness as a non-primordial experience of alien presence. Because foreign experience always presents itself as alien to my own primordial sphere of conscious life, the Other cannot, in principle, be originarily constituted through acts of cognition alone. Rather, what is authentically *fremde* must as well be co-constituted emotively in the order of experience. In fact, this is equally true for both cognition and feeling, without regard to Stein's distinction between them. The subject of empathy, Stein reminds us, is the Other, the *felt experience* of foreign givenness. (Empathy, to be sure, is not my primordial experience of the foreign subject's primordial experience but rather my primordial experience of an alien primordiality that is not mine.) In terms of both cognition and affectivity, this means that the primordiality of foreign experience can never be fully apprehended by me as the subject of *my* primordial experience. Alterity must always be given to me non-primordially, that is, *as foreign*. (Otherwise, the distinction between primordial and non-primordial experience would collapse.) The Other is announced primordially through a non-primordial experience.

The "non-primordial experience" is the experience of the bodily appearance of another ego seeming, for example, to be in joy. (Of course, as noted above I can always perceive or read or interpret the other's body language erroneously.) Nevertheless, the "primordial experience" that is announced but not accessed is the inner life of joy of the other ego. I see a smiling face that announces the joy that the Other experiences but with which I can only empathize. I empathize (non-primordial) the other's primordial joy. As Stein observes, empathy announces the other to me: "The subject of the empathized experience, however, is not the subject empathizing but *another*" (*Empathy* 10). Like Husserl, so too Stein addresses the unintuitability of the other's conscious life stream.

Upon closer inspection, we may now see that Stein's analysis follows Husserl's description of empathy up to this point rather tightly. Like Husserl, Edith Stein insists that primordial and non-primordial experiences co-constitute all genuine acts of empathy. Constitutionally speaking, the alterity of the Other lies outside my own primordial grasp, or else empathy could not be defined as a non-primordial experience that announces a primordial one. Edith Stein notes that the content of foreign experience always remains for the constituting ego a foreign experience (*fremde Erlebnis*): "And this is what is fundamentally new [in empathy] in contrast with the memory, expectation, or the fantasy of our own experiences. These two subjects [I and Thou] are separate and not joined together . . . by a consciousness of sameness or a continuity of experiences. And while I am living in the other's joy, I do not feel primordial joy. It does not issue live from my 'I'" (*Empathy* 10–11). According to Edith Stein, empathy *announces* the Other, it makes manifest what is not there, it makes possible the *im*possibility of the experience of foreign givenness *as such*. Hence, there consists a kind of two-sidedness to every description of the essence of empathic acts: (1) an experience of my own that (2) announces the experience of the human Other (*Empathy* 19). In every genuine encounter with foreign experience, I do not simply lose myself by becoming "at one" with the empathized subject, as Lipps suggested. Empathy means "transferring the self into the other's orientation" (*Empathy* 65), not losing myself *in* foreign experience. According to Edith Stein's observations, we may thus provisionally conclude that a robust phenomenological description of empathy needs to accomplish two distinct objectives. First, empathy stresses the inaccessibility of the Other's own conscious life stream. Second, empathy entails a felt experience relating to the constitution of the person in emotional experiences *as well as* cognitive descriptions of how I and Thou are analogically similar in spite of different streams of lived experiences (*Erlebnisse*). Following Husserl's analysis of intersubjectivity, Stein acknowledges that a full description of empathy needs to include an analysis of affectivity along with cognition. An analysis of foreign experience that does not address the reciprocal constitution of persons in terms of values of emotive givenness, along with an analysis of the act of empathic constitution of the other through feelings and embodiment, remains inadequate and incomplete.

Chapter Six

Embodiment, Temporality, and Emotions in Acts of Empathy

Introduction

For the most part, by "constitution" Husserl means passive synthesis, a kind of reception or recognition, as opposed to a more active sense of creation. Consequently, in formulating Husserl's description of constitution in terms of an epistemological focus, I mean to recognize that in "constitution" Husserl includes themes of transcendental intersubjectivity. In particular, these themes are explored at great length in Husserl's lectures on Nature and Spirit, *Ideas II*, and *Cartesian Meditations*. Husserl's unfinished notes and manuscripts concerning the lifeworld also give account of what Husserl designated as "social ontology." We explored some of these issues in chapter three of part one, and we will return again later in this study to explore these themes even further in part four in order to engage a deeper Husserlian analysis regarding the relationship between empathy, ethics, and transcendence. What we are attempting to describe, then, is not only a thematic discussion of Husserl's exploration of some of these themes with his students and colleagues, especially in the 1910s and 1920s, but also the way by which subsequent discussions of empathy return, in the end, to their Husserlian roots. For example, we have seen from the previous chapter that Edith Stein attempted to investigate the phenomenon of foreign experience largely along Husserl's own line of argument and that she also attempted to "push" Husserl's description of pairing with a close and detailed phenomenological description of constitution in terms of foreign experience. In order to better appreciate the complex issues centered in early twentieth-century empathy debates, a number of questions may now be raised: (1) Were the emotions and affectivity considered subordinate to a more rational and cognitive-based approach to constitution?[1] (2) If so, to what effect on the phenomenological method might a neglect of affectivity and the emotions have had on early accounts of transcendental constitution and subsequent evaluations in terms of givenness? (3) To what extent might exploring constitution in terms of a co-primordial givenness between affectivity and cognition contribute to a fuller and more robust understanding of roles that feelings and emotions might play in terms of intentionality? (4) In what sense were monadological models of constitution contaminated in the early half of the twentieth century by presuppositions and prejudices that also embraced dominant cultural hierarchies, including, for instance, German scholasticism and psychologism? For Stein, the answer to these (and similar) questions lies not outside Husserl's descriptive account of the constitution of the alter ego but *within* the language and imagery he used to describe the phenomenality of foreign experience. Although Husserl emphasizes the primacy of perception and develops an intersubjective consensus theory of truth, descriptions of empathy by both Stein and Husserl remain, at least at first glance, largely egological and monadological. With these criticisms in mind, let us return to Scheler's influence on Stein's dissertation project.

§1. Scheler's Notion of Psychic Causality

Might an entirely different kind of causality exist in the psychic domain that does not exist in the physical domain? This new kind of efficacy, Stein argues, would have to consist of "every past experience [that] can in principle have an effect on every future one without mediating connecting links, thus without being reproduced, either" (*Empathy* 72). Although Scheler says that psychic causality is not dependent on every previous experience, Stein claims that Scheler does not prove that there is a difference in the phenomenal structure of efficacy in the physical and in the psychic domains. Unfulfilled volitions, forgotten promises, experiences and decisions made without full consciousness of the psychological needs that underlie them do not merely disappear into oblivion. But neither do isolated past experiences determine my present experience, as, for example, happens within the physical chain of causes and effects. Stein draws on Scheler's observation that psychic causality is dependent on the totality of experiences that constitute an individual's entire life. An act of volition that was once conscious but is no longer conscious is *not* nothing. It remains passively *present*, a kind of background noise in my stream of lived experience:

> It has only gone out of the mode of actuality over into that of non-actuality, out of activity into passivity. Part of the nature of consciousness is that the *cogito*, the act in which the "I" lives, is surrounded by a marginal zone of background experiences in each moment of experience. These are non-actualities no longer or not yet *cogito* and therefore not accessible to reflection, either. In order to be comprehended, they must first pass through the form of the *cogito*, which they can do at any time. They are still primordially present, even if not actually, and therefore have efficacy. The unfulfilled volition is not dead, but continues to live in the background of consciousness until its time comes and it can be realized. Then its effect begins. Thus, it is not something past which affects the present, but something that reaches into the present. (*Empathy* 73)

In order to produce an effect, some sort of volition or fantasy or memory must be lived through again. This is the case with future events that "throw their shadows in advance." Turning again to Scheler's notion of the human person as a dynamic act-being, Stein recounts how William James, "under the influence of an unpleasant logic course he had to teach afternoons, undertook many unnecessary activities the entire day before, simply so that he would find no time for the burdensome preparation. Yet," she cleverly notes, James "did not 'think about it.'" What Stein describes is the psychic process by which we turn our attention to certain objects in order to escape other objects, whether those objects be physical or psychic. At the same time, the objects we are trying to avoid *do not vanish*. Although they are not present (inasmuch as we try to put them "out of our mind"), such objects remain in the background and influence our entire conduct, whether or not we are conscious of their effect. Strictly speaking, however, we cannot say that these causes affect present behavior, precisely because we are not at present conscious of them.

Further analyzing the structure of psychic lived experience, Stein notes that the object of avoidance relentlessly lurks in the shadows, constantly tending "toward going over into actual experience, toward pulling the 'I' into itself" (*Empathy* 73). Psychically speaking, such an object remains unseen, unfocused. It blends quietly into the wallpaper and remains there, unnoticed until fear finally surfaces again in a moment of anxiety or dread. Stein comments that "the fear constantly resists giving itself to this *cogito*" (*Empathy* 74); it remains blocked until it is pushed out into the stream of *actual* feeling.

§2. Notions of Temporality

James Hart contends that for Husserl "there is a sense in which the primal transcendental I as primal presencing is essentially uncreated."[2] According to Hart, Husserl's theory of temporality and inner-time consciousness points, curiously enough, to a prominent weakness in Husserl's own position regarding the genesis of the ego as a sort of transcendental *creatio ex nihilo*.[3] It is my contention that Edith Stein was aware of this problem and concerned with trying to help Husserl adequately address a solution to this question.[4] Turning to the issue of empathy, Stein originally intended to investigate how primal presencing is essentially constituted in terms of foreign experience, that is to say, in terms of alterity.[5] Following Husserl, by constitution Stein means to explore how we "see" essences of foreign experience by means of and on behalf of others who "stand in" for perspectives or variations not currently in view. Stein's primary goal is to investigate and describe how foreign experience is constituted as such. She wants to explore how the alter ego is constituted by my ego as a for-itself within my stream of consciousness. Similarly to how I cannot constitute my own participation in pairing effectively (that is to say, pairing requires the Other), I also cannot by myself constitute the origin or end of the transcendental Ego or the stream of lived time. For Stein, what I discover by encountering the Other is a felt sense of alterity that awakens within me a depth of myself that remains inaccessible and unrecognized apart from the Other.

Let us turn, then, to the significance that "temporality" plays in Stein's and Husserl's phenomenological descriptions of the constitution of the embodied self. For example, we note that Husserl's analysis of inner-time consciousness bespeaks a Now-point that is part of a stream of immediate presencings of retentions and protentions:

> We never have merely a Now-point and we exist in the past and future as immediately as in the present through our

retentions and protentions. In retaining and protending we do not make present nothing but rather what is absent. The actual Now is presenced, not from out of nothing but from out of the absent Just Past Now and absent Not Yet Now. These are, respectively, no longer actual or not yet actual; but this absence and non-actuality is not nothing. The actual Now is the immediate continuous successor of the Just Past Now. This is why we have not a staccato punctual Now-existence but a continuum of actual Nows.[6]

Stein concurs with Husserl's general analysis of temporality, but not entirely. Citing Husserl's description of activity and passivity, she argues that part of the nature of consciousness is that the *cogito*, the act in which the "I" lives, is surrounded by a "marginal zone of background experiences." In effect, this marginal zone constitutes each moment of experience *qua* moment. The following excerpt is worth repeating:

These are non-actualities no longer or not yet *cogito* and therefore not accessible to reflection, either. In order to be comprehended, they must first pass through the form of the *cogito*, which they can do at any time. They are still primordially present, even if not actually, and therefore have efficacy. The unfulfilled volition is not dead, but continues to live in the background of consciousness until its time comes and it can be realized. Then its effect begins. Thus, it is not something past which affects the present, but something that reaches into the present. (*Empathy* 73)

Stein's argument here is complex and concerns the notion of duration. Stein concedes to Husserl that "what is Now, or the momentary, has existence only in what has duration; what is actual now stretches forwards and backwards."[7] Thus far, Stein is clearly lodged in Husserl's camp. But notice how she subsequently directs emphasis away from Husserl's original intent. All objects are temporal, Stein tell us, insofar as they are actual in the Now of temporal existence. In effect, Stein agrees with Husserl that what is actual is what endures, though I would argue that her notion of temporality contains more of a Platonic realist meaning to it than does Husserl's. For Stein, objects are temporal insofar as their endurance is actual, whereas for Husserl, duration, although it can be reflected upon in the transcendental attitude, is given in direct experience. In a telling insight that anticipates to a striking extent Derrida's critique of Husserl's analysis of inner-time consciousness,[8] Edith Stein argues that only the absolute Now-point is itself radically and originarily *actual* in the sense of a pure actuality. Retention and protention, namely, what is just, just no longer, and what is just, just (but not quite) yet, are *not* actual in the order of experience:

> In Stein's ontological view all things, whether non-temporal or temporal, are pervaded by temporality, i.e., have duration only by hopping from one moment to the next; this having of duration is not something they give to themselves but rather they only appear to have it themselves and from themselves. For Husserl, temporality is basic because of the transcendental reduction where being and display are inseparable; for Stein temporality is basic because it is ontologically evident that everything is riddled with the contingency of Now, wherein each moment, although seemingly continuous with the next, is a novel grace in regard to what preceded. Some of Stein's formulations seem to tend to make out of duration a "mere appearance," whereas Husserl's view lets the thing's duration appear without problematizing the source of actuality in the Now.[9]

§3. The Problem of Representational Thinking

This distinction leads Stein to further question the sense by which the foreign living body is a bearer of phenomena of expression, which in a particular sense cuts to the very heart of empathic inter-activity. In *Logical Investigations*, Husserl makes a clear distinction between "sign" and "expression" or "symbol." Following Husserl's language, Stein notes that symbol means "that in something perceived there is something else and, indeed, we co-comprehend something psychic in it" (*Empathy* 76). On the other hand, a sign signifies "that something perceived says to me that something else exists"; for example, smoke is a sign of fire (*Empathy* 76). In a sign, what is co-given is an object of outer perception that leads to something hidden, foreign, *not yet perceived*. But inasmuch as symbols are conventional, a sign is primarily expressive (i.e., if smoke, then fire). A sign does not merely refer to something else. A sign announces what is *not* co-perceived, what remains indeterminate, alien, and unfulfilled. For Stein, a sign possesses a *moral quality* as well; it always points to something more than what is given: "The signal has a moment of ought, a demand in itself" (*Empathy* 79).

Consequently, expressions such as frowning lips, tears, gait, a bowed head, clenched fists, wrinkled eyebrows, and posture do not mean anything in and of themselves. For instance, I may (falsely) attribute the sense of sadness to tears, anger to a clutched hand, or even consternation or bewilderment to a furrowed brow. In each of these cases, Stein would certainly warn us against using implied symbols as signs.[10] The sad countenance ought not to mean sadness, nor blushing, shame: "When I 'see' shame 'in' blushing, irritation in the furrowed brow, anger in the clenched fist, this is a still different phenomenon than when I look at the foreign living body's level of sensation or perceive the other individual's sensations and feelings of life with him. In the latter case I comprehend the one with the other. In the former case I see the one through the other" (*Empathy* 75). Stein notes that the psychic is not only co-perceived with the bodily, but it is expressed *through* it. This means that the foreign living body is the bearer of psychic life. Embodiment is not symbolic, but rather *indicative*. "Symbolic and signal character are combined in a certain way in the purposeful externalization using the symbol as a sign. I now not only comprehend disapproval in the furrowed borrow but it intends to and ought to announce it" (*Empathy* 79).

In a similar way, words too function as signs. It is the case with expressive gestures, for example, that words proceed out of experience and adapt themselves to the expressed material. In terms of context, words *transform* experience: "Words point to the object through the medium of meaning, while the signal has not meaning at all but only the function of being significant. And words do not simply point to the circumstances as the signal does. What goes into them is not the circumstance, but its logico-categorical formation. Words do not signify, but express, and what is expressed is no longer what it was before" (*Empathy* 81). Naturally, Stein's analysis distinguishes between verbal and bodily expressions. "Understanding of a bodily expression is based on comprehending the foreign living body already interpreted as the living body of an 'I.' In other words, I project myself into the foreign living body, carry out the experience already co-given to me as empty with its countenance, and experience the experience ending in this expression." Stein calls the movement from the givenness of one occurrence to the givenness of another by its Husserlian name, "motivation," and contends that "the proceeding of one experience from another" is a pure and immanent experience (*Empathy* 83–84).

Husserl and Stein are seemingly in agreement that the Other appears through the givenness of experience of a foreign living body, an alter *ego*, a transcendental subject whom I am motivated to constitute via analogical apperception. For Stein, the alter ego is not merely constituted cognitively; the alter ego is constituted as well in a prejudicative, emotive experience of sensual expression. I "read" the other's bodily movements and facial expressions in precisely the same way that I read words on a page. Experience and understanding are not primordial; they must be empathized, interpreted, evaluated, shared. Words, expressions, tears, bodily movements, and so on are always directed toward someone and "thus refer to the relationship of the speaker to the hearer" (*Empathy* 83). As a hearer, of course, I can always be deceived; I can also be deceived about being deceived. Nevertheless, the speaker's intentions and expressions substantially assist in pointing toward the intuitive fulfillment of whatever words are spoken or read. What I am able to comprehend in any given sentence is the comprehension of the sentence, not the comprehension of the speaker. The speaker, Stein reminds us, is comprehended at the same time as the words. Of course, the speaker can be an individual subject as well as "a group of possibly changing subjects bound into one by a continuity of experience." Unlike signs, then, words are "always borne by a consciousness," they live " 'by the grace' of spirit" (*Empathy* 80).

According to Stein, such interpretive experience also applies when something psychic is expressed. For example, let us suppose that my friend tells me that he is sad. Without hesitating, I say that I understand immediately the meaning of his words, though of course I have no way of knowing whether he is lying or telling the truth. Therefore, the sadness I now "know" is not an "alive one" that rises before me as if it were apodictic. Like the backside of a building, which I do not see but rather apperceive, so too I apperceive my friend's sadness through his words and gestures. "In one case," Stein notes, "I am in the apophantic sphere, the realm of propositions and meanings, in the other case in immediate intuitive contact with the objective sphere" (*Empathy*,81). I do not know what the expressions or words or tears of the speaker mean in general but what they mean here and now in light of my own concrete givenness.

In order for me to understand and evaluate meaning, I must grasp an expression as a unity of intention. A word or gesture alone is senseless; it is made intelligible only when it is placed within a context, an environment. Like individual letters in a word, or individual words on a page, expressions remain meaningless unless they are contextualized and constituted by a particular environment—that is, through language, linguistic tradition, and laws of discourse. In a similar way that I must first learn the rules of grammar in a particular language in order to communicate with others intelligibly, so too I must learn to "read" a person's facial gestures, hand motions, bodily movements, and so on, within a social and cultural web of interconnected meanings and intuitions. "To be intelligible," Stein says, "means nothing more than to experience the transition from one part to another within an experiential whole" (*Empathy* 84). Of course, my "emotive experience" of another person is not apodictic, since the whole idea behind the experience of empathy is that the Other is *other*. Even the Other's tears may therefore hide a secret that, in principle, I may never know.

§4. Edith Stein's Phenomenology of Embodiment

Edith Stein follows the general direction of Husserl's notion of the foreign lived body (*Leib*) and argues that my own embodiment is not a *consequence* of constitution but is its condition of possibility. Meaning is enacted through embodied experience in that I experience both the living body of the Other and my own living body, by which I am motivated to posit another ego. To say that cognition is embodied means to say that cognition depends upon the perceptual and motor capacities of the body, and that cognition is thereby reciprocally intertwined with the body's environment. Similar to how Husserl argues that empathy is founded on the recognition of a pairing between my live body and the animate embodiment of the Other, so too Edith Stein adheres that the lived body is essential for every act of constitution. For Stein, embodiment is intersubjectively given at even the most fundamental levels, such that foreign embodiment is itself fundamentally *empathic*.

Edmund Husserl's analysis of the constitution of the psycho-physical individual turns on and begins with the absolutely unique and privileged body that "I" am, "I" alone and no one else in the universe, "I" who originally take myself as the only living body in the universe. In a similar way, Stein also begins with the living body as the zero point (*Nullpunkt*) of spatial orientation, the "grid" out of which all other things (including other bodies) appear orderly and given. Through pairing and analogical apperception, I come to experience the Other as a concrete individual, one who announces to my primordial experience the embodied manifestation of a non-primordial, foreign, constitutive phenomenon. The Other is always another embodied person—*Geist* or spirit—and never merely an ego. The other is an embodied yet mediated givenness who possesses his or her own particular face, set of values, and psycho-physical identity. Following Husserl, Stein argues that the living body "cannot be separated from the givenness of the spatial outer world" (*Empathy* 61). Hence,

> the other's physical body as a mere physical body is spatial like other things and is given at a certain location, at a certain distance from me as the center of spatial orientation, and in certain spatial relationships to the rest of the spatial world. When I now interpret it as a sensing living body and empathically project myself into it, I obtain a new image of the spatial world and a new zero point of orientation. It is not that I shift my zero point to this place, for I retain my "primordial" zero point and my "primordial" orientation while I am empathically, non-primordially obtaining the other one. On the other hand, neither do I obtain a fantasized orientation nor a fantasized image of the spatial world. But this orientation, as well as the empathized sensations, is con-primordial, because the living body to which it refers is perceived as a physical body at the same time and because it is given primordially to the other "I," even though non-primordially to me. (*Empathy*, 61–62)

According to Edith Stein, this orientation takes us a long way in constituting the foreign individual, for "by means of it the 'I' of the sensing, living body empathizes the whole fullness of outer perception in which the spatial world is essentially constituted" (*Empathy* 62). My living body is the *Nullpunkt* of orientation; through analogical appresentation the Other helps me "fill in" what I cannot see of myself. Therefore, I *need* the Other, not only to complete the apprehension of my own body but also to fulfill the world as a public (hence Objective) phenomenon. In this sense, the Other is co-primordial. Consequently, empathy as the basis of intersubjective experience is a condition of possibility of knowledge of an existing outer and objective world. For Stein, the world image that I empathize in the Other is not only a modification of my own image on the basis of the Other's orientation; my world image also varies with the way that I *interpret* his or her living body. Hence, empathy is significant for how I come to experience the real outer world through intersubjective experience. Empathy enriches "our own world image through another's" (*Empathy* 62–62).

§5. Corrections and Deceptions of Empathic Acts

In her analysis of empathy, Edith Stein argues that a genuine phenomenological description of embodiment also analyzes the fundamental, interpersonal, social structures of emotive, enfleshed experience. Stein begins with Husserl's description of the psycho-physical individual as *Leib*, that is, a composite of flesh and soul, and also embraces Scheler's model, which describes the human person as a network of values and act-orientations. As the surface of deep-felt emotive experiences, my body intertwines with other bodies in a dynamic and ever-expansive current, or flow, of consciously embodied social life.

For Stein, the constitution of foreign experience is founded on the constitution of the physical body. Hence, the givenness in outer perception of a physical body of a certain nature is a *presupposition* for the givenness of a psycho-physical individual (*Empathy* 87). As we noted earlier, empathy cannot guarantee apodicticity, regardless of whether foreign experience is constituted cognitively or emotively. Nevertheless, Stein insists, empathy *can* offer a "correction" as to how we "understand what is concealed behind a countenance." For example, "when I empathize the pain of the injured in looking at a wound, I tend to look at his face to have my experience confirmed in his expression of suffering. Should I instead perceive a cheerful or peaceful countenance, I would say to myself that he must not really be having any pain, for pain in its meaning motivates unhappy feelings visible in an expression" (*Empathy* 84–85). Similarly, "the harmony of empathy in the unity of a meaning also makes possible the comprehension of expressive appearances unfamiliar to me from my own experience and therefore possibly not experienceable at all." Acts of empathy can possess for Stein a *corrective* significance:

> I not only interpret single experiences and single-meaning contexts, but I take them as announcements of individual attributes and their bearers, just as I take my own experiences in inner perception. I not only comprehend an actual feeling

in the friendly glance, but friendliness as an habitual attribute. An outburst of anger reveals a "vehement temperament" to me. In him who penetrates an intricate association I comprehend sagacity, etc. Possibly these attributes are constituted for me in a whole series of corroborating and correcting empathic acts. But having thus gotten a picture of the foreign "character" as a unity of these attributes, this itself serves me as a point of departure for the verification of further empathic acts. . . . Thus we comprehend the unity of a character in each attribute, as we comprehend the unity of a thing in every material attribute. Therein we possess a motivation for future experiences. This is how all the elements of the individual are constituted in empathic acts. (*Empathy* 86)

Of course, "as in every experience, deceptions are here also possible" (*Empathy* 86). Because foreign psychic life is bound to the perceived physical body, the Other "stands before us as an object from the beginning. Inasmuch as I now interpret it as 'like mine,' I come to consider myself as an object like it" (*Empathy* 88). Empathy describes how I come to perceive the image the Other has of me, it serves as a basis for how I interpret the way in which I present myself to others, how I am seen by the Other. Just as the same natural object is given in as many varieties of appearances as there are perceiving subjects, so too there can be just as many interpretations of my psychic individual as I can have interpreting subjects. Whether cognitive or emotive or both, Stein is clear on this point, namely, that empathic acts "can prove to be in conflict with the primordial experiences so that this empathized 'interpretation' is exposed as a deception." In principle, Stein argues, "it is possible for all the interpretations of myself with which I become acquainted to be wrong" (*Empathy* 88).

§6. Constitution: Revisiting the Problem of Solipsism

Interestingly, Edith Stein's adherence to key concepts of Husserl's cognitive theory of transcendental intersubjective constitution involves, to some extent, both adherence to and a modification of it. In effect, Stein holds to Husserl's theory of constitution, though she redescribes implications of the transcendental ego in terms of the order of experience, that is, by offering descriptive analyses of the constitution of emotive acts and embodiment. James Collins, for one, notes that Stein refuses to accept Husserl's rather "easy solution" to the problem of the knowledge of givenness of other persons. In effect, "solipsism" was a problem that Collins observes bothered Husserl "down to his final years."[11] Accordingly, Stein confronts the problem of solipsism by turning "increasingly critical of the epistemological framework which led Husserl eventually to his principle of transcendental intersubjectivity."[12] One way for solipsism to be refuted is by modifying Husserl's strict cognitive account of ego-constitution with a co-constitutive theory of empathy that describes how other persons are originarily felt and emotively given in the order of experience. But before we can fully appreciate the implications of Stein's analysis of emotive givenness, we must first understand *why* Husserl's strict, cognitive theory of ego-constitution proved to be such an insurmountable problem, not only for Stein but for almost everyone influenced by Husserl's thought.

Let us revisit, again, Husserl's startling claim concerning the transcendental reduction in the Fourth Cartesian Meditation: "As ego," Husserl muses, "I have a surrounding world, which is continually 'existing for me'; and, in it, objects as 'existing for me'" (*CM* 68). He continues: "[B]y virtue of this proper essence, the ego likewise constitutes in himself something 'other,' something 'Objective,' and thus constitutes everything without exception that ever has for him, in the ego, existential status as non-Ego" (*CM* 85). Husserl's words present a serious challenge to our investigation of acts of empathy, in that they appear to diminish the significance of the pure or transcendental ego to that of mere solipsism. Does Husserl's application of the pure, transcendental ego in effect reduce the actual givenness of reality to *what I can know* of the world, such that the transcendental ego is the measure of all things? Is Stein's pure-I essentially the same as Husserl's transcendental ego? Or might her notion of the pure-I assist in modifying Husserl's epistemological description of ego-constitution precisely where it is most vulnerable? Let us look at these questions, and the issues raised by solipsism, more closely.

The word "solipsism" is derived from the Latin *solus* ("alone") and *ipse* ("self").[13] In its most basic articulation, solipsism is the belief that only the self is real. Solipsists are convinced that what I take to be "the world" is nothing more than a self-interpretation of my own experience, now imposed by my own ego as the subject of all possible knowledge. Clearly, we see how close solipsism stands to Husserl's theory of transcendental idealism, wherein I exist for myself and am continually given to myself, by experiential evidence, as "I myself." For Husserl, the method of transcendental reduction signifies that the concrete monad encompasses the whole field of actual and possible conscious life. Maurice Natanson calls Husserl's effort to begin with the transcendental ego, rather than with the social order, the "egocentric predicament." He illustrates the close connection between the solipsistic ego and Husserl's concrete monad:

> Within the immediacy of the self's perceptual experience, there is appreciation of sensations and ideas of the surrounding world which appear to be limited to the subject for whom there is experience—the individual. The colors, noises, tastes, odors, touch-sensations, as well as kinesthetic experience are all aspects of the individual's sensory apprehension, as are, it would also seem, the multitude of ideas, concepts, interpretations, and other constructions of cognition. But if the perceptual experience of the self includes the awareness it has of the rest of the world, how does the individual ever manage to go beyond his own subjectivity, how does he break out of the circle of his own consciousness? The "egocentric predicament" is nothing less than the question of whether the self is sealed off in such a way as to allow only self-knowledge.[14]

On the surface, the "egocentric predicament" appears dangerously solipsistic, though upon closer inspection we shall see that this is really not the case at all. For one thing, Husserl does not share Descartes's metaphysical doubt about whether there are "sky, air, earth, colors, shapes, sounds or any existences at all." The self is not the whole of reality; objects in the world are never reducible to mere "inventions of the mind." Neither, however, does Husserl share Locke's epistemological brand of empirical solipsism. Whereas knowledge for Locke is "nothing but the perception of the connection of an agreement, or disagreement and repugnancy of any of our ideas,"[15] Husserl maintains a more critical stance that affirms the primordial givenness of transcendental experience. For Husserl, ideas do not exist *in* the thinker's mind alone, such that communication *between* minds becomes at best a form of inference or statistical guesswork. What Husserl claims to have accomplished by his discovery of the transcendental ego is nothing less than to demonstrate once and for all that if the given of immediate experience is constituted in such a way as to yield doubt about the existence of a real world and of other selves, then it is constituted erroneously. The transcendental ego, in other words, makes possible the phenomenological attitude. Eugen Fink concurs:

> In radically bracketing belief in the world, the phenomenological reduction takes the one phenomenologizing out of the situation of intersubjective-communal reference to that which is existent in the world and accessible to everyone, and places him in the solitude of his transcendental egological existence [*Existenz*]. As phenomenologizing onlooker he consistently thematizes his own constituting life to gain a wealth of cohesive cognitions that in their systematic linkage comprise something in the manner of a *solitary, solipsistic* science. The *objects* of his cognitive life are at first not (*in any sense*) "intersubjective"; even the essential laws he sets forth are only pure possibility modifications of his *own* egological de fact existence, and do not in the least supply a validity that goes beyond the transcendental ego.[16]

In effect, Husserl presents the doctrine of the transcendental ego as a rejection of Cartesian systematic doubt. In so doing, he rejects any attempt to reduce the transcendental ego to a solipsistic self. Solipsism, Husserl argues, is self-contradictory. It is simply non-sensical, since it posits that nothing exists outside of the existing mind. But the transcendental ego reaches no such conclusion. Rather, the transcendental reduction merely makes possible the phenomenological attitude. Dorian Cairns notes: "The more detailed but primitive analyses of the *Ideen* have their place in the whole indicated clearly by the *Méditations Cartesiennes*. At the same time the *Méditations Cartesiennes* present in outline analyses of the awareness of 'other minds' and of 'the world as an intersubjective object,' important matters for forestalling the fear that phenomenology must end in solipsism."[17]

§9. The Environment and Foreign Experience

We have one more important issue yet to discuss. Edith Stein believes that the subject undergoing an experience of empathy must somehow incorporate certain aspects of the environment into one's own bodily schemata. Indeed, some of the theoretical similarities that exist between Stein and

Merleau-Ponty on this theme are indeed striking. For Merleau-Ponty, the lived body is not limited by the flesh, by skin. It necessarily extends to "the world beyond," literally, the cultural environment within which the lived body moves and acts. Stein, as well, claims that a "fusion of outer and bodily perception" is warranted "by the interpretation of our own living body as a physical body and our own physical body as a living body" (*Empathy* 58). Drawing from Husserl, Stein argues that empathy requires pairing and imaginative variation, what she calls "con-primordiality." This sense of the co-givenness of foreign varieties of experience in effect makes possible "the possibility of modifying real properties in fantasy while retaining [the original] type." In phenomenological terms, Stein is saying that the variability of foreign experience is inherently mixed with, though absolutely distinguished from, my own experience precisely on account of embodiment:

> Were the size of my hand, such as its length, width, span, etc. given to me as inalterably fixed, the attempt at empathy with any hand having different properties would have to fail because of the contrast between them. But actually empathy is also quite successful with men's and children's hands which are very different from mine, for my physical body and its members are not given as a fixed type but as an accidental realization of a type that is variable within certain limits. (*Empathy* 58–59)

If this were not the case, Stein concludes, then human persons would merely be unintelligible bundles, unrecognizable *nothings*, mere shapes without size or content. Without empathy, there could be no recourse to values or culture or language.

This is true for Stein in terms of inner life experience, too. When we experience fear, for example, "we turn our attention to another object [in order] to escape the fear, but it does not vanish. Rather, it remains 'in the background' and influences our entire conduct." Similarly, "I do not 'forget' my friends when I am not thinking of them. They then belong to the unnoticed present horizon of my world. My love for them is living even when I am not living in it. It influences my actual feeling and conduct" (*Empathy* 74). Stein's emphasis on living in "the background" or environment of one's own body (now writ large in terms of the interface of a multiplicity of bodies within one or several environments) means that consciousness is first and foremost a mode of being-in-the-world.

"I" and "Other" cannot be understood apart from that by which "we" inhabit and engage the world—namely, our bodies and, by extension, our embodied environments. Especially in reference to a much grander scale, Stein suggests that "I" and "Other" cannot be understood apart from empathy. As we will discuss further, empathy for Stein thus contains a hermeneutical principle; it is constitutive in terms of interpretation and meaning. This includes the social world, the "we-world" and its values and political bodies by which and within which we engage one another, namely, culture, language, technology, and art.[18]

Part Three

A Reversal of the Law of Empathy

Part Three

Introduction

Are there other ways of seeing or knowing that remain inaccessible to what is constituted or given cognitively? Might there be an emotive or affective capacity to consciousness as well that is not dependent on mental processes, a noncognitive capacity with its own stream of embodied experience? Would such an emotive capacity of a noncognitive stream of reflection perceive the world sui generis and outside what can be given cognitively or rationally? Grasped phenomenologically as *this* individual—that is, as *this* particular, embodied, conscious, living subject—such an emotive capacity of consciousness could open up new paradigms of experience and new appearances of phenomena that have been previously closed to analysis but that could be constituted by an inner feeling or noncognitive perception. What would a noncognitive experience look like? How could such "experience" be described without relying on rational discourse to set its meaning and limitations? What might a more dynamic model of consciousness—one that takes into account emotive constitution alongside cognitive constitution—reveal about the phenomenology of empathy as an experience of radical alterity? How might our understanding of ethics be challenged or even enlarged if concepts such as alterity and transcendence are reconceptualized as "events" in terms of an emotive and generative capacity of givenness? Questions such as these push language and discourse about consciousness to its limits, and possibly beyond. It is my argument that empathy describes a kind of experience of a non-experience and stretches language to a breaking point. What is experienced through acts of genuine empathy is the primordial experience of a non-primordial experience, an uncanny and embodied "event" or experience of *mysterium tremendum* that is as equally felt and constituted emotively as it is cognitively.

How might we encounter new approaches for raising questions about the roots of social ontology and the relationship between ethics and empathy? Our task remains oriented in the phenomenological method, insofar as we are exploring empathy as a phenomenon encountered through an experience of alterity, an experience of the Other—or, perhaps better stated, through the "experience of a non-experience." Empathy is given amidst the communicability of mundane reality, human striving, and social accomplishment. Our starting point is that the human person is a transcendent being that remains fundamentally a being in search—a being in search of meaning and the kinds of values that give meaning to one's life and one's choices and relationships. Ethical awareness thus reveals a kind of hierarchy of judgments involving the sorts of ethical actions by which human subjectivity is grounded. Consequently, human being-in-the-world cannot be adequately defined merely in terms of transcendental structures of consciousness. Being human means to exist as an embodied subject within social and spiritual horizons that incorporate ethical involvements in living-with-and-for-others. The individual does not exist in isolation as a disembodied ghost. Rather, the self is thrust into a field of embodied actions, the value of which is constituted via empathy through a conscious encounter with other embodied beings in the world, similar yet different from one's own.

A primary concern in this study has been to explore the phenomenology of empathy in terms of how a public world is given to consciousness in terms of transcendent reality, along with ways of describing how consciousness constitutes transcendence within the lived experiences of one's own finite and limited historical grounding. Subsequently, in part three, we will explore what is meant by transcendence, phenomenologically speaking, and how transcendence as a phenomenon appears in its non-phenomenality. Drawing principally from Heidegger, Levinas, and Derrida, we will explore ways by which empathy is given (or not given) emotively and cognitively. The question of the Other as an expression or trace of transcendent alterity will be a main focus of our inquiry, along with questions of how transcendence can be given, or expressed, or grasped, whether cognitively, emotively, or intuitively. Constituted by the experience of empathy, the Other as alter ego reveals ethical dimensions that remain inaccessible to the solitary ego apart from transcendent reality. In terms of givenness, this means that the self is not adequately given in terms of cognition alone. Defined in terms of a closed or self-sufficient monadological structure, the self or ego remains incomplete. Empathy requires a kind of "interior seeing *sui generis*," a kind of seeing that is co-constituted in terms of cognitive and emotive constitution. The self becomes authentic by engaging other centers of value that are experienced originarily as foreign experience. What is described in ethical terms as "empathy," then, is a process by which transcendence becomes recognizable precisely in its non-phenomenality through the givenness of the alterity of the Other qua other. Such givenness is enacted co-constitutively in terms of thinking and feeling. Understanding the phenomenology of empathy in terms of a constitutive and internal relationship between ethics and transcendence is the real subject of our inquiry in part three.

Consciousness is never barren or neutral; constitution is always generative. What is grasped or constituted or given by consciousness, then, is the Other as foreign object, grasped non-thematically as transcendence, that is, the Other as radical alterity. This means that the Other is engaged and encountered through empathy as a subject, a for-itself, as something that reveals another being that is like me, only different. In fact, what I encounter through empathy is that the being that is revealed as something like me is not a "what" or a "that" but a "who." What is given by empathy in terms of transcendence is the non-givenness or non-phenomenality of transcendence/alterity-itself, now recognized as a for-itself in its own right and integrity.

Acts of perception and givenness include a residue or trace of alterity. There is always something hidden in the givenness of every act. What is given by this trace is never given fully or adequately. Consciousness, then, requires a kind of hiding or taking-away in every act of givenness. The Other that is given both reveals and at the same time withholds that which makes the other *other*; otherwise, "I" and "other" would be the same. Such givenness or generativity of the experience of alterity is described phenomenologically in terms of transcendence. Empathy therefore exposes a kind of value-act, a revelation of non-relationality or nonappearance between two subjects, I and Other. Who is Other? Precisely the one who is similar to me, yet different. Phenomenologically speaking, alterity elicits a kind of givenness that manifests the nonappearance of transcendence. The Other is constitutive. This means that every I-Thou relationship signifies an ethical nonconformity between ego and alter ego. The experience of transcendence is precisely that which is given through the experience of alterity between I and Thou. The manifestation of difference, of alterity between Self and Other, reveals an ethical asymmetry that cannot be fully comprehended by cognition or analogical thinking alone. Empathy thus requires an emotive or felt component that is equally as primordial as cognition. In a constitutive sense, empathy apprehends alterity through the experience of transcendence. The nonappearance of transcendence in effect ensures that every I-Thou relationship, commonly referred to as empathy, becomes constituted ethically through a co-mingling of emotive and cognitive processes, and not merely by cognition alone.

Chapter Seven

Martin Heidegger's Critique of Empathy

§1. The Structure of Ready-to-Hand

The aim of *Being and Time* proports an analysis of the meaning of the Being of beings that was originally intended to be included in part three of Heidegger's magnum opus but was never written. Such a task, Heidegger notes, was to be found by way of an analytic of the Being of Dasein as temporality (part two), whose point of departure is the analysis of Dasein in its everydayness (part one), where the preliminary being is determined as care (*Sorge*), which itself starts out with the analysis of Being-in-the-world. Martin Heidegger organizes *Being and Time* according to a three-way movement that originates (1) from the entity (2) to its being structured (3) to that which provides the "key" or "principle" to its being structured. Published in Husserl's 1927 *Jahrbuch* edition, *Being and Time* is primarily concerned with analyzing the meaning of Being by way of an analysis of the structure of the worldhood of the world (what Husserl calls the "lifeworld"), in terms of being-with other persons in the world. One of Heidegger's primary goals is to provide an analysis of care in relation to the provisional being of Dasein. Hence, Heideggerian care marks a distinction between the ontic and the ontological, between (a) that which has to do with entities, with phenomena, with the totality of instruments and (b) that which has to do with the *logos* or structure ("being-structure") of those entities.

Many issues raised by Heidegger in *Being and Time* are complex, thought provoking, and worthy of intense scrutiny. Nevertheless, in this chapter we shall focus only on a few of these themes, and these only insofar as they contribute directly to the problem of empathy as articulated by Husserl's and Stein's phenomenological analyses. It is in the light of the theory of transcendental constitution that we shall consider Heidegger's important contribution to the historical and thematic study of empathy, namely, in terms of the question, Who is Dasein in its everydayness (*BT* 149)?

By way of introduction of our analysis, it is imperative to distinguish right from the start a primary difference between Husserl's and Heidegger's project. Whereas Husserl accepts the primacy of perception, Heidegger argues that perception is an abstraction. The world (*Welt*), Heidegger argues, is primarily given as the cultural and environmental setting for conducting business. He treats perception as a founded and derivative mode, achieved by turning off or disengaging Dasein's ongoing "concernful dealing" with the world; hence, perception is an abstraction; we do not "perceive" the hammer, we hammer with it; we never just "perceive" *mere things*, we "deal with them." Perception is therefore an abstraction that results from disengaging with the world and just looking at it. We do not perceive the world. Rather, we "use" instruments and equipment. Heidegger presents the "ready-to-hand" world as the world of instrumentality, the world of equipment, the world of what is given (*BT* 97). Hence, an important theme in *Being and Time* is for Heidegger to present Being-in-the-world in its everydayness (*Alltäglichkeit*), to lay bare a hermeneutics of facticity that describes "the way in which everyday Dasein always *is*" (*BT* 96).

Heidegger wants to bring the structure of ready-to-hand *back* to Dasein. By "ready-to-hand," he does not mean the "natural" world but the totality of tools and equipment that orient Dasein's involvements in the world. The purpose or projection of these involvements is described principally in terms of "that-for-the-sake-of-which" (*BT* 119) and includes the notion that the "instrumentality" of the world is the necessary horizon of Dasein's self-understanding. In other words, we understand the world as a referential system constituted by the use of equipment and tools. We perform tasks, but always in the implicit understanding that we have *of* Being.[1] For Heidegger, this implicit hermeneutics of facticity constitutes a set of a priori conditions by which Dasein understands the world in terms of itself, and itself in terms of its involvements in the world: "Thus anything constantly ready-to-hand of which circumspective Being-in-the-world takes account beforehand, has its place. The 'where' of its readiness-to-hand is put to account as a matter for concern, and oriented towards the rest of what is ready-to-hand" (*BT* 137). This emphasis away from the primacy of perception marks a decisive break by Heidegger from the theory of transcendental constitution as proposed by his philosophical mentor,

Edmund Husserl.² Contrary to Husserl's description, Heidegger argues that the world is never given as merely present-at-hand. Instead, what is given to Dasein is the referentiality of tools and equipment. Heidegger thus refers to equipment and tools (*Zeug/Werkzeug*) as entities "which we encounter in concern," as a pragmatic "in-order-to [*etwas um-zu*]" (*BT* 97). What alone appears to Dasein is the tool in terms of its being ready-to-hand. Material nature, therefore, is a constituted, higher-order abstraction founded upon that which alone is given, namely, the tool.

§2. Dasein as Directionality

Heidegger's critique of Husserl's primacy of perception may perhaps best be expressed as a rejection of monadism. For Heidegger, the world always appears as a with-world (*Mitwelt*), never as the world merely given to *me*. Others always present themselves as Being-for-one-another (*Für-einandersein*), Being-among-one-another (*Schon-sein-bei*), and Being-there (*Dasein*), though for Heidegger "the 'here' [*Hier*] does not mean the 'where' of something present-at-hand, but rather the 'whereat' [*Wobei*] of a de-severant Being-alongside, together with the de-severance" (*BT* 142). What Heidegger means by Being-alongside is that the world is always and already "made to fit" long before *individual* Dasein appears on the scene. Heidegger describes the with-world in terms of the spatiality of Being-in-the-world. The "world" *is* what is given to Dasein in the mode of care; it is that about which Dasein is concerned. Consequently, that about which Dasein cares is "in a world already *and must be* in it [in order for Dasein] to be able to orient itself at all" (*BT* 143).³

This is an important criticism to explore. According to Husserl's cognitive account of empathy, "I and Other" constitute (Objective) meaning in the world by means of intersubjectivity, whereas Stein privileges affectivity and the emotions in her analysis of reciprocal constitution. Heidegger rejects both of these models. Instead, he argues that we encounter other persons primarily, through our everyday dealings, on the one hand and spatiality on the other hand. Spatiality (*Räumlichkeit*) describes the lived, existential experience of whether things are close at hand or far away.⁴ On the basis of its character as Being-in-the-world, Dasein exists always in some particular oriented "place" in the chain of referents. Heidegger calls such oriented space the "lived world" and says that every lived world is charged with meanings that are oriented always in a particular "directionality" (*BT* 138).

Heidegger wants to eliminate Husserl's contention that pure consciousness needs to account for a body.[5] In effect, the Dasein-analytic makes it a point not to thematize the "body" or "embodiment" because it regards that as an anthropological approach and not an ontological one. Dasein brings things close-to-hand primarily through concern and care (*Besorgen, Sorge*). The principal task of Dasein is to let-things-be either near or far. Dasein allows an entity to be what it is. Such a task is not merely subjective but describes how Dasein lets the world present itself. In effect, Heidegger's argument is that Dasein is never quite "neutral." Dasein is always busy working at some task, it is always directed toward some place of concern in the referential system. This is what Heidegger means by directionality, namely that the Being of Dasein is orient*ing*. We come at the world always in terms of concern. Such "coming at" marks the orientedness of the world of our concern. Hence, it is Dasein's practical engagement with the world that arranges things concretely, pragmatically, concernedly: "When we let entities within-the-world be encountered in the way which is constitutive for Being-in-the-world, we 'give them space.' This 'giving space,' which we also call 'making room' for them, consists in freeing the ready-to-hand for its spatiality" (*BT* 146). How we learn to organize or "take" the world depends on those specific tasks that we bring *to* the world. Space—that is, a condition of possibility in which I and Other encounter each other—is inherently an *objective* presence, it is the way the world becomes manifest as an object of concern. *Ergo*, space (*Raum*) is not "in" the subject. Rather, space is in the world insofar as space has been disclosed by that Being-in-the-world that is constitutive for Dasein. In other words, Dasein is motivated to bring an a priori spatiality to the world.[6] As soon as Dasein comes-to-be, it "comes-to-be-in-the-world" as an entity that orients. Heidegger concludes that spatiality is therefore a constitut*ed* phenomenon. The "world" is precisely what Dasein learns to take *as* this oriented, near/far system of references: "Still less does space constitute the phenomenon of the world. . . . [S]pace is still *one* of the things that is constitutive for the world, just as Dasein's own spatiality is essential to its basic state of Being-in-the-world" (*BT* 148).

§3. The Question of the "Who" of Dasein

The question of the "who" of Dasein is next introduced by Heidegger in order to displace the theme of empathy as derivative and founded, summarily set in terms of the environment and spatiality. Heidegger's innovative question, "'Who' is Dasein in its Being-in-the-world?" proposes a response that is equally as elusive as every attempt to answer it. "Dasein," Heidegger says, "is an entity which is in each case I myself; its Being is in each case mine" (*BT* 150). The definition of Dasein introduced here indicates an ontologically constitutive state, but it does no more than "indicate" it. The question of the "who" is thus set in terms of the "I," the "subject," the "Self," and so functions primarily as a formal indicator.[7] In practical terms of everydayness, this means that the "who" is what maintains itself as something identical throughout all the changes in its experiences and relates itself to this changing multiplicity. Ontologically, Heidegger defines the "who" as what is constantly present-at-hand, a subject, an *I*: "As something selfsame in manifold otherness, it [the who] has the character of the Self" (*BT* 150).

In presenting the question of the "who" of Dasein in the light of his earlier analysis of tools, Heidegger notes that the Being of Dasein is always and necessarily characterized in terms of Being-with (*Mitsein*). Dasein shares the world with others. Phenomenologically speaking, this means that others are always and already in the world much in the same way that tools and equipment are already in the world long before individual Dasein ever takes explicit notice of them. In both cases, the world is given first and foremost as a shared world, a world that is "cut" for *us* and not merely "cut" for *me*. Heidegger's notion of the with-world refers to the world of practical involvement in which "we" always and already find ourselves busy and filled with worldly concern.

The Being of Dasein is *Mitsein*, though "Being-with" for Heidegger does not refer to the mode of authenticity but rather to a sense of the anonymous. Thrown into a with-world already always constituted by others, Dasein must learn to "catch up" with itself precisely by not being itself. Who is Dasein in its common everydayness? Ultimately, Heidegger answers, the "who" of everyday Dasein is not myself, but the *nobody* to whom every Dasein has already surrendered itself in the *they* (*BT* 166):

> It could be that the "who" of everyday Dasein just is not the "I myself." The word "I" is to be understood only in the sense of a non-committal formal indicator, indicating something which may perhaps reveal itself as its "opposite" in some particular phenomenal context of Being. In that case, the "not-I" is by no means tantamount to an entity which essentially lacks "I-hood"

[*Ichheit*], but as rather a definite kind of Being which the "I" itself possesses, such as having lost itself [*Selbstrerlorenheit*]. (*BT* 152)

According to Heidegger's analysis, the "who" of everyday Dasein is always already lost in the *they* (*das Man*) long before individual Dasein arrives on the scene. Whereas Husserl believed that empathy makes possible our objective knowledge of the natural (*Naturwissenschaften*) and social (*Geisteswissenschaften*) sciences, the notion of empathy was met with derision by Martin Heidegger, who rejected outright any theory that assigned to empathy a found*ing* mode. "This phenomenon," Heidegger argues, "which is none too happily designated as 'empathy [*Einfühlung*],' is then supposed, as it were, to provide the first ontological bridge from one's own subject, which is given proximally as alone, to the other subject, which is proximally quite closed off" (*BT* 162). His objection is that empathy is unnecessary because Dasein is always already given with others. If, on the other hand, empathy was a founding mode as Husserl proposed, then Dasein would be reducible to "publicness" (*die Offentlichkeit*), to being a mere Thing (*Ding*) in a world (*Welt*) in which "everyone is the other, and no one is himself" (*BT* 162).

What Heidegger says is that the "who" of everyday Dasein is never I myself, but the *they* of mass society. In its fallen everydayness, Dasein encounters Others as objects in the world, mere tools (*Zeugen*) for its use, as instruments that are always and already there in their Being-among-one-another (*Untereinandersein*) (*BT* 166). Others are always already given to Dasein environmentally, that is, in the fallenness of tools and their uses. Accordingly, the world in which Dasein finds itself is from the start always a with-world (*Mitwelt*), a world with Others, a world of tools, an environment constituted by the use of equipment. By Others (*Anderen*), Heidegger means *the ones among whom I am myself already lost*, astray, caught up with even before "I" come to be. "By Others," Heidegger notes, "we do not mean everyone else but me. . . . They are rather those from whom, for the most part, one does *not* distinguish oneself" (*BT* 154).

For Heidegger, Others are precisely those who are not different from me. Hence, he proposes a categorial rejection of the use of the term "empathy" for every theoretical explanation that describes the transcendental constitution of the alter ego. By dismissing analogical appresentation, Heidegger's task is to show not how others are constituted but how I can ever authentically hope to be myself (*mir selbst*) in the midst of the overwhelming presence of Others. What is primordially present for Heidegger, then, is my being always already in the world with others. In *Being and Time*, Heidegger defines empathy as an ontic structure that presupposes the ontological a priori structure of being-with: empathy is not a primordial existential phenomenon (*BT* 163). Therefore, it is in principle incoherent that there could exist any sort of private world at all. Because it is a founded mode, the main problem of empathy consists for Heidegger in the difficulty of authentic being-with. "Only on the basis of Being-with does 'empathy' become possible: it gets its motivation from the unsociability of the dominant modes of Being-with" (*BT* 162). In effect, *Being and Time* begins with an analysis of tools and then describes Dasein principally in terms of equipment and inauthenticity via the everyday Being-with of Others.[8]

§4. Heidegger's Critique of Empathy

The problem that plagues Husserl's theory of empathy, Heidegger argues, is that Husserl mistakenly began by thinking that Dasein is in each case one's *own*. For example, the theory of transcendental constitution starts by marking out and isolating the monadological "I" from all forms of alterity. Since monadology neglects to take into account the primordiality of the *they* in every event of constitution, Heidegger believes that Husserl's cognitive methodology is doomed from the start. In privileging monadology and the primacy of perception, Husserl has unintentionally burdened the task of transcendental phenomenology with having to find a way of getting over to other persons *from* this isolated subject.

Heidegger's rejection of Husserl's position is indeed striking. In effect, Heidegger holds that the world is *not* given to the constituting monad as the scene of intersubjective personal community. Rather, right from the very beginning of the world, *Others are already there*: the isolated monad is a fiction. By "Others" (*Anderen*), Heidegger does not mean, as Husserl does, everyone else but me, those over against whom the "I" stands out. Rather, "Others" for Heidegger are precisely those from whom, for the most part, one does *not* distinguish oneself. Hence, there are in Heidegger's analysis two equally primordial structures, namely "tools" and "others." By attacking the theory of transcendental monadology, Heidegger takes direct aim at Husserl's notion that the objective world is constituted intersubjectively through empathy. Instead, Heidegger argues, the "who" of everyday

Dasein is a Being-in-the-world that always and already takes the world as a with-world (*Mitwelt*), as the world that is always and already one I share with and alongside Others: "[In order] to avoid this misunderstanding[9] we must notice in what sense we are talking about 'the Others.' By 'Others' we do not mean everyone else but me—those over against whom the 'I' stands out. They are rather those from whom, for the most part, one does not distinguish oneself—those among whom one is too" (*BT* 154).[10]

"Who" is Dasein in its common, busy everydayness? According to Heidegger, Dasein is the "I," the subject, myself. Yet the moment the words "I," "subject," or "myself" are used, what is indicated is a metaphysics of presence, a persisting subjectivity that underlies all changes. Heidegger warns that the "who" of everyday Dasein is inherently inauthentic precisely because everyday Dasein confuses Being-with as a fixed substance (i.e., *ousia*, that which remains the same throughout every experience). Caught up with and for others, Dasein mistakenly equates the "who" of everyday Dasein with "I myself." What is striking here is Heidegger's insistence that inauthentic Dasein in fact denies its own entrapment in "everydayness" (*Alltäglichkeit*). Similar to Kierkegaard's notion that despair is the sickness unto death, everydayness is a thoughtless conformity to the world, a massive boredom and indifference toward life. By denying the overwhelming presence of the *they*, everydayness marks the "everyday" condition of Dasein as being lost, absorbed in the *they*. It thus remains structurally impossible for individual Dasein to ever be given as a worldless subject, as *solus ipse*, as merely I myself. The *they*—Others—are always there, much as Kierkegaardian despair is always there, *even when I am not conscious of being in despair*. What is needed, Heidegger contends, is an adequate phenomenological structure that can describe how Dasein is always already *with* Others.

§5. The Primordiality of "The They"

Others are given to us environmentally, that is, within the totality of tools and their usage. Heidegger thus proposes that there is no need to defend any sort of theoretical explanation of the constitution of other persons, as Husserl claims is necessary via the theory of analogical appresentation. The task of *Being and Time* is not to show that others are there, but how I can be myself in the overwhelming presence of Others: "According to the analysis which we have now completed, Being-with-Others belongs to the very Being of Dasein, which is an issue for Dasein in its very Being. Thus as Being-with, Dasein 'is' essentially for the sake of Others. . . . [T]his means that because Dasein's Being is Being-with, its understanding of Being already implies the understanding of Others. . . . Thus in concernful solitude the Other is proximally disclosed" (*BT* 160–61). Individual Dasein is therefore not what is given primordially; it is an abstraction. What is primordially given is my Being-in-the-world along with Others. "With" (*Mit*) constitutes for Heidegger the formal a priori structure of the world *as we find it*. Dasein is a priori oriented to Others; otherwise, Heidegger notes, I would not feel "lonely" when I am by myself: "The Other can *be missing* only *in* and *for* a Being-with. Being-alone is a deficient mode of Being-with; its very possibility is the proof of this" (*BT* 157).

Heidegger's critique of Husserl's theory of monadology is nearly complete. In section 26 of chapter four of *Being and Time*, he argues that we encounter the Other through the anonymity of mass society, the *they*, in a mode of indifference and passivity.[11] This means that even when Dasein explicitly addresses itself as "I here," such locative personal designation must be properly understood in terms of Dasein's existential spatiality. Dasein's "here" does not designate a certain privileged or primordial I-point of perception, but it is rather to be understood in terms of what Heidegger calls the "yonder" of the world that is ready-to-hand. This "yonder" (*das Dort*) refers to the dwelling-place of Dasein as *concern*: "The 'here' and the 'there' and the 'yonder' are primarily not mere ways of designating the location of entities present-at-hand within-the-world at positions in space; they are rather characteristics of Dasein's primordial spatiality. . . . [W]hen we interpret Dasein without any theoretical distortions we can see it immediately as 'being-alongside' the world with which it concerns itself, and as Being-alongside it spatially—that is to say, as desevering and giving directionality" (*BT* 155–56).

What Heidegger is driving at is the notion that Dasein understands itself "proximally and for the most part"[12] in terms of its world.[13] Yet—and this is Heidegger's point—even *if* Others are engaged as "themes" of study, they are never encountered as person-Things merely present-at-hand. Rather, we always meet and encounter other persons at work in the world, that is, primarily in the mode of Being-in-the-world. The Other is always encountered in his or her Dasein-with in the world through the mode of care.[14] Hence, the expression "Dasein" demonstrates that "in the first instance" this entity is unrelated to Others, though of course it is always related "with" Others in the sense that Dasein is essentially Being-with, an entity disclosed within-the-world alongside Others. What Heidegger emphasizes is the phenomenological assertion that "Dasein is essentially Being-with" has an existential-ontological meaning. Being-with is an existential characteristic of Dasein even when, factically speaking, no Other is present-at-hand or perceived. In a similar critique of Husserl's position made earlier by Max Scheler, Heidegger holds that even Dasein's Being-alone is Being-with in the world.[15] Heidegger thus concludes that "empathy" does not first constitute Being-with; on the contrary, only on the basis of Being-with does "empathy" become possible (*BT* 162).

§6. Everyday Being-One's-Self and "Das Man"

Rejecting outright the primordial role given by Husserl to the primacy of perception, Heidegger argues that neither *Einfühlung* ("empathy") nor *Erkennen* ("knowing in general") should be privileged or taken as primordial. Instead, he asserts that both knowing and empathy are constitut*ed* phenomena and not, as Husserl held, constitut*ing*: "The special hermeneutic of empathy will have to show how Being-with-one-another and Dasein's knowing of itself are led astray and obstructed by the various possibilities of Being which Dasein itself possesses, so that a genuine 'understanding' gets suppressed, and Dasein takes refuge in substitutes; the possibility of understanding the stranger correctly presupposes such a hermeneutic as its positive existential condition" (*BT* 163). One result of Heidegger's rejection of Husserl's law of empathy is his axiom that Being toward Others must be acknowledged as an autonomous, irreducible relationship of Being. But if Heidegger is right, that is, if *Einfühlung* is not a primordial existential phenomenon, then *who* is Dasein when Dasein is absorbed in the world of its concern? In other words, who is Dasein when it is not "itself?" *Who* is it, who takes Being as everyday Being-with-one-another (*BT* 163)?

The "who" of everyday Dasein is not *this* one, not *that* one, not oneself (*man selbst*), not some people (*einige*), and not the sum of all persons (*BT* 164). The "who" is the neuter, the *they* (*das Man*), similar to what Nietzsche called the "herd mentality." In effect, Heidegger argues, we "take pleasure and enjoy ourselves as *they* (*das Man*) take pleasure; we read, see, and judge about literature and art as *they* see and judge; we shrink back from the 'great mass' as *they* shrink back, we find 'shocking' what *they* find shocking" (*BT* 164), we even celebrate and hold worthy what *they* celebrate and honor. The *they* is no one, but rather a collective structure in which there are no individuals in particular. The *they*, in a manner of speaking, is the "it" that "runs with the crowd."[16] *Das Man* prescribes for Heidegger the kind of Being of everydayness.

As an indictment against mass society, Heidegger argues that "averageness" and "distantiality" are ways of Being of the *they*. The *they* constitute what is known as "publicness" (*die Offentlichkeit*). In effect, the realm of what is "public" becomes possible only in an advanced technological society of bourgeoises culture. That which is designated as exceptional gets "levelled down," everything that is primordial gets "glossed over as something that has long been well known"; even more, "everything gained by a struggle becomes just something to be manipulated" (*BT* 165). Cast in terms of "the Self of everyday Dasein" (*BT* 167), the *they-self* becomes quite problematic in Heidegger's later analysis of authenticity. In section 64 of *Being and Time* ("Care and Selfhood"), for instance, Heidegger says that authenticity is really an *existentiell* modification of *das Man*: "It has been shown that proximally and for the most part Dasein is not itself but is lost in the they-self, which is an *existentiell* modification of the authentic Self" (*BT* 365).[17]

What Heidegger means is that the *they* is not a genus or a universal subject to which individual Dasein belongs, a kind of plurality of subjects that hovers or floats "above" particular Dasein. Rather, the *they* is a primordial phenomenon that belongs to Dasein's positive constitution. In other words, the *they* is what happens when Dasein loses sight of its own everydayness. "Falling" therefore is both a distinctive and primordial mode of Dasein's Being-in-the-world. As with thrownness and projection, falling is neither an external nor accidental characteristic of Dasein. Hence, in the everyday world of fallenness, it is not "I" who understands but always the *they*. What gets understood in terms of the "what" of idle talk is merely what gets understood in a superficial manner through public discourse. I open my mouth, but the *they* speak.[18]

Heidegger notes that the constitution of how things get "cleared" or "opened" is through an authentic understanding that the primordial movement of Dasein in its own Being is its "downward plunge" (*Absturz*): "Dasein plunges out of itself into itself, into the groundlessness and nullity of inauthentic everydayness" (*BT* 223). This "plunge" downward, however, remains hidden from Dasein by the way that things have been publicly interpreted by the *they*, "so much so, indeed, that it gets interpreted as a way of 'ascending' and 'living concretely' " (*BT* 223). What this means for Heidegger is that Dasein *has not lost itself*, not even in the vast, overwhelming presence of the *they*. If Dasein were lost to itself, then the issue of its own authenticity could never be raised. Meaning, therefore, rises from everydayness, but only insofar as Dasein is aware of its own existential uprootedness. What rules the *they* according to Heidegger is not authenticity but idle talk (*Gerede*), curiosity (*Neugier*), and ambiguity (*Zweideutigkeit*),[19] namely, everything that belongs under the structure of "falling" and "thrownness." Inauthenticity is Dasein's primary ontological structure.[20]

§7. Authenticity and Inauthenticity

According to Heidegger, the possibility of "falling" surrounds Dasein; it enables Dasein to escape personal responsibility in favor of public interpretation. The *they* is what "tranquilizes" Dasein from itself. Hence, I escape from my own-most responsibility for myself precisely by getting lost in the public world of idle talk and curiosity. I find myself "delivered" over to the *they*. This, I submit, is precisely the point where Heidegger's rejection of Husserl's transcendental theory of empathy begins to break down under the weight of an inherent theoretical contradiction. The problem of authenticity, as Heidegger sees it, is that inauthentic everydayness encompasses *both* the natural attitude, the way things get done, and *at the same time* a flight from oneself. This means that inauthenticity must be taken as a positive structure that *makes* Dasein what it is. But if the *they* is what plunges Dasein into a whirlpool of inauthenticity in the first place, how can a flight from oneself be seen as something positive? How can Dasein "fall" into inauthenticity if Dasein is first and foremost always and already *in*authentic? Is there any hope for Dasein to achieve authenticity if it is primordially fallen in everydayness? Does "falling" (*Verfallen*) involve a fundamental ontological structure of the Being of Dasein?

In response, Heidegger turns to the theme of the call of conscience. Dasein, he notes, is "fallen" ontologically from the call of conscience to be or become authentic, but authenticity is itself a modification of the *in*authenticity into which Dasein is first thrown. What he means is that the world of everyday practices constitutes us culturally and socially and brings us into conformity with itself. The problem is that Heidegger himself fails to distinguish everydayness from inauthenticity. Everydayness is a positive structure, the cultural conditions that shape us, the language that we inherit, our traditions, symbols, myths, and heritage. But that all too positive structure induces us to conform to the world. Consequently, when conformity induces us to take conscious flight from our own personal responsibility, we fail to choose to be ourselves. Inauthenticity thus becomes manifest as irresolute conformist Dasein. Certainly it is true that you can't be both authentic and inauthentic at the same time, but you can modify your everydayness into authentic Being-in-the-world.

Thrown into the everyday world of idle talk, curiosity, and ambiguity, "Dasein has, in the *first* instance, fallen away (*abgefallen*) from itself as an authentic potentiality for Being its Self, and has fallen into the 'world'" (*BT* 220). Defining Dasein in terms of the *they*, Heidegger notes that "not-Being-its-self functions as a *positive* possibility of that entity which, in its essential concern, is absorbed in a world" (*BT* 220). However, if Dasein is lost in the *they* from the very beginning, then how can Dasein *find* itself except by way of differentiation? Paradoxically, this would mean that solicitous concern characterizes the way Dasein understands itself primordially in its Being-with Others. Yet if this is the case, then in what sense can Dasein ever be said to be authentically itself apart from the *they*?

These questions expose a tremendous tension that remains to great extent unresolved in Heidegger's critique of *Einfühlung*. Although he agreed with Husserl that the world is constituted, Heidegger did not believe that the world is constituted by a constituting ego or even a plurality of constituting egos. For Heidegger, the world is that in which Dasein is always and already at work, absorbed, concerned, lost alongside Others. The world is where Dasein finds it is already *there*. Where? No where, amidst no one, but *there* nonetheless, fallen amongst the *they*, defined by inauthenticity, curiosity, fallenness, tools, *interpretations*: "In falling, nothing other than our potentiality-for-Being-in-the-world is the issue, even if in the mode of inauthenticity. Dasein *can* fall only *because* Being-in-the-world understandingly with a state-of-mind is an issue for it. On the other hand, *authentic* existence is not something which floats above falling everydayness; existentially, it is only a modified way in which such everydayness is seized upon" (BT 224).

According to Heidegger, Dasein finds itself sucked into the *they* whether it wants to be or not, whether it chooses to be or not, whether it is aware of it or not. Consequently, what distinguishes authenticity from inauthenticity is how I gather myself together *after* being thrown. What Heidegger rejects from Husserl's transcendental model of empathy, then, is not simply the sense of primacy that Husserl affords to perception. He rejects Husserl's very notion of analogical apperception and the theoretical problems of understanding the psychical life of Others that Husserl's empathic model imposes. Heidegger's account of constitution may be said to be "more radical" than Husserl's only if he can show that a cognitively based "knowing of the world" is in fact *founded upon* Being-in-the-world.

§8. Several Implications Regarding Heidegger's Task

Whether Heidegger accomplishes this goal remains, in my mind at least, open to debate. On the one hand, Heidegger succeeds in inviting us back to what Kierkegaard liked to call the "existing individual" who lives in the world and does not just "look" at it. By rejecting Husserl's theory of empathy, Heidegger affirms the primordiality of Others, of publicness, of the *they* of mass culture. Dasein is a product of mass culture. Being swept-up in the power of the *they*, the level of discourse in mass culture becomes degraded, fallen, enmeshed in everydayness. On the other hand, although Heidegger emphasizes the presence of the *they* as the "who" of everyday Dasein, he largely fails to describe individual Dasein as an existing, truly primordial phenomenon. In effect, one could argue that Heidegger inadvertently exonerates the very Husserlian principle that he set out to undermine. By exposing what he saw as Husserl's obstinate attempt to privilege the primacy of perception, Heidegger succeeds in exposing the weakness in his own position, namely that if individual Dasein is equi-primordial, how is it possible for Dasein to ever attain authenticity in the light of being thrown, projected, and fallen?

Clearly, Heidegger's intent in *Being and Time* is not to describe how to think outside the hermeneutical circle, but rather to demonstrate that Dasein *is* this transcendental structure that interprets its own Being as essentially transcendent and projected (*BT* 362).[21] Dasein presupposes the world as subject, it understands itself as the horizon of the understanding and projecting of its own self-interpretation. Husserl's failure, according to Heidegger, is that he left the being of consciousness—that is, the primacy of "knowing"—unquestioned. By privileging cognition, Husserl neglected the more radical insight that "existence" posits the condition of possibility to be or not to be the project that Dasein always and already is. The world is neither a Cartesian *res* nor a receptacle. It is a dwelling, a place or, better yet, a state or disposition or mode of concern. By rejecting empathy as a found*ing* mode, Heidegger succeeds in demonstrating the insufficiency of describing Dasein as merely a zoological fact. Dasein is not a fact; Dasein has *facticity*. As soon as Dasein comes-to-be, Dasein discovers that it is already *there*, in the world, surrounded by the anonymity of *das Man*, determined by its own flight from freedom and responsibility. The only thing that Dasein is not free of is being "thrown" in the world.

The "Self" of authentic Dasein is thus always already elusive, concealed by the *they*, hidden by its own flight from itself. Authentic, individual Dasein is non-primordial: "*Authentic Being-one's Self* does not rest upon an exceptional condition of the subject, a condition that has been detached from the 'they'; *it is rather an existentiell modification of the 'they'—of the 'they' as an essential existentiale*" (BT 168). Heidegger's rejection of empathy violates the monadological foundation of Husserlian constitution. By denying the intersubjective and cognitive characteristics of analogical apperception, Heidegger reintroduces to our discussion different versions of (1) Scheler's thesis that an undifferentiated stream of "public life" exists prior to individual ego and (2) Stein's and Scheler's attempts to define "person" as a principle of active agency rather than in traditional terms of *cogito* or rational animal.

Still, for all its seductive allure, Heidegger's theory concerning the primordiality of Being-with-Others remains largely unsatisfying for a number of reasons. For one, since Dasein can never quite get rid of the *they*, then why would Dasein ever seek to find itself apart from Others unless publicness itself was a constitut*ed* mode of Being-in-the-world? Does the primordiality of Dasein's Being-in-the-world (i.e., its "circle of understanding"), effectually negate the possibility of its own genuine freedom? Second, Heidegger's analysis of the *they* is largely circular. If Dasein is primordially absorbed in the *they*, in what sense can care (*Sorge*) or the call to conscience manifest an existential structure of projection that would not merely be part of the originating circle? In other words, how can I ever hope to find myself apart from the *they* if the *they* is primordial to my own self-understanding?

Finally, and perhaps most important for our discussion, Heidegger's assault on empathy demonstrates a serious misunderstanding on his part as to the goal and spirit of Husserl's overall project. What Husserl is presenting is an account of givenness of the component strata of our knowledge of other persons. Similar to the existence of nature and the world, the Other is never in doubt for Husserl, but rather needs explaining. In effect, it is Heidegger who begs the question of other persons and *not Husserl*. If Dasein is always already marked by inauthenticity and constituted by the *they*, then in what sense can Dasein ever hope to escape from the domination and tyranny of Others? How can Dasein ever authentically "be" itself *apart from* Others if, in fact, its primary manner of Being-in-the-world is always in the mode of not-Being-itself, that is, of Being-with-Others?[22]

Despite the weaknesses that these queries reveal in Heidegger's position, his rejection of Husserl's cognitive theory of empathy has far-reaching implications for our discussion. Following Stein's emotive modification of Husserl's theory of transcendental constitution, Heidegger exposes the myth that "knowing" is the primary mode of Being-in-the-world even further. A more primordial role must be extended to the body, the emotions, and the community than Husserl's theory of cognition will allow. Rather than co-prioritizing cognition with the emotions as Stein did, Heidegger instead argues that Husserl's cognitive model of empathy must be definitively rejected altogether. He replaces cognition with a more primary *social* constitution theory based on a phenomenological analysis that describes how perception is constitut*ed* according to the use of tools and their environments, and thereby includes the emotions as a part of Dasein's *Stimmung* or moodedness.[23]

By rejecting the primacy of perception, Heidegger argues that Dasein first interprets the world through a series of tasks, obligations, and dispositions by which it is always and already given by the *they*. Knowing and empathizing are found*ed* modes of concern of Dasein's Being-in-the-world. Consequently, Husserl's self-proclaimed vocation to describe a "knower" who looks at a "pure known" is for Heidegger merely an attitude of what Sartre would call "bad faith." Such an attitude of ideception describes what it means to be lost in everydayness. Whether constituted cognitively or emotively, empathy signifies for Heidegger the primordial state of being fallen, of being lost in the *they*, of being inauthentic.

Chapter Eight

Emmanuel Levinas and the Face of the Other

Introduction

Martin Heidegger's rejection of empathy as a constituting mode of Being-in-the-world inspired other phenomenologists to critique even further the primacy of perception granted by Husserl in his theory of cognition. Shortly following the publication of *Being and Time* in 1927, many voices from the early Phenomenological Society at Göttignen, including those of Ingarden, Scheler, Reinach, Hedwig Martius, and Edith Stein, were eclipsed. The philosophical landscape in which phenomenology had flourished for three decades changed dramatically in the late 1920s and early 1930s. Edith Stein's emotive modification of Husserl's strict cognitive model of transcendental constitution was quickly eclipsed by talk of the lifeworld, modes of existence, *alethea*, and whispers of a new Power emerging in the heart of central Europe. In terms of philosophy, the years between 1927 and 1937 were marked especially by Heidegger's increasing influence over the direction of phenomenology in German-speaking circles, as well as the growing popularity of phenomenology outside Germany, especially in France.[1] And so it happened that a twenty-two-year-old freshman graduate student, shortly after finishing his undergraduate studies in Strasburg, ventured to Freiburg in 1928 to study phenomenology under the watchful eyes of Edmund Husserl and Martin Heidegger. Little could anyone foresee the radical new direction in which Emmanuel Levinas would soon take phenomenology.

In this chapter, we shall investigate the crucial argument put forth by Levinas in his original and complex work, *Totality and Infinity*, namely, that there never would be any experience of empathy if it were not for the fact that the Other *precedes* the ego. Through a reversal of the direction of Husserlian intentionality, Levinas argues that there is something more primordial to cognitive (Husserl) and emotive (Stein) constitution,[2] and that even Being-in-the-world (Heidegger) is a constitut*ed* phenomenon. What alone remains unconstitutable, Levinas surmises, is the Other's infinite alterity, the *face*. Through the constitutive phenomenality of the face of the Other emerges an epiphany, a radical encounter of the Other qua other.

The crux of Levinas's analysis rests in his belief that empathy is constituted by alterity, strangeness, difference. Empathy imagines the impossible; it grounds ethics in an ungrounded ground. Empathy constitutes a relation without relation, or, better still, a dis-relation between the Other's face and my own. To understand the severity of Levinas's insight, let us recall briefly Husserl's description of the constitution of the alter ego in the fifth of his *Cartesian Meditations*. There, Husserl argued that in order to understand how an alter ego could appear in my stream of lived conscious experience, a second reduction within the phenomenological *epoché* needs to be performed. This reduction to the sphere of radical privacy excludes everything that cannot be given immediately to the constituting subject. Within this pure methodological sphere of ownness, only my body is singled out as the unique, living object to which I can ascribe fields of sensation. I alone exist, whereas my knowledge of all others, including all conscious and cultural life, remains in abeyance, suspended. Through "mundanizing self-apperception," I am motivated to apperceive my body, which is worldly, and my psychic states, which themselves never appear in the world except through the mediation of a body (*CM* 96–100). Only my stream of conscious lived experience (*Erlebnis*) is given absolutely, whereas my body is apperceived. Once my own body is apperceived, I am then naturally motivated to constitute other persons. Husserl writes:

> Since . . . my animate organism is the only body that is or can be constituted originally as an animate organism . . . the body over there, which is nevertheless apprehended as an animate organism, must have derived this sense by an apperceptive transfer from my animate organism, and done so in a manner

> that excludes an actually direct . . . showing of the predicates belonging to an animate organism specifically, a showing of them in perception proper. (*CM* 110–11)

Husserl's description of the constitution of the alter ego as a for-itself within my own stream of consciousness describes how the body (*Körper*) of the Other appears in a phenomenal field. On the basis of passive synthesis and association, I am motivated to analogize a comprehensive "pairing" of the Other's body with my own (*CM* 111–12). Thus, the similarity between the Other's body and my own body motivates me to cognitively constitute the other as an animate or psychic (*Geist*) being like myself. Husserl notes that I am motivated to see the Other as "having a physical side that indicates something psychic appresentatively" (*CM* 114). The psychic life of the alter ego is "indicated somatically and in the conduct of the organism toward the outside world" (*CM* 120). The Other is someone standing "over there" who is analogically similar to the animate organism that *I* am standing "over here." I see the other *seeing me*.

In the preceding chapters we have noted Scheler's, Stein's, and Heidegger's criticisms of Husserl's position. The primacy that Husserl gave to cognition and acts of perception dominated empathy theory for almost a century. Levinas, too, speaks in no uncertain terms of the inadequacy of this model, though for Levinas the root problem of the phenomenology of empathy does not lie so much in Husserl's privileging of cognition as it does in its orientation. The main criticism offered by Levinas is that what phenomenologists have mistakenly presumed to be true is precisely the myth that needs to be dispelled, namely, the directionality of constitution and the conceptualization of intentionality itself. What Levinas holds is that only the primordial face-to-face encounter with the Other makes ethics possible. In *Of God Who Comes to Mind*, he writes:

> I can, to be sure, have the experience of another and "observe" his face and the expression of his gestures as a set of signs that informs me of the state of the soul of the other man, analogous to those that I experience. This is a knowledge by "appresentation" and "intropathy" [*durch Einfühlung*], to remain with the terminology of Husserl, who is faithful in his philosophy of the other to the idea that *all meaning begins in knowledge*. But against this conception of the relation of another we make

> the reproach that it persists not only in imagining this relation to the other as an indirect knowledge . . . but also in still understanding it precisely as knowledge. In this knowledge, obtained from the analogy between the behavior of a foreign body objectively given and my own behavior, there is formed only a general idea of interiority and of the I. The indiscernible alterity of the other is precisely missed.[3]

According to Levinas, Husserl's theory of analogical apprehension remains tied to a schematization of cognition that is itself largely based on assimilation. Such assimilation, Levinas holds, elicits a form of violence. I am motivated to understand the body (*Leib*) of the Other based on an analogy in which I see my body as like the Other's and the Other's body as like my own. Hence, it is only through the violent assimilation of the Other by the Same that I come to understand the actions of others. For Levinas, the being of the other is born of violence; the Other becomes meaningful only *in terms of my own*. Levinas charges that Husserl's notion of empathy in effect reduces the extent of what I can know about the world and the process of accumulating such knowledge. Empathy reduces difference to mere reciprocity and sameness. It violates the Other by limiting access to the Other and so reduces the way I imagine the Other as a response to external circumstances. Through the totalizing effects of empathy, the Other becomes cognized in terms of the responses that I would envision myself to make were I in a similar situation. Levinas thus rejects Husserl's attempt to reduce the radical alterity of the Other as something already identifiable and expected, namely, *a face similar to my own*.

For Levinas, Husserl's cognitive reductionism mistakenly holds that ethics is derived from within commonly accepted horizons established by the same. Analogical descriptions of the alter ego imply that the Other is constituted always in relation to *my* comprehension of the Other's subjectivity alongside the *Other's* (embodied) orientation to the world. Levinas sets ethics against what might be described as a derivative theory of knowledge. According to Levinas, genuine knowledge is not simply a matter of understanding the situation of the Other via the act of empathy. In this chapter, we will evaluate Levinas's understanding that ethics is "first philosophy" and explore his contention that ethics delimits the whole sphere of knowledge, that it debunks empathy as a crisis of violence vis-à-vis the emergence of genuine ethics as difference.

§1. The Problem of Transcendence

Levinas's reversal of the theory of intentionality is more radical than Stein's emotive modification of Husserl's position or Heidegger's outright rejection of *Einfühlung*. Genuine alterity calls attention to the fact that I can never truly know what it is like to "feel" what another feels, to walk in another's shoes, to act from the mental context of another person's environment, no matter how similar to my own. Empathy underscores that my own constitution of these experiences are quasi-experiences of alterity, at best. Paradoxically, unknowing becomes a condition of possibility of ethics, since it is precisely by acknowledging that I cannot know what it means to see the world through an Other's eyes that ethics becomes possible. Levinas poses a dilemma for describing the phenomenology of empathy. On the one hand, if empathy provides a description of alterity that takes into account the Other as a genuine for-itself, then ethics violates the inviolability of the Other. On the other hand, if empathy reduces the Other to a mere self-representational object, then any access given to the Other through empathy is merely fleeting, illusory, untrustworthy. Either way, Levinas says, Husserl's doctrine of empathy leaves open the problem of transcendence, that is to say, How can I ever understand the Other as a for-itself without having to assimilate the Other within my own stream of lived experience? Joseph Kockelmans describes the problem of empathy in terms of transcendence:

> When I try to understand the real meaning of this insight, I must come to the conclusion that transcendence, in whatever form it may manifest itself to me, is an immanent characteristic constituted within the sphere of the pure ego itself. Stated in another way, every possible sense and every imaginable being, whether it manifests itself as immanent or transcendent, falls within the domain of my transcendental subjectivity which ultimately constitutes all sense and Being. Once I understand this, I see also that every attempt to conceive the universe of true Being as something lying outside the universe of possible consciousness is nonsensical because true Being and consciousness belong together essentially and inseparably, being concretely one in the only absolute concretion of transcendental subjectivity . . . an "outside of consciousness" is certainly nonsense.[4]

Whether in terms of intersubjectivity (Husserl) or Being-in-the-world (Heidegger), and whether in terms of privileging cognition (Husserl) or co-privileging affectivity alongside cognition (Stein and Scheler), Levinas notes that, for Husserl, constitution always requires a horizon in which what is given is, in fact, given. Whatever is constituted within a horizon becomes part of that horizon. Outside of such horizon nothing can be intended, since then it would no longer be recognizable *as* what was intended. According to Levinas, such horizonal thinking violates the very essence of genuine alterity, since the condition of possibility of the wholly Other requires that the Other come from outside every horizon.

The problem of empathy becomes transformed by Emmanuel Levinas into an indictment against Western philosophy itself, along with every traditional notion of ethics as an enlightened will to power or a universalizing attempt to ground difference as categorical imperative. "Everyone will readily agree that it is of the highest importance to know whether we are not duped by morality," he says at the beginning of *Totality and Infinity*. Husserl's so-called benign quest for the pure, objective *eidos* breaks under the weight of Levinas's inversion of Husserl's transcendental model of empathy. Even Heidegger's attempt to think Being in terms of "the obscure fragments of Heraclitus" shows signs of stress at having been duped by philosophy's totalizing instinct. Ontology, Levinas concludes, remains just another word for the violence wrought by philosophy. *Esse* is *interesse*: "Essence is interest."[5]

Levinas is concerned above all with wrestling the fate of ethics away from the traditional opposition between theory and practice. The critique appears to be leveled as much against Husserl as Heidegger. Both philosophers, Levinas argues, are guilty of maintaining the formal structure of thought at the expense of ethics, Husserl in terms of the pure ego and Heidegger in terms of careful concern, publicness, and anguish before death. What is needed instead is a radical reversal of the very categories of thinking that philosophers have traditionally assumed make thinking possible, namely, interiority, truth, and essence. Because ethics begins with transcendence and not empathy, only ethics can render radical exteriority possible. This, in a nutshell, is Levinas's dream. He wants to use empathy against ethics in order to expose philosophy as the giver of violence. Levinas unmasks the harsh reality that underlies the West's essentialist dream of providing a sufficient reason for everything. He wants to expose the "secret" that lurks behind every ontotheological system and every attempt to pay homage to Being over beings, the Whole over the individual, empathy over difference.

The assimilation of what is strange and foreign within philosophy's dream of totalization engenders a false transcendence. False transcendence leads everything back to immanence, back to the self, back to the *cogito* as the (fictional) *giver* or grounding of transcendence. Beneath and more radical than the ego's intentional act directed toward the Other, Levinas argues, lies the more radical address of the self by the Other. This reversal in the direction of constitution away from empathy is what Levinas calls metaphysics. It elicits a desire that "tends toward something else entirely, toward the absolutely other" (*TI* 33). What Husserl means by empathy, then, gets reclassified by Levinas as a secondary, derivative phenomenon of the ego. What alone is primordial is interiority, the face of the Other, that is, precisely what cannot be constituted. Now, how do we constitute *that*?

§2. Hospitality to the Stranger

The language of *Totality and Infinity* is one of hospitality, at least in contrast to the later writings of Levinas that tend to be characterized by more violent imagery.[6] Levinas describes ethics as welcoming the stranger (the foreigner) into the realm of the same (the home). Ethics is thereby concerned with desire, transcendence, and *meta*-physics rather than ontology, that is, the science of the same. The Other announces ethics as the event of what is always inventive and unfamiliar, in a word, ethics lies *beyond* empathy: "The metaphysical desire does not long to return, for it is desire for a land not of our birth, for a land foreign to every nature, which has not been our fatherland and to which we shall never betake ourselves. The metaphysical desire does not rest upon any prior kinship. It is a desire that can not be satisfied. . . . The metaphysical desire has another intention; it desires beyond everything that can simply complete it" (*TI* 33–34). Ethics is an event of, by, and for the Other, the wholly Other. As such, ethics signals a happening of the impossible, an experience of excess, a "subjectivity [that] realizes these impossible exigencies—the impossible feat of containing more than it is possible to contain" (*TI* 27).[7]

In terms of excess, Levinas describes the face of the Other as an ethical relation that does not possess a *noetic-noematic* structure; it is ethical because the face always expresses more than can be expressed. "The essential of ethics," he says, "is in its *transcendent intention*" (*TI* 29). The face thus demands from me what is impossible for me to give: my home, my time, my self. The real subject of ethics is the nonappearing or transcendence of the Other. What Levinas seeks is not an apodictic account of the noetic-noematic correlation involved in every act of knowing but rather a phenomenological description of the face, that is, what turns on a phenomenon whose most salient feature is that the phenomenon never appears. In contrast to Husserl and his philosophy of horizons and lifeworlds, Levinas raises the question: What goes on beneath the movement of intentionality and makes intentionality possible as such?

What we may find most significant in terms of Levinas's critique of Husserl's phenomenology of empathy is not the noetic-noematic correlation but rather the breakup of the correlation between *noesis* and *noema*. Beneath every equilibrium lies a dis-equilibrium, a dis-proportion, upon which every formal structure of thought is founded (*TI* 28). This radical reversal of Husserl's position rejects out of hand Husserl's and Stein's description of how foreign consciousness gets constituted as a for-itself within my own stream of lived experience. Levinas dismisses all notions of intentionality that reduce thought to "an *adequation* with the object" on the grounds that such totalization does violence to the Other, to infinity. Contrary to Husserl, Levinas observes that intentionality "does not define consciousness at its fundamental level. All knowing *qua* intentionality already presupposes the idea of infinity, which is preeminently *non-adequation*" (*TI* 27). Such a principle of non-adequation means that the fundamental problem of constitution does not rest with the ego per se but rather with Husserl's theory of intentionality. While Levinas does not deny the existence of the personal ego, he opposes the argument that individual ego constitutes the Other. Rather, the ego is addressed or constitut*ed* by the Other. The advent of this event, Levinas observes, marks the origin of ethics:

> The metaphysical other is other with an alterity that is not formal, is not the simple reverse of identity, and is not formed out of resistance to the same, but is prior to every initiative, to all imperialism of the same. It is other with an alterity constitutive of the very content of the other. . . . The absolutely other is the Other [*L'absolument Autre, c'est Autrui*] . . . the Stranger who disturbs the being at home with oneself [*le chez soi*]. But Stranger also means the free one. Over him I have no

power [*pouvoir*]. He escapes my grasp by an essential dimension. . . . He is not wholly in my site. (*TI* 38–39)

The condition of possibility of transcending the circle of sameness remains structurally impossible for both Husserl and Heidegger, the latter on the condition of the hermeneutic spiral and the former in terms of intentionality. And this is precisely why Levinas defines ethics as first philosophy. By noting the impossibility of transcending the circle of sameness within the structures of Greek metaphysical thinking, Levinas proposes that authentic ethics needs to be *un*grounded in infinity, that is, in what lies outside every structural experience of empathic constitution. In effect, he weaves together three distinct threads into a profound reversal of the theory of empathy: (1) Hebrew nomadic spirituality, which affords a primordial sense of duty to the Other as a command to care for the stranger, the foreigner, the widow and orphan; (2) Descartes's Third Meditation, by which Levinas reverses Descartes's notion that the Infinite is an innate idea and instead argues that the idea of infinity is not merely cognitive but *experiential*, that the idea of infinity arises not from within the ego but wholly from *outside*, from what is exterior; and (3) Plato's notion of the Good beyond Being, from which Levinas argues that the Other comes from outside time in order to inaugurate something wholly and radically *new*.[8]

§3. Time and Infinity

Whereas Husserl's transcendental model of constitution posits an equilibrium between self and other, Levinas points instead to a *dis*-equilibrium between I and Thou that is constituted by time. According to Levinas, time is not an extension of the "Now" into the "just Now," as Husserl (and Stein) believed. Rather, time *is* the Other, time announces the Other in terms of what cannot be announced, namely, the Other as infinite, as transcendent, as radically alter. Manifest through structures of sociality, infinity makes time possible, it announces both the infinite alterity of the Other and the Other *as* infinite: "Infinity does not first exist, and *then* reveal itself. Its infinition is produced as revelation, as a positing of its idea in *me*. It is produced in the improbable feat whereby a separated being fixed in its identity, the same, the I, nonetheless contains in itself what it can neither contain nor receive solely by virtue of its own identity. . . . The idea of infinity (which is not a representation of infinity) sustains activity itself" (*TI* 27).

The experience of encountering the Other qua other propels human subjectivity toward an experience of infinity. Encountering the Other (literally) takes our breath away. For Levinas, the Other is like a hurricane that blows where it wills and cannot be bound by a neatly fashioned structure or restrictive horizon. Contradicting Heidegger, Levinas argues that the Other is not a tool or instrument or ground. Analogous, in a sense, to Irigiaray's notion of air, the concept of Levinas's *Other* contains no form.[9] In order to enclose air in a structured form, one must do violence against it: air simply spreads out, extends, expands, circulates, diffuses, sprawls, disseminates. Similarly for Levinas, the Other breaks up every formal structure of thought in which the Other is re-cognized. Hence, as a sort of arch-mediation, infinity constitutes the a priori condition of all possibilities, though it is not itself a *something*. Infinity is like time, like pure desire, in that it has no boundary, no borders, no limits. It is always present yet never fully *given*. The infinite hides always beyond every possible horizon, it remains veiled, secret, out of sight, waiting to make itself known precisely by concealing itself:

> The idea of Infinity *is revealed*, in the strong sense of the term. . . . But this exceptional knowledge is thus no longer objective. Infinity is not the "object" of a cognition (which would be to reduce it to the measure of the gaze that contemplates), but is the desirable, that which arouses Desire, that is, that which is approachable by a thought that at each instant *thinks more than it thinks*. The infinite is not thereby an immense object, exceeding the horizons of the look. It is Desire that measures the infinity of the infinite, for it is a measure through the very impossibility of measure. (*TI* 62)

Contrary to Husserl's doctrine of intentionality, Levinas holds that *I* do not constitute givenness and presence; rather, I am constituted *by* them. What I encounter in the Other is an infinite withdrawal, an inaccessibility, a nonappearing that reveals itself by hiding itself. The Other is therefore not constituted empathically, that is, via analogical apperception:

> But the relationship with this "thing in itself" does not lie at the limit of a cognition that begins as a constitution of a

> "living body," as according to Husserl's celebrated analysis in the fifth of his *Cartesian Meditations*. The constitution of the Other's body in what Husserl calls "the primordial sphere," the transcendental "coupling" of the object thus constituted with my own body itself experienced from within as an "I can," the comprehension of this body of the Other as an alter ego—this analysis dissimulates, in each of its stages which are taken as a description of constitution, mutations of object constitution into a relation with the Other—which is as primordial as the constitution from which it is to be derived. (*TI* 67)

The constitution of the alter ego within my stream of lived experience cannot be constituted through empathy as *merely another* ego, as Husserl famously claimed. Otherwise, the other ego would contain a trace of the same, that is, it would not be alter ego.

For Levinas, the Other qua other is wholly Other, infinitely Other, the Other as infinite alterity, a condition of possibility of ethics. Consequently, the face of the Other is not a phenomenon that can be analogically constituted by and for consciousness. Levinas holds that the face of the Other is not constitut*ed* at all but rather constitut*ing*. Taken this way, the face of the Other is the foundation of ethics in the sense that it is infinitely inaccessible and so cannot be constituted by my own self-interest. What is wholly inaccessible to me necessarily disrupts every linguistic attempt I make to define it. "Already of itself ethics is an 'optics'" (*TI* 29), Levinas notes. Ethics is a way of *unsaying* the said.[10] The face thus signifies an ethical claim, a living presence: "The face speaks . . . it is expression" (*TI* 66).

§4. Ethics as First Philosophy

"Infinity," Levinas posits, "is not commensurate with the soul. The idea of infinity does not proceed from the I" (*TI* 61). What he means is that neither intersubjectivity nor intentionality is capable of grounding the experience of transcendence. Ethics is not founded on a cognitive relationship between *noesis* and *noema*: "The quest for truth is an event more fundamental than theory, even though theoretical research is a privileged mode of the relation with exteriority we name truth" (*TI* 61). It is in the context of such primordial givenness that ethics is designated not as a truth relation but as "first philosophy," that is, what is prior to truth. What he means by "first philosophy" is that the "I" is constituted as a "me" in the ethical response, "Here I am," *me voici*. The Other comes over me, lays claim to me, and constitutes "me" as an ethical subject. Ethics thus reverses the intentional arrow of traditional metaphysics: "Transcendence designates a relation with a reality infinitely distant from my own reality, yet without this distance destroying this relation and without this relation destroying this distance, as would happen with relations within the same. . . . We have called this relation metaphysical" (*TI* 41–42).

Ethics (and not ontology) designates for Levinas what was traditionally referred to by the Greeks as first philosophy. His position stands in marked contrast to both Husserl and Heidegger. For Husserl, transcendental consciousness is first in the order of knowledge, whereas for Heidegger in *Being and Time*, what is primordial is the ek-static temporality of Dasein. According to Levinas, however, what holds priority is the ethical command by the Other upon me. Hence, although Levinas does not deny the importance of the existence of individual ego, he argues that the direction of Husserl's transcendental theory of constitution needs to be reversed. The ego constitutes the Other in neither a unilateral nor intersubjective sense. The command of the Other constitutes *me* in the accusative case and thereby makes possible the ethical subject as such.

Of course, at the same time that he criticizes Husserl, Levinas also criticizes Heidegger as well for not introducing the element of flesh into his discussion concerning the analysis of Dasein: "We live from 'good soup,' air, light, spectacles, work, ideas, sleep, etc. . . . These are not objects of representations. We live from them" (*TI* 110). In effect, Levinas says that Heidegger's schema of tools, care, and concern does not adequately illustrate the primordiality of Dasein's Being-in-the-world. "The bare fact of life," he says, "is never bare. Life is not the naked will to be, an ontological *Sorge* for this life. . . . Life is *love of life*, a relation with contents that are not my being but more dear than my being: thinking, eating, sleeping, reading, working, warming oneself in the sun" (*TI* 112). The Levinasian observation that the living body is missing entirely from *Being and Time* is well taken, especially noting that, for Heidegger, Dasein's only body seems to be an "agent body" that gets things done mainly by hammering nails into walls. Levinas notes that such instrumentality is not itself primordial. The privileging of care, like the privileging of perception, is constituted:

> [E]ven the hammers, needles, and machines are objects of enjoyment, presenting themselves to "taste," already adorned,

embellished. . . . Enjoyment is made of the memory of its thirst; it is a quenching. It is the act that remembers its "potency." It does not express (as Heidegger would have it) the mode of my implantation—my—in being, the tonus of my bearing. . . . Life is affectivity and sentiment; to live is to enjoy life. (*TI* 110–15)

In other words, if, as Heidegger argues, the structure of care is always care about my own being, then how is it at all possible for me to care or relate to Others whose own care is the care and concern of themselves?

On the contrary, first and foremost the body is flesh. At the heart of Levinas's critique is a corporeal-life philosophy that rejects at one and the same time both Husserl's strict model of cognitive constitution and Heidegger's theory that the essence of Dasein lies in its existence. In effect, Levinas rejects the very *idea* of constitution. By this I mean that Levinas discards outright any notion that purports that (1) the Other is constituted via analogical apperception and (2) the primordiality of the *they* pervades everyday Dasein in the mode of Being-in-the-world. Based solely on grounds that ethics is first philosophy, Levinas adjures that the infinite alterity of the Other cannot be reduced to an "I" that constitutes it. Levinas demands that "first philosophy" be defined in terms of ethics, by which he means "the calling into question of the same by the other." In other words, ethics alone "accomplishes the critical essence of knowledge" (*TI* 43). Ethics is privileged neither by tools and instrumentality on the one hand nor by the theory of monadological intersubjectivity on the other hand. Ethics is an event, a *rupture*. It elicits a de-privileging of cognition in the sense that it is not founded on prior knowledge, regardless of whether such knowledge is essential (Husserl) or pragmatic (Heidegger).

§5. A Critique of Representation

Husserl's *Cartesian Meditations* plays a dominant yet elusive role throughout *Totality and Infinity*. This can be evidenced primarily in the way that Levinas has interwoven three general themes: (1) the reversal of the theory of constitution; (2) the de-privileging of cognition; and (3) a reexamination of Husserl's notion of representation (*Vorstellung*). After examining the first two themes, let us next take a moment to examine the third theme. Concerning representation, Levinas writes:

> The Husserlian thesis of the primacy of the objectifying act—in which was seen Husserl's excessive attachment to theoretical consciousness . . .—leads to transcendental philosophy, to the affirmation (so surprising after the realist themes the idea of intentionality seemed to approach) that the object of consciousness, while distinct from consciousness, is as it were a product of consciousness, being a "meaning" endowed by consciousness. . . . But does the theory of mental images, betraying a confusion of the act with the object of consciousness, rest uniquely on a false description of consciousness inspired by the prejudices of a psychological atomism? (*TI* 123)

In his analysis, Levinas attempts to rework the entire framework of Husserl's doctrine of intentionality. He argues that representation, that is, the correlation between consciousness and objects, is a found*ed* mode: the object of representation is reducible to *noemata* (*TI* 124). Levinas claims that Husserl's yearning to discover the truly concrete apodictic subject that underlies all changes inadvertently caused him to fall victim to the very spirit of Cartesianism that he was in fact trying to avoid. "Descartes' clear and distinct idea manifests itself as true and as entirely immanent to thought: entirely present, without anything clandestine; its very novelty is without mystery" (*TI* 124). According to Levinas, intelligibility and representation are thematically equivalent. What is "intelligible" is what is re-presentable, namely, an "exteriority surrendering in clarity and without immodesty its whole being to thought, that is, totally present without in principle anything shocking thought, without thought never feeling itself to be indiscreet" (*TI* 124).

What Levinas seems to be driving at is the sense in which Husserl's doctrine of intentionality succeeds in marking the condition of possibility of determining the same amidst difference but does not mark the revelation or unconcealment of genuine alterity: "The intentional relation of representation is to be distinguished from every other relation—from mechanical causality, from the analytic or synthetic relation of logical formalism, from every intentionality other than representational—in that in it the same is in relation with the other but in such a way that the other does not determine the same; it is always the same that determines the other" (*TI* 124). In effect, Levinas underscores an apparent weakness in Husserl's theory of *epoché*. The Husserlian reduction does not allow the essence of genuine alterity to appear but instead demonstrates that the direction of intentionality of representational thinking always predetermines the Other in the light of the same. Consequently, even in the reduction, Levinas argues, the Other never appears in the context of the Other's own radical alterity but rather always appears as for-me. "Such is the movement of the Husserlian *epoché*, which, strictly speaking, is characteristic of representation. Its very possibility defines representation. . . . [I]n representation the same defines the other without being determined by the other" (*TI* 125).

By holding that "representation is the seat of truth" (*TI* 124), Husserl in effect succeeds in describing consciousness in terms of intentional directedness. The task Husserl originally set out to accomplish was the task of describing things themselves. In order to achieve this task, Levinas notes, the phenomenological reduction must itself be abandoned. Levinas holds that Husserl's notion of intentionality needs to be radically altered in order to "free" the object from the intentional gaze that constitutes every object by a subject. The Husserlian model that defines consciousness as always "consciousness *of* something" requires further analysis. The intended object can become clear and distinct only after it has been cut down to size precisely *in order for it to fit* representational thinking. Husserl failed to grasp this misstep in the phenomenological method, namely, that "in the intelligibility of representation the distinction between me and the object, between interior and exterior, is effaced" (*TI* 124). Focusing instead on clarity, Husserl appears to have lost the more radical sense of alterity that his own theory of intentionality had intended to discover. Objects are always inadequately given, Husserl argues, such that there remains an infinity of profiles of each object. Nevertheless, Levinas proposes, in principle phenomenology's infinite task could be carried out. Because Husserl's notion of empathy reduces alterity to clarity, intentionality in effect effaces the "disappearance of what could shock" (*TI* 124).

Levinas wants to expose what Husserl himself did not see in his own discovery of intentionality, namely, that representation is a pure present: "The positing of a pure present without even tangential ties with time is the marvel of representation . . . representation involves no passivity" (*TI* 125). Levinas notes that the structure of representation has a "positive condition in the other," in that what is represented in representation is not the same, but the Other. What Levinas means is that the structure of representation posits a nonreciprocal relation in which the I "loses its opposition to its object; the opposition fades, bringing out the identity of the I despite the multiplicity of its objects, that is, precisely the unalterable character of the I" (*TI* 126). The subject does indeed constitute its object by representation, which is Husserl's whole point. But at what cost? For Levinas, neither constitution nor representation are ultimate revealers of transcendence. Instead, Levinas asserts that Husserl missed entirely the important sense in which representation necessitates assimilation: "To reduce a reality to its content thought is to reduce it to the same" (*TI* 127). In effect, Levinas turns Husserl against Husserl. In discovering that any object represented or constituted by consciousness reduces that object to the transparency or clarity of the constituting subject,[11] Husserl failed to recognize that representation itself is *constitutive*.

§6. The Night Of *Il y a*

The meaning that Levinas appropriates by the use of various images of *il y a* (literally, "there is") is striking. *Il y a* manifests the night, it makes present the "nocturnal dimension of the future" (*TI* 142). Of course, the presence that arises behind such nothingness is neither a being in the sense of *res cogitans*, nor consciousness functioning in a void, as is the case when a person is hungry and the need for food is one's only goal (*TI* 134). *Il y a* pronounces an indeterminacy characterized by anonymity, shadows, absence.[12] Levinas likens such faceless, nameless, sheer existence to insomnia and says that in the *il y a* is wakefulness but not consciousness: "Wakefulness is anonymous. In insomnia it is the night itself that watches. It watches. In this anonymous nightwatch I am the object rather than the subject of an anonymous thought. I become aware of it in a movement in which the I is already detached from the anonymity. Thus, our affirmation of an anonymous vigilance goes beyond the phenomena, which already presupposes an ego. Yet, *il y a* is the dissipation of personages" (*EE* 66).

In *Existence and the Existent*, Levinas says that he is concerned with discovering the origin of the apparition of every existent, a "substantive in the heart of impersonal existence, a pure verb in the *il y a*" (*EE* 82). He argues that a verb is not simply the name for an action in the same way that a noun is the name for a thing. The function of a verb, he notes, "does not consist in naming, in producing language, in bringing-forth" (*EE* 82). Rather, in a verb "we are looking for the very apparition of the substantive: God, world, inanimate things, an object in opposition to the subject, extension in opposition to thought, matter in opposition to mind."

In order to describe such an apparition, that is, the apparition of the appearing of a nonappearing, Levinas sometimes uses the term *hypostasis*.

Etymologically, hypostasis comes from the Greek words *hypo*, meaning "under" and *stasis*, "standing." Hypostasis signifies the substructure or substance or essence of something that "under-stands" or "stands under" or remains concealed from what is visible. In the history of philosophy, hypostasis has traditionally designated the event "by which the act expressed by a verb became a being designated by a substantive. It thus signifies the suspension of the anonymous *il y a*, the apparition of a private domain, of a noun" (*EE* 83). Hypostasis designates a corruption in the history of Western philosophy. It signifies degeneration, in the sense that existence has become more and more associated with the personal "I" of an existent, a consciousness, a thinking-substance, a *person*.[13]

Levinas seeks to retrieve the anonymity of *il y a* before philosophy got hold of it and turned Being into beings, existence into *the existent*. But is such a pure experience of *il y a* possible? Levinas is quite aware that Husserl's notion of intentionality makes *il y a* an impossibility. The Husserlian doctrine of intentionality assumes I cannot have a pure experience of an Other that is not first constituted as *my* experience. Either an experience is *my* experience or it is no experience at all. Similarly, experience can either be described within language or it is rendered incoherent, incomprehensible, inconceivable. Levinas notes, however, that the experience of *il y a* is precisely the experience of a non-experience. *Il y a* announces a feeling of being engulfed by an anonymity of which I am not even aware. For Levinas, *il y a* is constitutive of such an *un*constitutable experience. The radical alterity of such strangeness is not cognizable. It grabs me from behind, its felt presence is itself surprise, a shock, a rupture to the system.

The formal structure of *il y a* thus contains no formal structure. It is a visitation that never arrives, an intention without a subject, a solicitation without petition. The experience of *il y a* in a sense *un*does the very doing of philosophy itself. What Levinas seeks is a way to affirm an experience of the wholly Other that both betrays and affirms every description of it. Such an experience of the inexperienceable rests solely in the enjoyment of B/being inundated by the elements.

§7. Alimentation and the Elements

The question that Levinas raises is whether representation is antecedent to activity. Is an overflowing saturation of life prior to constitution, or merely an effect of constitution? In what sense is Levinas justified in saying that life is *prior to* representation and that the body is prior to consciousness?

In effect, Levinas wants to find a corporeal, sensible sphere that exists prior to constitution and representation:

> The body is the elevation, but also the whole weight of position. The body naked and indigent identifies the *center* of the world it perceives, but, *conditioned* by its own representation of the world, it is thereby as it were torn up from the center from which it proceeded. . . . The body indigent and naked is not a thing among things which I "constitute" or see in God to be in a relation with a thought, nor is it the instrument of a gestural thought, of which theory would be simply the ultimate development. The body naked and indigent is the very reverting, irreducible to a thought, of representation into life, of the subjectivity that represents into life which is sustained by these representations and *lives of them*; its indigence—its needs—affirm "exteriority" as non-constituted, prior to all affirmation. (*TI* 127)

According to Levinas, the significance of the Husserlian *epoché* is the discovery of a surplus that is not constituted by representational thinking. *Epoché* announces a reversal in the direction of cognition; it lives from an excess not bound by the sufficiency of reason. "In 'living from . . . ,' " Levinas notes, "the process of constitution which comes into play wherever there is representation is reversed" (*TI* 128). In attempting to identify the founding stratum, Levinas rejects Husserl's thesis that there is a pre-perceptual field prior to constitution that is purely cognitive. Levinas here introduces the notion of alimentation or surplus or excess, what Jean-Luc Marion calls "saturation," in order to describe a different source of pre-conscious life that is sensuous, embodied, and nonintentional.[14]

The criticisms provoked by Levinas are of course not only directed against Husserl. Addressing Heidegger, Levinas uses the language of alimentation in order to describe how the world of enjoyment is given prior to representation, prior to concern, care, even utility. Being lost in pure enjoyment, for example, means that I do not constitute the element as a "thing" or a "tool" for use. Instead, I allow myself to be bathed in enjoyment, saturated in an elemental overflow or excess of pleasure. As a quality without support and a content without form, such indetermination of elements constitutes every experience in which I find myself, whether cognizant of their presence or not. Rather than having to figure out how to get outside an element in order to see it from different angles, the doctrine of alimentation implies that the object or element envelopes *me* and surrounds *me* in its entirely: "Hence we can say that the element comes to us from nowhere; the side it presents to us does not determine an object, remains entirely anonymous. It is wind, earth, sea, sky, air" (*TI* 132).

As a noncognitive experience of "being lost in the element," saturation marks an experience *before* representational thinking arrives on the scene. "It is not a question of a *something*," Levinas adds, "an existent manifesting itself as refractory to qualitative determination. Quality manifests itself in the element as determining nothing" (*TI* 132). Sunbathing, enjoying a spectacular glass of wine, standing at the edge of the sea, "losing myself" in an intimate embrace—each of these experiences gives witness to pure experience in which I find myself not constitut*ing* but, on the contrary, being enveloped, addressed, enraptured—in a word: constitut*ed*. Whereas for Heidegger, "the hammer" becomes invisible in its use, for Levinas even the work of hammering is completely saturated by the sensuous elements that surround it. The "blue sky" presents what Levinas calls a "pure quality" since its "blueness" is not constituted by individual ego or by a plurality of egos. The "blue" of the sky is not a thing; it is, phenomenologically speaking, an expanse of space and time, an inexhaustible element that comes *to me* and bathes me in its immensity (*TI* 132). The sky bathes the entire sensuous sphere of life, much like the smell of baking bread or roasting sweet garlic saturates the entire environment of one's home. For Levinas, bathing in the elements constitutes enjoyment, fertility, infinity, the future:

> But this overflowing of sensation by the element . . . is not a quality of something. The solidity of the earth that supports me, the blue of the sky above my head, the breath of the wind, the undulation of the sea, the sparkle of the light do not cling to a substance. They come from nowhere. This coming from nowhere, from "something" that is not, appearing without there being anything that appears—and consequently coming always, without my being able to possess the source—delineates the future of sensibility and enjoyment. (*TI* 141)

What is Levinas saying here? First, he is not disputing the notion of facticity. Rather, he thinks that Heidegger and Husserl have gotten it backward in a sense, Husserl by privileging perception and Heidegger by privileging instrumentality. Second, Levinas highlights their positions, not as two contradictory or even antagonistic theories but in order to show that Husserl and Heidegger in fact present very similar notions. Whatever their differences, Levinas muses, Husserl and Heidegger are Greek thinkers. They present two versions of a single theme, namely, the way that constitution gets the world done. Consciousness "cuts" things down to size, so to speak. Whether consciousness-as-subject constitutes knowledge of the world by perceiving concrete things (Husserl) or whether consciousness-as-subject uses things as tools *before* it perceives objects (Heidegger), the methodology is remarkably the same. Levinas holds that, either way, representation and intentionality essentially accomplish the same job. They both constitute objects in order to fit them to the world. Contrarily, Levinas's notion of the depth of the elements describes a noncognitive experience *before* representation takes place. The thing comes to me and addresses me; it has a face and speaks.

We may hence characterize the Levinasian notion of alimentation in terms of a profound tension between (1) the correlation between sensibility and the elements and (2) the *apeiron*, that is, what is ungraspable, unidentifiable, ineffable, indefinite. In the first sense, alimentation senses that it is always directed toward the pure enjoyment of bathing in the elements. Because sensibility is not at all the same as imperfect or implicit thought waiting to be clarified, it is irreducible to interiorization and mere enjoyment. In the second sense, Levinas notes that bathing in the elements can indeed be terrifying. Those things that I enjoy prior to representation can also menace, threaten, and destroy my very existence. Such brute facticity seemingly appears from nowhere, without explanation, without reason, without justification. It is *il y a*, the night, infinity, death, an experience beyond experience—in a word: *ethics*.

§8. The Face and the Ethics of Discourse

Levinas proposes a transcription of the fifth of Husserl's *Cartesian Meditations* into an ethics that turns on the phenomenon of the face, the phenomenon of precisely what can't be seen or touched, the phenomenon of what doesn't (and cannot) show up. He argues that neither vision nor sensibility grant genuine transcendence: "The relation with the Other alone introduces a dimension of transcendence" (*TI* 193). Hence, only the face leads to a relation *totally different* from every relative and egoist experience in the sensible sense of the term. This is accomplished by Levinas in primarily two different ways. First, he describes the face in terms of epiphany: "The Other remains infinitely transcendent, infinitely foreign; his face in which his epiphany is produced and which appeals to me breaks with the world that can be common to us" (*TI* 194). In this regard, the transcendence of the face appears precisely in its nonappearance and refusal to be comprehended. The face manifests what cannot be manifest, it leads to a sense of the incomprehensibility of the *aperion*. Second, Levinas describes the face as a condition of possibility of alterity itself. The face of the wholly other is not completely beyond experience; otherwise, we could not talk about it *as* epiphany. Yet the epiphany of the face is precisely the experience of our not having access to the appearing of its phenomenality. "The face is present in its refusal to be contained," Levinas notes, "[and] in this sense it cannot be comprehended, that is, encompassed" (*TI* 194). The face is a phenomenon wholly in recess. Levinas asks: How do we engage *that* sort of experience, namely, an epiphany that never arrives?

According to Levinas, we encounter the face of alterity as an ethical experience only in and through *language*. Of course, such an encounter between two (human) speakers does not constitute a difference between members of the same genus. On the contrary, "absolute difference, inconceivable in terms of formal logic, is established only by language. Language accomplishes a relation between terms that breaks up the unity of a genus" (*TI* 195). In other words, the encounter between two speakers is an ethical relationship, what Husserl called "intersubjectivity." It is a kind of social ontology by which the terms tend to withdraw from the relationship at the same time they establish the conditions of possibility of the relationship-itself: "The terms, the interlocutors, absolve themselves from the relationship. Language is perhaps to be defined as the very power to break the continuity of being or of history" (*TI* 195).

The incomprehensible givenness of the presence of such radical alterity is best described in terms of what remains essentially transcendent in every event of discourse about the Other. Levinas notes that the formal work of language "consists in presenting the transcendent" (*TI* 195). But the Other who is presented through signification is not contained or absorbed by the words that bear him. Levinas likens the Other to a position, never a negation. I am visited by something that interrupts what I attempt to gather. As interlocutor, the Other upsurges inevitably *behind the said*: "Words are said, be it only by the silence kept, whose weight acknowledges this evasion of the Other. The knowledge that absorbs the Other is forthwith situated within the discourse I address to him. Speaking, rather than 'letting be,' solicits the Other. Speech cuts across vision" (*TI* 195). What Levinas presents is an ethical rendering of Husserl's notion that the conscious stream of lived experience (*Erlebnis*) of the Other is inaccessible to me. Because the Other's stream and my stream of lived conscious life are separated by an abyss that neither of us can cross—for Husserl, there are "no canals" between different streams of consciousness—the inaccessibility of "I" and "Other" becomes for Levinas an *ethical* principle rather than an epistemological problem. When we encounter the Other, we are given the alterity of the Other, but precisely in terms of the Other's *not being present*, that is to say, what is given is the non-givenness of alterity. The Other is given only in language: "The formal structure of language thereby announces the ethical inviolability of the Other and, without any odor of the 'numinous,' his 'holiness'" (*TI* 195).[15]

Given to us in living speech, the face of the Other is the face of someone who speaks, who greets me from out of the depths, who calls me from the other shore toward which I set out but never quite arrive. The Other is someone who speaks from an interiority to which I have no access. To speak is like the giving of a gift that is neither expected nor anticipated. Always indicative of something else, something beyond what is present, the face of the Other does not merely express itself. The face of the Other *speaks*, it is a *living* self, distinguished from the trace it leaves behind in texts, in language, in expressions. Hence, the hidden givenness by which the face maintains a relation with me through discourse does not imprison the face in an economy of reciprocity. The Other, in effect, "remains absolute *within* the relation" (*TI* 195). What makes the relation ethical, Levinas contends, is that when the Other speaks, a relation is established between two absolutes, a relation that puts the "I" in question. This is the ethical moment that puts everything in question. The I emanates from the *Other*, not from the same. As a sign of both opposition *and* peace, presence *and* withdrawal, the face that speaks also keeps silent. Its secret, revealed yet hidden, is that the Other constitutes a moral summons that always proceeds from the other, never from me. Once the face speaks, the said becomes part of the world: "But the other absolutely other—the Other—does not limit the freedom of the same; calling it to responsibility, it founds it and justifies it. The relation with the other as face heals allergy. . . . This is the situation we call welcome of the face. The idea of infinity is produced in the opposition of conversation, in sociality.... But the relation is maintained without violence, in peace with this absolute alterity" (*TI* 197).

For Levinas, the significance of the face of the Other must be sought within the linguistic turn. Language, in a sense, interrupts itself; it suspends the economy of words and meanings, representation, analogy. Levinas muses that language disturbs "the being at home with oneself [*le chez soi*]" (*TI* 39). I have no power (*je ne peux pouvoir*) over language, just as I have no power over the Other, since language always escapes my grasp by an essential dimension, even when I use words and meanings at my own disposal. For this reason, the infinity of the Other is given to me linguistically: the face of the Other, which appears without my constituting it, speaks by calling my name. For Levinas, language imposes a relation between the same and the other in terms of vigilantly maintaining a radical sense of alterity that is prior to every initiative of the same. *L'absolument Autre, c'est Autrui*: "Language accomplishes a relation such that the terms are not limited within this relation, such that the other, despite the relationship with the same, remains transcendent to the same. The relation between the same and the other, metaphysics, is primordially enacted as conversation, where the same, gathered up in its ipseity as an "I," as a particular existent unique and autochthonous, leaves itself" (*TI* 39).

What Levinas thinks is essentially needed for ethics, therefore, is a relation between I and Other that is "maintained without violence, in peace with this absolute alterity" (*TI* 197). The face resists possession, not because it overpowers me with greater force, but because my own weakness and vulnerability cannot contain its own withdrawal in the sensible. In effect, I cannot bring the alterity of the Other under my power: Its very infinity makes it impossible for me to contain the face in any conventional or totalizing sense. When Levinas writes about language, he is thinking of the Other as the speaker and "I" as the addressee, that is, the one being addressed. The face "speaks to me ... and invites me to a relation incommensurate with a power exercised" (*TI* 198), it announces ethics by making possible the sphere of exteriority, it "shocks" into openness "the sensible appearance of the face" (*TI* 198). The epiphany of the face is ethical, not because it ensures an ethical relationship between two subjects but because it is an embodied, concrete command that overpowers me. The face comes from outside and fills me with respect; it announces what is foreign, transcendent, irreversibly unique; it commands: you shall not commit murder (*TI* 199)—that is, it commands that you be your brother's keeper.

§9. Time and Death

"Reason" is the name Levinas gives to openness to the Other, to infinity, to other others, to infinities of others. The name of reason *is* the wholly Other: its outer *sur*-face is the face of what is absolutely new, unconstitutable, inapproachable, primordial. Such infinity is not merely reminiscent of Descartes's innate idea. Infinity is constitutive of an ethical command that comes from outside the sphere of knowability. For Levinas, the infinite is not something I conjure up on my own. In every case, infinity, similarly as with time and death and the Other, is not mine. I *belong* to the Other, my time is claimed by the Other. In death the Other menaces me, threatens me, strikes me down like a thief. Death constantly stalks me. Like the face beyond the face, death is irreducible to the categories of neither being nor nothingness. Rather than isolating me from all others, death is a metaphysical structure of sociality that elicits from me the call for help.[16]

As noted earlier, Dasein for Heidegger is constituted always in the mode Being-toward-death (*Sein zum Tode*), such that death is its ownmost projection and anticipation. For Levinas, on the other hand, the being of subjectivity is not a projected movement *toward* death. Rather, it is a reversal, a retreat *away from* death. The time of death, like the time of war, suspends "everydayness." Hence, the time of death and suffering is extra-ordinary. Instead of signaling an ending, the experience of death constitutes the origin of authentic being, of real subjectivity:

> A being independent of and yet at the same time exposed to the other is a temporal being: to the inevitable violence of death it opposes its time, which is postponement itself. It is not finite freedom that makes the notion of time intelligible; it is time that gives a meaning to the notion of finite freedom. Time is precisely the fact that the whole existence of the mortal being—exposed to violence—is not being for death, but the "not yet" which is a way of being against death, a retreat before death in the very midst of its inexorable approach. In war death is brought to what is moving back, to what for the moment exists completely. (*TI* 224)

Death brings me into relationship with the Other, even against my will and better judgment. It carries me to the Other, to ethics, it promises me to a future that is never mine. In death, "the reality of a conscious being and its interiority, is recognized" (*TI* 224). Even my own death, Levinas notes, is never purely mine; it pertains to the Other, to other others, to generations of others: I am remembered, forgotten, haunted; obligated to the future, to time, to infinities of others who are always already yet to come. The appearance of the face announces the experience of death and vice versa. In both cases, the elemental phenomena of the elements constitute "first philosophy" in the Levinasian sense that the Other is the condition *of the condition* of every possibility. The face announces an ethical relation, the face is the ethical relation *itself* that announces the inauguration of time and death, of timeless death, of deathless time, that is, of *temporality*:

> To be temporal is both to be for death and to still have time, to be against death. . . . It is a relation with an instant whose exceptional character is due not to the fact that it is at the threshold of nothingness or of a rebirth, but to the fact that, in life, it is the impossibility of every possibility, the stroke of a total passivity alongside of which the passivity of the sensibility, which moves into activity, is but a distant imitation. Thus the fear for my being which is my relation with death is not the fear of nothingness, but the fear of violence—and thus it extends into fear of the Other, of the absolutely unforeseeable. (*TI* 235)

In his earlier work *Time and the Other* (1948), Levinas proposed that death is the absolutely other. Death comes from "outside" the circle of expectation and its approach exposes the truth that something absolutely alien is about to happen, something that escapes even the sovereignty of my own intentionality. In effect, death announces the possibility of *mysterium tremendum*, an encounter with something whose origin comes from outside the self. Death announces time, it makes possible the future, but not in the Heideggerian sense that the future is what comes from *out of me* in my Being-toward-death, that is, in the attitude of "resoluteness" that I project against the totalizing power of *das Nichts*. Rather, time is announced by death as the future that comes at me whether I will it or not. Death *is* ungraspability; it announces what remains always and wholly impossible, mysterious, incomprehensible, foreign. That is why death is never temporally present:

> The fact that [death] deserts every present is not due to our evasion of death and to an unpardonable diversion at the supreme hour, but to the fact that death is *ungraspable*, that it marks the end of the subject's virility and heroism. The now is the fact that I am master, master of the possible, master of grasping the possible, Death is never now. When death is here, I am no longer here, not just because I am nothingness, but because I am unable to grasp. (*T&O* 72)

In distinction from Heidegger, Levinas holds that death is "the impossibility of having a project" (*T&O* 74). As the event of enigma, of darkness, of the night, death announces the arrival of an Other who wholly disrupts every totality. The approach of death, moreover, is announced by a time outside my control. It indicates that we are "in relation with something that is absolutely other, something bearing alterity not as a provisional determination we can assimilate through enjoyment, but as something whose very existence is made of alterity" (*T&O* 74). The Other (*l'Autre*) that is announced in death is not merely unknown but unknowable. Hence, death is similar to an encounter with another person: "In the being for death of fear I am not faced with nothingness, but faced with what is against me, as though murder, rather than being one of the occasions of dying, were inseparable from the essence of death, as though the approach of death remained one of the modalities of the relation with the Other. The violence of death threatens as a tyranny, as though proceeding from a foreign will" (*TI* 234).

The radical alterity of the Other is announced by time, by death, by the time of death's (untimely) arrival; hence, death "precisely indicates that the other [*l'Autre*] is in no way another myself, participating with me in a common existence" (*T&O* 75). In his analysis of death, Levinas utterly redirects Husserl's arrow of intentionality. A "right relationship" with the Other, Levinas says, does not come about through empathy. On the contrary, it "is not an idyllic and harmonious relationship of communion, or a sympathy through which we put ourselves in the other's place" (*T&O* 75).[17] "On the contrary, we recognize the other as resembling us, but exterior to us; the relationship with the other is a relationship with a Mystery. The other's entire being is constituted by its exteriority, or rather its alterity, for exteriority is a property of space and leads the subject back to itself through light. . . . The relationship with the other will never be the feat of grasping a possibility. . . . The other is the future" (*T&O* 75–77). In effect, Levinas directs our attention to a centrifugal force constituted by the sphere of the same that constantly draws things unto itself. Contrarily, the Other is precisely what cannot be subsumed by the sphere of the same. The Other cannot be annihilated. In terms of ethics, death constitutes a structure of sociality; it elicits from me a "call for help."

Levinas understands death in precisely the opposite way from Heidegger. In *Being and Time*, Dasein is always already exposed to and projected toward death as its own-most possibility; whereas in *Totality and Infinity* the time of death announces the genuine beginning of subjectivity: "Time is precisely the fact that the whole existence of the mortal being—exposed to violence—is not being for death, but the 'not yet' which is a way of being against death, a retreat before death in the very midst of its inexorable approach" (*TI* 224). What Levinas means is that time constitutes the "I" that is in attendance at its own manifestation. This is the "living-I," a living subjectivity. Although Levinas borrows the theme of the "living-I" from Husserl, he reverses its directionality and says, in opposition to Heidegger, that death is not what I am in the mode of Being-toward-death, but what I am *given*. In other words, death and time are not understood as categories of being, nor are they reducible to categories of non-being. Rather, death and time constitute *me*, menace me, threaten me, stalk me, strike me in the (dead of) night like a thief: "The unforeseeable character of death is due to the fact that it does not lie within any horizon. It is not open to grasp" (*TI* 233).

Death is time's announcement of the shattering of the present moment. In death, the Other interrupts the sphere of the same and announces another positive infinity. Death thus appears as precisely what cannot appear, since it arrives from what is exterior from my own horizon of possibility. Death appears from outside the sphere of the same, outside every sphere. Death announces the unforeseeability of the approach of violence from outside the circle of every compossible reciprocity. For Levinas, death rejects empathy totally and out of hand.

Chapter Nine

Jacques Derrida and the Possibility of an Empathic Antipathy

Introduction

When all is said and done, does Levinas in fact support a version of empathy? Although he appears to reject empathy by reversing Husserl's arrow of intentionality, in the end does Levinas's notion of the face beyond the face, despite his stated intentions, betray some sort of transcendental symmetry, a kind of empathy that winds up privileging ethics over epistemology? In order for the Other to be *tout autre*, must the Other remain wholly outside every structure of expectation? Does the abandonment of all horizons of possibility lead to the mere dissolution of meaning altogether, to what is unintelligible, irrational, non-sensical? Is the absolutely wholly other, *l'infini*, as pure and radically other as Levinas wants us to think? Or could what Levinas calls the "positive infinity" of the infinitely other contain something that submits the Other in advance to the very violence of a horizon of expectation that he wants to reject? Might there be a *trace* of something in the wholly Other that doesn't quite belong to the Other but rather belongs to the same, to the structure of language, to the sphere of discourse? And might there be a relationship between such discourse and ethics? These are some of the questions we shall investigate in this chapter.

Derrida wrote *Violence and Metaphysics* in large part in response to Levinas's *Totality and Infinity*. In his essay, Derrida argues that what Levinas in fact means by the wholly Other is not quite as wholly other (*tout autre*) as Levinas initially assumed. On closer inspection, it appears that Derrida is arguing for a return of sorts to Husserl's model of empathic constitution via analogical imagination. In this chapter, we shall follow Derrida's attempt to criticize Levinas in light of Levinas's own earlier critique of Husserl. Because Levinas's notion of the wholly Other is a *human* other who shares something in common with me, Derrida argues that there must be a corresponding underlying sense of similarity between every I-Thou relation. What the Other shares in common with me is a trace of the same. Hence, Derrida concludes, the condition of possibility of recognizing the wholly Other requires the presence of a non-traceable trace. In every intuition, I recognize something of the same in the other without reducing the Other to the sphere of the same. This, it seems to me, is a form of empathy, at least insofar as empathy involves a certain analogy. But unlike Husserl's doctrine of analogical apperception, Derrida notes that Levinas's model of empathy is really a model of what I will call here "antipathy."[1] Paradoxically, he says that the wholly Other requires as a condition of possibility that the Other not be *wholly* other. Consequently, a transcendental symmetry in the order of knowledge makes possible an ethical asymmetry.

§1. The Task of Speaking Greek

In the last sections of *Totality and Infinity*, Levinas exposes the ontological separation between the "self" and "Other" in terms of *violence*. Anarchy, he insists, is "essential to multiplicity . . . [a] trembling and vertigo . . . [that] demands justice" (*TI* 294). Totality therefore arises out of a certain propensity to systematize what in fact resists totality. "The break-up of totality, the denunciation of the panoramic structure of being, concerns the very existing of being and not the collocation or configuration of entities refractory to system" (*TI* 294). The tension of expectation portends a call from beyond totality that breaks up every totalizing instinct. Such trauma must be capable of being heard without being audible, seen without being visible, known without being comprehended. What Levinas means is that there must inhere some sort of structure of expectation within every horizon of foreseeability. Such expectation breaks up the totality but is itself never fully exposed as being part of that totality. We shall designate this "structure of expectation" a *quasi*-transcendental, meaning that the condition of possibility that makes something possible is also what makes it impossible. A quasi-transcendental "supplies a condition under which something is constituted or constructible and at the same time through and through deconstructible."[2]

The face of the child, that is, the face of justice, the face beyond the face, functions as such a quasi-transcendental. As Levinas notes, the face overflows with meaning.[3] The face is excess, exterior. It lies beyond both Being and Totality and so represents a unique mode of signification that refuses identification with any essentialist or primordial core of identity.[4] According to John D. Caputo, the face is a quasi-transcendental because it functions as "a condition of or for entities, but is not an entity itself; a condition under which things appear, but too poor and impoverished, too unkingly, to dictate what there is or what there is not, lacking the power to bring what is not into being, lacking the authority to prohibit something from being."[5]

The face manifests a condition of possibility of expectation that lies outside every horizon of expectation. Without the face there is neither transcendence nor expectation, but only immanence. Although the face is never inscribed within the measured horizons of predictability, there must correspond some sort of structure within the horizon of knowability that allows the unexpected to be encountered *as such*. The face is a quasi-transcendental that allows something new or different to happen without any idea whether or what it will be or where it will lead.

For Levinas, language—like the face—functions as a quasi-transcendental. Since discourse describes the manifestation of contact between self and Other, it alone is the "Bonjour!" and "Welcome!" that grants infinite respect while retaining infinite distance. Speech belongs to the sphere of the impossible, of eschatological peace, of a future that always remains elusive. Speech "refuses vision," Levinas says, "because the speaker does not deliver images of himself only, but is personally present in his speech, absolutely exterior to every image he would leave" (*TI* 296). Discourse, then, is central to the art of philosophy. It constitutes a totalizing, a "naming" and "speaking" that does violence to the individual. It devours the Other. Hence, inasmuch as language aspires to speak clearly and distinctly, discourse "enlightens" the Other, it subsumes alterity by shining the "light" of Greek ontology onto the Other in order to *see* the otherness of the Other.[6]

For all his protestations to the contrary, Derrida notes, Levinas too is a Greek. How could he not be, Derrida wonders, since Levinas is the heir apparent of the two most Greek-thinking moderns of all? Heidegger and Husserl each preserved the structure of "inside-outside," the latter by the "enlightenment" of cognition and the former by "illuminating" the world as care. "In making the structure 'inside-outside' tremble at the point where it would have resisted Heidegger, Levinas in no way pretends to erase it, or to deny its meaning and existence" (*VM* 88). Levinas is seduced by the light, by the gods, by language and discourse, precisely in his desire to conceptualize the infinite positivity of the wholly Other. According to Derrida, Levinas's claim that he is able to glimpse the impossible through Plato's depiction of the Good "beyond" Being betrays the fact that he does not yet grasp the implications of what he himself has discovered. Similarly, his affinity to Descartes's assertion in the third of his meditations that the idea of Infinity is visited upon us shows that, when all is said and done, Levinas is as much a victim of the *telos* of a totalizing Greek vision that desires to catch a glimpse of *real* alterity as he is its messenger.

What gets revealed in Levinas's text, therefore, is for Derrida not so much a glimpse of the impossible—since to glimpse a pure vision of alterity would *be* impossible—but rather the proposition that the wholly Other is a relatively stable unit of meaning that has itself been constituted in the play of discourse. If the wholly Other were *wholly other*, then neither Plato nor Descartes would be able to catch even a glimpse of it. Consequently, an appearance of the wholly Other must somehow be possible, it must share a trace with what is similar to (yet different from) itself. Derrida's point is that the interior/exterior distinction that Levinas wants to maintain in fact does not hold. Rather, we need to understand that "interior" and "exterior" are mere expressions of a third potency, namely, writing. This is what Derrida calls *différance*, that is, the nameless name of an open-ended, uncontainable, generalizable and infinite play of traces and significations.[7]

According to Derrida, Levinas is fully aware of the incongruity of his own position. In fact, what Levinas designates as the positive infinity of *l'infini* becomes so utterly transcending that it denies even the possibility of its being conceived. "It is at this level that the thought of Emmanuel Levinas can make us tremble," Derrida warns. "At the heart of the desert, in the growing wasteland, this thought, which fundamentally no longer seeks to be a thought of Being and phenomenality, makes us dream of an inconceivable process of dismantling and dispossession" (*VM* 82). Derrida notes that the dream of Levinas is a dream that seeks to liberate thought from itself: "[F]or Levinas the sun of the *epekeina tes ousias* will always illuminate the pure awakening and inexhaustible source of thought" (*VM* 85). This means that philosophy is saturated by "the visage of being that shows itself in war" and "is fixed in the concept of totality which dominates Western philosophy" (*TI* 21).

Levinas's dream to dream outside the horizon of all possibility in effect betrays "the Greek ancestor of the Infinite which transcends totality (the totality of being or of *noema*, the totality of the same or the ego)" in the first place (*VM* 85). Derrida observes that the loftiest Greek dream of all is to dream in terms of what is non-Greek, namely, to subject radical alterity to what cannot be addressed, described, or represented. The appearance of such a non-phenomenon attempts to free the Other from "the neutral totality of the Same as Being or as Ego" (*VM* 85). Consequently, even Levinas's most lucid thought experiment to think alterity in terms of non-totalizing givenness "seeks to define itself, in its primary possibility, as metaphysical . . . hence, a Greek notion" (*VM* 83).

What Derrida discovers from Levinas is the most radical endeavor to think what is not yet possible to conceive. Derrida's response to Levinas is both unexpected and yet surprisingly conspicuous. In order to speak of the wholly Other, Derrida notes, one must in effect be able to speak of that which cannot be spoken. Derrida likens his own project to that of Meister Eckhart's. Noting the way that the Greek fathers of the Church and medieval philosophers of the *via negativa* address the name of God, Derrida paraphrases Eckhart by saying, "Transcendence toward Being, permits . . . an understanding of the word God . . . even if this understanding is but the ether in which dissonances can resonate. This transcendence inhabits and founds language" (*VM* 146). Derrida claims that real, adequate alterity can be addressed only in radical silence. The requisite for saying anything about the wholly Other is that one first has to say *that one cannot say* what one wants to say. Such auto-deconstructing discourse continuously tries to erase its own marks, its own effects, its own traces from every page. Nevertheless, such an epiphany "of a certain non-light before which all violence is to be quieted and disarmed—will still have to be exposed to a certain enlightenment" (*VM* 85). In other words, the dream of Levinas is the dream of every Greek metaphysician. It is the dream of absolute purity and unblemished innocence, the dream of the face of an infinitely wholly Other, a dream *without* discourse, a dream of the impossible. But it is a *dream* nonetheless:

> One anticipates that this metaphysics will have some difficulty finding its language in the medium of a traditional logos

entirely governed by the structure "inside-outside," "interior-exterior." . . . But will a non-Greek ever succeed in doing what a Greek in this case could not do, except by disguising himself as a Greek, by *speaking* Greek, by feigning to speak Greek in order to get near the king? And since it is a question of killing a speech, will we ever know who is the last victim of this stratagem? (*VM* 88–89)

What Derrida demonstrates is that the dream of the impossible always announces itself with language, with speech. Indeed, the impossible is a dream of language itself. Hence, when Levinas says that he dreams of a pure Other, Derrida responds that even the radical and purely, wholly Other of which Levinas dreams cannot rightfully escape discourse. Every Other betrays some kind of horizonality, some sort of structure even (especially) when dreaming about the *wholly* Other. Levinas's failure to think outside the horizon of discourse, Derrida concludes, proves that Husserl was right from the beginning. In effect we need some sort of "horizon" or "analogy" in order to speak or dream at all: the Other is like me, only different. What is most striking for Derrida is that Levinas himself saw this critique coming and prepared for it in *Totality and Infinity*. Derrida's critique is not a simple rejection of Levinas's position. He argues that the very idea of the wholly other is "incoherent" precisely so that he (Levinas) can reconstruct or rehabilitate it for a new purpose. Is Derrida justified in inferring from Levinas that there has to be a horizon of the same in order for the Other to appear as other, that is, as human? How does the event of the arrival of the wholly Other shatter the horizon of every expectation?

§2. The (Un)Wholly Other

According to Derrida, philosophy domesticates alterity and reduces it to its own terms. What Levinas is really talking about when he talks about the wholly Other, Derrida surmises, is a linguistic event, and this because Levinas has independently said that meeting the Other occurs in language. In effect, Derrida turns Levinas against himself. He is saying the Levinas is not in the position, and cannot use the strategy of, negative theology, viz., of saying that we have an experience of an infinite alterity but we just don't have the language to say it or describe it. Levinas deprives himself of such recourse because he argues that infinity—unlike the mystic's infinity—is delivered up to me in language, that is, in the Welcome! and Bonjour! of solicitation. When the other speaks to me, his speaking comes from an infinitely distant source.

Since the infinite Other approaches me in language, Derrida must show how the sphere of the same can be interrupted by the living saying, the moment of impossibility where infinity appears. Derrida begins by acknowledging that no vision, no singularity, no sense of representation or structure of correlation, neither the Jewish or Hebraic biblical tradition nor Hume's empiricism, nor even Christian traditions of mystical transcendence, can ever escape the overflowing reach of philosophy. Because not even phenomenology can address an unqualified, unconditional alterity, Derrida infers that the wholly Other *is* merely an other trace. In a purely logical-linguistic sense, the infinite positivity of the wholly Other is a contradiction in terms. Either the Other is wholly and unconditionally other—which is impossible, since nothing (not even the *wholly* Other) can escape the horizon of foreseeability, of knowability, of representation, of vision, of discourse—or else the Other contains a visible-linguistic trace, by which the Other is not wholly and unconditionally *other*. Speaking of Levinas, Edith Wyschogrod notes Derrida's point, namely that "the failure of representation to attain the other lies in its emphasis upon vision as the model for the understanding of language."[8]

What, then, is meant by the term: "wholly" other? For one thing, the wholly other is not the sky, a tree, a stone, an animal, God, a spirit. This must be the case, Derrida acknowledges, because I know that rocks, trees, stones, and so on do not have an interior life, and I know that I do and that the other one who is like me does also. The wholly other signifies an other *person*. Therefore, what appears to Levinas as "wholly" other is really based on analogy. If it were not for analogy, it would be impossible to speak of what is infinitely other. As Derrida notes in *Violence and Metaphysics*, there is no "outside" of violence. In effect, the very act of discourse constitutes violence. Discourse differentiates, it defines and constitutes meaning, it raises radical questions within a totalizing context of linguistic signs. Therefore, what Derrida wants is to push language to its limit precisely in order to expose the Levinasian sense of alterity that assumes some resistance to the other. What Levinas missed, however, was that every "push" beyond limit essentially remains within the domain *of* limit; hence, within the domain of language, intelligibility, speech, discourse, *totality*: "Incapable of respecting the Being and meaning of the other, phenomenology and ontology would be philosophies of violence.

Through them, the entire philosophical tradition, in its meaning and at bottom, would make the common cause with oppression and with the totalitarianism of the same. The ancient clandestine friendship between light and power, the ancient complicity between theoretical objectivity and technico-political possession" (*VM* 91).

Derrida argues that Levinas's notion of violence is really an arché-violence, a structure or articulation that is neither "good" nor "bad" but transcendental. Violence is wary of anything that proclaims itself as *presence*. There is, he argues, nothing outside of violence, no privileged position that stands exterior to language or writing or speaking or seeing. There is no a priori Archimedean point by which one is able to apprehend the totality without somehow still standing in it or somehow being conditioned by it. On the contrary, there is always a trace of violence even in every condition of possibility. There is no such thing as a pristine encounter with pure alterity (Levinas), no "pure" knowing or intending (Husserl), no "pure" way of Being-in-the-world through care (Heidegger). For Derrida, the notion of purity itself provides recourse to violence, it manifests a certain and particular kind of prejudice that privileges presence: "A light before neutral light, before the truth which arrives as a third party, the truth 'which we look toward together,' the judgmental arbitrator's truth. Only the other, the totally other, can be manifested as what it is before the shared truth, within a certain nonmanifestation and a certain absence. It can be said only of the other that its phenomenon is a certain nonphenomenon, its presence (*is*) a certain absence" (*VM* 91).

What Derrida argues is that the pure positive infinity of the wholly Other can never be grasped, except in a trace of its absence. As Derrida notes, Levinas's description of the Other's absence concerns "not pure and simple absence, for there logic could make its claim, but a *certain* absence" (*VM* 91). What does Levinas's description of absence entail? How might the notion of "absence" illuminate his more formal claim that philosophy is a radicalization of the ethical? Does Levinas succeed in dislocating the primordial notion of Greek *logos* by announcing his radically ethical and prophetic declaration in *Attic* speech?

§3. The (Secret) Violence of Light

Claiming that Levinas places the very concept of Western philosophy itself in question by raising the question of the alterity of the Other, Derrida effectually deconstructs the totalizing historicity of Greek thinking that underlies the Levinasian project. Derrida inhabits Levinas's text, in a manner of speaking, and lets the text "spin" itself out, much like discourse violates the sovereignty of everything that falls under its sway. "If the other could be possessed, seized, and known, it would not be the other," Derrida quotes from *Time and the Other*. Hence, "to possess, to know, to grasp are all synonyms of power" (*VM* 91). Turning to Levinas, Derrida notes that even Levinas recognized that there is no absolutely pure Other, that every other must be brought into the light in order to first be seen. The subject always has its own bearings; thus, light allows the subject to see and distinguish limits, to set marks and boundaries, to grope toward a horizon of intelligible visibility. Light illuminates knowing, Derrida argues. Intelligibility is always concerned with seeing, comprehending, grasping, en-lighten-ing: "To see and to know, to have and to will, unfold only within the oppressive and luminous identity of the same; and they remain, for Levinas, fundamental categories of phenomenology and ontology. Everything given to me within light appears as given to myself by myself. . . . What language will ever escape it? How, for example, will the metaphysics of the face as the epiphany of the other free itself of light? Light perhaps has no opposite" (*VM* 92). Because light makes knowing possible, it entails both power and violence. Levinas makes a distinction (which is itself an act of transcendental violence) between epiphany and phenomenon. A phenomenon is what appears or is constituted by the light, whereas an epiphany appears by not appearing.[9] According to Derrida, the distinction that Levinas makes between epiphany and phenomenon betrays philosophy's Greek dream for the absolutely pure and unmediated Other. He thinks that Levinas has gotten it half-right when he champions Heidegger's notion that Dasein must project a horizon in which entities can appear by its proper name, that is, violence. For Levinas, the wholly Other does not (and cannot) appear. Such visible "appearance" would in fact reduce the infinity of the face to triviality, to a kind of existence as an empirical manifestation of phenomenality.

Essentially, Levinas wants to describe an epiphany that remains hidden from the light. As a linguistic event, an epiphany reveals itself in the form of a "secret." By concealing itself, however, the non-phenomenality of the epiphany requires that the epiphany never quite appears but that it remains hidden, secret, concealed. What Levinas fails to ask, Derrida wonders aloud, is whether there *is* anything outside the light? Derrida's point is that without exposing the secret of the nonappearance of an epiphany as a secret, "parricide is philosophy's theatrical fiction" (*VM* 90). To understand the secret requires one to understand that the secret exists, that it is the secret of the existent, that the secret is (secretly) brought into the light. Otherwise, the secret—like the wholly Other—remains totally and irrevocably hidden, unconcealed, unthought, and in effect: unthink-*able*. Levinas's distinction between epiphany and phenomenon thus betrays for Derrida a dangerous and corrupt endeavor to keep secrets concealed, hidden—in a word, to keep them *secret*: "Without intermediary and without communion, neither mediate nor immediate, such is the truth of our relation to the other, the truth to which the traditional logos is forever inhospitable. This unthinkable truth of living experience, to which Levinas returns ceaselessly, cannot possibly be encompassed by philosophical speech without immediately revealing, by philosophy's own light, that philosophy's surface is severely cracked, and that what was taken for its solidity is its rigidity" (*VM* 90).

Derrida's description of the overwhelming violence of light and secrets means that when we speak of *lux et veritas* we are always dealing with a certain interpretation of things, a particular kind of (Greek) metaphysical striving for purity. Consequently, even Levinas's ethical dream for absolute purity is set within a metaphysical context that he himself did not create. When speaking of the face, for example, Levinas says that the other is always given in person *as other*, that is, "as that which does not reveal itself, as that which cannot be made thematic" (*VM* 103). Since the Other is shrouded in secrecy, Levinas argues that "the Other could not be constituted as an alter ego, as a phenomenon of the ego, by and for a nomadic subject proceeding by appresentative analogy" (*VM* 106). What he means is that all of Husserl's cognitive problems describing how the constituting ego can have genuine knowledge of a for-itself in its own stream of lived experience can be overcome only if the primary ethical relationship is recognized as the original face-to-face encounter. This ethical (as opposed to a merely epistemological) face-to-face encounter, Levinas adheres, is "the emergence of absolute alterity, the emergence of an exteriority which can be neither derived, nor engendered, nor constituted on the basis of anything other than itself" (*VM* 106).

The radical emergence of such an absolute outside, an exteriority infinitely overflowing the monad of the *ego cogito*, is, however, not quite as *autre* as Levinas would initially lead us to believe. Derrida notes that, for Levinas, the infinite(-ly other) cannot be an object because "it is speech, the origin of meaning and the world" (*VM* 106).[10] This means that some trace of empathy must exist between the Same and the Other since even the *idea* of a pure exteriority, in Levinas's own terms, is unsupportable. According to Levinas, exteriority is inextricably bound up with place, with body, with speech (*VM* 112). Speech, therefore, shatters every horizon from *within* rather than from without since there can be no possibility of an "outside" of the horizon. It follows, then, what Levinas means by Infinity (i.e., the infinitely other) really signifies a "finite totality." Otherwise, Derrida notes, what is *wholly* Other could never be recognized as a *person*. Derrida wants to show that for Levinas there is some kind of "analogy" or "symmetry" that exists between the same and the Other. Even the infinite positivity of the wholly Other cannot be banished outside the conceptual framework by which such banishment is proscribed by words.

In effect, Derrida thinks that Levinas has violated his own system. If he wants to talk about something absolutely other, Levinas needs language to do it. The Other is given in language, the Other is revealed in speaking to me. If the Other needs language in order to appear, then the Other, even the wholly Other, remains saturated in the presence of violence, the very violence that Levinas is attempting to transcend. According to Derrida, violence is the way we carve things up in a certain way, the way we "cut up" the world in and through language. Therefore, in every thought, in every dream, in every word, in every *Other*, there is both violence and mediation. Derrida concludes that either Infinity cannot be reduced to the alterity of the Other or it is impossible to speak of the Other at all: "As soon as one attempts to think Infinity as a positive plenitude (one pole of Levinas's nonnegative transcendence), the other becomes unthinkable, impossible, unutterable. Perhaps Levinas calls us toward this unthinkable-impossible-unutterable beyond (tradition's) Being and Logos. But it must not be possible either to think or state this call" (*VM* 114). Yet, as Levinas contends, we must be able to speak of the wholly Other, or else the wholly Other would not be the human other. Eternally exiled outside every context, every economy, every circle of reciprocity, the face of the anonymous, wholly Other would remain totally and irreconcilably unrecognizable, unknowable, ineffable—in a word, *inconceivable*.

§4. Of Violence and Metaphysics

For Derrida, of course, such an impossible infinity is a "false infinity," to use Derrida's account of Hegel's word (*VM* 119). An inconceivable infinity would be nothing less (and nothing more), than absolute silence, analogous in a sense to Levinas's notion of "real" peace. In effect, it would be nothing at all (*VM* 117), the absence of all economy (which is impossible). Levinas notes that real peace, like silence, "is the strange vocation of a language called outside itself by itself" (*VM* 117). Discourse is the medium of violence, it claims recourse to a "violence against violence" while at the same time it constitutes an economy of violence in the name of a pure, *non*violent essentialism. Levinas attempts to combat Greek light (i.e., philosophy as totality) with a certain other kind of other (Jewish) light (i.e., infinity). All the while, however, he forgets that the sun rises and sets on both Jews and Greeks. Levinas has apparently forgotten that even the philosopher who writes of the purity of silence from within his darkened monk's cell still writes with pen and ink, that is, from *within* history. Even Levinas must speak and write about the secret not merely to be understood but in order to understand.[11] The philosopher of infinite alterity always and already stands saturated by a kind of arché-violence that remains inescapable. Such an attempt to think ethics outside the boundary of metaphysics exposes the false infinity that grounds the descriptive event of the coming-to-be of "radical" alterity. As Derrida notes, Levinas's rejection of empathic association, his insistence that the wholly Other escape history, escape light and metaphysics, effectually perpetrates violence upon the very notion of transcendence that he is attempting to secure: "Within history which the philosopher cannot escape, because it is not history in the sense given to it by Levinas (totality), but is the history of the departures from totality, history as the very movement of transcendence, of the excess over the totality without which no totality would appear as such. History is not the totality transcended by eschatology, metaphysics, or speech. It is transcendence itself" (*VM* 117).

For Derrida, there is neither violence nor totality but rather various economies and multiplicities of more and less violence. Arguing that not even the impossible can escape the grasp of violence, Derrida sets out to retrieve Levinas's notion of infinite alterity and put it to work again, this time in service of the impossible. What Derrida wants is to keep all economies open. He thus turns to the structural idea of the wholly Other in order to accomplish the task that Levians began but did not achieve. Since philosophy tends to domesticate alterity, Derrida contends that the (secret) dream of Western philosophy is the desire to auto-deconstruct every economy. It is Levinas's notion of the wholly Other, of the impossible, of the infinite impossibility of a pure economy, that Derrida is convinced hints at the arché-violence that underlies every ethics (including Levinas's!)

and which alone shatters every metaphysics of presence. What Derrida *un*conceals is that Levinas's dream of *pure* gift, *pure* economy, *pure* alterity is but the secret dream of all metaphysicians. Hence the dream "to glimpse" the wholly Other in effect imprisons alterity within the confining horizon of the same. It totalizes rather than shocks the horizon in order to include that which resists inclusion. All there *is*, Derrida notes, is difference, that is, different economies, different horizons, different contingencies and com-possibilities: "Metaphysics is *economy*: violence against violence, light against light: philosophy (in general). . . . This becoming is war. This polemic is language itself. Its inscription" (*VM* 117).

What is remarkable in Derrida's critique of Levinas's reading of Husserl's theory of adequation is that in each principal move that *Totality and Infinity* makes in criticism of Husserl, Levinas in fact presupposes the truth of Husserl's claims. Hence, in this section we shall draw our attention to two important themes hinted at by Derrida: (1) First, that Levinas uses the method, not the content, of Husserl, and (2) second, that Levinas is in fact much further from Heidegger's rejection of empathy and much closer to Husserl's theory of apperception than he himself was aware. What Levinas has done is to give the fifth of Husserl's *Cartesian Meditations* an ethical status, but in a different and more radical way than either Edith Stein or Max Scheler were able to imagine decades earlier.

The main point of Derrida's argument in *Violence and Metaphysics*, it seems to me, is that Levinas has in fact misunderstood Husserl's notion of empathy and that, upon careful analysis, this misunderstanding serves a quite positive and productive purpose. Levinas's own desire to move beyond Husserl's cognitive account of intentionality further demonstrates to Derrida that Levinas has failed to comprehend the most radical character of Husserl's appreciation of alterity. What Levinas mistakenly argues is that, for Husserl, there is always adequation between *noesis* and *noema*, such that any idea of "infinity" always and already presupposes a "false infinity" that the subject gives itself. Derrida responds that there is no more characteristic a theme for Husserl than *in*adequation: "But is there a more rigorously and, especially, a more literally Husserlian theme than the theme of inadequation? Of the infinite overflowing of horizons? Who was more obstinately determined than Husserl to show that vision was originally and essentially the inadequation of interiority and exteriority? And that the perception of the transcendent and extended thing was essentially and forever incomplete? That immanent perception occurred within the infinite horizon of the flux of experience?" (*VM* 121).

In the light of Derrida's pointed criticism of Levinas, let us take a brief moment to reflect what Husserl was up to in the fifth of his *Cartesian Meditations*. Through greater and more detailed pairing, Husserl argues, the Other gets "filled in," so to speak, such that I am motivated to believe that the body that is before my eyes not only moves but "holds sway" over its space in much the same way that I hold sway over my own. Motivated to constitute a sense of subjectivity in an alien body that moves in the world in a manner similar to the way that I move, Husserl observes that I am further motivated to spontaneously posit the other body with consciousness. The Other, according to his or her own constituted sense, points me to myself. Husserl says that "the other is a 'mirroring' of my own self and yet not a mirroring proper, an analogue of my own self and yet again not an analogue in the usual sense" (*CM* 94). Through imaginative variation I meet a givenness that has a one-to-one likeness with me. This absolute "given" is expanded into an embodiment, a "worldifying mundanization" which is itself founded upon an apperceptive grasp of myself as embodied. Into this embodied self enters the Other: a spatial, physical, living body like mine, only different. What is physically seen is this bodily being, whereas what is apperceived is its ego. Husserl comments:

> [The Other] is therefore conceivable only as an analogue of something included in my peculiar ownness. Because of its sense-constitution it occurs necessarily as an 'intentional modification' of that Ego of mine which is the first to be Objectivated, or as an intentional modification of my primordial "world": the Other as phenomenologically a "modification" of myself (which, for its part, gets this character of being "my" self by virtue of the contrastive pairing that necessarily takes place). It is clear that, with the other Ego, there is appresented, in an analogizing modification, everything that belongs to his concretion: first, his primordial world, and then his fully concrete ego. In other words, another monad becomes constituted appresentatively in mine. (*CM* 115)

What Derrida discovers is that contrary to Levinas's reading, Husserl in fact respects transcendence and infinity. According to Husserl, only consciousness is given to itself, and this through the apparatus of retention and protention. Internal time consciousness, therefore, is the condition of possibility of my knowledge of phenomena, even that of infinity. Levinas's ethical demand that I give infinite respect to the Other is thus not possible without apperception and the given phenomenality of the Other's body. Such appearance is precisely what Levinas refuses to grant to the face. Levinas argues that the phenomenal appearance of the wholly Other would reduce the radical alterity of the Other to that of a mere analogue or appendage of the constituting-I: "According to Levinas, by making the other, notably in the Cartesian Meditations, the ego's phenomenon, constituted by analogical appresentation on the basis of belonging to the ego's own sphere, Husserl allegedly missed the infinite alterity of the other, reducing it to the same. To make the other an alter ego, Levinas says frequently, is to neutralize its absolute alterity" (*VM* 123). This, Derrida notes, is the fundamental disagreement between Levinas and Husserl, namely, Levinas's rejection of Husserl's description of the constitution of the alter ego within my stream of lived experience. According to Derrida, Levinas's misjudgment results from a perceptual blindness on Levinas's part concerning the radical asymmetry that exists for Husserl between Self and Other according to the theory of apperception. What Husserl thinks he discovered via his theory of transcendental constitution is a unique phenomenon, namely, something whose unique phenomenality is discovered by a non-phenomenality. If something is not constituted, Husserl holds, then there is no experience of it. But what remains unstated here is Husserl's more radical notion that the transcendental monad is not an enclosed totality but is in fact pervaded (even constituted, in a particular sense?) by alterity. Derrida is quick to point out that Husserl's notion of transcendental constitution needs to be properly understood by Levinas within the larger context of apperception. According to Derrida, Levinas missed entirely Husserl's insistence that apperception, although constitutive, does not inhere totalization. Apperception describes how the Other comes to be in the order of experience; it describes empathy in terms of nonviolence, difference, dissymmetry, transcendence, infinity:

> Constitution is not opposed to encounter. It goes without saying that constitution creates, constructs, engenders, nothing: neither existence, nor the fact, which is evident, nor even meaning, which is less evident but equally certain. . . . [L]et us recall this warning of Husserl's, among so many others: "Here, too, as concerns the alter ego, the 'constitution of consciousness' [*Bewusstseinleistung*] does not mean that I invent [*erfinde*] and that I make [*mache*] this supreme transcendence." . . . The

> *Cartesian Meditations* often emphasize that in *fact*, *really*, nothing precedes the experience of Others. (*VM* fn.44, 315–16)[12]

According to Derrida, the meaning that Husserl affords to the doctrine of constitution via his description of apperception is not accepted by Levinas on Husserl's own terms. What is constituted via apperception for Husserl is the knowledge *of the relation to the Other*, not the Other. Derrida agrees with Husserl in the sense that we could not possibly speak of the totally or wholly Other if there were not, first, a phenomenality of givenness by the Other. Derrida charges that Levinas has fundamentally misunderstood what Husserl means by "constitution." Had Levinas grasped Husserl's position, he would be forced to acknowledge how close their positions in fact are:

> By acknowledging in this infinitely other *as such* (appearing as such) the status of an intentional modification of the ego in general,[13] Husserl gives himself the *right to speak* of the infinitely other as such, accounting for the origin and the legitimacy of his language. He describes the phenomenal system of nonphenomenality. Levinas *in fact* speaks of the infinitely other, but by refusing to acknowledge an intentional modification of the ego—which would be a violent and totalitarian act for him—he deprives himself of the very foundation and possibility of his own language. (*VM* 125)

§5. An Empathic Antipathy

Because Levinas is blinded somewhat in his rejection of Husserl's theory of analogical appresentation, he fails to grasp that the whole structure of apperception in fact respects the radical alterity of the Other and allows the constituting Ego to experience such transcendence without initiating violence against it: "The necessary reference to analogical appresentation, far from signifying an analogical and assimilatory reduction of the other to the same, confirms and respects separation, the unsurpassable necessity of (nonobjective) mediation" (*VM* 124). On the one hand, the basis of Husserl's respect for alterity is that for him all material objects are infinite and transcendent. This means that, in principle at least, no material object can ever be adequately given; what is given is an infinity of adumbrations and apperceptions *of* objects.

As Derrida notes, Husserl's phenomenology marks the height of respect for genuine alterity in two important ways. First, material objects can never be adequately given; hence, they are *always* other. Second, what constitutes the "interiority" of the Other person cannot, in principle, be adequately given, hence the Other is *wholly* (though analogously) Other. Husserl's doctrine of apperception essentially preserves the irreducible alterity of the Other as a sign of infinite respect. Contrary to what Levinas thought, Husserl in fact argues that ethics is preserved precisely on account that the Other is wholly, originary, infinitely, and transcendently other and, at the same time, like me, only different. Derrida notes the following: "It would be easy to show the degree to which Husserl takes pains to respect, in its meaning, the alterity of the Other, particularly in the *Cartesian Meditations*. He is concerned with describing how the other as other, in its irreducible alterity, is presented to me. Is presented to me, as we will see later, as originary nonpresence" (*VM* 123). On the other hand, the whole force of Levinas's argument lies in his conviction that material objects are not transcendent, inaccessible, infinite. Derrida notes that Levinas will not grant transcendence to material objects precisely because of his insistence that ethics is first philosophy. Ethics gives transcendence, ethics *is* transcendence. By the very process of privileging ethics, however, Levinas winds up in effect of depriving himself of offering any real account of radical alterity. Speaking about the wholly Other requires violence (language). In point of fact, Levinas (as much as he resists admitting it), has no other choice than to speak about the wholly Other in terms analogous to Husserl's theory of apperception. The mistake that Levinas makes is that he thinks the theory of analogical apperception makes the Other a "clone" of the Self, another "me," a domestication and assimilation that gets devoured by a totalizing economy of light, of vision, of the same.

Yet as Derrida testifies, this is precisely what Husserl's theory of apperception does *not* do. If the Other were not already another ego, then it would not—it could not—be part of the world, as originary, as subject. What makes the Other *other* is that the wholly Other has a form like me yet different or, rather, as Derrida says, the Other is of the same form as I am (i.e., another ego), but the content is different. Derrida charges that Levinas failed to see the conclusion to his own argument, namely, that if the wholly Other is always the human other, then its condition of possibility is a transcendental symmetry between me and the wholly Other qua other. "If the other were not recognized as a transcendental alter *ego*," Derrida says, "it would be entirely in the world and not, as ego, the origin of the world. To refuse to see in it an ego in this sense is, within the ethical order, the very gesture of all violence. If the other was not recognized as ego, its entire alterity would collapse" (*VM* 125).

My argument is that either Levinas's position inheres a kind of analogy or empathy, or else it fails on account of its own internal inconsistency. Levinas is clearly justified to emphasize the radical inaccessibility of the Other in order to give the Other an ethical, rather than a merely epistemic, origin. But he fails to acknowledge that transcendental violence is the condition of recognizing ethical nonviolence. Ethical nonviolence presupposes the Other as another *person*. This means that the Other qua other is always the human other and must be pre-apprehended in a noncognitive, emotive, bodily attitude. According to Derrida, "[D]issymmetry itself would be impossible without this symmetry" (*VM* 126). Hence, transcendental symmetry makes possible ethical asymmetry. Of course, what Derrida is driving at is his notion that dissymmetry constitutes a new kind of *economy*, an economy that he defines as the transcendental symmetry of two empirical asymmetries:

> The other, for me, is an ego which I know to be in relation to me as to an other. . . . The movement of transcendence toward the other, as invoked by Levinas, would have no meaning if it did not bear within it, as one of its essential meanings, that in my ipseity I know myself to be other for the other. With this, "I" (in general: egoity), unable to be the other's other, would never be the victim of violence. (*VM* 126)

Derrida refers to the possibility of a "pre-ethical" violence in terms of "an irreducible zone of factuality, an original, transcendental violence, previous to every ethical choice, even supposed by ethical nonviolence" (*VM* 125). What he means is that, in virtue of transcendental symmetry, I recognize in the Other that I have come upon an abyss, an asymmetry that is not cognitive but *ethical*. Turning now to Levinas, Derrida distinguishes the "form" of the Other as an ego, and the "content" of the Other's being. The mystery that comes to me appears first and foremost as mystery, as abyss, as person, as dissymmetry. Otherwise, Derrida notes, the Other would merely be reducible as a mere tool, an object-for-me. Hence it would not be an ethical subject, an *other* in the proper Levinasian sense: "The infinitely other cannot be what it is—infinitely other—except by being absolutely not the same. That is, in particular, by being other than itself (non-ego). Being other than itself, it is not what it is. Therefore, it is not infinitely other, etc." (*VM* 126). Derrida notes the paradox that is constitutive in Husserl's notion of the "play of the Same." On the one hand, if the wholly Other is the same as me (i.e., an alter *ego*), then it is radically Other; on the other hand, if the wholly Other is radically other than me (i.e., it is a mere *object*), then the wholly Other is not radically, that is, wholly, *other*. Derrida notes that there could not possibly be a "play of the Same" if alterity itself was not already *in* the same. Therefore, in order for the Other to be radically and wholly other, there must be some sort of symmetry, an empathic antipathy, a trace of the Other in the same, and a trace of the same in the Other. Derrida warns:

> We must reverse the terms: "Other" is the name, "other" is the meaning of this unthinkable unity of light and night. What "other" means is phenomenality as disappearance. Is it a question here, of a "third route excluded by these contradictory one" (revelation and dissimulation, *The Trace of the Other*)? But this route cannot appear, cannot be stated as tertiary. If it is called "trace," the word can emerge only as a metaphor whose philosophical elucidation will ceaselessly call upon "contradictions." Without which its originality—that which distinguishes it from the *Sign* (the word conventionally chosen by Levinas)—would not appear. For it *must* be made to appear. And the phenomenon supposes original contamination by the sign. (*VM* 129)

§6. A Reversal of the Reversal

Derrida's analysis of Levinas is not in the end a critique of Levinas. In fact, Derrida claims, Levinas's descriptive ethical insight of the Other is not any less radical for all Derrida's criticisms. "Levinas's metaphysics in a sense presupposes—at least we have attempted to show this—the transcendental phenomenology that it seeks to put into question" (*VM* 133). The fact that appresentation, analogy, intentionality, and so on is violence escaped much of pre-Levinas phenomenology. Levinas "opens up" a dialogue between phenomenology and its other that puts phenomenology into radical question. Levinas puts phenomenology "on guard," so to speak. What Levinas exposes is Husserl's inability to see that there is no pure seeing. The wholly Other alerts us to the structural violence that is built into phenomenology via the phenomenological reduction: "This is the opening of a question, in the inversion of transcendental dissymmetry, put to philosophy as logos, finitude, history, violence: an interpellation of the Greek by the non-Greek at the heart of a silence, an ultralogical affect of speech, a question which can be stated only be being forgotten in the language of the Greeks; and a question which can be stated, as forgotten, only in the language of the Greeks. The strange dialogue of speech and silence" (*VM* 133). According to Derrida, what finally makes infinite respect possible for Levinas is precisely what he rejects from Husserl, namely, that the *wholly* Other be regarded as another person, an alter ego. Nevertheless, what Levinas unconcealed was the very violence of structure itself. The structure of the wholly Other continuously disturbs—it "makes tremble," to use Derrida's words—every discourse that tends toward an ultimate conclusion. Consequently, the wholly Other is a functioning idea that disturbs the tranquility and complacency of every structure, every discourse, every institution, every *eidos* as thought and representation.

Nevertheless, the very idea of the wholly Other is impossible, except (of course) in terms that speak meaningfully and ethically of empathic antipathy. It is precisely this notion of a "non-empathic analogy" or a "transcendental symmetry" in the order of knowledge that makes possible an *ethical* asymmetry. In a particular manner of speaking, Husserl's notion of transcendental empathy ensures that the wholly Other remains radically open toward the unforeseeable future always and already yet-to-come.

In the end, Derrida concludes, Levinas is right, in part, by his insistence that saying is always betrayed by the said: "We say the *dream* because it must vanish *at daybreak*, as soon as language awakens" (*VM* 151). Haunted always by the dream of purity, Levinas dreams "the dream of a purely heterological thought at its source. A *pure* thought of *pure* difference" (*VM* 151). According to Derrida, the problem with Levinas is not that Levinas's dream is a bad dream, not in the least. What Levinas needs to do is to learn to call things by their proper names. The dream that he calls metaphysics is called by history "radical empiricism" (*VM* 151). But even this dream is a good dream, the dream of the pure other, the dream of non-philosophy, the dream of transcendence. In trying to call things by their rightful names, Derrida calls this dream *Judaism*. It is fitting, then, that the patriarch of *this* dream, of the dream that dreams all things, of the dream that dreams to name all things, is Adam, to whom "Yahweh God brought all the wild beasts of the earth and all the birds of heaven to see what he would call them; each one was to bear the name the man would give it."[14]

Part Four

Conclusion:
Empathy, Ethics, and Transcendence

Part Four

Introduction

Living in a world with others requires rigorous analyses that describe how others are given or constituted by consciousness in cognitive and emotive acts, that is, as ethical subjects as opposed to objects of utility. In this study, we have attempted to formulate phenomenological descriptions of the constitution of the "I" (or "Ego") and "the Other" in constant reference to this important ethical residuum. This is because every act of constitution is itself revelatory of higher-order value-acts. In describing how the Other *qua* other gets constituted empathically, I mean to emphasize that consciousness reveals a kind of ethical horizon by which everything that is constituted gets constituted in terms of value through the unfolding of phenomenological givenness. By "phenomenological" is meant that consciousness is not to be understood as a concrete thing such as an object in a tangible or physical sense. To be conscious means always to be conscious *of* something *as* something. There is no inside or outside of consciousness. What is given or constituted by consciousness is a significative content or perception—the world as such—whether real or imagined. The Other is therefore given *as* something; the Other remains bound to the same constitutive laws of apperception and analogical pairing by which consciousness grasps every Other as meant, whether given cognitively or emotively. Every act of consciousness thus grasps the Other *qua* other as an ethical act, in the sense that every grasping requires value-orientation. Some of the overarching questions we want to raise in these final chapters are the following: Is the constitution of the Other through empathy essentially cognitive? Or might there be a noncognitive element, perhaps even an emotive element to the process of constitution? How does consciousness constitute experiences of transcendence and alterity when the givenness of the wholly Other has no phenomenal content? Can a reciprocal or mutual model of empathy adequately describe an experience or understanding of ethics that is both generative and constitutive and thereby rests outside pure rational analyses and discourse?

Several early phenomenologists, including Stein, Ingarden, Heidegger, and Scheler, held that in terms of intersubjectivity, perhaps the most primordial human experience, existentially speaking, is the fundamental awareness that I am never alone. The Other is always and already present. This sense of alterity is constitutive, regardless of whether the awareness is thematized within the temporal sphere of ownness or felt emotively as an impending threat of objectification by the look or felt presence of the Other. Alterity thus functions as a condition of possibility of every experience of transcendence. Without the emergent givenness of the Other *qua* other, there could be neither identity nor difference, but merely the same. The primordiality of givenness of alterity is what appears as signification. Alterity allows the Earth to be an earth, a realm of transcendence and an experiential horizon of possibility and infinite tasks. Empathy opens up the world in its intersubjective experienceability. It *feels toward* alterity as an uncanny and non-thematic manifestation of a non-originary experience by which the Other is recognized as primordial and originary. The limitless phenomenality of the objective world presupposes the possibility of multiple centers of meaning that reveal infinite centers of meaning that remain inaccessible to finite apprehensions. Constituted by an infinite play of intersubjective givenness, material and psychic phenomena manifest the emergent disclosure of transcendence *as such*. In this way, empathy is revelatory; it points to the emergent givenness of transcendence-itself without being able to grasp such radical alterity as such.

A main focus of this study has been concerned with describing the significance of social ontology, namely, the emergence of alterity by the transcendental Ego and the ethical implications that arise from epistemological concerns regarding how the Other is encountered or constituted within the phenomenological attitude. Empathy opens up multiple perspectives of meaning that explore what can be known and the limits of such knowing in terms of the primacy of givenness of ethics involved in every I-Thou relationship. For example, the question "How can I be certain that other persons exist or that an objective world is possible as an ontological reality outside my cognitive constitution of it?" involves ethical and not merely epistemological concerns. How the other is constituted demands the primacy of an ethical response. If constitution—as

I argue—is intersubjective and social in application, then every act of perception constitutes, at the same time, an act of apperception. Ethics presupposes the Other *qua* other. In a phenomenological sense, perception involves both epistemological and ethical implications. In terms of critical phenomenology, the look of the Other is never value-neutral; to "see" the Other means to-be-seen *by* the Other.

Empathy in terms of social ontology thus explores how the world is given to consciousness; it neither denies nor casts doubt on the objective givenness of the world *as such*. Classically formulated by Husserl in the order of knowledge, the phenomenology of empathy ensures the unknowability and primordiality of alterity by describing how the Other is constituted through pairing *as other*, that is, as a for-itself like me, only different. The phenomenal appearance of the Other thus marks the emergence of an event or unfolding or encounter of manifestation in terms of ethics as an abyss of expectation. Otherness is indicative, it points always to something beyond itself. The Other *qua* other initiates a kind of revelatory blindness or apophatic experience of transcendence. Such experience of the givenness of alterity anticipates an incomprehensibility of the meaning of the world alongside its social environments in which I exist: who I am, the limits of what I can know, how I should act. Consequently, empathy describes the givenness of the Other in terms of a feeling of uncanniness, a *mysterium tremendum*, an apophatic lack of apprehension that is at once both destabilizing and constitutive. Here, empathy engages ethics as a kind of first philosophy in a Levinasian sense; it announces a rupture and dis-rupture to every metaphysical order of things. It is this sense of givenness—that is, empathy as an ethical event of withholding or as the apophatic emergence of a cloud of unknowing—that in effect grounds the subject of our concluding inquiry.

I submit that what empathy makes manifest is that the Other is never given without some kind of accompanying ethical (dis-)orientation. Every act of givenness entails a genealogy or pre-cognitive stream or flow of nonconscious life by which the Other *as other* is both perceived and valued. A primary ethical analysis concerning the phenomenology of empathy, then, requires stepping outside merely binary-based ways of seeing and experiencing reality. The phenomenology of empathy explores ethics as first philosophy and not as a derivative of cultural ideology or as the artificial construction of social values writ large in terms of grand historical narratives. The emergence of a nonbinary relationship between ethics, ontology, and epistemology is therefore an underlying theme of the investigation of the phenomenology of empathy. How does the data of foreign experience point to differing structures of value-acts from which foreign experience is comprehended *as such*? The problem of empathy—that is, the phenomenological description of the givenness of other persons—must be recast in terms of intersubjectivity and the emergent ethical relationship between epistemology, ontology, and metaphysics. The question "How can I have knowledge of other persons?" poses an incomplete articulation of the problem unless two other questions are posed alongside it: (1) "What is the *origin* of such knowledge?" and (2) "How is experience of the Other gained and warranted in terms of ethical actions?"

Ethical questions concerning the givenness of other persons are particularly poignant in a post-9/11 world. In the increasingly violent decades since the barbaric attacks on the World Trade Center took place, the world has witnessed a profound proliferation of cultural violence, discrimination, and intolerance. Despite so-called self-evident truths of Enlightenment jurisdiction, what is often designated as "the Other" remains an object of fear and suspicion. In effect, through the lack of cultural empathy, the Other has effectively been disinvited from the totality of givenness of what can be known and loved. The epistemological extent by which foreign experience can be grasped, described, and comprehended remains a derivative appendage to the primarily ethical concern about how human persons are constituted at all. In other words, if the Other is absolutely other (*tout autre*) and thereby absolved from all relationality, to what extent is it possible for me to enter into a genuinely ethical relationship with another person in general and with persons who hold vastly different value systems than me in particular? The epistemological impossibility of establishing an ethical relationship with someone who does not share cultural or religious or political or social or economic or gender or racial assumptions describes, in a nutshell, the (impossible) task of this project. In effect, the phenomenology of empathy alludes to the primacy and the impossibility of ethics as an epistemological project in terms of the givenness of values and other persons.

Throughout our investigation, we have defined transcendence as the experience of fecundity, of a kind of radical alterity. Since transcendence points to what is not there, transcendence cannot be described adequately by recourse to language and the sufficiency of reason. Empathy attempts to articulate transcendence and the indescribability of the non-phenomenal appearance of the other *qua* Other in terms of a kind of radical alterity that itself must be investigated beyond totality and infinity, beyond language. Consequently, I submit that the phenomenology of empathy requires an account of consciousness that includes an encounter with the Other precisely in terms of radical alterity, immanence, and transcendence. Such encounter of a non-encounter means that constitution has to be rethought outside of traditional intellectual abstractions in order to expose the very limitations of cognition that empathy attempts to transcend. The self—that is, the "I" of human subjectivity—encounters other human beings "as-if" both similar to yet alien from itself. This "encounter" gives me a cognitive-based experience of the Other as a being similar to myself while, at the same time, *feels into* the Other an uncanny and unsettling experience of transcendence, a gut-based emotive experience of unfathomable mystery, an experience of such radical alterity that what is Other remains inarticulate precisely in order to preserve the mysterious transcendence and otherness of the Other *qua* other. Empathy announces that the Other *is not me*. My argument is that the phenomenology of empathy describes an emotive capacity that is mutually reciprocal alongside cognition but is not reducible to cognition. Every encounter with every other constitutes, at one and the same time, both a judgment upon the individual subject perceiving the Other as external to itself and a judgment that involves the objective nature of its own perceptive reality. Empathy "gives" the Other to me as an object of inquiry and, at the same time, withholds the Other via experience of transcendence. Through pairing and analogical variation, the Other's subjectivity is both given and withdrawn. The Other remains a being of inaccessibility, radical alterity, transcendence, and mystery. Empathy ensures that the transcendence of the Other remains a cloud of unknowing, that is to say, empathy ensures that the alterity of the Other remains other. Alterity is nonreducible; it is neither an object of value nor cognition. The phenomenology of empathy thus describes the origin of consciousness in terms of an infinite ethics and an impossible givenness rather than as an epistemological rule of cognition. As an ethical encounter grounded in the nonappearance of radical alterity, empathy opens up complexities of meanings and realms of mystery regarding the transcendence of the Other. Such radical alterity remains unrecognizable in terms of what can be given by cognition alone. In effect, what we are attempting to describe by empathy is how "the Other" is apprehended ethically through the nonappearance of transcendence. Given by the nonappearance of radical alterity precisely in its non-givenness, the Other is given by being other-than given, by being given in the trace of non-phenomenal transcendence.

As we have seen, themes and connections between empathy and ethics have been widely explored in the humanities and various social science fields, including law, sociology, women's studies, political science, social work, peace and conflict studies, psychology, and redistributive and transitional justice. Given the interdisciplinary nature of such research, it is essential to make a final phenomenological intervention in this important and timely conversation. By framing a discussion about ethics within phenomenology, we have been able to explore empathy according to three basic models or approaches by which philosophers within the phenomenological tradition have historically attempted to engage critical reflection of key issues. In the first model, we see that one could argue that empathy should be primarily understood as a particular act of mind that allows us to grasp the sense of what the other is experiencing, including ethical content. Here, one would need to show how, for example, Edmund Husserl held that empathy is not only an act rooted in consciousness but a transcendental condition of possibility of thinking itself. Second, we discussed how empathy can be amplified in a discussion of value-making and *ordo amoris*, for example, as developed in phenomenological descriptions of intersubjectivity, as with Max Scheler and Edith Stein, or in terms of fallenness and inauthenticity, as with Martin Heidegger. In this second model, the human person is constituted within a reciprocal nexus of social values and contagions. Described in terms of reciprocity, empathy moves from a transcendental and mainly epistemological framework to an ethical one. Third, we explored how empathy can be described as a unique ethical capacity that describes the Other as an experience of infinite transcendence and radical alterity. Consequently, empathy in this third model must be mobilized as a unique ethical power of human beings, thematized and situated with and against thinkers like Levinas and Derrida.

What is ultimately needed, however, is a fourth model that offers a clearer unpacking of what the ethical capacity of empathy looks like, distinguishing it, on the one hand, from sympathy and reciprocity and what others say about empathy, for example, in care ethics, while at the same time holding to the inherent tensions and apophatic limitations imposed by every I-Thou encounter that entails the a priori experiences of genuine transcendence and alterity. In the final section of this study, I shall articulate an intersubjective model of empathy that draws inspirationally from Edith Stein's social ontology in order to give voice to what I call an "ethics of infinite respect." A kind of ethics that remains rooted in various tensions in and against phenomenology itself would constitute a particular kind of *ethos* or way of grounding one's existential orientation in and to the world. Empathy defined phenomenologically in terms of self-transcendence would thus manifest a deconstructive kind of ethics, as opposed to an extrinsic and formalistic kind of ethics determined principally by concepts and rules.

Chapter Ten

Gender and Reciprocity

§1. A Review of Empathy

Let us take a moment to review the phenomenology of empathy as presented thus far, that is, in its historic and thematic development, especially in early twentieth-century social and philosophical thought centered around Husserl and his students and colleagues from the 1910s and 1920s. We began our discussion noting Husserl's keen opposition to psychologism and how he wanted to offer a strict epistemological account of constitution that did not reduce the knowledge we can have of objects (including other persons) to mere psychological states or moods. Husserl's goal was to present a phenomenological description as to how consciousness must unfold in the order of knowledge. In the fifth of his *Cartesian Meditations*, Husserl developed a theory of empathy that posits a monadological point of departure, meaning that the alter ego is constituted through an act of pairing and an "as-if" analogy motivated by an encounter within my stream of consciousness between my own live body and the perceived animate body of the Other. The description of the constitution of the Other by transcendental apperception defines Objectivity as the realm constituted by the public, by what is shared by a harmonizing synthesis of monads and described by Husserl as transcendental intersubjectivity. *Einfühlung* thus describes the process by which individual ego is motivated to apperceive alter ego as an embodied spiritual being, that is, as a for-itself like me, only different. Hence, the notion of Objectivity is founded on intersubjectivity, on a model of empathic reciprocity whose own cognitive roots draw from the rich soil of transcendental monadological constitution.

Reactions against Husserl's account of transcendental constitution dominated phenomenological discussions after the publication of *Ideen*. Edith Stein, for one, adhered to Husserl's realist phenomenology while also wrestling with what she perceived as Husserl's turn toward transcendental idealism. She was deeply concerned that Husserl's privileging of the transcendental Ego in descriptions of constitution weighed phenomenology down with charges of solipsism that resulted from Husserl's strict adherence to monadology. In her 1915 dissertation on empathy, Stein presented a largely Husserlian-inspired phenomenological description of *Einfühlung* that explored the givenness of foreign experience in terms of sociality, affectivity, memory, and human emotions. Drawing as well from Scheler's belief that a "social nexus" of *ordo amoris* presupposes an essential element of the human person, Stein attempted to flesh out Husserl's transcendental account of empathy—for example, as developed in his lectures on Nature and Spirit in the early 1910s (with which Stein was familiar) and as she was intimately aware as the first editor or redactor of what was posthumously published in 1952 as *Ideas II*—by redescribing the transcendental Ego in light of a pure-I in accounting for the givenness of foreign experience and "fellow-feeling." Influenced by both Scheler and Husserl, Stein sought in her early phenomenological works to identify different aspects of the constitution of the human person in terms of culture, community, and values, at least in terms of the givenness of foreign experience. On the one hand, she wanted to defend Husserl's description of egoic constitution against the indeterminacy of Scheler's "undifferentiated stream" of conscious life; on the other hand, she wanted to enrich Husserl's strict epistemological theory with Scheler's provocative idea that the *ordo amoris* grounds the givenness of foreign experience as such. Edith Stein was keenly aware of Husserl's lectures in the 1910s on intersubjectivity and equally familiar with ongoing revisions of his understanding of constitution throughout the 1920s. Since she served as Husserl's assistant and helped transcribe what was eventually published posthumously as *Ideas II* after writing her dissertation under his direction, I submit that Stein's initial understanding of the phenomenology of empathy was intrinsically related to Husserl's project, while also attempting to mark her own unique insights. In effect, Stein attempted to distance herself from Scheler's claim that there exists an *a priori* presence of the Other in one's own personal sphere of conscious experience while also attempting to temper Husserl's so-called transcendental turn that privileged the order of understanding over the order of experience.

Following Scheler's description of the human person in terms of *ordo armoris*, we can now note that Stein's descriptive analysis of constitution would be more radical than Husserl's strict epistemological description allows only if it can be shown how constitution intuits what is *different*, what is radically other, without having to subsume alterity within an epistemological horizon preset by language and discourse of the constituting Ego. In her doctoral dissertation, Stein appears to hint at such possibility but does not offer any concrete proposals as to how this might be achieved. Shortly afterward, in her Habilitation thesis written in 1919, she revisited this theme and further explored a reciprocal kind of relationship extant between individual and community.

Turning next to Heidegger, we noted that the stated rejection of empathy outlined in *Being and Time* is essentially a rejection of Husserl's confidence that the phenomenological reduction can provide philosophers with pure seeing or what Stein calls the pure-I. In opposition to Husserl and Stein, Heidegger holds that consciousness cuts the world to size by reducing it to a set of objects. In place of the phenomenological reduction, Heidegger substitutes an analysis of Dasein in its everydayness or what he terms the anonymity and inauthenticity of being-in-the-world. Rejecting Husserl's privileging of pure perception, Heidegger argues that Dasein is always already thrown among the of the public world. Long before individual Dasein arrives on the scene, he argues, Dasein is always already thrown into a common world in which Others are interpreted in the mode of tools and instrumentality. For Heidegger, empathy is a constitut*ed* mode of Being-with-Others.

Against Heidegger's ontological assimilation of the self by the *they*, Levinas argues that the very direction of intentionality needs to be reversed. In order to account for radical alterity, Levinas charges that all ontologies, including cognitive and emotive models of constitution, must effectively yield to ethics. Otherwise, the wholly Other becomes reduced to the Same by virtue of analogy, that is, according to a totalizing economy of apperception, assimilation, and articulation. Levinas reverses the Husserlian arrow of intentionality, effectually privileging ethics over epistemology. Finally, we noted that Derrida's criticism of Levinas's critique of Husserl's reduction maintains that *Totality and Infinity* in fact presupposes some sort of symmetry or analogy or "antipathy" that makes possible ethical asymmetry. In the end, Derrida surmises, nothing can escape the irreducible necessity of transcendental arché-violence, which of course is not to be confused with ethical violence.

§2. Empathy as Ethics

Several striking similarities in the phenomenology of empathy may now be noted between Husserl, Stein, and Levinas. First, we should note that each of these philosophers were exposed in their youth to a religiously Jewish inspired encounter with the natural world. Similarly, Scheler and Buber also drew from the rich heritage of Judaism and Rabbinic mysticism, which experiences reality in terms of mutuality rather than detachment. Second, it is important to observe that Stein, Husserl, and Levinas each suffered terribly at the hands of the National Socialist propaganda machine that dehumanized anyone considered "racially impure" according to its own insidious criteria. By the 1930s in Germany, the issue of the Other as an alien and foreign contagion bent on corrupting the mythic purity of the Aryan race began to take on a diabolical ferociousness that few could have foreseen twenty years earlier. Third, Husserl, Stein, and Levinas each believed that philosophy in general and phenomenology in particular could advance the personal and social forms of responsibility required for genuine ethical, cultural, and spiritual development. At the heart of their respective systems is the conviction that phenomenology is a life philosophy; that is, phenomenology is concerned with learning how to live as an integrated psycho-social, embodied, spiritual human being. And fourth, Husserl, Stein, and Levinas were each convinced that authentic self-development is intrinsically linked with the well-being of Others, with the primordiality of intersubjective communication.

In this regard, contributions to the phenomenology of empathy must be explored far beyond the scope of merely justifying why certain names should (or should not) be included in the philosophical canon.[1] I submit that the notion of empathy, for example, functions at heart as a kind of hermeneutic,[2] an attempt to understand the very nature of *understanding* itself. Predicated on intersubjective experience, empathy correctly grasps that "I" and "Other" are reciprocally constituted as being the same, yet different. What I propose is that a proper hermeneutic of empathy comprises ethical rather than merely epistemological implications.[3] In turning to Edith Stein as a source of reflection, we have noted that, for Stein, "ethical concern is deeply and thematically woven into . . . the ethical obligations arising in and with community, and the sense of communal responsibility for carrying out . . . social responsibility."[4] Empathy requires that the Other is (1) an irreducible subject who demands infinite respect and (2) the human subject toward whom I must show infinite concern.

Properly understood, the subject of such an ethics is not "a set of mere individual egos in monadic isolation, but a communal 'We-subject.'"[5] In effect, Stein's understanding of empathy *as how we understand* recognizes alterity and foreign experience as manifestations of a kind of givenness of transcendence. Such non-phenomenal givenness presuppposes a Husserlian understanding of hermeneutics and thus makes possible the phenomenology of social ontology as such. Mette Lebech notes, for example, that "Edith Stein's phenomenological perspective, accounting as it does in a unique way for both social construction and the phenomenon of valuation, lends itself not only to the integration of hermeneutical and phenomenological methods . . . but also to the analysis of human dignity in its phenomenal, personal and social dimensions. Stein's intersubjective values-theory . . . enables us to distinguish between the perspectives of the 'I' and the 'we,' while understanding both in their interdependence."[6] Although an ethics and a theory of understanding propose two different means, they tend to imply a unitive capacity in the way that alterity as transcendence is experienced as an ethical phenomenon, that is, as a hermeneutic of understanding.[7]

§3. Considerations of Gender in Acts of Empathy

The strict cognitive characteristic of Husserl's epistemological theory of ego constitution does not adequately account for affective phenomena such as how *emotions* and *feelings* experience the givenness of radical alterity and transcendence. Such an undertaking of affectivity, or what I call sensual empathy, was given scant attention in terms of constitution prior to Edith Stein's analysis: "This basic level of constitution has always been ignored so far" (*Empathy* 60). In modest ways, Stein seems to anticipate later phenomenological accounts of bodily constitution in terms of encountering the Other as foreign experience. In contemporary aspects, psycho-social impacts of gender and certain aspects of critical phenomenology have modified Husserl's "masculine model" of cognitive constitution even further. Hence, what might be described as a "feminine model"[8] of constitution involves emotive sensory impact and affective constitution, often focusing on first-person experience as opposed to third-person descriptive hierarchies. What results is not a rejection of Husserl but, I submit, a rather fascinating opportunity to explore deeper ethical insights into how gender and "other" differences contribute to contrasting images of the self.⁹ Carol Gilligan, for one, notes that ego psychologists have traditionally emphasized the role of the male self in determining the context from which people base decisions on ethical considerations. In her groundbreaking work, *In a Different Voice*, Gilligan rejects the notion that biology alone can adequately explain the development of the sexualized voice. She argues that women tend to focus on human bonds, relationships of care[10] and interdependence, and the feelings of the individual persons involved, whenever moral problems need to be resolved within the concrete context of a given situation. Conversely, men tend to focus on abstract principles and rational, cognitive rules (what the Frankfurt School calls "instrumental reason"), in order to establish an "ethic of justice and rights." Gilligan believes that women tend to emphasize a narrative of relationships that extends over time, whereas men tend to assume a truly just solution is one that is rationally and purely derived, one by which anyone following reason would necessarily arrive at the same conclusion—in a word, transcendental.

I propose that Carol Gilligan offers an interesting perspective of a reciprocally based account of empathy in the order of experience in contrast to Husserl's epistemological approach of monadological constitution in the order of knowledge. Gilligan, for example, argues that women tend to blur the relationship between self and other, not because they do not understand the Deuteronomic Law but because the very sense and preservation of bonds and relationships *constitutes* the meaning of justice. By learning to integrate one's love and hate for the same object, the feminine sense of justice tends to emphasize an experience of ambivalence and ambiguity that remains bound to every relationship. For men, autonomy is often equated with independence whereas moral judgment is relegated to a rigid symbolic equation. Contrarily for women, Gilligan notes, an emphasis is often placed on the intermingling of private and public, home and market, personal and social. Care for another person as subject and concern for another person's individual suffering mark the feminine sense of morality as reparation-oriented.

According to Gilligan, the male must learn to surpass all feminine traits within himself in order to claim his masculine identity and so assert himself *as* masculine. Hence, the male learns to subordinate his own emotive capacity to a higher cognitive realm as a matter of principle of reason. The feminine becomes an encounter of "otherness" *within* the male that the male must deny. We may now grasp an important characteristic concerning the nature of constitution itself. Rather than offering a theory of constitution that simply replicates Husserl's cognitive model, what I propose is a model of reciprocal givenness that attempts to draw a deeper significance of empathy in terms of the givenness of foreign experience as transcendence, as Stein herself seemed to hint in her dissertation but did not fully pursue. Turning again to Stein's project as a guide, such a model of empathy highlights the ethical relationship between empathy and transcendence beyond how *Einfühlung* has traditionally been approached, judged, and resolved in terms of the constitution of the alter ego. How might a reworking of Stein's articulation of the givenness of foreign experience, now writ in context of alterity and the transcendence of the Other, help us better grasp some of the keen ethical insights drawn from contemporary social ontology?

As a first step, let us agree that, for Stein, the human person is more than a *res cogitans* or a clear and distinct idea or an epistemological principle of self-sufficiency that must be defended at all costs. On the contrary, as we have shown, alterity is an experience of transcendence that as such cannot be fully exhausted or described within the order of knowledge. As Levinas notes, every genuine experience of transcendence carries with it an ethical and therefore radical sense of alterity; otherwise, what is "other" would only have the appearance of being other. And yet, what is radically Other must nevertheless include a trace of sameness, as Derrida argues, otherwise the wholly Other would remain unrecognizable such that any ethical asymmetry would be shattered. What is needed, then, phenomenologically speaking, is an ethics that constitutes the impossible, that is to say, an ethics that frees the alter ego from all rational, ordered, universal, and cognitive conventions and yet remains recognizable in the order of experience. Such a radical ethics of infinite capacity would clearly push Stein's notion of foreign experience to the breaking point. My point is that ethics requires transcendence, ethics is a command that we ascribe alterity beyond the order of understanding. What we discover in the order of experience is that alterity is always already visited upon us as a condition of every possibility. Ethics in its most radical form is concerned with what is infinitely other: it seeks the lost coin, the lost son, the lost sheep; it abandons the ninety-nine for the one; or, as Kierkegaard perused, ethics acknowledges that the individual is higher than the universal. Hence, the subject of ethics, phenomenologically speaking, concerns what is natural, pre-rational, chaotic, subjectivity, affectivity, emotional, pre-conscious—that is to say, the pre-thematic conditions that presuppose and thereby violate every strict cognitive model that describes empathy merely as an act of understanding. Such an undertaking would tend to reimagine transcendental constitution in a way that no longer appears to privilege self-sufficiency over interdependence, transcendancy over nurturance, universality over relatedness, cognition over affectivity, rationality over nature, culture over personal, the theoretical over the particular. What gets exposed by a more radical interpretation of empathy as an encounter with foreign experience is an ethics that co-privileges the order of experience with the order of understanding.

Let us again turn to Edith Stein for inspiration. In her analysis of empathy, Stein anticipates to some extent Maurice Merleau-Ponty's classic critique of Husserl by nearly two decades and, I submit, offers a reinterpretation of embodiment that can propose new insights into social ontology. She argues that a genuine phenomenological description of embodiment should be concerned with analyzing the fundamental, interpersonal, social structures of emotive, enfleshed experience. Consequently, although Stein follows Husserl's description of the psycho-physical individual as *Leib*, the composite of flesh and soul, I also read Stein in terms of anticipating to some extent Merleau-Ponty's phenomenology of flesh. For Merleau-Ponty, "I live in my body" means that the lived body is an entity that can never be known or defined in a completely objective way. Similar to Stein's rich description of embodiment and her rejection of the "body as object," what emerges phenomenologically (as both Stein and Merleau-Ponty note) is a unity of a single, integrated blending of mental, physical, spiritual, and emotional capacity structured around a unitive core identity, what Stein calls the "pure-I" of I myself. A description of enfleshed experience in terms of constitution could, phenomenologically speaking, deemphasize the primacy that Husserl affords to the role of cognition in terms of the constitution of foreign experience in the order of understanding.

Tellingly, Edith Stein also embraces Scheler's model, which describes the human person as a network of values and act-orientations, a play of deep-felt emotive experience that "emerges out of herself" and intertwines with other bodies in a dynamic and ever-expansive current, or flow, of consciously embodied social life. This stream or current of lived experience constitutes meaning intersubjectively, and it therefore offers a more critical approach to experiences of radical alterity than Husserl's epistemological structure appears to allow.

§4. Implications of an Emotive Motification of Husserl's Position

As early as 1915 in her refutation of Lipps, Edith Stein had argued that empathy is primarily a manner of appearing of *foreign* experience: "Strictly speaking, empathy is not a feeling of oneness" (*Empathy* 17). What this means is that, for Stein, empathy does not describe how foreign consciousness becomes "one" with me, but rather how we are different. Thus, empathy does not mean that I can "get inside the other's head" (as Lipps had proposed) but that I can only posit another primordial sphere to which I do not have intuitive or primordial access by processes of pairing, apperception, and analogy. Similar to Husserl, for Stein, empathy is a condition of possibility that makes cognition of foreign experience possible. But more than Husserl's order of understanding will allow, what I want to do is push what Stein means by "foreign experience" to a more radical level. How could "foreign experience" be described if it were so foreign, so radically other, that it resisted every attempt to define it? In other words, how might transcendence appear as the wholly Other, that is, in its non-phenomenality? To what extent can the non-givenness of the Other be a felt or affective presence of genuine alterity that arises from outside the egoic stream of consciousness?

Ethically speaking, empathy announces the Other by announcing what cannot be announced within the realm of reason and thought; that is to say, empathy announces the experience of a non-experience, the experience of the impossible, the non-givenness of a non-experience of a genuine encounter with a foreign subject *as such*. Accordingly, empathy constitutes what is other through a felt sense of dread or anxiety or uncanniness. What is important to note here, however, is that, phenomenologically speaking, what empathy constitutes is my awareness of the feeling of dread, not its object. The object of dread or anxiety or uncanniness is always already other-than what can be constituted since the object encountered is no object at all. What is given is the non-givenness of the origin of an affective awareness of transcendence. Like Levinas's face of the Other, the *mysterium tremendum* is visited upon me, disturbs my peace, renders every attempt to cognitively grasp such radical alterity as artificial and inconclusive. Otherwise, I could not know that the Other is a foreign experience, alien to my sphere of ownness. In a manner of speaking, Stein helps us deconstruct Husserl's notion of monadological constitution by pointing, perhaps blindly and pushing her analysis to a breaking point, to the unfolding of a co-primordial givenness of a *felt* experience of transcendence as a kind of non-thematic *un-knowing* in the order of understanding.

In terms of the natural attitude, alterity is always already present in the world before philosophy arrives on the scene. In the order of understanding, this means that theories of pairing and analogical imaginative transference is a constitut*ing* act, regardless of whether what is constituted is cognitively or emotively based. In either case, as Husserl noted, reciprocal constitution is a condition of possibility of describing an account of the constitution of the alter ego in my stream of consciousness through the motivation of pairing. However, what is meant by "empathy" in the order of understanding is not quite what is meant by "empathy" in the order of experience. By describing the transcendental intersubjective constitution of the Objective world through *Einfühlung*, it becomes clear that empathy is not used in a completely univocal sense in the two different orders of understanding and experience. In the order of understanding, empathy refers to a strictly cognitive or epistemological process by which the Other must be constituted as alter ego in my stream of consciousness. It describes how the other is re-*cognized* through paring "as its own originary source, but apprehended in a non-originary way."[11] In being motivated to pair my live body with the animate body of another live body like me, only different, the Other emerges as a subject analogous to my own self. Empathy "does not produce something novel over against the self."[12] Conversely, in the order of experience, emphasis is not placed on how the Other is re-cognized by me; rather, empathy describes the mode by which I come to experience *my own feelings* either originarily or mediatedly through my encounter with the source of radical transcendence, now enfleshed in a body like mine, only different.

If empathy announces a certain distance between I and Thou, then its task is to distinguish the other *from* me. This requires an ethical act. Consequently, we need to assign to empathy not merely cognitive status but as well an emotive or affective quality that describes the non-givenness and non-communicability of transcendence in terms of empathy as foreign experience. It is important to note that I am not proposing a rejection of Husserl's epistemological position, but rather to modify it and point it in a different direction in order to address and reorient some inherent tensions within Husserl's description of the order of understanding in terms of ethics and transcendence. For example, in speaking of empathy as a non-originary experience that points to an originary experience, I submit that what is given in empathy, in its origin, is wholly and radically transcendent from me. My argument is that we appear to have stumbled upon a significant problem regarding empathy as the givenness of foreign experience, the gravity of which neither Stein nor Husserl nor Scheler recognized in their timely discussions concerning the givenness of foreign experience as such. Upon closer inspection, however, it appears that what is originarily primordial as the wholly Other cannot be fully recognized, comprehended, or constituted cognitively. Alterity requires that there must as well be an affective or emotive co-constitutive element in the order of experience that is at least as equi-primordial as what is cognized—whether thematically or non-thematically—in the order of understanding.

We catch a small glimpse of this early on in Stein's dissertation. Following Husserl, Edith Stein acknowledges that the significance of empathy is to show that one cannot identify with the Other, which is the Lipps position they both reject. Rather, one must posit the Other as *ganz Anderes*. But is cognitive constitution as described in the order of understanding adequate for describing the Other as another thinking, conscious ego? It appears to me that a description of the constitution of the Other within my stream of consciousness in the order of understanding neglects an important element by which the nonappearance of the radical alterity of the Other in terms of the non-givenness of foreign experience must be preserved in the order of experience. I submit that what is required in every act of givenness is a phenomenological description of the nonappearance of transcendence, that is to say, a description that takes into account an affectivity that feels-into the givenness of alterity in a way that cannot be adequately thematized through the order of understanding alone. It is this affective capacity of constitution in the order of experience that needs to be explored and co-privileged along with cognition in order for an "ethics of empathy" to emerge in its radical otherness.

§5. The Significance of Affective Constitution in the Order of Experience

For Husserl, empathy may best be described as an experience of understanding (*Verstehen*) of a foreign self. Nevertheless, we have seen that empathy indelibly announces experiences of transcendence through feelings of uncanniness, of mystery, of an unfulfilled intuition (*Anschauung*), all of which may or may not be thematized through mental acts of cognitive description. Any attempt to rethink Husserl's theory of constitution outside the bounds of cognition would violate the order of understanding by which transcendental ego constitutes both the Other and the world as meaningful. But what about the order of experience? Although a theory of empathy in the order of understanding requires affectivity to be at least equally as co-constitutive as cognition, such notion of givenness could result in accusations of phenomenological heresy.[13] Notwithstanding, I propose that the order of experience engages a far richer and more complex understanding of the givenness of alterity, even radical alterity, than a pure epistemological model can (possibly) allow. Consequently, Husserl's epistemological theory of the constitution of the alter ego already at play in the *Ideas* of 1913 and in his lectures at Göttingen in the early-mid 1910s seemingly gave way to more complex descriptions of the lifeworld alongside growing emphases on intersubjectivity and social ontology at Freiburg in the 1920s and 1930s. It is a "felt" experience of a more radical sense of givenness of alterity that I now wish to explore. This less cognitively focused approach toward describing the appearance of transcendence requires learning "to speak of empathy as a 'blind' or 'empty' mode of knowledge that 'reaches' the experience of the other without possessing it."[14]

The tension between appearance and nonappearance of transcendence and the givenness of foreign experience in the order of experience is subtle, but important. Consequently, I now want to advert to the implications of what appears to lie fallow and perhaps unrecognized, though potential, drawing from Stein's analysis of empathy. I submit that (1) emotive givenness of foreign experience is at least as equi-primordial as the cognitive constitution *of* that experience and (2) non-primordial, foreign experience announces a primordial one.

Although Stein never quite comes out and shows her hand—perhaps she simply did not want to confess her "heresy" to the Master—it seems to me that an argument can be made that Stein's understanding of empathy as the givenness of foreign experience at least allows one to explore modifying a more robust epistemological approach of constitution by recasting constitution in the order of experience. "This *basic level of constitution*," Stein tells us, "has always been ignored so far" (*Empathy* 60).[15] Here, Stein is referring directly to "the empathizing of feelings" of foreign consciousness. She offers a rather interesting comment, though she does not underscore its significance: "On the other hand, our preceding demonstrations show that sensations cannot be assessed quite so narrowly. Emotional reasons should not cause us to separate what essentially belongs together. The comprehension of foreign experiences—be they sensations, feelings, or what not—is a unified, typical, even though diversely differentiated *modification of consciousness* and requires a uniform name. Therefore, we have selected the already customary term 'empathy' for some of these phenomena" (*Empathy* 60). Although the mention of affective or sensual empathy is intriguing, little further mention is made of it again, either by Stein or Husserl, apart from how emotions are given in terms of constitution, except of course in the final few pages of her dissertation, as discussed above.[16] Similarly, while Stein implies that foreign experience includes sensations, feelings, and emotions along with cognition, she does not adequately describe the implications of what this might mean in terms of the constitution of foreign experience. Still, it seems evident that if the constitution of foreign experience is not limited to cognition alone, then what is meant by transcendence described solely in the order of understanding remains deficient, lacking, and inferior without understanding of some sort of affective or emotive component to the theory of constitution in the order of experience. I believe this is what Edith Stein meant when she called the emotive component of constitution a "modification of consciousness." Although she does not spell it out in detail, Stein's (like Husserl's) account of constitution seems deficient unless the emotive is somehow co-given along with the cognitive in every genuine empathic act of foreign experience. Sensations, feelings, and emotions given in the order of experience "modify" the pure grasping of cognition given in the order of understanding. Of course, for Husserl (and Stein) constitution is not primarily cognitive or creative, but more like reception and recognition. It is nonetheless difficult to conjecture whether Stein and her contemporaries appreciated the implications of what a modification of Husserl's analysis of constitution might entail in order to account for a more radical sense of alterity and transcendence in the givenness of foreign experience. What does seem clear, however, is that although Husserl's work on emotions is important, Scheler and Stein, and others who shared their concerns, contributed tremendously to pushing Husserlian descriptions of pairing and empathy to profound new levels of insight regarding social ontology and critical phenomenology, especially in terms of ethics and transcendence.

§6. Emergence of Ethics as Social Ontology

Ethics requires that the cognitive distinctness that exists between I and Thou is not something that needs to be "overcome" in terms of abstract thinking. Such distinctness is constitutive of the a priori experience of solidarity itself. To be "one" with another person does not mean that I must shed my own skin and enter into the skin of another in order for there to exist genuine fellow-feeling. Rather, solidarity implies imaginative variation, an ethical apperception and sense of pairing that takes the historical givenness of I and Other (and other Others) in a serious and absolutely irreducible context. Such givenness of reflexive empathy "both precedes and transcends the circumstantial, variable factors—that is, the political, ideological, or historical shifting conditions that incessantly affect and transform human relationships."[17]

My contention here is that the phenomenology of empathy "emphasizes the interdependence of self and other in terms of ethical self-education."[18] Rachel Brenner seems to concur with this observation and further notes that empathy between I and Thou is an essential condition of possibility of my own ethical subjectivity. "This interdependence is indispensable to the self's autoperception as an unfolding personality. Only through the empathic encounter with the other can I see myself as I am from a detached point of view."[19] In effect, experiences of what we might call "reflexive empathy" enable me to obtain a better understanding of myself, and not merely a cognitive grasp of the Other. "This new self-knowledge offers a corrective to self-deception and allows me to develop my ethical potential."[20] Stein concurs that empathy can give me a more honest understanding of myself, since empathy contains dialogical and reciprocal aspects of self-correction. Descriptions of epistemological constitution do not engage alterity in its more radical givenness as foreign experience. Hence, empathy as the experience of foreign experience grasped in the order of experience emphasizes *ethical* aspects of difference and asymmetry.

Nevertheless, despite their differences in degree on this issue, for Stein, as for Husserl, the constituting "I" is constituted in its subjectivity via an empathic recognition of sameness and reciprocity, what Husserl calls pairing, in every ethical encounter with a Thou. On the one hand, what makes ethics possible is a recognition of reciprocity and sameness-in-difference between the "I" and foreign experience. On the other hand, Levinas observes that sameness and reciprocity do not permit the possibility of ethics. For Levinas, the Other is the absolute origin of ethics, since ethics requires that what is foreign must break or crash into the world always already predisposed to what is given. Opposed to Husserl's model of empathy that privileges being *with* the Other, Levinas argues instead that ethics is essentially being *for* the Other. By reversing the Husserlian arrow of intentionality, Levinas declares that ethics is prior to truth, prior to ontology, in the sense that ethics requires that I place the interest of the Other above my own personal (i.e., metaphysical) self-interest. Yet, as Derrida has pointed out, such ethical asymmetry is possible only on principle of a prior recognition of analogical symmetry. Whereas Husserl's model of empathy is based on pairing and Scheler's model of empathy tends to blur I and Thou in an undifferentiated stream, and whereas Heidegger's rejection of empathy appears to beg the question of others by stressing the primordiality of the they, Derrida's critique of Levinas's reversal of intentionality brings into the light a certain unnoticed affinity—though to vastly different degrees—of what is meant by the radical alterity of "foreign experience" between Derrida and Stein.

In this sense of the givenness of alterity, Stein and Derrida appear to share several important aspects in their respective approaches to what I call an ethics of infinite respect. Both see the phenomenology of empathy in terms of an ethical being *for*, as opposed to merely being "with," the Other. For Edith Stein and Jacques Derrida, the model and language of explication is different, but the equi-primordial co-privileging of self and Other hold several tensions in common. For Derrida, analogical *symmetry* is the condition without which ethical asymmetry is impossible; whereas for Stein, *solidarity* means that the Other is constitutive of the essential coming-to-be of the "I" as an ethical event constituted in the order of experience and not merely in the order of understanding. For both phenomenologists, the "I" appears to be *itself* as being-*for-the-other* in terms of constituting a "common ground" by which analogy (Derrida) and empathy (Stein) make possible ethics as phenomena.[21]

While I think a certain affinity between Stein, Levinas, and Derrida is worth pursuing, I do not want to imply that the similarity between analogy, ethics, and empathy is all-inclusive. There are significant differences between these three authors and their respective themes, especially in terms of Derrida's notion of transcendental arché-violence and Levinas's reversal of Husserl's arrow of intentionality, as well as Stein's enduring adherence to Husserl's methodology. Nevertheless, it appears to me that the notion of empathy—understood in its complex unfolding as explicated by Husserl and his students and colleagues in the 1910s and 1920s—continues to offer important correctives and insights in contemporary social ethics. In its broadest sense, empathy encompasses both analogy and ethics; it grasps what is similar yet acknowledges what must remain different and unthematized in every apperception. Stein's deference to the living body and her seeming openness to co-privilege the emotions in the order of experience underlines a deepening awareness of the role that alterity as foreign experience plays in every social ontology.

Empathy, therefore, unfolds or explicates or makes known a kind of transcendence in the givenness of the non-givenness of foreign experience. Empathy preserves the non-reducibility of what cannot be grasped in every individual human person; it makes present the nonappearance of alterity in the unfolding of being-for-Others. According to Brenner, "Stein suggests that ethical self-actualization takes place in growing self-consciousness, a process contingent on one's participation in society and on the empathic perception of the other."[22] Along with Derrida and Levinas, it is important to point out that Stein too rejects the notion that ethical self-actualization is achieved by the anonymity of the constituting monad alone. The I *needs* the Other in order to be itself. Without alterity, apart from transcendence, the I remains unfinished, incomplete; it needs the Other in order to be *ethical*, in order to be a *person*.

Chapter Eleven

Empathy and an Ethics of (In)Finite Respect

§1. A Proposal for a New Paradigm of Ethics

Because foreign experience presents itself as alien to my own primordial sphere of conscious life, the Other cannot, in principle, be originarily constituted through acts of cognition alone. Rather, I submit that genuine alterity and what is authentically other or *fremde* must as well be co-constituted in terms of affectivity in the order of experience. The unfolding of a primordial experience of a non-primordial experience was addressed by Husserl through pairing in his description of constitution and thus is a condition of possibility of empathy in the order of understanding. What is meant by "foreign experience," of course, includes what has been described throughout this study in terms of transcendence and ethics. By transcendence is meant the non-phenomenality of what is given precisely in terms of its non-givenness, that is, in terms of alterity and what must remain unthematized except as a felt experience of an apophatic non-experience, what might be described in terms of a *via negativa* or *mysterium tremendum*, and by ethics is meant the givenness of response to the transcendent needs of the other. Consequently, we have sketched the givenness of foreign experience incrementally, centered on historical and thematic descriptive accounts of empathy proposed by Husserl and several of his students and colleagues in the 1910s and 1920s.

First, we explored how Edith Stein offers an approach to the phenomenology of empathy that acknowledges Husserl's emphasis on constitution in the order of understanding while also attempting to describe emotions, feelings, and embodiment in the order of experience. Stein's model of empathy remains phenomenologically viable within an egological and monadological model of constitution yet, at the same time, addresses empathy as the givenness of foreign experience. Second, we saw how Levinas approaches ethics by describing radical alterity in terms of transcendence. As a command imposed from "on high," transcendence grounds ethics as first philosophy by imposing upon me both a demand from and a response to the unconditional needs of the Other. As we saw, this Levinasian sense of ethics as radical alterity in effect reverses Husserl's arrow of intentionality. And third, Derrida proposes a kind of asymmetrical antipathy that describes a trace of sameness within every encounter with alterity; otherwise, as Derrida notes, what Levinas described as the wholly other would be so radically and incomprehensible other that it would be impossible to encounter, let alone engage. Similarly, I have argued that Scheler's notion of an "undifferentiated stream" of consciousness between I and Thou is not only not practical but non-sensical. As Stein points out, if there is no distinction between "I" and "Other" in my own stream of conscious life, then I and Thou become interchangeable and nondifferentiated. Such a blending between I and Thou would sweep away all distinctions and violate not only the phenomenological method but every possible difference by which "I" and "Other" can claim autonomy and freedom in terms of bodily and psychic energy. In a similar capacity, Heidegger's description of the *they* in terms of the ontological structure of Dasein and the call to conscience denigrates empathy to a mere attitude or disposition of inauthentic Dasein.

Another way of describing ethics must be found that takes alterity as a constituti*ng* phenomenon in the order of experience. A description of transcendence as a non-phenomenal phenomenon must include alterity as felt experience that, at the same time, escapes full cognitive thematization, similar in terms of intentionality to what Rudolf Otto described as an experience of the numinous. Phenomenologically speaking, this means that every non-fathomable feeling in the order of experience must contain some level of positivity in the order of understanding, otherwise it could not be registered, either cognitively or affectively, as a phenomenon. The phenomenology of empathy thus requires at least a trace of reciprocity, what we earlier designated (for Derrida) as a kind of ethical asymmetry or shared capacity for intersubjectivity and communication, including an essential acknowledgment of solidarity as being-*for*-the-Other, as opposed to merely being-with-others. Without the givenness of these conditions, solidarity and reciprocity lack any kind of transcendental imperative needed to mark empathy as an ethical phenomenon. The givenness of these phenomena asserts that transcendence is never reducible to mere abstraction, to what is required by apodictic laws of cognition and logic. Rather, the Other is an a priori, pre-thematic condition of possibility, a for-itself like me, only different, another "I" who calls me into ethical existence by virtue of the fact that the Other is given to me always already embodied and in and through language. By speaking, the Other comes to me from an infinitely distant source that is both recognizable and strange.

These dual notions of (1) the constitution of the human person in affective or emotional experience and (2) "reciprocal solidarity" offer a significant contribution toward fulfilling each of the conditions outlined above.[1] Even more, a descriptive account of empathy that takes seriously the notion of transcendence in the order of experience prefigures several important aspects of contemporary "cultural feminism" in a number of important ways. For example, as Nel Noddings's observes in her landmark study of the ethics of care,[2] men's moral development differs significantly from that of women, such that women's empathic proclivity tends toward a unity of reflection, judgment, and emotion. Noddings's emphasis on care and the capacity by which care invites us to enter into a rich emotional life of intersubjective relationships with others offers an interesting insight into Stein's attempt to modify Husserl's strict cognitive approach of constitution with a turn toward feelings and emotions. "For Stein, the emotions are a way to know the soul of another, an intersubjective knowledge."[3] Antonio Calcagno muses that "Stein's reformulation of intentionality as care" suggests that, for Stein, "insofar as women are more empathic and more aware of the emotional life of others, one could insert 'care' as another descriptor of the female capacity for empathy."[4] This is an interesting observation and one that I support enthusiastically. Calcagno concludes: "Though Stein does not develop this point fully, one can perhaps see in her work an anticipation of the connection between feminism and the ethics of care."[5] I submit that Noddings's, as well as Gilligan's, observations appear to tie in with Stein's own emphasis on the central role and irreducibility by which the lived body constitutes acts of meaning through emotive and cognitive constitution. By exploring the connection between the rational and the moral, as well as implications of this connection regarding the genesis and status of genuine community, we may begin to see that the criterion of rationality is constitutive of the moral sphere and vice versa.[6]

What does this mean in terms of our discussion on empathy? For one, an ethics that addresses transcendence and otherness as a priori offers important contributions to contemporary feminism, since it questions the privileged status of a purely rationalist model of moral epistemology based on a strictly cognitive analysis. By attempting to include the constitution of the human person in emotional experience, our study of empathy anticipates to a large extent Gilligan's own "postmodern move of arguing that there are different patterns of moral reasoning."[7] Susan Hekman argues that what Gilligan demonstrates is that the "rationalist, abstract, universalizing pattern of moral reasoning is one way of moral reasoning, but it is neither the only nor the superior way. She shows that the contextual, relational model that characterizes women's moral reasoning is just as valid as the rationalist model."[8] The theoretical psychological view of the feminine gender, which traditionally sees the self as "oriented towards relationships and interdependence,"[9] is greatly enriched by an analysis of an ethics of empathy that argues in favor of the dis-privileging of the abstract masculine model of epistemology against the contextual feminine model of emotive constitution.[10]

I submit that the solidarity and symmetry that exists between I and Thou is not accidental but primordial. In an ethical sense, this notion of solidarity runs counterpart to Levinas's theory that the face of the Other impels me to become an ethical subject, though of course Levinas does not mean "subject" in the strict Cartesian sense of a "pure knower" who discovers truth through abstract rationality. Empathy constitutes the absolute singularity of my own unique personhood, it calls into question the care and concern I show for all those who are like me, yet different.[11] Without the wholly Other, I am *nothing*, not in the sense that I would cease to exist but in the more existentially significant sense that "who" I am is constituted in the order of self-experience and not merely in the order of understanding.

In circling back to Husserl and his early students and colleagues gathered around him at Göttingen and Freiburg in the 1910s and 1920s when he was lecturing on constitution, an important question needs to be raised: To what extent was Edith Stein aware of the radical direction in which Husserl's thinking could be taken? Such a question may be impossible to answer, but it appears to me that she remained too loyal a Husserlian to be able to anticipate, let alone pursue, the radical Levinasian direction in which Husserl's early description of the lifeworld and subsequent ethical analyses could be pushed. Levinas goes beyond Husserl in a more decisive way than Stein seems prepared to go, at least during the years 1913–1922, when she was most immediately under Husserl's intellectual influence. Nevertheless, I think it is important to note that Stein's contributions to the empathy project are profound. She attempts neither to synthesize the intricate ruminations of Husserl and Scheler into a "middle way" nor to reduce the constituting/constituted subject into a passive recipient of social forces.

Nevertheless, it is my position that Stein anticipates, though to a less radical degree, an analogous move made later by Heidegger, Levinas, and Derrida, and others.[12] Turning to the order of experience, Stein largely describes human subjectivity in terms of social and emotional reciprocity. In this way, the intersubjective is always already in place, and all relations are mediated, in a sense, by the public rather than the merely constituting monad. As with Levinas, so also for Stein there are some truths of myself that I simply cannot know from myself alone. The Other is a condition of possibility of ethical, religious, and existential meanings, especially as the Other opens up whole worlds of values in terms of creativity and fidelity that "I"-alone cannot have access to by myself.[13] Similarly, as Susan Bordo notes, the emergence and revaluation of epistemological and ethical perspectives underscores the fact that "different voices" describe elements of a social construction, characteristic of certain (though not all) forms of gender organization, and not merely the reified dualities of an "eternal feminine" and "essential masculine" nature.[14] Bordo writes: "That voice, which classical as well as contemporary writers identify as feminine, claims a natural foundation for knowledge, not in detachment and distance, but . . . in closeness, connectedness, and empathy."[15]

This last observation, of course, does not mean that Stein foreshadowed the brilliant exegesis done on Husserl by Derrida and Levinas[16] or foresaw all the intricacies that Husserl's epistemological project would anticipate in light of emerging trends in critical phenomenology; even less did she solve all the problems raised in her dissertation and Habilitation thesis. As noted in part two, Stein's model of empathy does not repudiate Husserl's theory of monadology but enriches it. Consequently, she is far less suspicious of "dialogue" and "community" than is the case with either Derrida or Levinas. In this way at least, I think it is fair to describe Edith Stein's descriptive account of empathy as a kind of ethics, a "model of reciprocity" that remains vulnerable to Levinas's critique of Martin Buber's overall project:

> To Buber, the *Thou* that the *I* solicits is already, in that appeal, heard as an *I* who says *thou* to me. The appeal to the *Thou* by the *I* would thus be, for the *I*, the institution of a reciprocity, an equality or equity from the start. Whence the understanding of the *I* as *I*, and the possibility of an adequate thematization of the *I*. The idea of the *I* or of a Myself in general is immediately derived from that relation: a total reflection on myself would be impossible and thus the elevation of the Myself to the level of the concept, to Subjectivity above the lived centrality of the *I*. . . . In my own analyses, the approach to others is not originally in my speaking out to the other, but in my responsibility for him or her. That is the original ethical relation. That responsibility is elicited, brought about by the face of the other person, described as a breaking of the plastic forms of the phenomenality of appearance. . . . Here, then, contrary to Buber's I-Thou, there is no initial equality. (Is the use of the familiar I-Thou form justified?) Ethical inequality: subordination to the other, original diacony: the "first person accusative" and not "nominative."[17]

Stein's emphasis on dialogue and community is as much the effect of a false sense of cultural optimism shared by many phenomenologists in the 1910s and 1920s[18] as it is a reluctance on her part to ask Levinas's more radical question, and here we may include Husserl's and Stein's as well, namely, "Does Buber's language so faithful to the novelty of the relation with others in contrast with the knowledge going toward being, break entirely with the priority of ontology?"[19] In effect, Edith Stein contributed a thorough and comprehensive phenomenological analysis on the problem of empathy and successfully raised questions related to Husserl's epistemological approach to constitution in terms of emotions and the primacy of community, as outlined previously.[20] What Stein failed to see, however, is similar to what Michael Murray acknowledges Gadamer also failed to see in Murray's critique of *Truth and Method*, namely, that the very concept of dialogue "depends upon dubious metaphysical postulates that are idealizing, reductive, and domineering." Murray continues, "Contrary to the postulates of dialogue, in real conversation partners often speak at cross-purposes, about diverse objects with conflicting interests, in languages that divide up speakers into incompatible groups, pursuing multiple and happenstantial aims. At its philosophical core, dialogue is really monological, the same seeking the same, and this shows in its axiomatic reduction of the partners to two, a binary relation excluding thirds and manys and meant to climax in the victory of agreement."[21]

What the phenomenology of empathy needs in order to respond to the infinite respect required by an ethics that takes the radical transcendence of the Other seriously is what Derrida calls the "field of the innumerable," that is, a way to overcome the exclusion of other others, of "thirds and manys."[22] Such inclusive non-exclusion posits an explicit assumption in every I-Thou relation, and I do not think an ethics of infinite respect can afford an exception to this rule. In the end, we are left in the wake of Husserl's *epoché*, facing the impossibility of what remains indeterminate and indescribable in every attempt to provide order to understanding. What is needed is what Kierkegaard called "fear and trembling," a kind of non-thematic, nonappearance that cuts through every cognitive analysis and washes against the tides of meaning and signification. But how to speak of what is unspeakable, unthinkable, unknowable? Even Gadamer notes that the notion of dialogue automatically presupposes that the two speakers speak the same language: "Only when two people can make themselves understood through language by talking together can the problem of understanding and agreement even be raised."[23] What is needed for a new kind of ethics that acknowledges empathy as the givenness of foreign experience is a new kind of language, or at least a new understanding of ethics as the limit of language. What is needed is a deepening retrieval of Stein's notion of empathy as foreign experience, a kind of understanding of alterity that requires further explication of constitution in the order of experience.

Every I-Thou relationship is an ethics of transcendence, even radical transcendence, since what is given in the Other is precisely a felt sense of what is not present, that is, the other's radical alterity, what remains *in pectore*, in one's heart, so to speak, and thus constitutes a non-phenomenal phenomenon revealed to no one. Stein appears to point toward this insight when she says that empathy opens up worlds of meanings hitherto closed to us: "Since the experience of value is basic to our own value, at the same time as new values are acquired by empathy, our own unfamiliar values become visible. When we empathically run into ranges of value closed to us, we become conscious of our own deficiency or disvalue. Every comprehension of different persons can become the basis of an understanding of value" (*Empathy* 116). We may thus conclude that worlds and meanings become accessible through empathy precisely in their non-accessibility. The world is never fully given, it is apprehended through pairing and imaginative variation, "as-if," but only haphazardly, perspectively, analogically. What is constituted in the order of understanding, then, always already includes what is not given, since the world always already escapes my grasp. This, I submit, is what Stein pointed to in her description of empathy as foreign experience, though the grasping of such radical and infinite otherness remains elusive and unthematized. In terms of ethics, empathy is constitutive. What is given in ethics, phenomenologically speaking, is the non-phenomenal givenness of the Other, that is to say, what is given in empathy is foreign experience, apprehended through modes of affectivity, transcendence, and traces of alterity, a kind of hermeneutic that opens up phenomenology as an infinite task.

§2. Is Empathy a Quasi-Transcendental?

What does it mean to say that empathy functions as a sort of hermeneutic? As Petr Urban notes, "The question of how the world can be given to us as an objective world appears for Stein, as well as for Husserl, as inseparably connected with the question of how we can know and understand others as subjects who relate to the same shared world as we do. Stein conceives of the act of understanding or knowing the other subject as an act of empathy (*Einfühlung*).[24] Hence, to understand another person means to "come to an understanding about the subject matter, not to get inside another person and relive his experiences [*Erlebnisse*]."[25] Empathy opens up realms of values hitherto closed off, values that may be constituted in emotional (as opposed to strictly cognitive) experience, such as indicated by Levinas's notion of being bathed in the elements and Stein's example of being transformed by someone else's joy. In speaking of "mass" and "social" contagions in her Habilitation treatise published in 1922, Stein inadvertently acknowledged her own growing frustration with Husserl's monadology on the one hand and Scheler's notion of an undifferentiated stream of pre-conscious life on the other hand. Nevertheless, it appears that even Stein herself fails to grasp the significance of her own ambivalence toward her two mentors. What she needs is Derrida's notion that difference is not a *binary relation*. "The other is not one of two, does not depend upon a common ground or an idol of consensus, and is not governed by a dialectic. The other is plural others—in their withholding and yielding, inaccessibility and accessibility, contentiousness and consent."[26]

Exploring Derrida's complex critique of Husserl in terms of the other, Michael Murray notes that "the *secret* of dialogue—secret since contrary to its outward significance and even hidden to itself—is its actually *monological* character. In this vein we could say that dialogue exhibits, trades upon, the structure of a monologue. . . . [Hence], the claim made is not that dialogue is not really possible, but that it is possible only in the form of monologue . . . that dialogue is possible only for those who already share a unity and have a common language, and precisely *not* between those who do not so share or speak the same language."[27] For Derrida, the exercise of dialogue within every so-called community tends to perpetuate a similarity of exclusivity between the same and the same. In the end, Derrida's critique of Levinas's (secret) longing for symmetry reveals a monological voice that makes dialogue and empathy possible *as such*.

By attempting to retrieve a more radical sense of alterity than monadology appears to allow in the order of understanding, what I propose is that empathy must essentially include what cannot be included, namely, the possibility that every understanding shared between I and Other, whether cognitive or emotive, can ultimately fail and lead to an abyss of misunderstanding. Empathy does not mean that I understand someone as if I can speak from their own experience, that is, in an apodictic sense. Rather, empathy points to the order of experience, to what Stein termed "foreign experience," to a felt experience of incomprehensibility that is constitutive in every act of apprehension. Empathy entails the impossible. Empathy entails an act of interpretation, a kind of pairing or imaginative variation of what it would be like were I to step inside another person's skin, knowing all along that this is precisely what I can never do.

We may thus conclude that empathy is structured by what Derrida calls the impossible: both an affirmation of what it is like to be another along with the affirmation that it is impossible to know that. The significance of empathy lies not in what is imagined or comprehended in terms of analogizing the Other, but in what is left behind, what remains unfinished, deficient, tentative, *other*. Empathy points not to clarity and distinctness but to what is always held back in secrecy, not to the circularity of all understanding or the immanence of dialogue but rather to infinity and even to infinities *beyond* infinity that make it impossible to close the circle or to reach the other shore. The condition of possibility of empathy is the condition of its impossibility. In this sense, one could argue that, rightly understood, empathy is a quasi-transcendental.

The notion that empathy manifests the givenness of the impossible is perhaps best characterized by Jean-Luc Marion, who holds that givenness "does not limit itself to the very restricted case of the phenomena of revelation but defines in a universal way all phenomenality."[28] Although the face of the Other first addresses me, what the face signifies is not an I-Thou relation but a relation with "thirds and manys," with other others and infinities of others. What, then, is given in acts of empathy? Drawing from Marion, let us say that the Other is given and, at the same time, is constituted by a secret, given in the mode of a non-givenness, which is what apperception means. The Other *comes to me* as a given, "thus from and within a givenness."[29] Yet, what is given when the face beyond the face speaks is not the Other but the givenness of the command of ethics to listen, interpret, judge, (mis)understand, respond. What is given in empathy is precisely what cannot be given: the Other as the subject of an ethical address. In effect, it is the address from the Other that gives me *to* myself, that "constitutes" me, so to speak, in empathy, that is, as a being *for* others.

The infinity of the Other is thus revealed as a condition of possibility of an I as ethical subject-*for*-the-Other. Levinas wonders, "Is not the *for the other* itself of sociality concrete in *giving*, and does it not presuppose *things*, without which, empty-handed, the responsibility for others would be but the ethereal sociality of angels?"[30] Empathy points me in the direction of transcendence, that is to say, in the direction of the infinite only once the Other opens her mouth and speaks. Empathy, therefore, is constituted ethically by acts and responses. First, I must look into the eyes of the Other and recognize the one standing beside me. Second, I allow the Other to speak. Third, I allow myself to be moved by the Other, and only then should I attempt to respond. If I attempt to respond to the Other without recognizing her radical alterity *qua* other, I will eventually learn to resent and hate the Other, who will be seen by me primarily as an object of endless obligation. Again, we turn to Husserl, whose description of constitution in terms of pairing and analogical variation entails recognition and reception. When I "see" the other, I do not just see him; I "see" him seeing me. We are "as-if," one (un)like the other.

§3. Empathy, Transcendence, and Imagination

Clearly, one of my goals in this book has been to introduce Edith Stein's work on empathy to a broader audience and to place it in conversations with Husserl and his students and colleagues, as well as the wider phenomenological tradition, including points of similarity with ethics, deconstruction, and contemporary feminist thought. In that vein, it is important to offer some final reflections outlining how the phenomenology of empathy can enrich the field of critical phenomenological research. To begin, let us note that empathy requires at least five essential ethical qualities: (1) an emphasis on intersubjectivity, (2) a recognition of the particularity of others, (3) the complementarity of "play" between individual and community, (4) a rejection of the privileging of cognition over affectivity, and (5) the significance of the "first-person" embodied, concrete Other as opposed to, say, the notion of a "generalized other" or a "third-person" autonomous alter ego.[31]

Consequently, the phenomenology of empathy cannot be described in strictly epistemological terms; it must include an ethical description as well. What is important in understanding empathy is not so much whether the Other is given cognitively or emotively, but rather that the Other is given *at all*. What this means in terms of ethics is that any notion of the autonomous ego—the fully individuated and somehow disembodied "third-person" subject—"is not in any *a priori* sense a moral or human given." Barbara Marshall notes that several contemporary feminist theorists "have begun to articulate conceptions of autonomy that are premised not simply on separation but also on the experiences of mutuality, relatedness and the recognition of an other as a full subject. This entails not a rejection of the concept of autonomy, but a critical reinterpretation."[32]

What this means is that the thing, the *what*, the object of my intention, namely, the object of duty, say, or perhaps the object of my love, whatever it is to which I offer ultimate concern, constitutes *me*. This is what thematically distinguishes first-person critical phenomenology from third-person epistemological phenomenology. In effect, empathy does not tell me who or what I am but rather *whose* I am. To whom do I belong? To whom am I committed? Empathy does not allow me to "stand in for someone else," but rather it awakens in me a deepening awareness that every act of cognition, every act of feeling and intelligibility, every conversation and affective moment of mutual understanding must of itself be necessarily oriented as a first-person event and irreducibly appropriated as *mine*. In empathy I am never simply "given" the Other. The Other is given, but what is given is given as necessarily transcendent and irreducibly *other*, grasped as beyond my grasp, contextualized in particular linguistic and social frameworks that mark the limitations of what I can know. Despite the multiplicity of ways that I am engaged by the Other, empathy requires that I am always already involved in a moral and political context that acquires an image of the Other *that is itself* constituted from my own unique, embodied, particular, concrete standpoint. In this important aspect, empathy is constitutive.

Arne Johan Vetlesen concurs. "Empathy," he attests, "originates and is fostered within a small-scale setting, where communication takes place on a face-to-face basis and where the participants are physically co-present. The genuinely *moral* significance of empathy lies in its other-directedness."[33] Although he does not mention Stein's work directly, Vetlesen nevertheless concludes that, as with Stein, empathy "takes an act of imagination of mental abstraction to extend one's empathy to unknown and nonexperienced others. . . . *This extension is exactly what takes place in solidarity.*"[34] Vetlesen further notes that empathy as an ethical event of transcendence challenges us to respond "in a morally appropriate manner to what happens to abstract and absent others with whom we have never interacted . . . it is not a one-sidedly or even predominantly a cognitive accomplishment; rather, it is a complex process involving the interplay of cognitive and emotional faculties."[35]

The similarity between Vetlesen's observations and the description of the constitution of the human person in emotional or affective experience may offer an insight into overcoming cultural distances as well. Could the imaginative adaptation of a foreign perspective help bring light and intelligibility to what appears on the surface to the perceiver as merely random, or incomprehensible, or even capricious acts of violence? Does empathy require that we extend an ethic of solidarity to those who live outside our particular cultural and linguistic and religious communities? Is there an epistemological justification for implementing such exclusion, or is Levinas right, namely, that ethics precedes epistemology? In an age of biotechnological terror, in which entire populations are held hostage by suspicion and misunderstanding and where foreign cultures and even rival political perspectives are viewed with mistrust and grave apprehension, the answer to this question seems most urgent. In our analysis, we have shown that Husserl's privileging of epistemology in his description of constitution is not sufficient for appreciating adequately the phenomenology of empathy in all its *otherness* and complexity.

My argument is that a proper phenomenological description of empathy is required for developing bonds of respect toward persons with whom we, at least initially, may be inclined to dismiss or even dislike, to those often designated as "other others." Empathy is a condition of possibility by which the self is invited (rather, commanded) "to extend one's empathy to unknown and nonexperienced others (or, to be more precise, to secondary, as opposed to primary experienced others)."[36] As Vetlesen notes, "It is not only that ego's empathy relates to alter, sets up a relation, and establishes some emotional tie and personal bond between the two; it is also that the very origin and initial cultivation of ego's capacity for empathy can be traced back to an interpersonal relation . . . as the setting that is the *conditio sine qua non* for the emergence of empathy."[37] I submit that what is needed to understand the relationship between empathy and transcendence as a form of ethics is less emphasis on constitution as cognition and more emphasis on constitution as reception and recognition. In proper perspective, it seems to me that Stein's work on empathy and community ultimately elucidates the formal role that Husserl assigned to pairing. What is given in pairing is not prioritizing either oneself or the other, but the mutually reciprocal situation in which each begins to distinguish one from the other. Rightly understood, what Husserl means by pairing in the Fifth Meditation is similar to what Stein means, for example, when she distinguishes one's own feelings of grief on behalf of the unit (or state) at an experience of loss and what one feels at the grief of loss on behalf of oneself. Empathy commands that I take seriously not merely the appearance of the Other, which happens under the conditions of the constituting ego, but the Other as *revelation*, that is, the manifestation of the transcendence of the Other *on its own terms*.[38]

§4. Empathy and the Analogical Imagination

A reciprocal theory of empathy requires adherence that some sort of symmetry is necessary for ethical asymmetry. To this end, I have attempted to balance Husserl's largely epistemological description of constitution with reference to another side to Husserl's description of constitution, one that sees constitution less as cognition and more as recognition. I think this emphasis is in part what Edith Stein also saw as a "missing lacuna" in Husserl's description of empathy, namely, the role of empathy as a condition of possibility of ethics. Perhaps what is most surprising in all of this is how Husserl, Stein, and Levinas each advance, to a more or lesser degree, the idea that the Other as transcendent not only can appear in terms of immanence but in fact must do so. Otherwise, as Derrida notes, the Other simply will not appear at all. Pairing and analogy is a constitutive condition of possibility of givenness and manifestness of the alter ego in its otherness as well as its similarity. Apart from the conditions of the possibility of givenness, the Other could not be revealed or manifested qua other, at least not in a phenomenological sense. It is therefore this sense of the givenness of the hiddenness of transcendence that makes empathy, and therefore ethics, possible as such.

What is significant here is that by pointing to analogy as the necessary condition of the possibility of having knowledge of the Other *qua* other, we turn again not only to Husserl but to Husserl's teacher, Franz Brentano, and even to his source of inspiration, St. Thomas Aquinas.[39] *Adequatio rei et intellectus* was Aquians's mantra, adhering to the notion that the understanding of the knower must be adequate to the thing to be known.[40] Essentially, Thomas argued that all knowledge—including even knowledge of God as wholly/Holy Other—is a matter of reception and, as such, must appear always in terms of immanence, that is, according to the mode or condition of the perceiver. In Timothy McDermott's modern translation of the *Summa*, Aquinas notes the following:

> [O]ur bodily eyes do not perceive peoples' life directly: rather, as soon as our senses perceive the people, some other cognitive power accompanying our senses perceives their life. To be known a thing must be present in the knower, so how it is known depends on how it can be present, given the ways in which knower and known exist (Ia, 12.4). . . . Human minds, existing in bodies, know first the natures of material things, and by knowing the natures of what they see derive some knowledge of what they cannot see . . . by way of analogies. (Ia,84.7)[41]

What Thomas is driving at is his notion that the other, every other, the human other, even the (w)holy Other, that is, even Levinas's notion of the Infinite, *must* appear in terms and conditions that the active intellect can understand and (ap)perceive according to its own appropriation, hence, within a horizon of possibility: *Unde ens est proprium obiectum intellectus* (Ia,5.2). Aquinas himself argues not only that "the thing known is in the knower according to the mode of the knower" but that "the knowledge of every knower is according to the mode of its own nature" (Ia,12:4).[42]

A similar insight may be attributable according to St. Thomas's account of analogy. For Thomas, apperception and analogical imagination constitute what may be described as the very quintessence of Husserl's description of the appearance of transcendence, now set in terms of the description of the alter ego as depicted in the fifth of his *Cartesian Meditations*. Based in pairing and analogy, empathy is the necessary condition of possibility of every appearance of transcendence in terms of what is given as different, other, foreign. Taken in this context, alterity, even the most radical alterity of the *tout autre*, must reveal itself always in terms and conditions of possibility required by the perceiver. Therefore, it is necessary for the Infinite to appear in its (non-)phenomenality in order for the perceiver to grasp the transcendent *at all*. According to Levinas, however, the possibility of the Infinite condescending to the conditions of the finite perceiver violates the very essence of the Infinite's own infinity, it "undoes" the absolute ethical transcendency required for it to be wholly Other.

Well, it *almost* violates its own infinity, as Derrida so cleverly notes. We may finally conclude that empathy is an appearing that is not an appropriation, a giving that also remains a withholding, a "feeling-into" foreign experience that does not blur the distinction between I and Other but rather *constitutes* the ego as an ethical being, a value-being, an embodied act-being of infinite concern *for the Other*. Drawing on Edith Stein's description of empathy, we acknowledge that the Other cannot be reduced to a foreign experience that is merely apperceived cognitively by the constituting ego, but it must as well adhere to some aspect of the constitution of the person in terms of a felt or affective experience of alterity or transcendence. Of course, Stein's analysis of the reciprocal relationship between individual and community was somewhat compromised by her painstaking attempts to steer clear of Scheler's own pitfalls regarding his belief in an undifferentiated stream of conscious life between I and Thou. Nevertheless, my argument is that Stein points us in the right direction, though her own thinking was not quite radical enough to escape the *tout autre* from appearing within the conscious life of the pure-I. Only Levinas's reversal of the direction of intentionality, carefully construed from Heidegger's earlier rejection of empathy in *Being and Time*, raises the issue of ethics in the most radical way by allowing the wholly Other to appear on the Other's own terms. Yet even here Derrida notes that the manifestation of the Infinite must be given to the perceiver in light of some sort of analogy, that is, according to the mode of reception of the perceiving intellect, as both Aquinas and Brentano foreshadow.

To paraphrase the German-Jewish philosopher Franz Rosenzweig, who died in 1929: I and Other "exclude one another, but they supplement each other."[43] The phenomenology of empathy is a lived experience of finitude that *presupposes* Infinity, it points to the Other as an inexhaustible source, an "icon" (in Richard Kearney's classic sense),[44] as that which transcends the givenness of transcendence and evades every attempt to define and comprehend it. As a hermeneutics of suspicion, empathy captures "finitude" as the finite binary of the Infinite. In other words, empathy puts one at risk to the wholly/Holy Other by raising the preeminent ethical question "*Whose* am I?" To whom do I belong? To whom am I responsible? To whom do I give my time, my respect, my *life*? The possibilities are indeed infinite. All we can do is try to be ready. For whom? For what?

The infinite. And what is that?

We do not know, we *cannot* know.[45] Consequently, we must conclude our own contributions to the phenomenology of empathy in the spirit of Stein's own analysis of foreign experience, that is, by leaving the answering of this question to further investigation and satisfying ourselves here with a *non liquet*, "It is not clear."

The readiness is all.[46]

Notes

Introduction

1. The thematic of "person-in-the-world" is thoughtfully presented by Mary Catherine Baseheart in her early description of Edith Stein's phenomenology of empathy. I remain indebted to many of the themes and analyses introduced by Baseheart, who authored some of the earlier scholarly works centered on Stein written in English. See, especially, Baseheart's *Person in the World: Introduction to the Philosophy of Edith Stein* (Dordrecht: Kluwer Academic Press 1997).

2. Ongoing research concerning Husserl's "social ontology" continues to flourish, especially as a result of the publication of *Husserliana* volumes XIII, XIV, and XV, as well as new investigations into critical phenomenology. We will explore some of the themes and implications raised in Husserl's posthumously published works later by contemporary scholars, such as Dan Zahavi, Natalie Depraz, Dermot Moran, and others. However, our main focus in this study remains those primary texts written by Husserl and published during his lifetime, which were accessible to Husserl's students and colleagues.

3. Themes concerning the intersubjective "we-world" include an impressive and robust contemporary body of investigative research that explores empathy and social ontology, as noted, for example, in *Phenomenology of Sociality: Discovering the "We,"* eds. Thomas Szanto and Dermot Moran (London: Routledge, 2016). Another important resource to our discussion, and one that continues to make a profound impact on my own thoughts and development concerning the subject, was a 1988 Yale graduate philosophy seminar on Sartre's *Being and Nothingness* with Prof. Maurice Natanson, including Natanson's rich commentaries on the social phenomenology of the American sociologist Alfred Schütz. Both Natanson's and Schütz's observations have contributed to my own deepening understanding of the phenomenology of the human sciences and figure significantly in the background of many reflections and insights underlying this project.

4. A detailed discussion of the historical setting of *Einfühlung* by Lipps and others will be covered in part two.

5. Rosenburg was convicted of "crimes against humanity" at the conclusion of his trial at Nuremberg and executed in 1946.

6. As a consequence of racial policies of National Socialism, Husserl's position as Rector was revoked and his work had to be secretly smuggled out of Germany to Holland following his humiliating departure from Freiburg University; Levinas was imprisoned in a Nazi concentration camp; Edith Stein and her younger sister Rosa died together in a gas chamber in Auschwitz. The list of victims from Hitler's anti-empathy policies is legion.

7. I am following here a line of thought noted by a number of contemporary Stein scholars, including Mary Catherine Baseheart, Angela Ales Bello, Antonio Calcagno, and Dermot Moran, amongst others, regarding Stein's interpretive attempt to reconcile different phenomenological emphases between Husserl and Scheler and other "early phenomenologists." We will return to this theme later in the study.

Part One

1. Colin Davis, *Levinas: An Introduction* (Notre Dame, IN: Notre Dame University Press, 1996), 3.

Chapter One

1. Maurice Natanson, *Edmund Husserl: Philosopher of Infinite Tasks* (Evanston, IL: Northwestern University Press, 1973), 5.

2. Wolfgang Walter Fuchs, *Phenomenology and the Metaphysics of Presence* (The Hague: Martinus Nijhoff, 1976), 1.

3. Natanson, *Edmund Husserl*, 94.

4. What I say here, of course, is indebted to Jacques Derrida's defense of Husserl in light of Levinas's critique. See Derrida's essay *Violence and Metaphysics*.

5. Herbert Spiegelberg holds that three distinct phases mark the overall development of Husserl's thinking: (1) the pre-phenomenological period, covering most of the Halle years and up to the first volume of *Logical Investigations* (1894–1900); (2) the "transitional" period beginning with Husserl's first years in Göttingen and including the second volume of *Logical Investigations* (1901–1906); and (3) the period of "pure phenomenology" as the universal foundation of philosophy and science. From 1907 to 1938, a new spirit of transcendental idealism culminated in Husserl's Freiburg period. See Herbert Spiegelberg, *The Phenomenological Movement: A Historical Introduction*, 2nd ed. (The Hague: Martinus Nijhoff, 1969).

6. Edith Stein, *On the Problem of Empathy*, trans. Waltraud Stein. *The Collected Works of Edith Stein: Volume III* (Washington, DC: ICS Publications, 1989), 3.

7. Joseph Kockelmans, "Intentional and Constitutive Analyses," in *Phenomenology: The Philosophy of Edmund Husserl and Its Interpretations* (New York: Doubleday, 1967), 138.

8. A detailed analysis of Husserl's distinction may be drawn from "Lecture One." See Edmund Husserl, *The Idea of Phenomenology* (The Hague: Martinus Nijhoff, 1970), 13–21.

9. Of course, for Husserl, intuitions may be adequate or inadequate, depending on whether the intuitions are fulfilled. Even "essential" intuition is still intuition, and the eidetic object is still an object.

10. See especially sect. 24 of the first volume of Husserl's *Ideas*.

11. Marvin Farber, "The Ideal of a Presuppositionless Philosophy," in *Philosophical Essays in Memory of Edmund Husserl* (Cambridge, MA: Harvard University Press, 1940), 44ff.

12. Iso Kern, "Three Ways to the Transcendental Phenomenological Reduction," in *Husserl: Expositions and Appraisals*, eds. Frederick Elliston and Peter McCormick (Notre Dame, IN: University of Notre Dame Press, 1977), 129.

13. Natanson, *Edmund Husserl*, 175.

14. Natanson, 82.

15. This is a criticism raised against Husserl's notion of *transcendental intuition* by Edith Stein and other members of the Göttingen Circle, as well as by Merleau-Ponty. According to Husserl, the "pure I" operates in the transcendental sphere and sees in an unmediated fashion. For Stein, such transcendental *purity* is always an impossibility, since "seeing" requires always an enfleshed embodiment. Hence, Husserl's "transcendental Ego" is descriptive.

16. Fuchs, *Phenomenology and the Metaphysics of Presence*, 10.

17. Marvin Farber, "The Ideal of a Presuppositionless Philosophy," in Kockelmans, *Phenomenology*, 47.

18. We will return to the theme of Cartesian dualism later in this study.

19. Natanson, *Edmund Husserl*, 100.

20. Fuchs, *Phenomenology and the Metaphysics of Presence*, 12.

21. J. N. Mohanty, *Phenomenology: Between Essentialism and Transcendental Philosophy* (Evanston, IL: Northwestern University Press, 1997), 1.

22. Emmanuel Levinas, *Theory of Intuition in Husserl's Phenomenology*, trans. André-Orianne (Evanston, IL: Northwestern University Press, 1995), 158.

23. From April 26 to May 2, 1907, Husserl delivered five lectures in a series that was subsequently edited by Walter Biemel and published in 1950 under the title *Die Idee der Phänomenologie*.

24. Michael F. Andrews, "Edmund Husserl: Empathy and the Transcendental Constitution of the World," in *Analecta Husserliana LXXIX* (Dordrecht: Kluwer Academic Publishers, 2004), 217–37. This chapter highlights several revised and amplified ideas from this article.

25. Mohanty, *Phenomenology*, 63.

26. The critical issues posed by "solipsism" are not resolved in this investigation.

27. Here I am following an argument initiated by Landgrebe's reading of Husserl. See Michael Theunissen, *The Other: Studies in the Social Ontology of Husserl, Heidegger, Sartre, and Buber* (Cambridge, MA: MIT Press, 1984), 16.

28. In effect, this question poses for Husserl the main task of the Fifth Cartesian Meditation.

29. The word *monad* is primarily used by Husserl to emphasize its Leibnizean roots. This will be clarified in the following pages.

30. It is important to recognize that Husserl translators use both "ego" and "Ego" throughout the fourth meditation. Lowercase "ego" signifies "an ego," whereas uppercase "Ego" signifies the "personal" Ego. Note, however, that Husserl is nowhere saying that two different egos exist in the same subject simultaneously. Rather, ego/Ego are two distinct aspects of constitutional analysis. They represent two different approaches or ways of speaking about subjectivity: mundanely ("ego") and transcendentally ("Ego").

31. "Identity pole" and "substratum of habitualities" are not opposed to the concrete Ego; rather, they are ingredients of it.

32. Note especially that (b) is a reversal of Husserl's earlier position (a).

33. Andrews, "Edmund Husserl," in *Analecta Husserliana LXXIX*, 221.

34. Husserl introduces a second reduction in *Cartesian Meditations V* that goes beyond what he describes in terms of the "first" reduction. For now, it is important to note that Meditations I–IV remain essentially monadological and within the "transcendental attitude"; whereas the Fifth Cartesian Meditation introduces a second reduction to the sphere of ownness.

35. Joseph Kockelmans, "Husserl's Transcendental Idealism," in Kockelmans, *Phenomenology*, 184.

36. The term "psychological reduction" does not appear in Husserl's earlier works but gradually came into use around 1906 when he wanted to make an explicit distinction between descriptive and empirical psychology. Between 1906 and 1916, Husserl often used the expressions "phenomenological" and "transcendental" interchangeably, though after 1916 the term "phenomenological reduction" is used for what he earlier called "the psychological reduction."

37. To confuse the situation even more, Husserl also refers to the "eidetic reduction" as the method of "ideating abstraction" and "free variation."

38. See especially Edmund Husserl, *IoP*, 4ff.

39. It is this point, of course, against which Emmanuel Levinas will later protest the ethical implications of Husserl's epistemological methodology.

40. Husserl, *IoP*, 6.

41. Peter Pietersma, "Husserl's Views on the Evident and the True," in Elliston and McCormick, *Husserl: Expositions and Appraisals*, 43.

42. Flows of acts of consciousness (*Erlebnisse*) are not totally arbitrary; however, they are structured according to habitualities, densities, predelineations, and cultural ways of seeing things. According to the theory of constitution, "habits" are immanent transcendencies that are built up and structure the flow of consciousness by virtue of the constitution of temporality. These multiple modes of consciousness break down into particular types or categories (i.e., formal and transcendental logic, ideal logic, culture), each type calling for intentional analysis of the noetic-noematic structure. This is the primary task of the transcendental reduction. Because the *cogitatum* is never present "as a finished datum" (*CM* 45), there is always more work to be done. Whereas every *cogito* is a meaning of its meant, this "something meant" is always more than what at that moment is meant explicitly (*CM* 46). We discover through the transcendental reduction that constitution remains always *unfinished*, an infinite task.

43. Henry Pietersma notes that "these considerations of course involve the idealism of the Husserlian position: the scope of the mind defines reality. To be sure, Husserl recognizes a kind of transcendence. But what he has in mind is simply the fact that something may lie beyond the scope of a particular epistemic situation or even a finite series of such situations. It is a transcendence that calls for further exploration." See his discussion in "Husserl's Views on the Evident and the True," in Elliston and McCormick, *Husserl: Expositions and Appraisals*, 43.

44. Maurice Natanson, *The Journeying Self: A Study in Philosophy and Social Role* (Reading, MA: Addison-Wesley Press, 1970), 10.

45. Taken in this context, I submit that Heidegger may not have grasped how radical and original Husserl's own project was.

46. Husserl himself says as much: "Questions of universal genesis and the genetic structure of the ego in his universality, so far as that structure is more than temporal formation, are still far away; and, indeed, they belong to a higher level" (*CM* 76–77).

47. Here I am referring to the Göttingen and Munich Circles, which included Max Scheler, Edith Stein, Theodor Conrad, Hedwig Conrad-Martius, Roman Ingarden, Adolf Reinach, Alexander Pfänder, Gerda Walther, and others, each of whom opposed from differing viewpoints Husserl's recasting of phenomenology in terms of transcendental idealism.

48. For a more elaborate analysis of the charge of solipsism raised by Heidegger against Husserl, as well as Husserl's response, see Andrews, "Edmund Husserl," in *Analecta Husserliana LXXIX*, 217–37.

49. Broadly speaking, Husserl returns to the theme of a "properly hermeneutic approach" in his later writings, notably his essay on "The Origin of Geometry" (1936). In this text, Husserl develops this theme in relation to historicity, intersubjectivity, and "the interweaving of original formations and sedimentations of meaning." Janet Donohoe, *Husserl on Ethics and Intersubjectivity: From*

Static to Genetic Phenomenology (Amherst, NY: Humanity Books, 2004), 95. See also Husserl, "The Origin of Geometry," in *The Crisis of European Sciences and Transcendental Phenomenology*, trans. David Carr (Evanston, IL: Northwestern University Press, 1970), 371.

50. A genetic account of the Ego implies a description of the Ego with its history, i.e., the Ego as monad, the I as subject. In *Cartesian Meditations*, Husserl proposes a genetic analysis of the ego alongside a static analysis of intersubjectivity as well.

51. Andrews, "Edmund Husserl," in *Analecta Husserliana LXXIX*, 223.

52. Of course, what Husserl means by the empirical ego and the transcendental ego are not two different egos but rather two ways of experiencing the same ego.

53. What I say here, of course, is indebted to Jacques Derrida's defense of Husserl in light of Levinas's critique, as will be discussed in part three. See Derrida's essay *Violence and Metaphysics*.

54. As we will discuss, a description of the constitution of "higher-order" objects engenders the main task of the fifth of Husserl's *Cartesian Meditations* as well as *Ideen II*.

Chapter Two

1. The character of "thingly" transcendence is the theme of *Cartesian Meditations* I–IV. In the Fifth Meditation Husserl now turns his attention to a particular theme of transcendence: specifically, the transcendental human subject.

2. The distinction I wish to draw here is between the notion of "the other" as thingly transcendence (e.g., the world, objects, things, values, ideas) and "the Other" as an individual human transcendental subjectivity, that is, the personal Ego as concrete monad.

3. The multiplicity of intentionalities belonging to every act of thought (*cogito*) implies an inner-lived experience that has its own intentional horizon of references. These references correlate to other potentialities of consciousness that are, in turn, constituted by that experience (*CM* 44–46). Objects exist "for me" insofar as they are constituted as intentional objects, whether such objects are real or imagined.

4. Husserl notes that all traditional theories of knowledge have merely attempted to ask and answer the question of the Other within the natural attitude.

5. As we saw in chapter one, the problem with Descartes was that he formulated the question of transcendence *within* the natural attitude. In asking how I—a natural human being in the world—can get "outside" my island of consciousness, Descartes in fact presupposed the existence of an "outside world" that he was now putting into question. In Husserl's view, the phenomenological

reduction alone brings to light that conscious life by which transcendental questions about the possibility of transcendental knowledge can be asked. World and consciousness belong together *essentially*; everything that exists, whether immanent or transcendent, real or imagined, exists for the ego.

6. Maurice Natanson, *The Journeying Self: A Study in Philosophy and Social Role* (Reading, MA: Addison-Wesley Press, 1970), 28.

7. Natanson shares his distaste for solipsism with many other philosophers. Bertrand Russell, for instance, is said to have once remarked in amusement about Mrs. Christine Ladd-Franklin, who, professing to be a solipsist, was surprised that there were no others who shared her point of view.

8. Natanson, *The Journeying Self*, 30.

9. Natanson, 30.

10. We will return to the ethical concerns raised by the issue of "sociality" later. It is interesting to note, however, that Natanson anticipates Levinas's argument against Husserl in at least one sense, namely that the Other inaugurates an ethical command: thou shalt honor thy father and mother.

11. David Carr, "The 'Fifth Meditation' and Husserl's Cartesianism," from *Philosophy and Phenomenological Research* 34 (1973): 21.

12. This means that the transcendental-I no longer experiences the world in the natural attitude as a private world, but rather as an intersubjective one.

13. Husserl notes: "Thus peculiarly involved with animate organisms, as 'psychophysical' Objects, they are *in the world*. On the other hand, I experience them at the same time as *subjects for this world*, as experiencing it (this same world that I experience) and, in so doing, experiencing me too, even as I experience the world and others in it" (*CM* 91).

14. Anthony Steinbock, *Home and Beyond: Generative Phenomenology After Husserl* (Evanston, IL: Northwestern University Press, 1995), 65.

15. To be a subject means to have experiences, and to be experienced as a subject means to be experienced as having experiences.

16. Natanson, *The Journeying Self*, 34; and Rudolf A. Makkreel, "How is Empathy Related to Understanding?," in *Issues in Husserl's Ideas II*, eds. Thomas Nenon and Lester Embree (Dordrecht: Kluwer Academic Publishers, 1992), 199–212.

17. Husserl's goal is to describe the essential structure of givenness of the alter ego; hence, the description of alter-ego constitution remains for him a static analysis throughout. Concerns raised by virtue of a "genetic approach" will be discussed in detail later in this chapter.

18. The question of the viability of this second reduction is important here, especially since many members of the Göttingen Circle refused to follow Husserl on the grounds that such a reduction leads unequivocally to a form of transcendental Idealism. In part two we will look at this problem in more detail. Nevertheless, here Husserl takes for granted the feasibility of the reduction to

ownness without taking into account the strong objections put forward by Max Scheler, Roman Ingarden, and Edith Stein.

19. Joseph Kockelmans, *Edmund Husserl's Phenomenology* (West Lafayette, IN: Purdue University Press, 1994), 25.

20. Paul Ricoeur, *Husserl: An Analysis of His Phenomenology* (Evanston, IL: Northwestern University Press, 1967), 118.

21. Ricoeur, 120.

22. David Bell, *Husserl* (London: Routledge Press, 1990), 225.

23. Bell, 225.

24. Frederick Elliston, "Husserl's Phenomenology of Empathy," in *Husserl: Expositions and Appraisals*, eds. Frederick Elliston and Peter McCormick (Notre Dame, IN: University of Notre Dame Press, 1977), 221.

25. Michael Theunissen, The Other: Studies in the Social Ontology of Husserl, Heidegger,Sartre, and Buber (Cambridge, MA: MIT Press, 1984), 57.

26. Husserl distinguishes what is properly "my own" from what is alien, foreign, other: *Fremde*.

27. I am using the word "it's" body here, precisely in order to draw attention to one of the unresolved difficulties implicitly implied by Husserl's position—namely, Is the body which I encounter as Other an "it" until I constitute it sexually as a "his" or "her?" The implications to Husserl's assignation of an anonymous ego, that is, a faceless, sexless, nameless *transcendental* ego, is of tremendous interest.

28. Husserl's distinction between "thing-body" as *Körper* and "animate-body" as *Leib* becomes extremely significant in light of his theory of the constitution of the cultural world. This distinction will be discussed in more detail concerning *Ideas II* and the unique role that the body plays in every theory of empathic constitution.

29. Here I am merely drawing out some of the implications of Husserl's position. The question of embodiment will be central in our discussion of *Ideas II*.

30. Theunissen, *The Other*, 146.

31. See *The Other* 144–47 for the whole of Theunissen's argument.

32. The account of Husserl's description of appresentation is drawn from an earlier discussion of similar themes. See Michael F. Andrews, "Edmund Husserl: Empathy and the Transcendental Constitution of the World," in *Analecta Husserliana LXXIX*, ed. A. T. Tymieniecka (Dordrecht: Kluwer Academic Publishers, 2004), 229.

33. Ricoeur, *Husserl*, 124.

34. Ricoeur, 124–25.

35. Andrews, "Edmund Husserl," in *Analecta Husserliana LXXIX*, 230.

36. Andrews, 231.

37. Ricoeur, *Husserl*, 128.

38. Ricoeur, 128–29.

39. Quentin Lauer, "Intersubjectivity: The Other Explained Intentionally," in *Phenomenology: The Philosophy of Edmund Husserl and Its Interpretation*, ed. Joseph Kockelmans (Garden City, NY: Doubleday, 1967), 167.

40. Andrews, "Edmund Husserl," in *Analecta Husserliana LXXIX*, 232. The next several sentences are drawn from an earlier discussion concerning similar themes.

41. Ricoeur, *Husserl*, 129.

42. Andrews, "Edmund Husserl," in *Analecta Husserliana LXXIX*, 230. The discussion that follows in this paragraph is drawn from an earlier discussion of similar themes.

43. Ricoeur, *Husserl*, 131.

44. Ricoeur, 131.

45. Husserl calls the relationship between two egos one of "reciprocity." However, following Edith Stein and others from the Göttingen Circle, I question Husserl's terminology. "Reciprocity" ensures the apodictic co-primordiality between two distinct egos. Husserl makes clear that although the alter ego is empirically distinct from my own, it is transcendentally and derivatively constituted *by me*.

46. Lauer, "Intersubjectivity," 170.

47. This, of course, is the quintessential reference from which Jean-Paul Sartre develops his notion of "the look of the Other," though here without its more existentially confrontational aspect. See part three of *Being and Nothingness*, "The Existence of Others."

48. According to the "linguistic argument" put forward by Merleau-Ponty and others, what constitutes the individual ego is *language*. Because everything is already said in a language, language is by necessity *public*. Hence, what is public makes possible the privacy of individual ego. For Merleau-Ponty, consciousness is always already engendered as a public phenomenon.

49. Theunissen, *The Other*, 147.

Chapter Three

1. The movement from the sphere of the ego to the sphere of Others is in fact what Husserl *means* by "culture."

2. Quentin Lauer, "Intersubjectivity: The Other Explained Intentionally," in *Phenomenology: The Philosophy of Edmund Husserl and Its Interpretations*, ed. Joseph Kockelmans (Garden City, NY: Doubleday, 1967), 176.

3. Lauer, 176.

4. For additional insight and further exploration of similar themes regarding the collaborative relationship between Stein and Husserl, see Antonio Calcagno, "Assistant and/or Collaborator? Edith Stein's Relationship to Edmund Husserl's

Ideen II," in *Contemplating Edith Stein*, ed. Joyce A. Berkman (Notre Dame, IN: University of Notre Dame Press, 2006), 243–70.

    5. Husserl gave the Cartesian lectures in Paris almost twenty years after he first began writing the text that was later posthumously published by the Leuven Archives in 1952 as *Ideas II*.

    6. I am here reminded of the Hollywood fad to provide "prequels" to the moviegoing public, that is, films that are made after the original but whose storyline takes place before the original.

    7. The translator's introduction at the beginning of *Ideas II* offers a good general overview of some of the editorial complications that surrounded the organization and eventual publication of this text. See *Ideas Pertaining to a Pure Phenomenology and to a Phenomenological Philosophy*, vol. 2, trans. Richard Rojcewica and André Schuwer (Dordrecht: Kluwer, 1982), xi–xvi.

    8. Elizabeth Ströker, *Husserl's Transcendental Philosophy*, trans. Lee Hardy (Stanford: Stanford University Press, 1993), 130–31.

    9. This is Husserl's attempt to distance himself from the "a priorism" imposed on the things-themselves by Kant's categorical framework.

    10. Notice how similar Husserl's position is to psychologism at this point. Note as well the difficulty Husserl had in trying to distance himself from psychologistic thinkers (such as Stern), who saw in Husserl's phenomenology a kinship with psychologism.

    11. Although they are never limited by mere sociological distinctions, such experience nevertheless constitutes "an intuitively given articulation of experienced reality" such that it "precedes all thinking, and especially all scientifically theorizing thinking" (*Ideas II* 67–69).

    12. "What psychical being 'is,' experience cannot say in the same sense that it can with regard to the physical. The physical is simply not experienced as something that appears; it is 'vital experience' and vital experience seen in reflection; it appears as itself through itself, in an absolute flow, as now and already 'fading away,' clearly recognizable as constantly sinking back into a 'having been.' The psychical can also be a 'recalled,' and thus in a certain modified way an 'experienced'; and in the 'recalled' lies a 'having been perceived.' It can also be a 'repeatedly recalled,' in recollections that are united in an act of consciousness which in turn is conscious of the recollections themselves as recalled or as still retained. In this connection, and in this alone, can the a priori psychical, in so far as it is the identical of such 'repetitions,' be 'experienced' and identified as being. Everything psychical which is an 'experienced' is, then, as we can say with equal evidence, ordered in an overall connection, in a 'monadic' unity of consciousness." Edmund Husserl, "Philosophy as Rigorous Science," in *Phenomenology and the Crisis of Philosophy*, trans. Quentin Lauer (New York: Harper and Row, 1965), 107–8.

13. Husserl distinguishes the Body as *Leib* from the mere materiality of *Körper* in the following way: "Sheer material things are only moveable mechanically and only partake of spontaneous movement in a mediate way. Only Bodies are immediately spontaneously ('freely') moveable, and they are so, specifically, by means of the free Ego and its will which belong to them" (*Ideas II* 159).

14. The distinction made between "physical" and "spiritual" is akin to Husserl's earlier distinction between the "empirical ego" and the "transcendental ego." There are not two entities, but one singular identity apprehended and described from the perspective of two distinct attitudes.

15. Husserl continues: "In this regard a distinction is to be made between the physical 'I can' (the Bodily and the one mediated by the Body) and the spiritual. I have power over my Body, I am the one who moves this hand and who can move it, etc."

16. "*A faculty* [e.g., motivation] *is not an empty ability but is a positive potentiality*, which may now happen to be actualized but which is always in readiness to pass into activity, into an activity that, as it is lived, refers back to the corresponding subjective ability, the faculty. The motivation, however, is, for consciousness, something open, understandable; the "motivated" decision as such is clear in view of the kind and the power of the motives" (*Ideas II* 267).

17. Husserl, "Philosophy as Rigorous Science," 117ff. Note Husserl's comment here: "Not without misgivings, it is true, does one consider psychology, the science of the 'psychical,' merely as a science of 'psychical phenomena' and of their connections with the body."

18. The emphasis here is my own.

19. Of course, the basis for this is laid by Husserl in the Fifth Cartesian Meditation. He is doing in *Ideas II* what he said could be done in the fifth of his *Cartesian Meditations*.

20. Of course, the intersubjectively constituted Objective world remains absolutely separate from the *merely* subjective sphere constituted by the solitary ego. In the sphere of ownness, what is given to each ego originarily is given to no other subject; hence, every alter ego has its own set of appearances that are exclusively given in its own unique sphere of originary experience.

21. We must remember, of course, that for Husserl social constitution is a derivative experience of monadology. We will return to this important distinction in the following sections.

22. In this sense, we could say that empathy is constitutive; it constitutes an act of genesis.

23. Husserl asks, "What is this social experience? . . . What is 'given' I can represent intuitively modified, I can produce intuitive variation-forms of marriage [and friendship or civic duty or any sort of civil modification] and consequently can grasp various essential differentiations of 'marriage [etc.],' and in that way, I

have, e.g., material for comparative evaluations. . . . If I cannot do it exhaustively, then it suffices, if need be, that I employ examples" (*Ideas II* 210–11).

24. This, of course, will be the line of argument directed *contra* Husserl by Levinas.

25. I am indebted in this and the following section to three anonymous reviewers for a number of helpful comments.

26. In the same way that my body is constituted by me as both a for-itself (in that it is mine) and a for-others (in that I am always conscious of being seen by Others), so the body of the alter ego is constituted by me as a for-itself (in that it has an originary sphere of ownness that remains inaccessible to me) and a for-others (in that I am always conscious of the Other's body as an object that presents itself before me). In this sense, I and Other share a "mutual relation of understanding."

27. Here I am indebted to J. N. Mohanty's essay "Husserl on Relativism in the Late Manuscripts," in *Husserl in Contemporary Context*, ed. Burt C. Hopkins (Dordrecht: Kluwer Academic Publishers, 1997), 181–88.

28. See *Husserliana XIII* 70.

29. Dermot Moran, "The Problem of Empathy: Lipps, Scheler, Husserl and Stein," in *Amor Amicitiae: On the Love That Is Friendship; Essays in Medieval Thought and Beyond, in Honor of the Rev. Professor James McEvoy*, eds. Kelly Thomas and Phillip Rosemann (Leuven: David Brown Book Company, 2004), 292.

30. Moran, 292.

31. Alfred Schutz, *Collected Papers Vol. I: The Problem of Social Reality*, ed. Maurice Natanson (The Hague: Martinus Nijhoff, 1962), 126.

32. Without "the Other," all that could possibly exist is *the same*. The Other *is* difference, alterity, possibility. The question may now be raised: Can the Ego alone constitute the Other? How can "difference" arise from what is already given? Does the doctrine of transcendental monadological constitution reduce ethics to a merely abstract form of arbitrary personal preference?

33. Wolfgang Walter Fuchs, *Phenomenology and the Metaphysics of Presence: An Essay in the Philosophy of Edmund Husserl* (The Hague: Martinus Nijhoff, 1976), 70.

34. Although we will return to this theme again, it is important to note the excellent historical and exegetical accounts that have influenced my own understanding of the development of Husserl's grasp of the phenomenology of empathy, including (but not limited to): (1) Dan Zahavi's essay "Empathy, Embodiment and Interpersonal Understanding: From Lipps to Schutz," *Inquiry: An Interdisciplinary Journal of Philosophy* 53, no. 3 (2010): 285–306; (2) J. N. Mohanty's *Edmund Husserl's Freiburg Years: 1916–1938* (New Haven, CT: Yale University Press, 2011); (3) Sebastian Luft's *Subjectivity and Lifeworld in Transcendental Phenomenology* (Evanston, IL: Northwestern University Press, 2011); and (4) Antonio Calcagno's

Lived Experience from the Inside Out: Social and Political Philosophy in Edith Stein (Pittsburgh: Duquesne University Press, 2014).

35. Of course, this distinction is epistemological, not ontological. If it were otherwise, Husserl would be forced to conclude that any reduction—indeed, any act of seeing whatsoever—would merely be a *solus ipse* activity, hence absurd, irrational, and unintelligible.

36. My emphasis on "alterity" here is intentional and not merely semantic, as I will explore the theme of alterity in detail later in this study. For now, I want to highlight that, for Husserl, phenomenology does not merely "prioritize the question of appearance" but attempts "to eliminate the claim that phenomenology is a subjectivism." That is to say, Husserl's phenomenology is more than "egology." See, for example, Leonard Lawlor's review of *Transcendence et Incarnation: Le Statut de L'intersubjectivité comme Alterité a Soi chez Husserl*," by Natalie Depraz, Continental Philosophy Review 34 (Dordrecht: Kluwer Academic Publishers, 2001), 103–11.

37. Edmund Husserl, *The Basic Problems of Phenomenology: From the Lectures, Winter Semester 1910–1911*, trans. Ingo Farin and James Hart, *Husserliana Collected Works, Vol. XII* (Dordrecht, 2006), 5–10.

38. Janet Donohoe, *Husserl on Ethics and Intersubjectivity: From Static to Genetic Phenomenology* (Amherst, NY: Humanity Books, 2004), 78.

39. Husserl, "The Origin of Geometry," in *The Crisis of European Sciences and Transcendental Phenomenology*, trans. David Carr (Evanston, IL: Northwestern University Press, 1970), 353–60. Hence, this book will be referred to as *Crisis*.

40. *Crisis*, 377.

41. Edmund Husserl, *On the Phenomenology of the Consciousness of Internal Time (1893–1907): Collected Works Vol. IV*, trans. John Barnett Brough (Dordrecht: Kluwer Academic Publishers, 1991), 28.

42. See Lawlor, review of *Transcendence et Incarnation*, 103–4.

43. Maurice Natanson, *Edmund Husserl: Philosopher of Infinite Tasks* (Evanston, IL: Northwestern University Press, 1973), 96.

44. Natanson, 95.

45. William R. McKenna, *Husserl's "Introductions to Phenomenology:" Interpretation and Critique*, Phaenomenologica Series, vol. 89 (Dordrecht: Springer, 1982), 10.

46. McKenna, 12.

47. Natanson, *Edmund Husserl*, 95.

48. The notion of a "we-world" is a philosophically rich concept and will be explored in greater depth later in this study. For now, I wish to highlight several important accounts by which this term has grown in significance, in particular among Stein scholars. See esp. Timothy Burns, "On Being a 'We': Edith Stein's Contributions to the Intentionalism Debate," *Human Studies: A Journal for*

Philosophy and the Social Sciences 38, no. 4 (2015): 529–47; Emanuele Caminada, "Edith Stein's Account of Communal Mind and its Limits: A Phenomenological Reading," *Human Studies: A Journal for Philosophy and the Social Sciences* 38, no. 4 (2015): 549–66; Dan Zahavi, "You, Me, and We: The Sharing of Emotional Experiences," *Journal of Consciousness Studies* 22 (Copenhagen: University of Copenhagen, 2015): 84–101.

49. I am here drawing on Natalie Depraz's notion of "ipseic flux," namely, the concept that the ego actualizes itself by turning back on itself and grasping itself as becoming-other. See, in particular, Natalie Depraz, *Transcendence et Incarnation: Le Statut de L'intersubjectivité comme Alterité a Soi chez Husserl* (Paris: Vrin, 1995), 330–38.

50. Peter Costello, "Toward a Phenomenology of Community: Stein and Nancy," in *Emotion, Space, and Society* 13, ed. Danielle Drozdzewski (November 2014): 122. https://doi.org/10.1016/j.emospa.2013.12.005.

51. *CM* 112.

52. See Lawler, review of *Transcendence et Incarnation*, 109.

53. The designation "early phenomenology" mainly describes the philosophical movement composed of students who studied with Edmund Husserl as well as his colleagues who were part of the Göttingen Circle, as well as students from the University of Munich who studied under the influence of Theodor Lipps. In particular, please refer to the "realistic phenomenology" of Adolf Reinach and Hedwig Conrad-Martius, "Über Phänomenologie," in *Anthologie der Realistischen Phänomenologie*, eds. Josef Seifert and Cheikh Mbacké Gueye (Frankfurt: Ontos Verlag, 2009), 423–48. I argue that the designation of "early phenomenology" should also include the influence of Franz Brentano and major and minor figures from the period, including Reinach, Scheler, Stein, Pfänder, Ingarden, ("the early") Heidegger, Hedwig Conrad-Martius, Gerda Walther, and Hans Lipps, amongst others. See Kimberly Baltzer-Jaray, "Introduction to the Early Phenomenology: Munich and Göttingen," from *Questiones Disputatae: The Early Phenomenology in Munich and Göttingen* 3, no. 1, ed. Kimberly Baltzer-Jaray (Steubenville, OH: Franciscan University of Steubenville, Fall 2012), 4–6.

54. Angela Ales Bello, "Edmund Husserl and Edith Stein: The Question of the Human Subject," *American Catholic Philosophical Quarterly* 82, no. 1 (Winter 2008): 143–44.

55. Recent contributions exploring the important relationship between ethics, emotional constitution, and social ontology include Dan Zahavi, the director of the Center for Subjectivity Research, established in 2002 in Denmark, whose work concerns the intersection between philosophy of mind and phenomenology and focuses on social emotions, collective intentionality, and "theory of mind" debate. See, in particular, Dan Zahavi, *Subjectivity and Selfhood: Investigating the First-Person Perspective* (Cambridge, MA: MIT Press, 2006) and *Self and Other: Exploring Subjectivity, Empathy, and Shame* (Oxford: Oxford University Press, 2014); Peter Costello: "Toward a Phenomenology of Community," 121–33 and

Layers in Husserl's Phenomenology: On Meaning and Intersubjectivity (Toronto: University of Toronto Press, 2012); Antonio Calcagno, *The Philosophy of Edith Stein* (Pittsburgh: Duquesne University Press, 2007).

56. Costello, "Toward a Phenomenology of Community," 121–33, 124.
57. Costello, 124.
58. Zahavi, *Subjectivity and Selfhood*, 124.
59. Natanson, *Husserl*, 108.
60. Roman Ingarden, *On the Motives which Led Husserl to Transcendental Idealism*, trans. J. E. Llewelyn, Phaenomenologica Series, vol. 64 (Dordrecht: Springer, 1975), 21.
61. See Ingarden, *On the Motives*, chap. four, "The results of the investigations into outer perception and the constitutive analysis of objects of the real world," 13–33.
62. Husserl, *IoP*, 50.
63. Paul Ricoeur, *Husserl: An Analysis of His Phenomenology* (Evanston, IL: Northwestern University Press, 1967), 71–72.
64. Husserl, *IoP*, 50.
65. Husserl, *IoP*, 58.
66. Natanson, *Husserl*, 109–10.
67. Derrida concurs, as noted in his comparison between Scheler and Husserl on the theoretical constitution of the infinity of the face. Citing Scheler and in anticipation of Levinas, Derrida notes: "I see not only the eyes of an other, I see also that he looks at me." See page 98, *VM*.
68. Rudolf A. Makkreel, "How Is Empathy Related to Understanding?," in *Issues in Husserl's Ideas II*, eds. Thomas Nenon and Lester Embree (Dordrecht: Kluwer Academic Publishers, 1992), 202.
69. *CM* 129–30.
70. As noted, much of Husserl's work on intersubjectivity, composed of lecture notes, manuscript drafts, and unfinished texts remained largely unpublished during his lifetime. A collection of these unpublished manuscripts was edited by Iso Kern and published in 1973 in volumes XIII, XIV, and XV of *Husserliana*: (1) *Zur Phänomenologie der Intersubjektivitä: Erster Teil (1905-1920)*; (2) *Zweiter Teil (1921-1928)*; and (3) *Dritter Tiel (1929-1935)*. Although important implications and references regarding these texts are examined in this chapter, the focus of inquiry of our study mainly concerns Husserl's public works that would have been published and therefore widely circulated and familiar to Husserl's colleagues and students in the 1920s and 1930s.
71. *Les Figures de L'Intersubjectivité Étude des Husserlaiana XIII-XIV-XV zur Intersubjektivität* (Archives de Philosophie 55, no. 3, July–Sept. 1992): 479–98, esp. 483–84 (my translation).
72. Donohoe, *Husserl on Ethics and Intersubjectivity*, 103.
73. *CM* 124; Donohoe, 103.
74. Donohoe, 103.

75. Makkreel, "How Is Empathy Related to Understanding?," 208.
76. Makkreel, 210.
77. Makkreel, 210; Theunissen, *The Other: Studies in the Social Ontology of Husserl, Heidegger, Sartre, and Buber* (Cambridge, MA: MIT Press, 1984), 72.
78. Makkreel, "How Is Empathy Related to Understanding?," 212.

Part Two

1. The topic of Edith Stein's dissertation, *Zum Problem der Einfühlung*, will be the subject of investigation in chapter five. In a letter to Fritz Kaufmann, dated August 16, 1916, regarding her assistantship to Husserl, Edith Stein comments that Husserl had confided to her that he was very satisfied with her thesis and that "indeed a good bit of it coincided with essential portions from Part II of *Ideen*" (*Letters* 1). The original letter is available at the Archivum Carmelitanum Edith Stein, Köln, Germany.

2. On January 12, 1917, Stein wrote to Kaufmann, "As far as my work [with Husserl] is concerned, the difficulties are even greater than appeared at first" (*Letters* 5). The original letter is available at the Archivum Carmelitanum Edith Stein, Köln, Germany.

3. The implications to Stein's rejection of what she believed was Husserl's Idealist position will be explored later. For now, I wish only to alert the reader to Edith Stein's rejection of Idealism (*Letters* 5). The original letter was published by Roman Ingarden in *Philosophy and Phenomenological Research*, vol. 23, 1962.

4. As we saw in part one, Husserl's phenomenological description of empathy is complex and involves appresentation, that is, a process of presentification whereby I apprehend another body as belonging to another subject. Through appresentation, I come to recognize the other as an embodied subject who is an "analogue" of myself: the other subject is not *here*, but over *there*. As we shall see, for Edith Stein this means that the other is recognized as its own originary source, as primordial, yet apprehended in a non-originary way, or non-primordially. As Rudolf Makrkreel notes, Husserl's phenomenological description of empathy thus remains deficient if it merely describes empathy's "cognitive status"; what is needed is to also give an account of empathy's "emotive quality." Rudolf A. Makkreel, "How is Empathy Related to Understanding?," in *Issues in Husserl's Ideas II*, eds. Thomas Nenon and Lester Embree (Dordrecht: Kluwer Academic Publishers, 1992), 200.

5. "Within the continental tradition, and especially within phenomenology, since Husserl has re-introduced the notion, the manner in which one person understands another, or engages with others has been usually treated under the general heading of 'empathy,' or *Einfühlung* (a term that originated in nineteenth-century German philosophical aesthetics and psychology.... The possibility and nature of sharing of intentions, emotions, and actions have been the object

of increased attention within recent analytic philosophy, especially in a field that is now standardly referred to as 'social ontology'—a label, incidentally, that was first used by Husserl in a manuscript from 1910." For a historic overview of the thematic of "collective intentionality," see Thomas Szanto and Dermot Moran, "Introduction: Empathy and Collective Intentionality: The Social Philosophy of Edith Stein," *Human Studies: A Journal for Philosophy and the Social Sciences* 38, no. 4 (2015), 146.

6. Issues revolving around Husserl's so-called transcendental turn and implications involving Idealism will be explored in parts two and three of this study. For additional analyses, see Dan Zahavi, *Husserl's Legacy: Phenomenology, Metaphysics, and Transcendental Philosophy* (Oxford: Oxford University Press, 2017), esp. chap. 3, "The Transcendental Turn," 51–76.

7. This list of students and colleagues who regularly engaged Husserl on these issues, though certainly not exhaustive, includes the main authors who make up the focus of our upcoming reflections.

8. See, for example, (1) "Stein's conception of emotions can only be understood as embedded in the larger context of early phenomenological theories. Stein was participating in a change of paradigm on affectivity that took place at the beginning of the twentieth century and which was initiated by Brentano and his students. According to this new paradigm, emotions are not mere subjective, qualitative, or some irrational bodily states but intentional mental acts that are built upon cognitions and are directed towards the world, revealing us what is valuable and how to act accordingly. This change of paradigm, in which the world-directedness of emotions plays a central role, is described in the current debate as 'affective intentionality'" (486); and (2) "It was in this context [at Göttingen] of a strong intellectual exchange that Stein forged her work on empathy and her theory of the emotions. The 'constellation' of authors working on these themes and exchanging ideas and arguments, who are thus the interlocutors of Stein, are those, aside from Husserl, Alexander Pfänder and Max Scheler, who offered systematic theories of emotions and of sentiments (Gesinnungen) respectively, as well as Moritz Geiger, who provided an account of the unconscious and the awareness of feelings" (487). Ingrid Vendrell Ferran, "Empathy, Emotional Sharing, and Feelings in Stein's Early Work," *Human Studies: A Journal for Philosophy and the Social Sciences* 38, no. 4 (2015): 481–502.

9. Descriptions of what a "reciprocal model of empathy" might or should entail will be explored in detail in parts two and three. For now, I merely want to raise the issue that the thematic of reciprocity offers important and normative insights about the givenness of empathy for phenomenologists in general, but especially as described by Edith Stein in her own analysis. For example, Robert Costello notes: "As Stein documents quite well in the beginning of her work on community, a phenomenologist is concerned with the 'constitution of objects in consciousness' as a series of 'reciprocal adaptations' or 'coherences.'" "Toward a Phenomenology of Community: Stein and Nancy," *Emotion, Space, and Society* 13, ed.

Danielle Drozdzewski (2014): 121–33, https://doi.org/10.1016/j.emospa.2013.12.005. See also Edith Stein, *Philosophy of Psychology and the Humanities*, trans. Catherine Baseheart and Marianne Sawicki, in *The Collected Works of Edith Stein: Volume VII* (Washington, DC: Institute of Carmelite Studies [ICS] Publications, 2000), 7.

10. My argument here is not that Husserl does not describe phenomena of sentient reality but that his description remains largely based in descriptive terms on a cognitive model of constitution; that is, Husserl is primarily concerned with describing how one ego enters into and understands the conscious life of another ego. This noetic act describes *Einfühlung* as a process of mutual understanding by which one monad recognizes and shares a lifeworld with another monad. Yet, in terms of feelings and sentient reality, it could be argued that Stein's emphasis on the nature of the lived experience of community "brings to the fore a crucial difference." This "distinction" in Stein's understanding of empathy engages a higher social objectivity of communal life that "was not addressed fully by her contemporaries." As Antonio Calcagno notes, Stein's focus on communal lived experiences and her analyses of the phenomena of feelings (e.g., "sadness" in *Philosophy of Psychology and the Humanities* and "joy" in *On the Problem of Empathy*) suggests that, "unlike Husserl, Stein places much weight on her analysis of feelings." *The Philosophy of Edith Stein* (Pittsburgh: Duquesne University Press, 2007), 34.

11. Other scholars have also raised this point by arguing that distinctions or descriptions of "feminizing and masculinizing elements constitutive of the human person . . . are not to be found in *Ideas II* or in Husserl's other works." Consequently, "Stein manages to recast the notion of the emotional" such that "Stein is to be read as presenting general sketches of the feminine. . . . Within the dynamic of intersubjectivity, Stein sees woman as more capable of empathy." See, for example, Calcagno, *The Philosophy of Edith Stein*, 70–72.

12. For this line of argument, I am indebted to Carol Gilligan, *In a Different Voice: Psychological Theory and Women's Development* (Cambridge, MA: Harvard University Press, 1996). Other scholars have also commented on Stein's affinity toward exploring the co-primacy that emotions and affectivity afford in recognizing alterity and difference and how this relates to a perspective of ethical responsibility, for example, in terms of the development of a "feminist ethics" or pluri-egological accounts of the genesis of genuine community and shared lifeworld experiences. See, for example, (1) Antonio Calcagno, *The Philosophy of Edith Stein*, 63–79; (2) Peter Costello, "Toward a Phenomenology of Community," 121–33; (3) Petr Urban, "Care Ethics and the Feminine Personalism of Edith Stein," *Philosophies* 7, no. 60 (2022): 1–14, https://doi.org/10.3390/philosophies7030060; and (4) Kathleen Haney and Johanna Valiquettte, "Edith Stein: Woman as Ethical Type," in *Phenomenological Approaches to Moral Philosophy: A Handbook*, eds. John Drummond and Lester Embree (Dordrecht: Springer, 2002), 451–73.

13. The words "numinous" and "*mysterium tremendum*" come to mind here. Of course, concerning what is genuinely other, we must "bear always in

mind that these expressions do not hit with precision, but merely hint at what is really meant." Rudolf Otto, *The Idea of the Holy: An Inquiry into the Non-Rational Factor in the Idea of the Divine and its Relation to the Rational*, trans. John Harvey (London: Oxford University Press, 1958), 50ff. A more radical sense of alterity will be explored by Levinas in part three.

14. Following Husserl, Edith Stein agrees that knowledge of the Other qua other is constituted in the order of cognition. But she also appears to infer, along with Scheler, that the order of affectivity is equi-primordial as that of cognition.

15. Timothy Burns, "From I to You to We: Empathy and Community in Edith Stein's Phenomenology," in *Empathy, Sociality, and Personhood: Contributions to Phenomenology* 94, eds. E. Magrì and D. Moran (Cham: Springer International, 2017), 127–42.

16. Mary Catherine Baseheart notes that Stein "made several attempts to habilitate at German universities, but sexism and anti-Semitism blocked the way." "Edith Stein's Phenomenology of the State," in *Reinterpreting the Political: Continental Philosophy and Political Theory*, ed. Lenore Langsdorf (Albany: State University of New York Press, 1998), 59ff.

17. In Stein's case, her voice was indeed silenced on account of her "otherness"—first, as a woman, and later, as a Jew.

18. Antonio Calcagno, "Assistant and/or Collaborator? Edith Stein's Relationship to Edmund Husserl's *Ideen II*," in *Contemplating Edith Stein*, ed. Joyce A. Berkman (Notre Dame, IN: University of Notre Dame Press, 2006), 243–70.

19. On this point, I am indebted to the generative research of recent Stein scholars, whose writings and research projects continue to explore influences and probe implications concerning Stein's social, phenomenological, and political philosophy while she was a student and collaborator of Husserl, and beyond. Several scholarly investigations from the 1990s and 2000s that investigate important persons, ideas, and philosophical themes that influenced Stein's intellectual development and thereby continue to shape her philosophical legacy include Angela Ales Bello, *Edith Stein: Patrona d'Europa* (Casale Monferrato, IT: Edizioni Piemme, 2000); Mary Catherine Baseheart, *Person in the World: Introduction to the Philosophy of Edith Stein* (Dordrecht: Kluwer Academic Publishers, 1997); Sarah Borden, *Edith Stein* (New York: Continuum, 2003); Antonio Calcagno, *Lived Experience from the Inside Out: Social and Political Philosophy in Edith Stein* (Pittsburgh: Duquesne University Press, 2014); Antonio Calcagno, *The Philosophy of Edith Stein* (Duquesne, PA: Duquesne University Press, 2007); Hilda Graef, *The Scholar and the Cross: The Life and Work of Edith Stein* (Westminster, MD: Newman Press, 1955); Josephine Koeppel, *Edith Stein: Philosopher and Mystic* (Collegeville, MN: Liturgical Press, 1990); Alasdair MacIntyre, *Edith Stein: A Philosophical Prologue, 1913–1922*; Marianne Sawicki, *Body, Text, and Science: The Literacy of Investigative Practices and the Phenomenology of Edith Stein* (Dordrecht: Kluwer Academic Publishers, 1997).

20. For a helpful general introduction to the thought of Max Scheler, see *The Mind of Max Scheler* (Milwaukee: Marquette University Press, 1996); and *Max Scheler: A Concise Introduction into the World of a Great Thinker* (Pittsburgh: Duquesne University Press, 1965), both by Manfred S. Frings.

21. In part three, I will follow Levinas's rejection of Husserl's notion of cognitive constitution, but for very different reasons from those of Stein and Scheler. Levinas not only reverses the "directional arrow" of intentionality; he also rejects out of hand *any* founding mode of empathy—whether cognitive or emotive.

Chapter Four

1. I mention this fact only as an interesting piece of historical information. However, I think it is worth noting the influence of Jewish thought on early twentieth-century phenomenology. A further note may be added here as well, in that Emmanuel Levinas also comes to Husserlian phenomenology via an appropriation of a more evident Jewish (and in his case, specifically rabbinical) ethical influence.

2. Eucken was an early and enthusiastic supporter of the League of Nations. See Manfred S. Frings, *The Mind of Max Scheler* (Milwaukee: Marquette University Press, 1996), 9.

3. Scheler described his own personal life as "wrapped in weaknesses and guilt" that often led "easily to lustful inclinations." He married three times and divorced twice due to his involvement in several public extramarital affairs, including one in 1919 with his young student assistant at the University of Cologne, Maria Scheu, whom he later married.

4. Cardinal Eugenio Pacelli, the soon-to-be Pope Pius XII, was the Vatican's nuncio to Bavaria and, subsequently, to the new German Republic in 1920. As papal secretary of state from 1930 to 1939, he fashioned concordats between the Holy See and both Austria and National Socialist Germany. In 1939 Edith Stein (then Sister Benedicta of the Cross) wrote a personal letter to Pope Pius XII urging him to publish a Papal Encyclical denouncing the anti-Semitism that had been openly flourishing in his former archdiocese for decades; she received a "formal blessing" for her and her family in response.

5. Due to scandal, Scheler was not allowed to lecture publicly at Göttingen. As a result, he met with the members of the Göttingen Philosophical Circle at various hotels and cafes. Stein notes in her autobiography that, on at least one occasion, Adolf Reinach "had to make the preparations for Scheler's guest lectures" (*LJF* 258–79).

6. On account of the cloud of scandals that surrounded him, for many years Scheler was unable to secure a full-time teaching position at any university.

7. It was Reinach who formally introduced Edith Stein to Husserl; she and Reinach and his wife, Anna, became great friends. When Adolf Reinach

died on the Western Front in 1917 (he was thirty-five years old), Husserl asked Edith Stein to represent the Göttingen Circle at his funeral. Her letters and *Autobiography* illustrate a rich and profound friendship with both Adolf and Anna Reinach, who were equally instrumental in Stein's faith conversion. According to Stein, it was Reinach who advised and prepared students for Husserl's Göttingen classes, much as Edith Stein would later do herself at Freiburg. (*Nota bene*: After many years of neglect, a critical edition of Reinach's works is now available in German. A notebook of Edith Stein's notes on Reinach has been discovered that was written in her own hand and dates from 1914. Edith Stein was responsible for assisting Anna Reinach in the compilation of her husband's papers shortly after Adolf Reinach's untimely death.)

8. This distinguished group of early phenomenologists did not constitute a collection of mere professional colleagues; many of them remained lifelong friends, even when they disagreed sharply on philosophical matters. Edith Stein maintained a prolific correspondence with several members of the Göttingen Circle until her death in 1942. Hedwig Conrad-Martius ("dear Hattie," as Edith Stein called her) was Stein's sponsor for the Christian sacrament of Baptism and a most intimate friend; Roman Ingarden became Edith Stein's spiritual and intellectual companion; Fritz Kaufmann testified that Stein's letters helped him survive the horrors of the trenches; finally, letters between Hans Lipps and Edith Stein, as well as Edith Stein's correspondence with Edmund and Malvina Husserl, are particularly noteworthy.

9. Although Stein wrote her doctoral thesis under Husserl's direction, this was the real focus of her own dissertation interests.

10. Stein's rather telling observation continues: "Although Scheler had never been in any of Husserl's classes, Husserl was convinced of Scheler's dependency" (*LJF* 259).

11. A description of Scheler's emphasis on the "emotive" rather than the "cognitive" sphere of constitution will be the focus of this chapter.

12. We should remember that Scheler was greatly influenced by contemporary French philosophy, most notably that of Bergson and, to a lesser extent, that of Maurice Blondel. Like Blondel, Scheler argues that even if we do not act, something acts in us or outside us, and almost always against us. In an important sense, then, Blondel's theory that "I act before knowing what action is" anticipates Scheler's and Stein's argument that "I" exist prior to my own cognitive experience of myself.

13. In this sense, Scheler followed the seventeenth-century French mathematician and philosopher Blaise Pascal, who—mirroring St. Augustine—said, "The heart has reasons that reason knows not of." In a translation of his essay "Leibe und Erkenntnis," in *Gesammelte Werke*, vol. 6, *Schriften zur Soziologie und Weltanschauungslehre*, Scheler quotes Pascal directly: "Blaise Pascal, in his 'Conversation on the Passions of Love,' dared to assert the clear, incredibly resonant

proposition, 'Love and reason are one and the same.' Pascal's deeper meaning was that love first *discloses* objects, which appear to the senses and which reason later judges" (*FKV* 147).

14. Manfred Frings, *Max Scheler: A Concise Introduction into the World of a Great Thinker* (Pittsburgh: Duquesne University Press, 1965), 40.

15. Frings, 40.

16. "For it is our *whole* spiritual life—and not simply objective thinking in the sense of cognition of being—that possesses 'pure' acts and laws of acts which are, according to their nature and contents, *independent* of the human organization" (*FE* 63).

17. Frings, *Max Scheler: A Concise Introduction*, 70.

18. By "act-being," we need to make sure that "being" should not be taken as a noun but as a verb. The verb *be-ing* in Scheler's sense remains "commensurate to the temporality itself of the person. It prevents the world from being taken as a noun that could lead to the implication that the person has a 'substance,' a conclusion to which Scheler strongly objects." Frings, *The Mind of Max Scheler*, 44.

19. Frings, 9.

20. Several similar themes are explored in an earlier essay attempting to explore Scheler's and Stein's descriptions of the genesis of community. See Michael F. Andrews, "Edith Stein and Max Scheler: Ethics, Empathy, and the Constitution of the Acting Person," *Quaestiones Disputatae: A Journal of Philosophical Inquiry and Discussion; The Early Phenomenology of Munich and Göttingen* 3, no. 1, ed. Kimberly Baltzer-Jaray (Steubenville, OH: Franciscan University Press, 2012), 33–47.

21. Here, Husserl compares "Indian" and "Greek" world-historical perspectives and notes that "the Greek notion can be seen to have a deep commonality with the Indian. First, love is understood intellectually, as dependent on the progress of knowledge" (*FKV* 148–52).

22. See St. Augustine, *The City of God*. There is a further similarity here as well with St. Thomas Aquinas's doctrine that the will tends toward the Good once the Good has been apprehended by the intellect. Like Augustine and St. Thomas, Scheler holds that *love* precedes and determines even the "ideas" that God wills into existence.

23. Remember, of course, that Husserl concludes the Fifth Cartesian Meditation by paying homage to the Saint of Hippo: "Noli foras ire," says Augstine, "in te redi, in interiore homine habitat veritas."

24. Frings, *Max Scheler: A Concise Introduction*, 69.

25. Frings, 67.

26. Frings, 68.

27. Frings, *The Mind of Max Scheler*, 43.

28. As we shall see shortly, Stein argues along much the same lines as these general critiques brought against Husserl by his critics. The fifth and sixth of the

Investigations were harshly received, if not downright rejected, by Ingarden, Stein, Reinach, Martius, Scheler, Kroye, and Kaufmann, not to mention Heidegger, Levinas, Merleu-Ponty, Sartre, etc.

29. Paul Ricoeur, *Husserl: An Analysis of His Phenomenology* (Evanston, IL: Northwestern University Press, 1967), 6.

30. Wolfgang Walter Fuchs, *Phenomenology and the Metaphysics of Presence: An Essay in the Philosophy of Edmund Husserl* (The Hague: Martinus Nijhoff, 1976), 55.

31. Derrida himself makes use of the inadequacy of Husserl's theory concerning "signs," "expressions," and "signification" throughout *Speech and Phenomena*. See especially his essay "The Voice that Keeps Silent."

32. It is not Husserl's thesis that an object only exists on the ground of the rationality of a thinking subject. Nevertheless, without such consciousness, the object cannot be meant, or intended; hence, the object is *meaningless*. Essentially, this is what Husserl means by the *noetic-noematic* correlation. The act (*noesis*) is on one side, and the material of the act (*noema*) is on the other side: each is co-constitutive.

33. According to Mohanty, the common error of Idealism consists in reifying the empirical ego as the transcendental ego, i.e., in ascribing "the constituting function to the empirical ego (resulting in empirical idealism, psychologism, and such philosophical mistakes)." J. N. Mohanty, *Phenomenology: Between Essentialism and Transcendental Philosophy* (Evanston, IL: Northwestern University Press, 1997), 93.

34. The confusion tied to the transcendental ego becomes even more acute when we take into consideration Husserl's theory of intersubjective constitution as outlined in *Ideas II*. The constitution of material and animal nature and the constitution of the spiritual world makes the Other a necessary co-constitutive partner in the meaning-making of the world. Nevertheless, it is the tactile experience of my Body as a zero-point of orientation that motivates a unique sense of the primordial givenness of my own corporeal identity. The Other is founded through analogical transference, in the sense that I am only *subsequently* motivated to constituted other Bodies as zero-points of tactile orientations similar to my own. What is originary, then, is the transcendental ego. The transcendental-I is a condition of possibility of Objective constitution.

35. Michael Theunissen, *The Other: Studies in the Social Ontology of Husserl, Heidegger, Sartre, and Buber* (Cambridge, MA: MIT Press, 1984), 110.

36. It is important to keep in mind that the sphere of ownness is a product of the strict end, the *telos*, the finality (*Engebnis*) of Husserlian methodology: the transcendental-*I* never exists as a realistic entity. Rather, the transcendental ego marks the origin of constitution, it makes manifest the conditions of possibility by which the Other is given to me, it posits the essential prerequisite that makes empathy and motivation conceivable in the first place.

37. Maurice Natanson, *Edmund Husserl: Philosopher of Infinite Tasks* (Evanston, IL: Northwestern University Press, 1973), 102.

38. James G. Hart, *The Person and the Common Life: Studies in a Husserlian Social Ethics* (Dordrecht: Kluwer Academic Publishers, 1992), 144.

39. The question of the intentional meaning of "I" will be explored further by Edith Stein, who, following Max Scheler, argues that the pure-I of transcendental Idealism is merely fictional. For Stein, the transcendental-I *presupposes* the *a priori* of embodiment. Scheler's and Stein's distinction between the concepts "I" and "person" will be explored later.

40. In volume I of the *Investigations*, Husserl wrote against psychologism. The constitution of a thing, the world, objects, etc. is not constituted by psychic intention. What is a mathematical entity? For Husserl, it cannot be the final form of mental activity, or else it would be merely psychologistic. Rather, the early Husserl shows that mathematical and logical entities *have their own meaning*, a meaning that is not based on the fact that there is someone in the world who first has to think this out in such and such a manner. Hence, Husserlian realism posits more of a Platonic understanding of meaning than what is normally granted by an idealist approach. There is an idea (i.e., a mathematical or logical truth) that exists for itself, and not because it is first constituted by consciousness. This signifies Husserl's early radical realist-ontological position; it is not yet *transcendental*.

41. Teresia Renata Posselt, *Edith Stein*, trans. C. Hastings and Donald Nicholl (London: Sheed and Ward Publishers, 1952), 22–25.

42. Henry Pietersma, "Husserl's Views on the Evident and the True," 38.

43. Biemel further points out that Husserl's *habilitation* (in which he supported the thesis that arithmetic must be approached originally as psychologism) was itself severely critiqued by Frege. This may be one reason why Husserl gradually came to the conclusion that "psychologism" poses a great tragedy for the foundation of philosophy. Frege's criticism, in fact, became a catalyst for Husserl's writing *The Idea of Phenomenology* in 1907.

44. Ricoeur, *Husserl: An Analysis*, 4–5.

45. J. N. Mohanty, "Husserl's Theory of Meaning," in *Husserl: Expositions and Appraisals*, eds. Frederick Elliston and Peter McCormick (Notre Dame, IN: University of Notre Dame Press, 1977), 35.

46. By characterizing Husserl as a Kantian, Scheler takes up Dilthey's claim that "in the veins of the knowing subject as constructed by Locke, Hume, and Kant [for Scheler, this list includes Husserl as well], there was no real blood." J. N. Mohanty, *Phenomenology*, 14–24.

47. Frings, *The Mind of Max Scheler*, 25.

48. Scheler is actually closer to Husserl on this than he would care to admit. For Husserl, values *presuppose* acts of cognition—they are not given "in" or "by" cognition. In other words, Husserl argues throughout *Ideas I* that you first have to know what it is that you value.

49. Frings, *The Mind of Max Scheler*, 30.

50. Scheler himself admits of his indebtedness to Nietzsche's theory of *resentiment* on this issue.

51. In this section, Scheler is consciously drawing on the work of Edith Stein, which we will discuss in the next chapters. See Scheler's footnote 1 from chapter II, "The Nature of Sympathy."

52. For all his effort to distance himself from Husserl's cognitive analysis, in the end Scheler's position regarding emotive constitution stands remarkably close to Husserl's cognitive theory of analogical apperception.

53. The position of Theodore Lipps will be reviewed in detail in the following chapter.

54. Frings, *The Mind of Max Scheler*, 82. It should be noted, however, that Scheler is not quite being fair to Husserl on this point. For example, Husserl's theory of transcendental apperception does not involve a conscious logical act of analogizing. Rather, as we noted in part one, apperception occurs pre-predicatively. It is *not* a conscious or "active" inference.

55. Interestingly, Scheler inverts Buber's "I-Thou" reference to "Thou-I," thereby emphasizing the significance of the Thou, the Other, in ethical relationships.

56. Frings, *The Mind of Max Scheler*, 83.

57. Frings, *Max Scheler: A Concise Introduction*, 57.

58. Frings, *The Mind of Max Scheler*, 84.

59. Frings, 85.

60. We need remember that, for Husserl, the lonely, isolated Ego is hypothetically, if not experientially, possible. For Scheler, an "I" apart from a "Thou" is *unthinkable*.

61. *The Nature of Sympathy* was first published by Scheler in 1913, the same year that Husserl published his theory of transcendental Idealism in *Ideas I*.

Chapter Five

1. Please note that in the English translation the editor mistakenly translates *Erfahrung* as "perceiving" rather than "experiencing."

2. See Edith Stein, *On the Problem of Empathy*, trans. Waltraud Stein. *The Collected Works of Edith Stein: Volume III* (Washington, DC: ICS Publications, 1989), xiii, "Preface to the First and Second Editions."

3. Included here are Scheler, Reinach, Hedwig Martius, Hans Lipps, Roman Ingarden, et al.

4. Although there is no evidence that Husserl made any mention of Stein's dissertation in his own works, Scheler publicly acknowledges the importance to him of Stein's research on two occasions in *The Nature of Sympathy*. In a footnote reference to her research, Scheler says that Stein's work has "decisively refuted"

the problem of "vicarious feeling" that Theodore Lipps's work had previously presented. See *The Nature of Sympathy* (Hamden, CT: Archon Books, 1973), 13, fn.1.

5. To a great extent, this was Husserl's argument raised against the problem of "psychologism" in his essay "Philosophy as a Rigorous Science."

6. Roman Ingarden, *The Cognition of the Literary Work of Art*, trans. Ruth Ann Crowley and Kenneth Olson (Evanston, IL: Northwestern University Press, 1973), 3.

7. Theodore Lipps's work was primarily psychologistic in nature, whereas Scheler focused primarily on the theme of sympathy (*Mitfühlung*), not empathy (*Einfühlung*), as noted above.

8. That Lipps provided for Stein her "point of departure" is not mere conjecture. Regarding her dissertation, she writes: "Almost immediately, I was given another bitter pill to swallow: [Husserl] required that . . . I had to make a thorough study of the long list of works by Theodor Lipps" (*LJF* 269–70).

9. Rudolf Makkreel, "How Is Empathy Related to Understanding?," in *Issues in Husserl's Ideas II*, eds. Thomas Nenon and Lester Embree (Dordrecht: Kluwer Academic Publishers, 1992), 199.

10. Makkreel, 200.

11. Stein's indebtedness to Husserl in this matter is clear. During her years in Freiburg, she was the editor of Husserl's *Phenomenology of Internal Time Consciousness*. For a fuller elucidation of this problem, see Stein, *On the Problem of Empathy*, 8–11.

12. Stein continues: "This 'present' [of fantasy time] does not indicate a present of objective time but an experienced present which in this case can only be objectified in a 'neutral' present of fantasized time." For a fuller explanation, see Stein, *On the Problem of Empathy*, 8–11.

13. Perhaps the best example of empathic literature, one which Stein curiously omits, is religious literature. In the ancient Christian tradition of *lexio divina*, for example, the reader is swept up into the story such that the penitent him/herself *feels* Christ's suffering, or Peter's sorrowful betrayal, or Mary Magdalen's joy on Easter Sunday. One might in fact classify Ignatius Loyola's entire *Spiritual Exercises* as an exercise in empathy. In the *Spiritual Exercises*, a retreatant's interior modes of consolation and desolation are drawn from an empathic encounter with other persons through prayer.

Chapter Six

1. It is important to note that an interest in the relationship between emotions, cognition, and constitution was not unique to Edith Stein but shared as a theme and area of profound interest by many of Husserl's students and colleagues and, to great extent, by Husserl himself. Petr Urban comments that

"Stein's ethical views draw heavily on the personalist ethics developed by Edmund Husserl and Max Scheler. Yet . . . Stein enriches the personalist perspective of her phenomenological companions by a unique feminist tweak." Hence, a richer and more comprehensive understanding of Stein's contributions to the debate is essential. Urban continues: "Stein shares and further develops the view of other early phenomenologists that it is through emotions that a person grasps 'the meaning of another being in relation to its own being, and then the significance of the inherent value of exterior things, of other persons, and impersonal things [96].' Emotions are the 'essential organ for comprehension of the existent in its totality and its peculiarity [96],' and through emotions, we open ourselves to the world of values that Stein takes to be present in the world of persons. It is important to stress that by 'emotions' Stein does not mean fluctuating states of sentiment, although emotions may include sentiment. Stein relates the primordial recognition of others to the emotions as a peculiar spiritual capacity, present both in self-knowledge and empathy. What we ought to be and do shows itself to us through the feelings we develop in encountering the experiences and actions of other persons. In line with the emotional value realism of Scheler, Stein claims that the structure of personal depth and periphery is mapped out in response to a range of values and that the person ought to be affected in the deepest way by the highest values. On the top of the hierarchy of values resides the absolute value of the human person: the human person is more precious than all objective values [256]." Petr Urban, "Care Ethics and the Feminine Personalism of Edith Stein," *Philosophies* 7, no. 60 (2022): 1–14, https://doi.org/10.3390/philosophies7030060. Quotations referenced in Urban's text are from Edith Stein, *Essays on Woman*, 2nd ed., trans. Fred Mary Oben (Washington, DC: ICS Publications, 1996).

2. James G. Hart, "Contingency of Temporality and Eternal Being: A Study of Aspects of Edith Stein's Phenomenological Theology as It Appears Primarily in *Endliches und Ewiges Sein*," in *Eighteenth Annual Symposium of the Simon Silverman Phenomenology Center* (Pittsburgh: Duquesne University, 2001), 58.

3. Many phenomenologists, including Scheler, Merleau-Ponty, Sartre, Heidegger, and Levinas, also draw attention to this point of vulnerability in Husserl's position.

4. Although Edith Stein did not edit Husserl's lectures on inner-time consciousness until after her dissertation was defended, she nevertheless had access to Husserl's lecture notes. As a student and active member of the Phenomenological Society at Göttingen and later in Freiburg, she was most certainly aware of details regarding Husserl's position.

5. Husserl's problem is apparent: If "primal presencing" is constituted first in my sphere of ownness, then how could presencing, in principle, be at one and the same time both constituted and "primal?"

6. Hart, "Contingency of Temporality and Eternal Being," 58.

7. Hart, 58.

8. Derrida's critique will figure in our discussion of Levinas's "reversal of the direction of intentionality" in part three.

9. Hart, "Contingency of Temporality and Eternal Being," 59.

10. I am reminded here of T. S. Eliot's poem "Gerontion": "Signs are taken for wonders, 'We would see a sign!' The word within a word, unable to speak a word, Swaddled with darkness."

11. James Collins, *Crossroads in Philosophy* (Chicago: H. Regnery Co., 1969), 86.

12. Collins, 86.

13. Paul Edwards, ed., *The Encyclopedia of Philosophy*, vol. 7 (New York: MacMillan, 1967), 488. Apparently, the earliest use of a cognate of the English term "solipsist" is ascribed to the apostate Jesuit priest Giulio Clemente Scotti, who used the word in a 1652 treatise entitled *La Monarchie des solipes*. While the work itself described a kingdom of "self-seekers," it was aimed by Scotti as a satire against the Jesuits. (Edwards notes that, for some time after Scotti's work was published, Jesuits in France were often subject to the epithet "solipsistes.") The work was no doubt in part directed as a farce of the "Two Kingdoms Meditation," which greets the Jesuit retreatant at the beginning of the Second Week of the *Spiritual Exercises*. See St. Ignatius Loyola, *The Spiritual Exercises*, ed. David Fleming (St. Louis, MI: Institute of Jesuit Sources, 1989).

14. Maurice Natanson, *The Journeying Self: A Study in Philosophy and Social Role* (Reading, MA: Addison-Wesley Press, 1970), 28.

15. John Locke, *An Essay Concerning Human Understanding* (Indianapolis: Hackett Publishing, 1980); see chap. IV, 1.2.

16. Eugen Fink, *Sixth Cartesian Meditation* (Bloomington: Indiana University Press, 1995), 122–23.

17. Dorian Cairns, "The Fundamental Philosophical Significance of Husserl's *Logische Untersuchungen*," *Husserl Studies* 18, vol. 1 (Dordrecht: Kluwer Academic Publishers, 2002), 48.

18. The thematic of a "we-world" is richly described in terms of social ontology and critical phenomenology. See, for example, Dan Zahavi, "You, Me, and We: The Sharing of Emotional Experiences," *Journal of Consciousness Studies* 22 (Copenhagen: University of Copenhagen, 2015): 84–101; and Timothy Burns, "On Being a 'We': Edith Stein's Contributions to the Intentionalism Debate," *Human Studies: A Journal for Philosophy and the Social Sciences* 38, no. 4 (2015): 529–47.

Chapter Seven

1. Heidegger's theory of hermeneutics in *Being and Time* suggests that there never exists an "uninterpreted" or "presuppositionless" world of "mere presencing," upon which we place interpretations. Rather, the world always and already appears

to Dasein as the world of practical involvement. "Meaning" casts or projects a phenomenon into view, such that it rises up into appearance. "Meaning" is what makes the hermeneutical act possible, it is a horizonal framework of Dasein in which the intelligibility of something is understood. For Heidegger's articulation of the issue, see esp. *Being and Time* 90ff.

2. The rift that ensued between Husserl and Heidegger is legendary, owing much to Heidegger's displeasure of Husserl's transcendental turn.

3. Heidegger's colorful notion of spatiality effectually completes the hermeneutical circle initially described above. For Heidegger, understanding (*Verstehen*) does not imply needing to "step outside" the circle of understanding, but rather to enter into the circle correctly. The hermeneutical circle, properly understood, *makes meaning possible*. It is a condition of possibility of the framework or structure of intelligibility; it is what illuminates the structure of the thing and lets it (the thing) disclose *itself*. See *Being and Time* 194–95.

4. We will discuss Heidegger's notion of "inauthenticity" in the next section, in context of his notion of the *they* of everydayness.

5. As we saw in our analysis of Husserl's notion of the constitution of the alter ego in part one, this is a concern in the fifth of Husserl's *Cartesian Meditations*.

6. Here, Heidegger clearly rejects Kant's notion that space is an a priori category.

7. A *formal indication* is Heidegger's substitute for the traditional "concept." Unlike the traditional concept, which is a universal that "contains" particulars under it, the formal indication simply points to a concrete singularity that exceeds it and that it cannot contain but simply indicates in a more or less empty way. "Existence" and the "I" are prominent examples of formal indications in *Being and Time*.

8. Of course, Heidegger is not describing a chronological priority but a thematic one.

9. Heidegger is directing his criticism against Husserl's theory of the constitution of other persons through analogical apperception.

10. Heidegger later notes in the text that the words "with" and "too" need to be understood existentially, not categorially.

11. For Heidegger, even the mode of "active interest" is fueled by a desire to dominate others, though the possibility always remains that a positive relation between two sources of authentic freedom in terms of productive communication can free the Other for their concern. The vast majority of human experience, however, is based on inauthenticity, in which I lose "myself" in the mass contagion of the they.

12. Heidegger uses the phrase "proximally" in order to describe the spatial sense of what is nearest at hand, familiar, right under our nose, while "for the most part," with which it is always associated, has the temporal sense of what we do routinely and everyday. Together "proximally and for the most part" make up our inauthentic everyday self, but definitely not our "primordial" self.

13. In Heidegger's terminology, we could say that the Dasein-with of Others is often encountered in terms of what is ready-to-hand within-the-world. "One's own Dasein, like the Dasein-with of Others, is encountered proximally and for the most part in terms of the with-world with which we are environmentally concerned. When Dasein is absorbed in the world of its concern—that is, at the same time, in its Being-with towards Others—it is not itself" (*BT* 163).

14. "If Dasein-with remains existentially constitutive for Being-in-the-world, then, like our circumspective dealings with the ready-to-hand within-the-world (which, by way of anticipation, we have called 'concern'), it must be Interpreted in terms of the phenomenon of *care*; for as 'care' the Being of Dasein in general is to be defined. Concern is a character-of-Being which Being-with cannot have as its own, even though Being-which, like concern, is a *Being towards* entities encountered within-the-world" (*Being and Time* 157).

15. Heidegger emphasizes the point that even if ten or a hundred human beings stand "beside" me, Dasein can still be alone. Being-with and the facticity of "living amongst" or with others is not based on numbers of subjects or objects of concern.

16. Again, the imagery invoking Nietzsche's "herd mentality" is intentional.

17. The "existential" (*Existenzial*) is the formal indication, the general ontological structure of Dasein as "existence," while "existentiell" is the unique singularity, the way someone with a proper name embodies their existential structure. *Existentiell* does not mean a mood, the "they" or fallen everydayness. One might be authentic or inauthentic in one's *existentiell* being. Finally, "existential" (*existenzial*) is used by Heidegger as an adjective to describe the formula for the structure of care as Being-alongside.

18. Perhaps it is better to say, "I open my mouth, but the *they* speaks."

19. In particular, "curiosity" is for Heidegger tied up with sight and understanding (*BT* 214ff). Curiosity is a mode of understanding of the *they*, namely, how you understand when you don't understand anything. Similar to Kierkegaard's notion of aesthetic existence, the *they* who indulge in curiosity need constantly to be entertained.

20. Refer to *Being and Time* sections 35–38 for Heidegger's detailed analysis of each of these themes. My intent in this chapter is not to present a comprehensive exegesis of Heidegger's magnum opus, but rather to demonstrate that, for Heidegger, "Dasein's facticity is such that *as long as* it is what it is, Dasein remains in the throw, and is sucked into the turbulence of the 'they's' inauthenticity" (*BT* 223).

21. Heidegger says: "When one talks of the 'circle' in understanding, one expresses a failure to recognize two things: (1) that understanding as such makes up a basic kind of Dasein's Being, and (2) that this Being is constituted as care. To deny the circle, to make a secret of it, or even to want to overcome it, means finally to reinforce this failure. We must rather endeavour to leap into the 'circle,' primordially and wholly, so that even at the start of the analysis of Dasein we make sure that we have a full view of Dasein's circular Being" (*BT* 363).

22. Another important and related issue here is the Wittgensteinian one, namely, that you can't have a "private language." To have a language means to engage in a public practice through public discourse. The implications to Wittgenstein's argument, however, would take us down another road entirely.

23. "As *existentialia*, states-of-mind and understanding characterize the primordial disclosedness of Being-in-the-world. By way of having a mood, Dasein 'sees' possibilities, in terms of which it is. In the projective disclosure of such possibilities, it already has a mood in every case" (*BT* 188).

Chapter Eight

1. Heidegger's influence was quickly on the rise not only in Germany but in Austria, Switzerland, and France, and this in terms of not only philosophy but theology as well.

2. Although this may be true genetically, what is presented by Husserl in the Fifth Meditation and by Stein in her work *On The Problem of Empathy* is not a genetic account but a static description of how other persons are constituted by individual ego.

3. Emmanuel Levinas, *Of God Who Comes to Mind*, ed. Bettina Bergo (Stanford: Stanford University Press, 1998), 161.

4. Joseph Kockelmans, "Husserl's Transcendental Idealism," in *Phenomenology: The Philosophy of Edmund Husserl and Its Interpretations* (Garden City, NY: Doubleday, 1967), 184.

5. Emmanuel Levinas, *Otherwise than Being or Beyond Essence*, trans. Alphonso Lingis (Duquesne, PA: Duquesne University Press, 1998), 4.

6. For example, one of the predominant themes of *Otherwise than Being* is the sense that I am "held hostage by the Other."

7. Although I have found no evidence in the literature comparing Levinas to Edgar Allan Poe, the opening lines to Poe's "The Raven" take on a rather fascinating ethical significance in light of Levinas's analysis: "Once upon a midnight dreary, while I pondered, weak and weary, Over many a quaint and curious volume of forgotten lore—While I nodded, nearly napping, suddenly there came a tapping, As of some one gently rapping, rapping at my chamber door. 'Tis some visitor,' I muttered, 'tapping at my chamber door—Only this and nothing more.'"

8. These three themes repeatedly appear throughout *Totality and Infinity*. Here, I wish only to highlight the importance they bear on Levinas's initial project.

9. Here I am indebted to Luce Irigaray's *The Forgetting of Air in Martin Heidegger*, trans. Mary Beth Mader (Austin: University of Texas Press, 1999).

10. Levinas's cryptic remark on page 30 of *Totality and Infinity* refers to the continual interruption of "the saying" by the dogmatism of "the said." Levinas draws profoundly on the difference between "the saying" and "the said" in *Otherwise than Being*; here, he merely alludes to it.

11. Husserl's response to Levinas would no doubt be that the *object* is transcendent. If the object was completely transparent, then it would *be* "in" my conscious stream, which of course is a conclusion to which Husserl is vehemently opposed. This theme will be raised again in more detail in response to Jacques Derrida's critique of Levinas in the following chapter.

12. In *Existence and Existents*, Levinas likens *il y a* to the impersonal form: "It rains; it is warm." What is the "it" in "it rains?" The weather? (The "weather" cannot rain.) *Il y a* refers, in general, to that term with which we are unable to fix a substantive. The following discussion will try to make this clear.

13. The theological history of the philosophical concept of *hypostasis* is loaded with confusion. At the Council of Nicea in 325, "hypostasis" was used to speak of the three *hypostaseis* ("persons") of God in one being. Then, in 451, the Council of Chalcedon declared that Christ is one *hypostasis* (person) possessing two *physeis* (natures). The Aristotelean notion of *hypostasis* stressed the unifying principle of individuation, whereas Cyril of Alexandria defined the doctrine of the hypostatic union in terms of the "uniting" of the divine and human natures of Jesus Christ in one person, or *hypostasis*. As with the term transubstantiation, Levinas freely uses many theological (and even specifically Christian) themes, though of course he gives them different emphases.

14. Such a pre-perceptual field is similar to Heidegger's notion of the use of tools—(and even somewhat similar to Stein's notion of the co-primordiality of affectivity)—but neither Heidegger nor Stein present as radical a position as Levinas requires. Similarly, Husserl also speaks of a pre-perceptual field of "passive genesis." Before I form a judgment that "X" is on the table, Husserl says, I have the raw perceptual experience that has not yet been logically or grammatically formed. There is a pure sense (*Sinn*) that has not yet become *Bedeutung*. Nevertheless, for Levinas the reversal of constitution is much more radical than Husserl's notion of passive constitution. Derrida, for his part, argues that there really is no pre-perceptual, pre-linguistic sphere. The linguistic has saturated the thing all the way down, such that it (the thing) is unrecognizable outside language.

15. Here, Levinas is referring to the dialogical model of the "I-Thou" relationship subscribed by Martin Buber. See also his earlier comments on Buber's analysis, 68ff, "Separation and Discourse" in *Totality and Infinity*.

16. The similarity and dissimilarity between Levinas and Heidegger is particularly noticeable in this context. Like Heidegger, Levinas argues that the "we" is more primordial than the "I." But whereas for Heidegger the *they* (*das Man*) of everydayness make manifest Dasein's inauthentic Being-in-the-world, for Levinas "other others" constitute the formal structure of the infinite, which makes possible the origin of ethics. Like death, the face of the Other commands, at one and the same time, both infinite respect and infinite distance.

17. In the English edition, Levinas's word for empathy is translated as "sympathy," which of course also brings Max Scheler into the heart of his crit-

icism. Still, it seems evident that Levinas means to criticize Husserl's notion of *Einfühlung*, especially since it was Levinas who first translated the fourth and fifth of Husserl's *Cartesian Meditations* into French in 1931.

Chapter Nine

1. An allusion is drawn here between Derrida and Kierkegaard who, in *The Concept of Anxiety*, describes anxiety as "a sympathetic antipathy and an antipathetic sympathy," that is, a simultaneous feeling of attraction and repulsion. See Sören Kierkegaard, *The Concept of Anxiety*, trans. Howard V. Hong and Edna H. Hong (Princeton, NJ: Princeton University Press, 1980), 42.

2. John D. Caputo, *The Prayers and Tears of Jacques Derrida: Religion Without Religion* (Bloomington: Indiana University Press, 1997), 12. Caputo notes: "A transcendental condition is a sufficient and enabling condition; a quasi-transcendental condition is insufficient and equi-disabling, seeing that the effect that it makes possible is also made unstable."

3. Emmanuel Levinas, *Ethics and Infinity: Conversations with Philippe Nemo* (Pittsburgh: Duquesne University Press, 1985), 86ff.

4. Emmanuel Levinas, "Substitution," in *Basic Philosophical Writings* (Bloomington: Indiana University Press, 1996), 85.

5. Caputo, *The Prayers and Tears of Jacques Derrida*, 13.

6. For a critical study of the denigration of vision in twentieth-century French thought, see Martin Jay, *Downcast Eyes: The Denigration of Vision in Twentieth-Century French Thought* (Berkeley: University of California Press, 1994). "A great deal of recent French thought in a wide variety of fields is in one way or another imbued with a profound suspicion of vision and its hegemonic role in the modern era." Jay's goal is to "explore more explicit manifestations of hostility to visual primacy in the work of artists and critics like . . . Emmanuel Levinas" (14).

7. See John D. Caputo, and Jacques Derrida *Deconstruction in a Nutshell: A Conversation with Jacques Derrida*, ed. John D. Caputo (New York: Fordham University Press, 1997), 105.

8. Edith Wyschogrod, *Emmanuel Levinas: The Problem of Ethical Metaphysics* (New York: Fordham University Press, 2000), 153.

9. As discussed earlier, for Levinas the face is never merely a phenomenon, but an epiphany in precisely this sense, namely, that the face cannot be seen; it is inscribed in inscrutability, it *makes* an epiphany, it *sees*.

10. By "world" Derrida means a synthetic unity of expressions and experience.

11. In the chapter entitled "Infinity and the Face," Levinas writes: "Absolute difference, inconceivable in terms of formal logic, is established only by language. . . . Language is perhaps to be defined as the very power to break the continuity of being or of history" (*TI* 195).

12. Husserl says, for example: "Accordingly *the intrinsically first other* (the first 'non-Ego') *is the other Ego*. And the other Ego makes constitutionally possible a new infinite domain of what is 'other': an *Objective Nature* and a whole Objective world" (*CM* 107).

13. See *CM* 115.

14. Genesis 2:19.

Chapter Ten

1. Mette Lebech adds: The "post-modern dimensions [of Stein's phenomenology] allow . . . for a systematic investigation of social construction within a decisively pluralistic phenomenological perspective" and "constitutes a prolongation of Husserl's phenomenology that is particularly apt to meet a contemporary demand for critical objectivity." *On the Problem of Human Dignity: A Hermeneutical and Phenomenological Investigation* (Würzburg: Königshausen and Neumann, 2009), 20.

2. There is a rich and substantive relationship between "hermeneutics" and "phenomenology," broadly conceived, especially in terms of continental (European) thought. The roots of this relationship are planted in the soil nurtured by Schleiermacher, Gadamer, Heidegger, Dilthey, Ricoeur, and Husserl, and include, for example, the problem of "empathy" as an encounter of meaning and interpretation with alterity (i.e., of "other persons"). Husserl's notion of a "fusion of horizons" of various lifeworlds was clearly the milieu in which Edith Stein was intellectually formed and, as we have seen earlier, the theme of hermeneutics was unquestionably a focus of Husserl and Heidegger and other early phenomenologists (including Stein) in terms of trying to describe how meaning is shared or constituted in an intersubjective we-world.

3. A number of contemporary Stein scholars have pointed to Stein's own hermeneutical development, both in terms of her understanding and interpretation of foreign experience as well as its ethical manifestations and implications. In particular, Edith Stein's description of empathy, now set in terms of hermeneutics or interpreting how meanings and understanding get constituted between persons, offers important insights into a topic that has a long history in phenomenology, particularly amongst European Stein and "early phenomenology" scholars. (Although much of this work is not yet translated into English, there are robust scholarly discussions about these themes by members of the Centro Italiano di Ricerche Fenomenologiche, especially under the leadership of Professoressa Angela Ales Bello.) While it is beyond the capacity of this study to explore the theme in greater detail, future research on this topic will contribute to important understandings of the rich ethical and hermeneutical dimensions of empathy. Ales Bello's scholarship in this area is an important resource regarding the development of Stein's "early phenomenology" as a student and colleague of Husserl to her later

writings, especially set within the European tradition. See, for example, Angelo Ales Bello, "Edith Stein's Contribution to Phenomenology," *Analecta Husserliana: Yearbook of Phenomenological Research LXXX; Phenomenology World-Wide*, ed. Anna-Teresa Tymieniecka (Dordrecht: Kluwer Academic Publishers, 2002), 232–40; "Edmund Husserl and Edith Stein: The Question of the Human Subject," trans. and ed. Antonio Calcagno, *American Catholic Philosophical Quarterly* 82, no. 1 (Winter 2008), 143–60; "From Empathy to Solidarity. Intersubjective Connections According to Edith Stein," *Life: In the Glory of its Radiating Manifestations; Analecta Husserliana XLVIII*, ed. Anna-Teresa Tymieniecka (Boston: Kluwer Academic Publishers, 1996), 367–75; "Ontology, Metaphysics, and Life in Edith Stein," *Contemplating Edith Stein*, ed. Joyce A. Berkman (Notre Dame, IN: University of Notre Dame Press, 2006), 271–82.

    4. William Tullius, "Person in Community, Repentance, and Historical Meaning: From an Individual to a Social Ethics in Stein's Early Phenomenological Treatises," in *Ethics and Metaphysics in the Philosophy of Edith Stein*, eds. Michael F. Andrews and Antonio Calcagno (Cham: Springer Press, 2022), 86.

    5. Tullius, 77.

    6. Lebech, *On the Problem of Human Dignity*, 20.

    7. Several contemporary scholars have examined the interplay between phenomenology and hermeneutics centered around Husserl, Stein, and other early phenomenologists. See Angela Ales Bello, "Phenomenology as Archeology vs. Contemporary Hermeneutics" in *Husserl's Legacy in Phenomenological Philosophies: New Approaches to Reason, Language, Hermeneutics, the Human Condition. Book 3: Analecta Husserlianana XXXVI*, ed. Anna-Teresa Tymieniecka (Dordrecht: Springer, 1991), 3–15; Domenica Jervolina, "Ricoeur and Husserl: Towards a Hermeneutic Phenomenology," in *Husserl's Legacy in Phenomenological Philosophies*, 23–20; Michele Keuter Petersen, *A Hermeneutics of Contemplative Silence: Paul Ricoeur, Edith Stein, and the Heart of Meaning* (Lanham, MD: Lexington Books, 2021); Anna Maria Pezzella, *L'antropologia Filosofica di Edith Stein* (Rome: Citta Nuovo Editrice, 2003); Urbano Santes, "The Hermeneutical Derivation of Phenomenology," in *Husserl's Legacy in Phenomenological Philosophies*, 83–91; Marianne Sawicki, *Body, Text, and Science: The Literacy of Investigative Practices and the Phenomenology of Edith Stein* (Dordrecht: Kluwer Academic Publishers, 1997); Robert Sweeney, "Phenomenology and Hermeneutics," in *Husserl's Legacy in Phenomenological Philosophies*, 17–22; Daniela Verducci, "Il Valore della vita come di senso nella post-modernità: Max Scheler, Edith Stein, Anna-Maria Tymieniecka," in *Fenomenologia della vita: Senso, Valore, Cura* (Lanciano, IT: Caralla Press), 2022.

    8. As noted earlier, a number of scholars have also explored this distinction found in Stein's writings between "masculine" and "feminine" traits, notably in her analyses of woman and the structure of the human soul, education, and vocation. Antonio Calcagno asks, "Finally, there is the question of feminine consciousness

and personal identity. If it is true that a woman is defined as having a unique soul by virtue of her womanhood, then it follows that the 'I' of the woman is differentiated accordingly. Can phenomenology, or Husserl, really speak of a gender-neutral 'I,' especially if male and female are differentiated essentially, as Stein holds? She maintains that feminine consciousness and personal identity affect the way women should be educated and how they view the world." *The Philosophy of Edith Stein* (Pittsburgh: Duquesne University Press, 2007), 75. See also Petr Urban and Lizzie Ward, eds., *Care Ethics, Democratic Citizenship and the State* (Cham: Palgrave MacMillan, 2020).

9. I am indebted in this discussion to Carol Gilligan, who claims, in her 1982 book *In a Different Voice*, that women tend to think and speak in different ways than men when confronted with similar moral dilemmas. For a more detailed examination of Carol Gilligan and Nel Noddings in light of similar themes related to Edith Stein, see Petr Urban, "Care Ethics and the Feminine Personalism of Edith Stein," *Philosophies* 7, no. 60 (2022): 1–14, https://doi.org/10.3390/philosophies7030060.

10. We will explore the "ethics of care," including important contributions from Carol Gilligan and Nel Noddings, in more detail later in this chapter and in the next.

11. Rudolf Makkreel, "How Is Empathy Related to Understanding?," in *Issues in Husserl's Ideas II*, eds. Thomas Nenon and Lester Embree (Dordrecht: Kluwer Academic Publishers, 1992), 200.

12. Makkreel is of course quoting Husserl here and further notes that "this is, of course, the basis for the common criticism of Husserl that his solipsistic beginning cannot really give him access to the other." Makkreel, 200.

13. One is reminded here, as noted earlier, of Stein's own self-confessed "heresy" against the Master regarding her notion of constitution.

14. Makkreel, 200.

15. The emphasis is mine.

16. Stein calls this part of the chapter "The Consequence of Sensual Empathy and Its Absence in the Literature on Empathy Under Discussion."

17. Rachel Feldhay Brenner, *Writing as Resistance: Four Women Confronting the Holocaust; Edith Stein, Simone Weil, Anne Frank, Etty Hillesum* (University Park: Pennsylvania State University Press, 1997), 34.

18. Brenner, 34.

19. Brenner, 34.

20. Brenner, 34.

21. In a particular manner of speaking, being *for* the Other befits Levinas as well, but only where there is a certain sacrifice of the self to the Other. In effect, Levinas rejects Buber's "I-Thou" relation and says that we cannot address the Other with such intimacy because of the Other's infinite distance.

22. Brenner, 38.

Chapter Eleven

1. Some themes discussed in this section over the next several pages are also explored in terms of Stein's understanding of the "personal attitude." See Michael F. Andrews, "Applications for New Paradigms of Empathy," in *Ethics and Metaphysics in the Philosophy of Edith Stein*, eds. Michael F. Andrews and Antonio Calcagno (Cham: Springer Nature, 2022), 232–37.

2. For a more detailed analysis of distinctions between male and female approaches to an "ethics of care," see Nel Noddings, *Caring: A Feminine Approach to Ethics and Moral Education* (Berkeley: University of California Press, 1984).

3. Antonio Calcagno, *The Philosophy of Edith Stein* (Pittsburgh: Duquesne University Press, 2007), 76.

4. Calcagno, 76.

5. Calcagno, 76.

6. Susan Hekman, *Gender and Knowledge: Elements of a Postmodern Feminism* (Boston: Northeastern University Press, 1990), 54.

7. Hekman, 56–57.

8. Hekman, 56–57.

9. Carol Gilligan, *In a Different Voice: Psychological Theory and Women's Development* (Cambridge, MA: Harvard University Press, 1993), 22.

10. Petr Urban also explores similar themes in his descriptive analysis of "an ethics of care" that he juxtaposes with Stein's description of woman. See, for example, Petr Urban, "Edith Stein's Phenomenology of Woman's Personality and Value," in *Alles Wesentliche Lässt Sich Nicht Schreiben: Leben und Denken Edith Steins im Spiegel Ihres Gesamtwerks*, eds. Stephan Regh and Andreas (Freiburg: Verlag Herder, 2016), 538–55.

11. Here, the work of Nel Noddings helps us draw an important correlation between Stein and Levinas. According to Noddings, "[T]he cared-for need not be one-caring in order to constitute the relation." What she means is that the Thou "is a necessary condition for the one-caring to be in a relation of caring." Like Levinas's notion of the elements, in a way, Noddings argues that the one-caring "is engrossed; the cared-for *fills the firmament.*" Hence, for Noddings the ethical command—what she calls the "I must"—"arises directly and prior to consideration of what it is that I might do. The initial feeling is the I must." Hence, the primordial ethical response is *felt*, it is *emotive* and not necessarily a rational, reasoned or even cognitive response. She concludes: "I have no difficulty in considering it as innate. Indeed, I am claiming that the impulse to act in behalf of the present other is itself innate. . . . [T]his strong desire to be moral is derived, reflectively,

from the more fundamental and natural desire to be and to remain related. To reject *the feeling* when it arises is either to be in an internal state of imbalance or to contribute willfully to the diminution of the ethical ideal." Nel Noddings, *Caring: A Feminine Approach to Ethics and Moral Education* (Berkeley: University of California Press, 1984), 69–83.

12. Andrews, "Applications for New Paradigms of Empathy," 234.

13. We may thus note a striking similarity here between Stein and Sartre ("the Look"), Gabriel Marcel ("creative fidelity"), and even Ignatius Loyola (the use of "colloquy" and imaginative variation in the *Spiritual Exercises*). In the case of each of these authors, the Other is not simply cognitively constituted but is rather constitutive of the world of values, which she presents to me and which I could not possibly obtain without her. Hence, the Other (whether human or divine) calls me into a reciprocal relationship of ethical fidelity that is simply impossible without the Other's constituting it. Jonathan Spence, for example, captures the significance of empathy as a means used by Jesuit spiritual directors to impel retreatants to "feel-into" the sufferings of Christ so as to be transformed interiorly by this experience, and not just on a cognitive level. For Ignatius, such self-abandonment is not self-directed but Other-directed; hence the need for a knowledgeable spiritual director to help the retreatant discern between different levels of authentic motivations. Describing how Matteo Ricci used the Exercises to dialogue with leaders of the sixteenth-century Ming dynasty, Spence writes: "The scriptural context was reinforced by the acts of memory.... Several exercises were designed to force the faithful *back to presence* at the acts of Christ's life and passion, so that *they felt* and saw every blow that the soldiers landed on Christ's body." Jonathan Spence, *The Memory Palace of Matteo Ricci* (New York: Penguin Books, 1984), 50.

14. Susan Bordo, *The Flight to Objectivity: Essays on Cartesianism and Culture* (Albany: State University of New York Press, 1987), 113.

15. Bordo, 112.

16. Andrews, "Applications for New Paradigms of Empathy," 235.

17. Emmanuel Levinas, "Apropos of Buber: Some Notes," in *Outside the Subject*, trans. Michael Smith (Stanford: Stanford University Press, 1994), 43–44.

18. Andrews, "Applications for New Paradigms of Empathy," 236.

19. Levinas, "Apropos of Buber: Some Notes," 47.

20. By all accounts, Stein was noted as an excellent reader of Husserl and was the invited "Husserl expert" at the Société Thomiste conference in Juvisy in September 1932 (*Letters* 117).

21. Michael Murray, "Against Dialogue," in *Reinterpreting the Political: Continental Philosophy and Political Theory*, ed. Lenore Langsdorf (Albany: State University of New York Press, 1998), 183.

22. Andrews, "Applications for New Paradigms of Empathy," 236.

23. Hans-Georg Gadamer, *Truth and Method* (New York: Continuum, 1998). See 383–88.

24. Petr Urban, "Care Ethics and the Feminine Personalism of Edith Stein," *Philosophies* 7, no. 60 (2022): 1–14, https://doi.org/10.3390/philosophies7030060. See esp. "Stein's Personalist Ethics," sect. 3.1.

25. Gadamer, *Truth and Method*, 83.

26. Murray, "Against Dialogue," 191.

27. Murray, 189.

28. Jean-Luc Marion, "Sketch of a Phenomenological Concept of Gift," in *Postmodern Philosophy and Christian Thought*, ed. Merold Westphal (Indianapolis: Indiana University Press, 1999), 123.

29. Marion, 130.

30. Levinas, "Apropos of Buber," 48.

31. The notion between the description of a "first-person" experience and a "third-person" narrative marks a boundary in contemporary critical phenomenology. As a "first-person" critical analysis, descriptions of the Other as an embodied subject necessitate further discussions about biological physical differences in terms of male, female, and intersex embodiment, whereas issues of gender and sexual identity are marked by "third-person" variations of cultural roles, expressions, and assumptions.

32. Barbara Marshall, *Engendering Modernity: Feminism, Social Theory and Social Change* (Boston: Northeastern University Press, 1994), 101.

33. Arne Johan Vetlesen, *Perception, Empathy and Judgment: An Inquiry into the Preconditions of Moral Performance* (University Park: Pennsylvania State University Press, 1994), 326.

34. Vetlesen, 327. The italics are in the original.

35. Vetlesen, 327–28.

36. Vetlesen, 327.

37. Vetlesen, 327.

38. This distinction, as noted previously in this chapter, refers to the distinction between "first-person" critical phenomenology and "third-person" analysis, respectively.

39. In her 1929 essay "Husserl and Aquinas: A Comparison," Edith Stein describes the close affinity between Husserl and St. Thomas on a number of important issues. "For someone coming from the thought of Edmund Husserl it is not at all easy to find a way into that of St. Thomas. We may perhaps find a link in connection with Franz Brentano. Husserl himself described in his reminiscences how Brentano's manner of handling philosophical issues had won him over for philosophy. . . . But where did Brentano get the unrelenting exactness in his reasoning that captivated Husserl and struck him so as novel in philosophy? Where did his crystal-clear concept formation come from? Was it

not his scholastic heritage? Brentano had been brought up in the austere school of traditional Catholic philosophy and its manner of thinking had shaped his mind. And in Husserl we find something like it in the precision of his thought and in the economy of his language." Stein, *Knowledge and Faith*, trans. Walter Redmond, *The Collected Works of Edith Stein: Volume VIII* (Washington, DC: ICS Publications, 1986), 6–7.

40. Thomas Aquinas, *Introduction to St. Thomas Aquinas*, ed. Anton C. Pegis (New York: Modern Library, 1948), Ia,12 (esp. 12.3 and 12.4).

41. Thomas Aquinas, *Summa Theologiae: A Concise Translation*, ed. Timothy McDermott (Westminster, MD: Christian Classics, 1991), 27, 131–32.

42. These quotes are taken from Aquinas, *Introduction to St. Thomas Aquinas*.

43. Friedrich Georg Friedmann, "On the Beatification of Edith Stein," in *Never Forget: Christian and Jewish Perspectives on Edith Stein*, ed. Waltraud Herbstrith (Washington, DC: ICS Publications, 1998), 120. While Rosenzweig's comment implicitly concerns the relationship between Judaism and Christianity, it seems appropriate to expand upon his quote in this context.

44. I bring to the reader's attention a wonderful grasp of this issue in Richard Kearney's *The Wake of Imagination*. See esp. 132–38, "Iconography and Iconoclasm." Describing the creation of an icon, Kearney quotes from another source: "The fact that the icon was executed on a two-dimensional surface was an essential reminder that it was representing another reality which could not be substituted for by the art-work itself. . . . Icons are not meant to create a subjective mood or even a pious response in the mind of the beholder. . . . The icon is meant to be a window onto another world, not really a thing in itself. As a material object it is no more than a prism or a focus which concentrates energy in a way that allows our vision to transcend it and go beyond . . . it should become *transparent*." Kearney, *The Wake of Imagination* (Minneapolis: University of Minnesota Press, 1988), 135–36.

45. Otherwise, if an answer to what the Infinite "is" *were* clearly given, it would not *be* the Infinite. After all, St. Thomas Aquinas himself claimed that the "ultimate in human knowledge of God [i.e., the (w)Holy Other] is to know that we do not know him (*De Potentia*, 7,5)."

46. William Shakespeare, *Hamlet*, eds. Barbara Mowat and Paul Werstine (New York: Simon and Schuster, 2012), act 5, sc. 2, 273.

Selected Bibliography

Ales Bello, Angela. "Analisi fenonemologica della voluntà. Edmund Husserl e Edith Stein" [Phenomenological Analysis of the Will]. Per la filosofia 11, no. 31, 1994: 24–29.

———. "Coscienza e solidarietà in Edith Stein" [Consciousness and Solidarity in Edith Stein]. Etica e società contemporanea I, *Studi Tomistica*, vol. 48. Edited by A. Lobato. Vatican City: Libreria Editrice Vaticana, 1992: 137–143.

———. *Edith Stein: Patrona d'Europa*. Casale Monferrato, IT: Edizioni Piemme, 2000.

———. "Edith Stein's Contribution to Phenomenology." In *Analecta Husserliana: Yearbook of Phenomenological Research LXXX: Phenomenology World-Wide*. Edited by Anna-Teresa Tymieniecka. Dordrecht: Kluwer Academic, 2002: 232–240.

———. "Edmund Husserl and Edith Stein: The Question of the Human Subject." *American Catholic Philosophical Quarterly*, vol. 82, no. 1. Edited by Robert E. Wood and Antonio Calcagno. Charlottesville, VA: Philosophy Documentation Center, 2008: 143–160.

———. "From Empathy to Solidarity: Intersubjective Connections According to Edith Stein." In *Life: In the Glory of Its Radiating Manifestations; Analecta Husserliana XLVIII*, Edited by Anna-Teresa Tymieniecka. Boston: Kluwer Academic Publishers, 1996: 367–375.

———. "Ontology, Metaphysics, and Life in Edith Stein." In *Contemplating Edith Stein*. Edited by Joyce A. Berkman. Notre Dame, Ind: University of Notre Dame Press, 2006: 271–282.

———. "Phenomenology as Archeology vs. Contemporary Hermeneutics." In *Husserl's Legacy in Phenomenological Philosophies: New Approaches to Reason, Language, Hermeneutics, the Human Condition: Analecta Husserliana XXXVI*, no. 3. Edited by Anna-Maria Tymieniecka. Dordrecht: Springer, 1991: 3–15.

———. "The Study of the Soul Between Psychology and Phenomenology in Edith Stein." In *Eighteenth Annual Symposium of the Simon Silverman*

Phenomenology Center. Edited by Daniel Martino. Pittsburgh: Duquesne University Press, 2001: 3–17.

Andrews, Michael F. "Applications for New Paradigms of Empathy." In *Ethics and Metaphysics in the Philosophy of Edith Stein*. Edited by Michael F. Andrews and Antonio Calcagno. Cham, Switzerland: Springer Press, 2022: 232–237.

———. "Edith Stein and Max Scheler: Ethics, Empathy, and the Constitution of the Acting Person." In *Quaestiones Disputatae: A Journal of Philosophical Inquiry and Discussion: The Early Phenomenology of Munich and Göttingen*, vol. 3 no. 1. Edited by Kimberly Baltzer-Jaray. Steubenville, OH: Franciscan University Press, 2012: 33–47.

———. "Edmund Husserl: Empathy and the Transcendental Constitution of the World." In Analecta Husserliana LXXIX. Edited by A.T. Tymieniecka. Dordrecht: Kluwer Academic Publishers, 2004: 217–237.

———. *Ethics and Metaphysics in the Philosophy of Edith Stein: Applications and Implications*. Edited by Michael F. Andrews and Antonio Calcagno. Volume 12 of "Women in the History of Philosophy and Sciences" series. Cham, Switzerland: Springer Press, 2022.

Aquinas, Thomas. *Introduction to St. Thomas Aquinas*. Edited by Anton C. Pegis. New York: Modern Library, 1948.

———. *Summa Theologiae: A Concise Translation*. Edited by Timothy McDermott. Westminster, MD: Christian Classics, 1991.

Arnold, Thomas. "The Object(s) of Phenomenology." *Human Studies: A Journal for Philosophy and the Social Sciences* 36, no. 2, 2020: 105–122.

Baltzer-Jaray, Kimberly. "Introduction to the Early Phenomenology: Munich and Göttingen." *Quaestiones Disputatae: The Early Phenomenology in Munich and Göttingen*, 3, no. 1. Edited by Kimberly Baltzer-Jaray. Steubenville, OH: Franciscan University of Steubenville Press, 2012: 4–6.

Balzer, Carmen. "The Empathy Problem in Edith Stein." In *Husserlian Phenomenology in a New Key. Book 2: Phenomenology in the World Fifty Years after the Death of Edmund Husserl: Analecta Husserliana XXXV*. Edited by Anna-Teresa Tymieniecka. Dordrecht: Kluwer Academic Publishers, 1991: 271–278.

Barry, William, and William Connolly. *The Practice of Spiritual Direction*. Minneapolis: Seabury Press, 1982.

Baseheart, Mary Catharine. "Edith Stein's Phenomenology of the State." In *Reinterpreting the Political: Continental Philosophy and Political Theory*. Edited by Lenore Langsdorf. Albany: State University of New York Press, 1998: 51–63.

———. "Edith Stein's Philosophy of Community." *The Personalist Forum* 8, no. 1 (1993): 163–73.

———. "Edith Stein's Philosophy of the Person." In *Edith Stein Symposium* (Carmelite Studies 4). Edited by John Sullivan. Washington, DC: ICS Publications, 1987: 34–39.

———. *Person in the World: Introduction to the Philosophy of Edith Stein*. Dordrecht: Kluwer Academic Publishers, 1997.

Beckmann, Beate. "Phänomenologie des religiösen Erlebnisses im Auschluss an Adolf Reinach und Edith Stein" [Phenomenology of Religious Experience According to Adolf Reinach and Edith Stein]. *Teresianum* 50, nos. 2–3, 1999: 299–317. See also "Fenomenologia dell'esperienza religiosa secondo Adolf Reinach ed Edith Stein." In *Edith Stein: Testimone di oggi profeta per domani*. International Teresianum Symposium. Edited by J. Sleiman and L. Borriello. Vatican City: Libreria Editrice Vaticana, 1998: 317–337.

Behnke, Elizabeth. "Edmund Husserl's Contributions to the Phenomenology of the Body in Ideas II." In *Issues in Husserl's Ideas II: Contributions to Phenomenology* 24. Edited by Thomas Nenan and Lester Embree. Dordrecht: Kluwer Academic Publishers, 1996: 135–160.

Bell, David. *Husserl*. London: Routledge, 1990.

Berkman, Joyce A. *Contemplating Edith Stein*, editor. Notre Dame, IN: University of Notre Dame Press, 2006.

Birkenbeil, Edward J. "Dr. Edith Stein: Assistentin, Lehrerin, Dozentin" [Dr. Edith Stein: Assistant, Teacher, Instructor]. *Edith Stein: Leben, Philosophie, Vollendung. Abhandlungen des internationalen*. Edith Stein Symposium, Würzburg, November 2–4, 1990. Edited by Leo Elders. Würzburg: Naumann, 1991: 95–110.

Borden Sharkey, Sarah. *Edith Stein*. New York: Continuum, 2003.

Bordo, Susan. *The Flight of Objectivity: Essays on Cartesianism and Culture*. Albany: State University of New York Press, 1987.

Buber, Martin. *I and Thou*. Translated by Walter Kaufmann. New York: Charles Scribner's Sons, 1970.

Burns, Timothy. "From I to You to We: Empathy and Community in Edith Stein's Phenomenology." *Empathy, Sociality, and Personhood: Contributions to Phenomenology* 94. Edited by E. Magrì and D. Moran. Cham: Springer International, 2017: 127–42.

———. "On Being a 'We': Edith Stein's Contributions to the Intentionalism Debate." *Human Studies: A Journal for Philosophy and the Social Sciences* 38, no. 4, Dordrecht: Springer Nature Press, 2015: 529–547.

Cairns, Dorion. *Conversations with Husserl and Fink*. The Hague: Martinus Nijhoff, 1976.

———. "The Fundamental Philosophical Significance of Husserl's *Logische Untersuchungen*." *Husserl Studies* 18, no. 1. Edited by Lester Embree, Fred Kersten, and R. M. Zaner. Dordrecht: Kluwer Academic Publishers, 2002: 41–49.

Calcagno, Antonio. "Assistant and/or collaborator? Edith Stein's relationship to Edmund Husserl's Ideen II." In *Contemplating Edith Stein*. Edited by Joyce A. Berkman. Notre Dame, IN: University of Notre Dame Press, 2006: 243–270.

———. *Lived Experience from the Inside Out: Social and Political Philosophy in Edith Stein*. Pittsburgh: Duquesne University Press, 2014.

---. *The Philosophy of Edith Stein*. Pittsburgh: Duquesne University Press, 2007.

---. "Thinking Community and the State from Within." *American Catholic Philosophical Quarterly* 82, no. 1. Edited by Robert E. Wood and Antonio Calcagno. Charlottesville, VA: Philosophy Documentation Center, 2008: 31–45.

Caminada, Emanuele. "Edith Stein's Account of Communal Mind and its Limits: A Phenomenological Reading." *Human Studies: A Journal for Philosophy and the Social Sciences* 38, no. 4. Edited by Thomas Szanto and Dermot Moran, 2015: 549–566.

Caputo, John D. *The Prayers and Tears of Jacques Derrida: Religion Without Religion*. Bloomington: Indiana University Press, 1997.

Caputo, John D. and Derrida, Jacques. *Deconstruction in a Nutshell: A Conversation with Jacques Derrida*. Edited by John D. Caputo. New York: Fordham University Press, 1997.

Carr, David. "Cogitamus Ergo Sumus: The Intentionality of the First-Person Plural." In *Interpreting Husserl*. Dordrecht: Kluwer Academic Publishers, 1987: 281–296.

---. "The 'Fifth Meditation' and Husserl's Cartesianism." *Philosophy and Phenomenological Research* 34, no. 1, 1973: 14–35.

---. *Time, Narrative, and History*. Bloomington: Indiana University Press, 1986.

Cohen, Joseph and Moran, Dermot. *The Husserl Dictionary*. London: Continuum, 2012.

Collins, James. "Edith Stein and the Advance of Phenomenology." *Thought* 17, 1942: 685–708.

---. "Edith Stein as a Phenomenologist." In *Three Paths in Philosophy*. Chicago: Henry Regnery Co., 1962. Published in 1969 as Crossroads in Philosophy: 85–105.

---. "The Fate of Edith Stein." *Thought* 18, 1943: 384.

---. "Review of Edith Stein *Werke II*." *Modern Schoolman* 29, 1952: 139–145.

Conrad-Martius, Hedwig. "Edith Stein." *Archives de Philosophie* 22, no. 2, 1959: 163–174.

---. "Meine Freudin Edith Stein" [My Friend Edith Stein]. *Hochland* 51, no. 1, 1958: 38–46. Reprinted in *Briefe an Hedwig Conrad-Martius* (Munich: Kosel, 1960). Translated as "La Mia Amica Edith Stein," in *Edith Stein* (Rome: Città Nuova Editrice, 1997): 78–89.

Conway, Mary Devereaux. "Edith Stein: A Woman of Today." *Magnificat* 95, 1955: 51–55. Reprinted as "Edith Stein: (Sister Benedicta Teresia, O.C.D.)," in *Book of Catholic Authors (5th Series): Informal Self-Portraits of Famous Modern Catholic Writers*. Edited by Walter Romig. Frosse Pointe, MI: Romig, 1957.

Costantini, Elio. "Einfühlung und Intersubjektivität bei Edith Stein und bei Husserl." In *The Great Chain of Being and Italian Phenomenology: Analecta Husserliana*, XI. Edited by Anna-Teresa Tymieniecka. Boston: Reidel, 1981: 335–339.

Costello, Peter. *Layers in Husserl's Phenomenology: On Meaning and Intersubjectivity*. Toronto: University of Toronto Press, 2012.

———. "Toward a Phenomenology of Community: Stein and Nancy." In *Emotion, Space, and Society*, vol. 13. Edited by Danielle Drozdzewski. https://doi.org/10.1016/j.emospa.2013.12.005: Elsevier, 2014: 121–133.

Cross, Nancy M. "A Higher Middle Ground: Blessed Edith Stein's Feminism." *Review for Religious* 48, 1989: 86–94.

Davis, Colin. *Levinas: An Introduction*. Notre Dame, IN: Notre Dame University Press, 1996.

Depraz, Natalie. *Transcendence et Incarnation: Le Statut de L'intersubjectivité comme Alterité a Soi chez Husserl*. Paris: Vrin, 1995.

Depraz, Natalie, and Zahavi, Dan, editors. *Alterity and Facticity: New Perspectives on Husserl*. Dordrecht: Kluwer Academic Publishers, 1998.

Derrida, Jacques. "Violence and Metaphysics: An Essay on the Thought of Emmanuel Levinas." *Writing and Difference*. Chicago: University of Chicago Press, 1978.

Descartes, René. *Meditations on First Philosophy*. Indianapolis: Hackett Publishing, 1993.

Donohoe, Janet. *Husserl on Ethics and Intersubjectivity: From Static to Genetic Phenomenology*. Amherst, NY: Humanity Books, 2004.

Edwards, Paul, ed. *The Encyclopedia of Philosophy* 7. New York: MacMillan, 1967: 488.

Elliston, Frederick A. "Husserl's Phenomenology of Empathy." In *Husserl: Expositions and Appraisals*. Edited by Frederick Elliston and Peter McCormick. Notre Dame, IN: University of Notre Dame Press, 1977: 213–231.

Fabro, Cornelio. "Edith Stein, Husserl e Martin Heidegger." *Humanitas*, 33, n.4. Brescia: Humanitas, 1978: 485–517.

Failla, Mariannina. "Phenomenology and the Beginnings of the Moral Problem: Dilthey, Brentano, Husserl." In *Phenomenology in a New Key: Analecta Husserliana XXXV*. Edited by Anna-Teresa Tymieniecka. Dordrecht: Springer, 2012: 53–65.

Farber, Marvin. "The Ideal of a Presuppositionless Philosophy." In *Philosophical Essays in Memory of Edmund Husserl*. Edited by Marvin Farber. Cambridge, MA: Harvard University Press, 1940: 44–64. Reprinted in *Phenomenology: The Phenomenology of Edmund Husserl and Its Interpretations*. Edited by Joseph Kockelmans. Garden city, NY: Doubleday and Company, 1967: 37–57.

Feldhay Brenner, Rachel. "Edith Stein: A Reading of her Feminist Thought." *Studies in Religion/Sciences religieuses* 23, no. 1, 1994: 43–56.

———. "Ethical Convergence in Religious Conversion." In *The Unnecessary Problem of Edith Stein*. Edited by Harry J. Cargas. Lanham, MD: University Press of America, 1994: 77–102.

———. *Writing as Resistance: Four Women Confronting the Holocaust; Edith Stein, Simone Weil, Anne Frank, Etty Hillesum*. University Park: Pennsylvania State University Press, 1997.

Fetz, Reto Luzius, Matthias Rath, and Peter Schulz. "Ich, Seele, Selbst. Edith Steins Theorie personaler Identität" [I, Soul and Self: Edith Stein's Theory of Personal Identity]. In *Studien zur Philosophie von Edith Stein*. International Edith Stein Symposium, Eichstätt, 1991. Phänomenologische Forschungen, Bd. 26/27. Freiburg: Alber, 1993: 386–419.

Fidalgo, António. "Edith Stein, Theodor Lipps und die Einfühlung problematik" [Edith Stein and Theodor Lipps and the Problem of Empathy]. In *Studien zur Philosophie von Edith Stein*. Freiburg: Alber Press, 1993: 90–106.

Fink, Eugen. *Sixth Cartesian Meditation: The Idea of a Transcendental Theory of Method*. Translated by Ronald Bruzina. Bloomington: Indiana University Press, 1995.

Fornaro, M. "Il pensiero di Edith Stein" [The Thought of Edith Stein]. *Humanitas* 31, 1976: 997–999.

Friedmann, Friedrich Georg. "On the Beatification of Edith Stein." Translated by Susanne Batzdorff. In *Never Forget: Christian and Jewish Perspectives on Edith Stein*. Carmelite Studies 7. Edited by Waltraud Herbstrith. Washington, DC: ICS Publications, 1998: 109–120.

Frings, Manfred S. *Max Scheler: A Concise Introduction into the World of a Great Thinker*. Pittsburgh: Duquesne University Press, 1965.

———. *The Mind of Max Scheler*. Milwaukee: Marquette University Press, 1996.

Fuchs, Wolfgang Walter. *Phenomenology and the Metaphysics of Presence: An Essay in the Philosophy of Edmund Husserl*. The Hague: Martinus Nijhoff, 1976.

Gadamer, Hans-Georg. *Truth and Method*. New York: Continuum, 1998.

Galeazzi, U. "La lezione di Husserl nell'itinerario di ricerca di Edith Stein" [The Lectures of Husserl in the Research of Edith Stein]. *Hermeneutica* 9, 1989: 163–186.

Garcia, Laura. "The Primacy of Persons: Edith Stein and Pope John Paul II." *Logos: A Journal of Catholic Thought and Culture* 1, no. 2, 1997: 90–99.

Geneviève, Soeur. "Édith Stein critique de Martin Heidegger." *Carmel: Revue trimestrielle de spiritualité chrétienne* 89, no. 3, 1998: 91–107.

Gerl-Falkovitz, Hanna-Barbara. "Edith Stein e la donna" [Edith Stein and Woman]. *Humanitas* 42. Brescia: Humanitas, 1987: 332–354.

Gilligan, Carol. *In A Different Voice: Psychological Theory and Women's Development*. Cambridge, MA: Harvard University Press, 1993.

Godschmidt, Tyron, and Kenneth L. Pearce, editors. *Idealism: New Essays in Metaphysics*. Oxford: Oxford University Press, 2017.

Grace, Madeleine. "Edith Stein and Simone Weil: A Study in Commitment." *Teresianum* 44, no. 1, 1993: 199–219.

Graef, Hilda. *The Scholar and the Cross: The Life and Work of Edith Stein*. Westminster, MD: Newman Press, 1955.

Haney, Kathleen. "Empathy Revisited." In *Eighteenth Annual Symposium of the Simon Silverman Phenomenology Center*. Edited by Daniel Martino. Pittsburgh: Duquesne University Press, 2001: 18-33.

———. *Listening to Edith Stein: Wisdom for a New Century*. Carmelite Studies 12. Edited by Kathleen Haney. Washington, DC: ICS Publications, 2018.

———. "Logos and the Empathic Life." In *Manifestations of Reason: Life, Historicity, Culture; Analecta Husserliana XL*. Edited by Anna-Teresa Tymieniecka. Dordrecht: Kluwer Academic Publishers, 1993: 319-333.

Haney, Kathleen and Valiquettte, Johanna. "Edith Stein: Woman as Ethical Type." In *Phenomenological Approaches to Moral Philosophy: A Handbook*. Edited by John Drummond and Lester Embree. The Netherlands: Springer Dordrecht, 2002: 451-473.

Hart, James G. "Contingency of Temporality and Eternal Being: A Study of Aspects of Edith Stein's Phenomenological Theology as it Appears Primarily: *Endliches und Ewiges Sein*." In *Eighteenth Annual Symposium of the Simon Silverman Phenomenology Center*. Edited by Daniel Martino. Pittsburgh: Duquesne University Press, 2001: 34-68.

———. *The Person and the Common Life: Studies in a Husserlian Social Ethics*. Dordrecht: Kluwer Academic Publishers, 1992.

Hegel, G. W. F. *Hegel's Lectures on the History of Philosophy*, vol. III. Translated by K. S. Haldane and Frances Simson. London: Routledge, 1955.

Heidegger, Martin. *Basic Problems of Phenomenology*. Bloomington: Indiana University Press, 1983.

———. *Being and Time*. Translated by John Maquarrie and Edward Robinson. Oxford: Blackwell, 1992.

———. *Logic: The Question of Truth*. Translated by Thomas Sheehan. Indianapolis: Indiana University Press, 2010.

Hekman, Susan. *Gender and Knowledge: Elements of a Postmodern Feminism*. Boston: Northeastern University Press, 1990.

Herbstrith, Waltraud, editor. *Aus der Tiefe leben: Ausgewahlte Texte zu Fragen der Zeit, Mit zahlreichen erstveroffentlichten Texten* [From a Profound Life: Texts and Questions on Time, with an Anthology of Texts by Stein]. Munich: Kosel-Verlag, 1988.

———. *Denken im Dialog: Zur Philosophie Edith Steins* [Thinking in Dialogue: On the Philosophy of Edith Stein]. Tübingen: Attempto Verlag, 1991.

———. "Edith Stein: A Challenge for Our Times." Translated by Teresa Kinnear. *Mount Carmel* 25, no. 2, 1977: 93-106.

Hughes, J. "Edith Stein's Doctoral Thesis on Empathy and the Philosophical Climate from which It Emerged." *Teresianum*, 36, 1985: 455-484.

———. "Edith Stein's Doctoral Thesis on Empathy." *Mount Carmel* 36, 1987 121-144.

Husserl, Edmund. *The Basic Problems of Phenomenology: From the Lectures, Winter Semester 1910-1911*. Husserliana Collected Works, Vol. XII. Translated by Ingo Farin and James Hart. Dordrecht: Kluwer Academic Publishers, 2006.

———. *Cartesian Meditations: An Introduction to Phenomenology*. Translated by Dorion Cairns. Dordrecht: Kluwer Academic Publishers, 1995.

———. *The Crisis of European Sciences and Transcendental Phenomenology*. Translated by David Carr. Evanston, IL: Northwestern University Press, 1970.

———. "Empfehlung für eine Habilitation Edith Stein" [Recommendation for the Habilitation of Edith Stein]. In *Edith Stein: Ein neues Lebensbild in Zeugnissen und Selbstzeugnissen*, ed. Waltraud Herbstrith. Freiburg: Herder, 1983; and Mainz: Matthias-Grünewald, 1993. Translated as "Raccomandazione per l'ablitazione di Edith Stein," in *Edith Stein: Vita e Testimonianze* [Edith Stein: Life and Testimony] (Rome: Città Nuova Editrice, 1997).

———. *The Idea of Phenomenology*. Translated by William Alston and George Nakhnikian. The Hague: Martinus Nijhoff, 1970.

———. *Ideas Pertaining to a Pure Phenomenology and to a Phenomenological Philosophy: First Book*, vol. 1. Translated by F. Kersten. In *Collected Works: General Introduction to a Pure Phenomenology*. Netherlands: Springer [Martinus Nijhoff Publishers], 1982.

———. *Ideas Pertaining to a Pure Phenomenology and to a Phenomenological Philosophy: First Book*, vol. 2. Translated by Richard Rojcewica and André Schuwer. *Collected Works: General Introduction to a Pure Phenomenology*. Dordrecht: Kluwer Academic Publishers, 1989.

———. *Ideas Pertaining to a Pure Phenomenology and to a Phenomenological Philosophy: Second Book*, vol. 3. Translated by Richard Rojcewica and André Schuwer. *Collected Works: Studies in the Phenomenology of Constitution*. Dordrecht: Kluwer Academic Publishers, 1989.

———. *Logical Investigations: Volume Two*. Translated by J. N. Findlay. London: Routledge and Kegan Paul Press, 1970.

———. *On the Phenomenology of the Consciousness of Internal Time (1893–1917)*: Collected Works 4. Translated by John Barnett Brough. Dordrecht: Kluwer Academic Publishers, 1991.

———. "Philosophy and the Crisis of European Man." In *Phenomenology and the Crisis of Philosophy*. Translated by Quentin Lauer. New York: Harper and Row, 1965.

———. "Philosophy as a Rigorous Science." In *Phenomenology and the Crisis of Philosophy*. Translated by Quentin Lauer. New York: Harper & Row, 1965.

———. *Zur Phänomenologie der Intersubjektivität: Erster Teil: 1905–1920*. Husserliana XIII. Edited by Iso Kern. Leuven: Springer / Husserl Archives of the Higher Institute of Philosophy of the Catholic University of Leuven, 1973.

———. *Zur Phänomenologie der Intersubjektivität: Zweiter Teil: 1921–1928*. Husserliana XIV. Edited by Iso Kern. Leuven: Springer / Husserl Archives of the Higher Institute of Philosophy of the Catholic University of Leuven, 1973.

———. *Zur Phänomenologie der Intersubjektivität: Dritter Teil: 1929–1935*. Husserliana XV. Edited by Iso Kern. Leuven: Springer / Husserl Archives of the Higher Institute of Philosophy of the Catholic University of Leuven, 1973.

Ingarden, Roman. *The Cognition of the Literary Work of Art.* Translated by Ruth Ann Crowley and Kenneth Olson. Evanston, IL: Northwestern University Press, 1980.

———. "Edith Stein on Her Activity as an Assistant of Edmund Husserl." Translated by Janina Makota. *Philosophy and Phenomenological Research* 23, no. 2, 1962, 155–175.

———. *On the Motives which Led Husserl to Transcendental Idealism.* Translated by J.E. Llewelyn, Phaenomenologica Series 64. Dordrecht: Springer, 1975.

———. "Über die philosophischen Forschungen Edith Steins" [About the Philosophical Research of Edith Stein]. Sonder-Abdruck aus bd.26, 1979: 2–3.

———. "Zu Edith Steins Analyse der Einfühlung und des Aufbaus der menschlichen Person" [On Edith Stein's Analysis of Empathy and the Construction of the Human Person]. In *Denken im Dialog: zur Philosophie Edith Steins.* Edited by Waltraud Herbstrith. Tübingen: Attempto Verlag, 1991: 72–82.

Irigaray, Luce. *The Forgetting of Air in Martin Heidegger.* Translated by Mary Beth Mader. Austin: University of Texas Press, 1999.

Jay, Martin. *Downcast Eyes: The Denigration of Vision in Twentieth-Century French Thought.* Berkeley: University of California Press, 1994.

Jervolina, Domenica. "Ricoeur and Husserl: Towards a Hermeneutic Phenomenology." In *Husserl's Legacy in Phenomenological Philosophies: New Approaches to Reason, Language, Hermeneutics, the Human Condition: Analecta Husserliana* 36, no. 3. Edited by Anna-Maria Tymieniecka. Dordrecht: Springer, 1991: 23–20.

Johann, Robert. *The Meaning of Love: An Essay Towards a Metaphysics of Intersubjectivity.* Glen Rock, NJ: Paulist Press, 1966.

Kaufmann, Fritz. "Review of Edith Stein Werke Band II." *Philosophy and Phenomenological Research* 12, 1952: 572–577.

Kearney, Richard. *The Wake of Imagination.* Minneapolis: University of Minnesota Press, 1988.

Kern, Iso. "The Three Ways to the Transcendental Phenomenological Reduction in the Philosophy of Edmund Husserl." In *Husserl: Expositions and Appraisals.* Edited by Frederick Elliston and Peter McCormick. Notre Dame, IN: University of Notre Dame Press, 1977: 126–159.

Kerremans, Ilse. "Edith Stein: een heilige voor onze tijd" [Edith Stein: A Holy One Among Us]. *Aggiornamento* 30, no. 3, 1998.

Kersey, Ethel. "Edith Stein." In *Women Philosophers: A Bio-Critical Source Book.* Edited by Ethel Kersey. New York: Greenwood Press, 1989.

Kierkegaard, Sören. *The Concept of Anxiety: A Simply Psychologically Orienting Deliberation on the Dogmatic Issue of Hereditary Sin.* Translated by Howard V. Hong and Edna H. Hong. Princeton, NJ: Princeton University Press, 1980.

———. *Fear and Trembling.* Edited by Howard V. Hong and Edna H. Hong. Princeton, NJ: Princeton University Press, 1971.

———. *The Sickness Unto Death.* Edited by Howard V. Hong and Edna H. Hong. Princeton, NJ: Princeton University Press, 1971.

Kinkaid, James. "Phenomenology and the Stratification of Reality." *European Journal of Philosophy* 28, no. 4, 2020: 892–910.
Kockelmans, Joseph. *Edmund Husserl's Phenomenology*. West Lafayette, IN: Purdue University Press, 1994.
———. "Husserl and Kant on the Pure Ego." In *Husserl: Expositions and Appraisals*. Edited by Frederick Elliston and Peter McCormick. Notre Dame, IN: University of Notre Dame Press, 1977: 269–285.
———. "Husserl's Transcendental Idealism." *Phenomenology: The Philosophy of Edmund Husserl and Its Interpretations*. Edited by Joseph Kockelmans. Garden City, NY: Doubleday, 1967.
———. "Intentional and Constitutional Analyses." *Phenomenology: The Philosophy of Edmund Husserl and Its Interpretations*. Edited by Joseph Kockelmans. Garden City, NY: Doubleday, 1967.
Koeppel, Josephine, OCD. *Edith Stein: Philosopher and Mystic*. Collegeville, MN: The Liturgical Press, 1990.
Landgrebe, L. "Über die Arbeit, die Edith Stein für Edmund Husserl geleistet hat" [Concerning the Work that Edith Stein Attended for Husserl]. In *Edith Stein—eine grosse Glaubenszeugin. Leven. Neue Dokumente. Philosophie*, edited by Waltraud Herbstrith. Annweiler: Thomas Plöger, 1986.
Lasky, Dalls. "Empathy, Creativity, Reason." In *Manifestations of Reasons: Analecta Husserliana XL*. Edited by Anna-Teresa Tymieniecka. Dordrecht: Springer, 1993: 335–342.
Lauer, Quentin. "Intersubjectivity: The Other Explained Intentionally." In *Phenomenology: The Philosophy of Edmund Husserl and Its Interpretations*. Edited by Joseph Kockelmans. Garden City, NY: Doubleday, 1967.
Lawlor, Leonard. Review of *Transcendence et Incarnation: Le Statut de L'intersubjectivité comme Alterité a Soi chez Husserl*, by Natalie Depraz. Continental Philosophy Review 34. Dordrecht: Kluwer Academic Publishers, 2001: 103–111.
Lebech, Mette. "Heidegger and the Meaning of Being." In *The Philosophy of Edith Stein: From Phenomenology to Metaphysics*. Bern: Peter Lang, 2015.
———. *On the Problem of Human Dignity: A Hermeneutical and Phenomenological Investigation*. Würzburg: Königshausen and Neumann, 2009.
———. "Why Do We Need the Philosophy of Edith Stein?" *Communio* 38, no. 4, 2011: 682–726.
Lembeck, Karl-Heinz. "Die Philosophie Edith Steins." *Zeitschrift für Katholische Theologie* 3, 1990.
———. "Die Phänomenologie Husserls und Edith Stein." *Theologie und Philosophie* 63, 1988: 182–202.
———. "Von der Kritik zur Mystik. Edith Stein und der marburger Neukantianismus" [From Critic to Mystic: Edith Stein and Marburg Neo-Kantianism]. In *Studien zur Philosophie von Edith Stein*.

Lenz-Médoc, Paulus. "L'idée de l'état chez Edith Stein" [The Idea of the State in Edith Stein]. *Les études philosophiques* 11, no. 3, 1956: 451–457.

Levinas, Emmanuel. *Collected Philosophical Papers*. Translated by Alphonso Lingis. Dordrecht: Kluwer Academic Publishers, 1987.

———. *Discovering Existence with Husserl*. Translated by Richard Cohen and Michael Smith. Evanston, IL: Northwestern University Press, 1998.

———. *Entre Nous / On Thinking of the Other*. Translated by Michael B. Smith and Barbara Harshav. New York: Columbia University Press, 1998.

———. *Ethics and Infinity: Conversations with Philippe Nemo*. Translated by Richard Cohen. Pittsburgh: Duquesne University Press, 1985.

———. *Existence and Existents*. Translated by Alphonso Lingis. The Hague: Martinus Nijhoff, 1978.

———. *Of God Who Comes to Mind*. Edited by Bettina Bergo. Stanford: Stanford University Press, 1998.

———. *Otherwise than Being or Beyond Essence*. Translated by Alfonso Lingis. Duquesne: Duquesne University Press, 1998.

———. *Outside the Subject*. Translated by Michael Smith. Stanford, CA: Stanford University Press, 1994.

———. "Substitution." In *Basic Philosophical Writings*. Edited by Adriaan T. Peperzak, Simon Critchley, and Robert Bernasconi. Bloomington: Indiana University Press, 1996.

———. *Theory of Intuition in Husserl's Phenomenology*. Translated by André-Orianne. Evanston, IL: Northwestern University Press, 1995.

———. *Time and the Other*. Translated by Richard Cohen. Pittsburgh: Duquesne University Press, 1987.

———. *Totality and Infinity*. Translated by Alphonso Lingis. Pittsburgh: Duquesne University Press, 1969.

Lindblad, Ulricka Margareta. "Rereading Edith Stein: What Happened?" *Theology* 99, 1996: 269–276.

Linssen, Michael. "Arbeitsbericht über die Edition der Werke Edith Steins durch das 'Archivum Carmelitanum Edith Stein'" [Working Report Concerning the Work of Edith Stein Published through the Edith Stein Carmelite Archive]. In *Edith Stein: Leben, Philosophie, Vollendung; Abhandlungen des internationalen*. Edith Stein Symposium, Würzburg, November 2–4, 1990. Edited by Leo Elders. Würzburg: Naumann, 1991.

———. "Das Archivum Carmelitanum Edith Stein" [From the Edith Stein Carmelite Archive]. *Edith-Stein-Jahrbuch V*. Würzburg: Echter, 1999.

Locke, John. *An Essay Concerning Human Understanding*. Indianapolis: Hackett Publishing, 1980.

Loyola, Saint Ignatius. *The Spiritual Exercises*. Edited by David Fleming. St. Louis, MI: Institute of Jesuit Sources, 1989.

Luft, Sebastian. *Subjectivity and Lifeworld in Transcendental Phenomenology.* Evanston, IL: Northwestern University Press, 2011.

Lynch S. J., William F. *Images of Hope: Imagination as Healer of the Hopeless.* Notre Dame, IN: University of Notre Dame Press, 1974.

Lyotard, Jean-Francois. *Phenomenology.* Translated by Brian Beakley. Albany: State University of New York Press, 1991.

MacIntyre, Alasdair. *Edith Stein: A Philosophical Prologue, 1913–1922.* New York: Rowman and Littlefield, 2007.

Madison, Gary. "Phenomenology and Existentialism: Husserl and the End of Idealism." In *Husserl: Expositions and Appraisals.* Edited by Frederick Elliston and Peter McCormick. Notre Dame, IN: University of Notre Dame Press, 1977: 247–268.

Makkreel, Rudolf. "How Is Empathy Related to Understanding?" In *Issues in Husserl's Ideas II.* Edited by Thomas Nenon and Lester Embree. Dordrecht: Kluwer Academic Publishers, 1992: 199–212.

Marcel, Gabriel. *Creative Fidelity.* Translated by Robert Rosthal. New York: Crossroad Publishing, 1982.

Marini, A. "Edith Stein e il 'monogramma interiore' di Husserl" [Edith Stein and the "Interior Voice/Monogram" of Husserl"]. In *Per la Fenomenologia della Coscienza Interna del Tempo.* Milan: F. Angeli Editore, 1985.

Marion, Jean-Luc. "Sketch of a Phenomenological Concept of Gift." In *Postmodern Philosophy and Christian Thought,* edited by Merold Westphal. Indianapolis: Indiana University Press, 1999.

Marshall, Barbara. *Engendering Modernity: Feminism, Social Theory and Social Change.* Boston: Northeastern University Press, 1994.

McKenna, William R. *Husserl's "Introductions to Phenomenology:" Interpretation and Critique,* Phaenomenologica Series 89. Dordrecht: Springer, 1982.

Merleau-Ponty, Maurice. *Phenomenology of Perception.* London: Routledge, 1962.

———. *The Visible and the Invisible.* Translated by Alfonso Lingis. Evanston, IL: Northwestern University Press, 1968.

———. "What Is Phenomenology?" *Phenomenology: The Philosophy of Edmund Husserl and Its Interpretations.* Edited by Joseph Kockelmans. Garden City, NY: Doubleday, 1967.

Metzger. "Correspondence between Husserl and Metzger." *The Human Context: Man and His World.* London: Chaucer Publishing, 1972.

Mohanty, J. N. "Consciousness and Existence: Remarks on the Relation Between Husserl and Heidegger." *Man and World* 11, 1978: 324–335.

———. *Edmund Husserl's Freiburg Years: 1916–1938.* New Haven, CT: Yale University Press, 2011.

———. "Husserl on Relativism in the Late Manuscripts." In *Husserl in Contemporary Context.* Edited by Burt Hopkins. Dordrecht: Kluwer Academic Publishers, 1997.

———. "Husserl's Theory of Meaning." In *Husserl: Expositions and Appraisals*. Edited by Frederick Elliston and Peter McCormick. Notre Dame, IN: University of Notre Dame Press, 1977: 18–37.

———. "Husserl's Transcendental Phenomenology and Essentialism." In *Review of Metaphysics* 32, no. 2, 1978: 299–321.

———. *Phenomenology: Between Essentialism and Transcendental Philosophy*. Evanston, IL: Northwestern University Press, 1997.

Moran, Dermot. "Immanence, Self-Experience, and Transcendence in Edmund Husserl, Edith Stein, and Karl Jaspers." *American Catholic Philosophical Quarterly* 82, no. 2, 2008: 265–291.

———. "The Problem of Empathy: Lipps, Scheler, Husserl and Stein." In *Amor Amicitiae: On the Love That Is Friendship; Essays in Medieval Thought and Beyond, in Honor of the Rev. Professor James McEvoy*, edited by Kelly Thomas and Phillip Rosemann. Leuven: David Brown Book Company, 2004: 269–312.

Murray, Michael. "Against Dialogue." In Langsdorf, *Reinterpreting the Political: Continental Philosophy and Political Theory*.

Natanson, Maurice. *Edmund Husserl: Philosopher of Infinite Tasks*. Evanston, IL: Northwestern University Press, 1973.

———. *The Journeying Self: A Study in Philosophy and Social Role*. Reading, MA: Addison-Wesley Press, 1970.

Neyer, Maria Amata. *Edith Stein: Ihr Leben in Dokumenten und Bildern*. Würzburg: Echter, 1990. Translated by Waltraut Stein as *Edith Stein: Her Life in Photos and Documents* (Washington, DC: ICS Publications, 1999).

Noddings, Nel. *Caring: A Feminine Approach to Ethics and Moral Education*. Berkeley: University of California Press, 1984.

Nota, John [Jan] H. "Edith Stein by One Who Knew Her." *Mount Carmel* 46, no. 2, 1998: 4–13.

———. "Edith Stein, Max Scheler, Martin Heidegger." In *Edith Stein: Leben, Philosophie, Vollendung: Abhandlungen des internationalen*. Edited by Leo Elders. Würzburg: Naumann, 1991: 227–236.

———. "Edith Stein and Martin Heidegger." In *Edith Stein Symposium* (Carmelite Studies 4). Edited by John Sullivan. Washington, DC: ICS Publications, 1987: 50–73.

Oben, Freda M. *Edith Stein: Scholar-Feminist-Saint*. Staten Island, NY: Alba House, 1988.

———. "Edith Stein the Woman." From *Edith Stein Symposium*. (Carmelite Studies 4). Edited by John Sullivan. Washington, DC: ICS Publications, 1987: 3–33.

Ogletree, Thomas W. *Hospitality to the Stranger: Dimensions of Moral Understanding*. Philadelphia: Fortress Press, 1985.

Ott, Hugo. "Edith Stein and Freiburg." Translated by Susanne Batzdorff. In *Never Forget: Christian and Jewish Perspectives on Edith Stein*. Carmelite Studies

7. Edited by Waltraud Herbstrith. Washington, DC: ICS Publications, 1998: 135–138.

———. "Die Randnotizen Martin Honeckers zur Habilitationsschrift 'Potenz und Akt'" [Martin Honeckers's Notes on Stein's Habilitation "Potency and Act"]. In *Studien zur Philosophie von Edith Stein*, from Internationales Edith-Stein Symposium Eichstätt, 1991. Freiburg: Albert, 1993: 140–146.

Otto, Rudolf. *The Idea of the Holy: An Inquiry into the Non-Rational Factor in the Idea of the Divine and its Relation to the Rational*. Translated by John Harvey. London: Oxford University Press, 1958.

Petersen, Michele Keuter. *A Hermeneutics of Contemplative Silence: Paul Ricoeur, Edith Stein, and the Heart of Meaning*. Lanham, MD: Lexington Books, 2021.

Pezzella, Anna Maria. *Edith Stein Fenomenologa* [Edith Stein's Phenomenology]. Rome: Pontificia Università Lateranense, 1995. Also published as "Edith Stein Fenomenologa," *Aquinas* 37, no. 2, 1994: 353–376.

———. *L'antropologia Filosofica di Edith Stein*. Rome: Citta Nuovo Editrice, 2003.

Pietersma, Henry. "Husserl's Views on the Evident and the True." In *Husserl: Expositions and Appraisals*. Edited by Frederick Elliston and Peter McCormick. Notre Dame, IN: University of Notre Dame Press, 1977: 38–53.

Posselt, Teresia Renata. *Edith Stein*. Translated by C. Hastings and Donald Nicholl. London: Sheed and Ward Publishers, 1952.

Przywara, Erich and Leroux, Henri. "Edith Stein et Simone Weil: Essentialism et existentialisme analogie." In *Les Études Philosophiques* 11. Paris: Presses Universitaires de France, 1956: 458–472.

Reinach, Adolf and Conrad-Martius, Hedwig. "Über Phänomenologie." In *Anthologie der Realistischen Phänomenologie*. Originally published in 1956. Edited by Josef Seifert and Cheikh Mbacké Gueye. Frankfurt: Ontos Verlag, 2009.

Ricoeur, Paul. *Husserl: An Analysis of His Phenomenology*. Evanston, IL: Northwestern University Press, 1967.

Ryan, Francis. *The Body as Symbol*. Washington, DC: Corpus Books, 1970.

Santes, Urbano. "The Hermeneutical Derivation of Phenomenology." In *Husserl's Legacy in Phenomenological Philosophies: New Approaches to Reason, Language, Hermeneutics, the Human Condition: Analecta Husserliana* 36, no. 3. Edited by Anna-Maria Tymieniecka. Dordrecht: Springer, 1991: 83–91.

Sartre, Jean-Paul. *The Transcendence of the Ego*. New York: Noonday Press, 1957.

Sawicki, Marianne. *Body, Text and Science: The Literacy of Investigative Practices and the Phenomenology of Edith Stein*. Dordrecht: Kluwer, 1997.

———. "Edith Stein's Philosophy of Psychology and the Humanities: The Jahrbuch Treatises of 1922." In *Eighteenth Annual Symposium of the Simon Silverman Phenomenology Center*. Edited by Daniel Martino. Pittsburgh: Duquesne University Press, 2001: 69–92.

Scheler, Max. *The Nature of Sympathy*. Hamden, CT: Archon Books, 1973.

———. *On Feeling, Knowing, and Valuing*. Chicago: University of Chicago Press, 1992.

Schmidtt, Richard. "Husserl's Transcendental-Phenomenological Reduction." *Phenomenology: The Philosophy of Edmund Husserl and Its Interpretation*. Edited by Joseph Kockelmans. Garden City, NY: Doubleday, 1967: 58–68.

Schulz, Peter. "Il concetto di coscienza nella fenomenologia di Edmund Husserl e di Edith Stein" [The Concept of Consciousness in the Phenomenology of Husserl and Stein]. Translated by Anna Maria Pezzella. *Aquinas* 39, no. 2, 1996.

Schutz, Alfred. *Collected Papers Vol. I: The Problem of Social Reality*. Edited by Maurice Natanson. The Hague: Martinus Nijhoff, 1962.

Secretan, Philibert. "Essence et personne: Contribution a la connaissance d'Edith Stein" [Essence and Person: Contributions to the Understanding of Edith Stein]. *Freiburger Zeitschrift für Philosophie und Theologie* 26, 1979: 481–504.

———. "Individuum, Individualität und Individuation nach Edith Stein und Wilhelm Dilthey" [The Individual, Individuality, and Individuation According to Stein and Dilthey]. In *Studien zur Philosophie von Edith Stein*, from Internationales Edith-Stein Symposium Eichstätt, 1991. Freiburg: Alber Press, 1993: 148–169.

———. "Personne, individu et responsibilité chez Edith Stein" [Person, Individual and Responsibility according to Edith Stein]. In *The Crisis of Culture: Analecta Husserlian V*. Edited by Anna-Teresa Tymieniecka. Dordrecht: Reidel, 1976: 247–258.

———. "The Self and the Other in the Thought of Edith Stein." In *Analecta Husserliana VI: The Self and the Other: The Irreducible Element in Man*. Edited by Anna-Teresa Tymieniecka. Dordrecht: Reidel, 1977: 87–98.

Shakespeare, William. *Hamlet*. Edited by Barbara Mowat and Paul Werstine. New York: Simon & Schuster, 2012.

Smith, Arthur David. *Routledge Philosophy Guidebook to Husserl and the Cartesian Meditations*. London: Routledge, 2003.

Sokolowski, Robert. *Husserlian Meditations*. Evanston, IL: Northwestern University Press, 1973.

———. *Presence and Absence*. Bloomington: Indiana University Press, 1978.

Spence, Jonathan. *The Memory Palace of Matteo Ricci*. New York: Penguin Books, 1984.

Spiegelberg, Herbert. *The Phenomenological Movement: A Historical Introduction, Volume One*, second edition. The Hague: Martinus Nijhoff, 1969.

———. *The Phenomenological Movement, Volume Two*. The Hague: Martinus Nijhoff, 1969.

Spinelli, Nicola. "Husserlian Essentialism." *Human Studies: A Journal for Philosophy and the Social Sciences* 37, no. 2, 2021: 147–168.

Stein, Edith. *Essays on Woman: Second Revised Edition*. Translated by Freda Mary Oben. *The Collected Works of Edith Stein: Volume II*. Washington, DC: ICS Publications, 1996.

---. "Husserl and Aquinas: A Comparison." In *Knowledge and Faith*. Translated by Walter Redmond. *The Collected Works of Edith Stein: Volume VIII*, 1–64. Washington, DC: ICS Publications, 1986.

---. *Life in a Jewish Family (1891–1916): An Autobiography*. Translated by Josephine Koeppel. *The Collected Works of Edith Stein: Volume I*. Washington, DC: ICS Publications, 1986.

---. *On the Problem of Empathy*. Translated by Waltraud Stein. *The Collected Works of Edith Stein: Volume III*. Washington, DC: ICS Publications, 1989.

---. *Philosophy of Psychology and the Humanities*. Translated by Mary Catharine Baseheart and Marianne Sawicki. *The Collected Works of Edith Stein: Volume VII*. Washington, DC: ICS Publications, 2000.

---. *Self-Portrait in Letters: 1916–1942*. Translated by Josephine Koeppel. *The Collected Works of Edith Stein: Volume V*. Washington, DC: ICS Publications, 1993.

---. "Ways to Know God: The 'Symbolic Theology' of Dionysius the Areopagite and Its Objective Presuppositions." In *Knowledge and Faith*.

---. *Woman*. Translated by Freda Mary Oben. *The Collected Works of Edith Stein: Volume II* (second edition). Washington, DC: ICS Publications, 1996.

Steinbock, Anthony. *Home and Beyond: Generative Phenomenology After Husserl*. Evanston, IL: Northwestern University Press, 1995.

Ströker, Elizabeth. *Husserl's Transcendental Philosophy*. Translated by Lee Hardy. Stanford, CA: Stanford University Press, 1993.

Sweeney, Robert. "Phenomenology and Hermeneutics," in *Husserl's Legacy in Phenomenological Philosophies: New Approaches to Reason, Language, Hermeneutics, the Human Condition: Analecta Husserliana 36, no. 3*. Edited by Anna-Maria Tymieniecka. Dordrecht: Springer, 1991: 17–22.

Szanto, Thomas. "Collective Emotions, Normativity, and Empathy: A Steinian Account." *Human Studies: A Journal for Philosophy and the Social Sciences* 38, no. 4. Dordrecht: Springer Nature Press, 2015: 503–527.

Szanto, Thomas and Moran, Dermot. "Introduction: Empathy and Collective Intentionality: The Social Philosophy of Edith Stein." In *Human Studies: A Journal for Philosophy and the Social Sciences* 38, no. 4. Dordrecht: Springer Nature Press, 2015: 445–461.

---. Editors. *Phenomenology of Sociality: Discovering the "We."* London: Routledge, 2016.

Taipale, J. "Empathy and the Melodic Unity of the Other." *Human Studies: A Journal for Philosophy and the Social Sciences* 38, no. 4. Dordrecht: Springer Nature Press, 2015: 463–479.

Taylor, Charles. "Responsibility for Self." In *The Identities of Person*. Edited by A. O. Rorty. Berkeley: University of California Press, 1976.

Theunissen, Michael. *The Other: Studies in the Social Ontology of Husserl, Heidegger, Sartre, and Buber*. Cambridge, MA: MIT Press, 1984.

Tilliette, Xavier. "Edith Stein." In *Études* 369. Paris, 1988: 347–358.
———. "Edith Stein et la philosophie chrétienne: À propos d'Être fini et Être eternel" [Edith Stein and Christian Philosophy: From Finite Being to Eternal Being]. *Gregorianum* 71, 1990: 97–113.
———. "La filosofia Cristiana di Edith Stein." *Aquinas* 32, 1989: 131–137.
———. "La filosofia cristiana secondo Edith Stein." *Aquinas* 37, no. 2, 1994: 389–394.
Trizio, Emiliano. "Husserl's Early Concept of Metaphysics as the Ultimate Science of Reality." In *The New Yearbook for Phenomenology and Phenomenological Philosophy* 17. Edited by Timothy Burns, Thomas Szanto, Alessndro Salice, Maxime Doyon, and Augustin Dumont. London: Routledge, 2019. Previously published in *Phainomenon* 26, 2017: 37–68.
Tullius, William. "Person in Community, Repentance, and Historical Meaning: From an Individual to a Social Ethics in Stein's Early Phenomenological Treatises." In *Ethics and Metaphysics in the Philosophy of Edith Stein*. Edited by Michael F. Andrews and Antonio Calcagno. Cham, Switzerland: Springer Press, 2022: 73–87.
Urban, Petr. "Care Ethics and the Feminine Personalism of Edith Stein" [https://doi.org/10.3390/philosophies7030060], *Philosophies* 2022, 7, 60. Edited by Maurice Hamington and Maggie FitzGerald. Basel, Switzerland: Open Commons Attribution, 2022: 1–14.
———. "Edith Stein's Phenomenology of Woman's Personality and Value." In *Alles Wesentliche Lässt Sich Nicht Schreiben: Leben und Denken Edith Steins im Spiegel Ihres Gesamtwerks*. Edited by Stephan Regh and Andreas Speer. Freiburg im Breisgau, Germany: Verlag Herder, 2016: 538–555.
Varela, Francisco, Evan Thompson, and Eleanor Rosch. *The Embodied Mind: Cognitive Science and Human Experience*. Cambridge, MA: MIT Press, 1991.
Vendrell Ferran, Ingrid. "Empathy, Emotional Sharing, and Feelings in Stein's Early Work." *Human Studies: A Journal for Philosophy and the Social Sciences* 38, no. 4, 2015: 481–502.
Verduci, Daniela. "Il Valore della vita come di senso nella post-modernità: Max Scheler, Edith Stein, Anna-Maria Tymieniecka." In *Fenomenologia della vita: Senso, Valore, Cura*. Lanciano, IT: Caralla Press, 2022: 175–197.
———. "Life and Human Life in Max Scheler: Phenomenological Problems of Identification and Individualization." In *Life: The Outburst of Life in the Human Sphere; Phenomenology of Life and the Sciences of Life. Book 2: Analecta Husserliana LX*. Edited by Anna-Teresa Tymieniecka. Dordrecht: Kluwer Academic Publishers, 1999: 71–92.
Vetlesen, Arne Johan. *Perception, Empathy and Judgment: An Inquiry into the Preconditions of Moral Performance*. University Park: Pennsylvania State University Press, 1994.

Wippel, John F. *The Metaphysical Thought of Thomas Aquinas: From Finite Being to Uncreated Being*. Monographs of the Society for Medieval and Renaissance Philosophy, no. 1. Washington, DC: Catholic University of America Press, 2000.

Wojtyla, Karol (Pope John Paul II). "Apostolic Letter." Reprinted in *Catholic Dossier* 7, no. 6, 2001: 26–31.

Wyschogrod, Edith. *Emmanuel Levinas: The Problem of Ethical Metaphysics*. New York: Fordham University Press, 2000.

Zahavi, Dan. "Empathy, Embodiment and Interpersonal Understanding: From Lipps to Schutz." *Inquiry: An Interdisciplinary Journal of Philosophy* 53, no. 3, 2015: 285–306.

———. *Husserl's Legacy: Phenomenology, Metaphysics, and Transcendental Philosophy*. Oxford: Oxford University Press, 2017.

———. *Husserl's Phenomenology*. Stanford: Stanford University Press, 2003.

———. *Self and Other: Exploring Subjectivity, Empathy, and Shame*. Oxford: Oxford University Press, 2014.

———. *Subjectivity and Selfhood: Investigating the First-Person Perspective*. Cambridge, MA: MIT Press, 2006.

———. "The Three Concepts of Consciousness in *Logische Untersuchungen*." *Husserl Studies* 18, no. 1, 2002: 51-64.

———. "You, Me, and We: The Sharing of Emotional Experiences." *Journal of Consciousness Studies* 22. Copenhagen: University of Copenhagen, 2015: 84–101.

Zhok, Andrea. "The Ontological Status of Essences in Husserl's Thought." In *The New Yearbook for Phenomenology and Phenomenological Philosophy* 11. Edited by Burt Hopkins and John Drummond. London: Routledge Press, 2012: 96–127.

Index

adequatio, 11; *adequation rei et intellectus*, 276. See also Aquinas, St. Thomas

adequation, 20, 35, 196, 229

affectivity, 8, 15, 102, 129, 145, 147, 150, 175, 194, 201, 248, 251, 253, 254, 257, 258, 263, 270, 273, 295n8, 296n12, 297n14, 310

alimentation, 205–208. See also *il y a*

alter ego, 7, 37–41, 44–63, 79–83, 88, 91, 97, 103, 106, 114–116, 123, 125, 128, 130–131, 150, 152, 156, 170–171, 178, 190–192, 199, 226, 231, 233, 235–236, 247, 253, 256, 258, 273, 276–277, 285n17, 287n45, 289n20, 290n26, 307n5. See also ego; transcendental ego

alterity, 2, 3, 6, 9–12, 15–18, 37–39, 42, 44, 46–47, 53–54, 57, 63–64, 77, 83, 85–88, 96, 103, 105, 119, 128–130, 135, 146, 152, 169–172, 179, 190–214 passim, 219–235 passim, 239–244, 249–264, 269–272, 277, 290n32, 291n36, 296n12, 297n13, 312n2; absolute alterity, 211, 226, 231; infinite alterity, 190, 197, 199, 201, 222, 228, 231; radical alterity, 10, 17, 88, 169, 171, 192, 203, 205, 209, 214, 221, 228–233, 240–244, 249, 251, 254–258, 261, 264, 269, 272, 277

analogical apperception, 7, 48–51, 81, 84, 88, 118–121, 128, 131, 156, 185, 187, 198, 201, 218, 233, 303n52, 307n9

analogical appresentation, 51, 56, 158, 178, 180, 231–232

analogical transference, 45, 51, 53, 60–61, 79, 82, 84, 301n34

analogy, 6, 10, 49, 52, 54, 56–57, 61, 85–93 passim, 121–128 passim, 133, 143, 192, 211, 218, 222–223, 226–227, 234–236, 247, 249, 255, 261, 276–277. See also Aquinas, St. Thomas

animate nature, 71–72, 75. See also Nature

antipathy, 10, 217–218, 232, 235–236, 249, 264, 311n1

apeiron, 208

apophatic, 11, 241, 244, 263

apperception, 6–7, 10, 47–55 passim, 59–60, 81, 84–88, 103, 117–123 passim, 128, 131, 136, 139, 156, 158, 185, 187, 190, 198, 201, 218, 229–233, 239, 241, 247, 249, 255, 260, 262, 272, 276, 303n52, 303n54, 307n9 appresentation, 50–53, 56–57, 59, 64, 78, 158, 178, 180, 191, 231–232, 235, 286n32, 294n4

Aquinas, St. Thomas, xi, 276–277, 317n39, 318n40, 318n41, 318n42, 318n45. See also *adequatio*; *adequatio rei et intellectus*; adequation; analogy

arché-violence, 224, 228, 249, 261

asymmetry, 10, 172, 218, 231, 234, 236, 249, 253, 260–261, 264, 275

assimilation, 95, 105, 128, 130, 192, 195, 204, 233, 249. See also economy

authenticity, 117, 183–186

autonomy, 76, 102, 112, 252, 264, 273

bad faith, 188

being qua being, 31; being-with, 139; being-with-others, 126

being-there, 52, 175. See also *Dasein*

Bell, David, 44

Bello, Angela Ales, 89, 280n7, 292n54, 297n19, 312n3, 313n3, 313n7

Biemel, Marly, 168

Biemel, Walter, 118, 281n23

binary, 5, 11, 241, 269–270, 278

body of the other, 5, 7, 52–54, 57, 81, 91, 105, 157, 199, 247. See also embodiment; incarnation; *Körper*; *Lieb*; my body

Bordo, Susan, 267, 316n14, 316n15

Brenner, Rachel, 260, 262, 314n17, 314n18, 314n19, 314n20, 315n22

Brentano, Franz, 15, 276–277, 292n53, 296n8, 317n39

Buber, Martin, 250, 268, 282n27, 286n25, 294n76, 301n35, 310n15, 316n17, 316n19, 317n30

Cairns, Dorian, 163, 306n17

Calcagno, Antonio, 265, 280n7, 287n4, 293n55, 296n10, 296n11, 296n12, 297n18, 297n19, 313n3, 313n4, 313n8, 315n1, 315n3, 315n4, 315n5

Caputo, John D., 219, 311n2, 311n5, 311n7

care, 102, 104–106, 173, 175–176, 181, 183, 187, 197, 200–201, 206, 220, 224, 244, 252, 265–266, 296n12, 302n48, 305n1, 308n14, 308n17, 308n21, 314n8, 314n9, 314n10, 315n2, 315n10, 317n24; ethics of care, 265, 314n10, 315n2, 315n10. See also Gilligan, Carol; Noddings, Nel

Cartesian Meditations, 6–7, 25, 27, 66–67, 76, 85–86, 89, 97, 102, 104, 136, 149, 190, 199, 201, 208, 229–233, 247, 277, 282n34, 284n50, 284n54, 284n1, 289n19, 307n5, 311n17. See also Fifth Cartesian Meditation

Climacus, Johannes, 51. See also secret

cogitationes, 26–27. See also cogito

cogito, 21, 26–27, 70, 141, 151–153, 187, 195, 226, 283n42, 284n3. See also *cogitationes*

cognition, 2, 8, 10–11, 17, 23, 25, 63, 91, 101–102, 104, 111, 113–114, 117, 119, 122, 128–130, 134, 145, 147, 150, 157, 162, 171–172, 186, 188–194 passim, 198, 201, 206, 220, 243, 254–259 passim, 263, 265, 273, 275, 297n14, 300n16, 302n48, 304n6, 304n1

Collins, James, 161, 306n11, 306n12

concrete monad, 27–28, 82, 162, 294n2. See also monad

consciousness, 2, 7, 9, 16, 18–51 passim, 61–62, 66, 69, 71, 74, 76–77, 82, 85–93 passim, 112–121 passim, 125–127, 137–138, 142–143, 145–146, 150–156, 162, 164, 169–171, 176, 186, 191, 193, 196, 199–205,

208, 210, 230–231, 239, 241, 243–244, 247, 249, 255–259, 262, 264, 283, 284n3, 284n5, 285n5, 287n48, 288n12, 289n16, 291n41, 292n48, 295n9, 301n32, 302n40, 304n11, 305n4, 306n18, 313n8, 314n8
consciousness is the body, 74
constitution, 2, 6–11, 15, 20–230 passim, 35, 37, 39, 41, 44, 48–49, 54–97 passim, 101–106, 109, 111–113, 116–117, 119, 121, 123, 128–131, 133, 136, 143, 147, 149–150, 152, 157, 159–161, 169, 171, 174–175, 178–180, 183, 186–191, 193–201, 204–206, 208, 218, 230–232, 239–240, 243, 247–249, 251–260, 263–266, 268–269, 272, 274–275, 277, 281n24, 283n42, 284n54, 285n17, 286n28, 286n32, 289n21, 290n32, 292n55, 293n67, 295n9, 296n10, 298n21, 299n11, 300n20, 301n34, 301n36, 302n40, 303n52, 304n1, 307n5, 307n9, 310n14, 314n13; ego-constitution, 44, 49, 63, 161; transcendental constitution, 6, 7, 10, 13, 20, 23, 101, 105–106, 111, 117, 128, 150, 174, 178–179, 188–189, 231, 248, 254, 281n24, 286n32
contagion, 16, 106, 140–142, 244, 250, 270, 307n11
Costello, Peter, 88–89, 292n50, 293n55, 294n56, 294n57, 295n9, 296n12
cultural sciences, 117. See also *Geist*; *Wissenschaft*
cultural world, 7, 58, 61, 66, 76–78, 82–84, 286n28. See also intermonadic community; public world; spiritual world; we-world; with-world
current of community, 9; current or flow of social life, 159, 254; current of lived experience, 254

das Ich, 26, 127, 129, 131
das Man, 178, 182–183, 187, 310n16
Dasein, 52, 173–188, 200–201, 212, 215, 225, 249, 264, 307n1, 308n13, 308n14, 308n15, 308n17, 308n20, 308n21, 309n23; the "who" of everyday Dasein, 177–178, 180, 182, 186. See also being-there
death, 6, 92–93, 180, 194, 208, 212–215, 299, 310; death and time, 215; being-toward-death, 212–213, 215
deduction, 21–22
Depraz, Natalie, 88, 95, 279n2, 291n36, 292n49
Derrida, Jacques, 3, 10, 16, 18, 22, 67, 84, 94, 170, 217–236, 244, 249, 261–264, 267, 269, 271, 275, 277, 301n31, 310n14, 311n1, 311n2, 311n5, 311n7, 311n10
Descartes, Rene, 24–25, 35, 63–64, 66, 162, 197, 202, 212, 220, 284
Dilthey, William, 134–135, 302n46, 312n2
dissymmetry, 231, 234, 236. See also symmetry
Donohoe, Janet, 86, 96, 282n49, 291n38
duration, 153–154. See also now-point; pure present; temporality

Eckhart, Meister, 221
economy, 78, 103, 210, 211, 228–229, 233–234, 249, 318n39; economy of sameness, 78, 103; economy of reciprocity, 210; economy of words, 211; economy of violence, 228; pure economy, 228–229; metaphysics is economy, 229; totalizing economy, 233, 249. See also assimilation
ego, 7, 11, 17, 25–63, 69–76, 79–92 passim, 96–97, 103–106, 109, 114–123 passim, 126, 128–131, 143, 146, 150, 152, 156–163, 170, 178,

ego *(continued)*
185, 187, 190–200, 204, 207, 221, 226, 230–236, 239–240, 247–253, passim, 256–258, 274, 275–277, 281n15, 282n30, 282n31, 283n46, 284n50, 284n52, 284n2, 285n5, 285n17, 286n27, 287n45, 287n48, 287n1, 289n13, 289n14, 289n20, 290n26, 290n32, 292n49, 296n10, 301n33, 301n34, 301n36, 303n60, 307n5, 309n2, 312n12; Cartesian ego, 28; concrete ego, 26–28, 33, 39, 230, 282n31; living ego, 44; personal ego, 27, 196, 282n30, 284n2. *See also* alter ego; transcendental ego
egocentric, 6, 44
egocentric predicament, 162. *See also* solipsism
eidetic, 10, 24, 29–33 passim, 71–72, 118, 281n9, 282n37
Einfühlung, 3, 7, 9, 66, 68, 77–78, 95, 121, 134, 136, 140, 178, 182, 185, 191, 193, 247–248, 253, 256, 270, 279n4, 294n1, 294n5, 296n10, 304n7, 311n17
Elliston, Frederick, 44–46, 281n12, 282n41, 283n43, 286n24, 302n43
embodiment, 2, 8, 46–48, 58, 105, 147, 149, 155, 157, 159, 161, 164, 176, 230, 254, 264, 281n15, 286n29, 290n34, 302n39, 317n31. *See also* body of the other; incarnation; *Lieb*
emotions, 2, 8–9, 15, 89, 102, 104–105, 109, 112, 149, 175, 188, 248, 251, 259, 262, 264–265, 268, 292n55, 294n5, 295n8, 296n12, 304–305n1
empirical ego, 34, 117, 284n52, 289n14, 301n33
epiphany, 190, 209, 211, 221, 225–226, 311n9. *See also* revelation

epistemology, 2–6 passim, 8–11, 16–17, 24, 29–32, 39, 63–64, 77, 83–89, 101, 103–104, 113, 118–123 passim, 128, 149, 161–162, 210, 217, 226, 240–244, 247–260 passim, 266–268, 273–275, 282n39, 291n35
epoché, 24, 29–31, 39, 117, 141, 190, 202–203, 206, 269
Erleben, 133, 140
Erlebnis, 34, 43, 47–51, 57, 84, 103, 117, 125, 138–139, 146–147, 190, 210, 270, 283
essence, 8, 21–25, 46, 48–49, 53, 71–72, 87, 89–90, 110–111, 120, 135–143 passim, 146, 152, 161, 194, 201–202, 205, 214, 277, 309n5
everydayness, 173–174, 177–178, 180, 183–188 passim, 212, 249, 307n4, 308n17, 310n16
evidence, 26–27, 43, 48, 102, 114, 126, 161, 288n12, 303n4, 309n7; *Evidenz*, 26
excess, 58, 62, 195, 206, 219, 228
experience of a non-experience, 2, 18, 169–170, 205, 255, 263
external perceptions, 51

face of the other, 9–10, 18, 190, 195, 199, 209–211, 221, 227, 255, 266, 268, 272, 310n16. *See also* I-Thou; *tout autre*; wholly other
fellow-feeling, 119–124 passim, 128, 248, 260
field of localization, 73
field of the innumerable, 269
Fifth Cartesian Meditation, 7, 37, 44, 58, 64–65, 86, 88, 91, 130, 282n28, 282n34, 289n19, 300n23. *See also Cartesian Meditations*
Fink, Eugen, 88, 95, 163, 306n15
first body, 48
first intersubjective object, 57

Index | 341

first philosophy, 10, 192, 197, 199–201, 213, 233, 241, 264; ethics is first philosophy, 10, 201, 233
foreign experience, 5, 9–11, 18, 63, 90, 119, 121, 123, 129, 135, 139–152 passim, 159, 163–164, 171, 242, 248, 251, 253–264, 269–271, 277, 278, 312n3
Freiburg, 4, 6, 20, 66–67, 97, 101, 189, 258, 266, 280n6, 280n5, 290n34, 299n7, 304n11, 305n4
Frings, Manfred, 111–112, 115, 119, 126–127, 298n20, 298n2, 300n14, 300n15, 300n17, 300n18, 300n18, 300n24, 300n25, 300n26, 300n27, 302n47, 303n49, 303n54, 303n56, 303n57, 303n58, 303n59
Fuchs, Walter, 22, 83, 115–117, 280n2, 281n16, 281n20, 290n33, 301n30

Gabelsberger, 93–94
Gadamer, Hans Georg, 268–269, 312n2, 317n23, 317n25
Geist, 35, 78, 158, 191; *Geisteswissenschaften*, 20, 76, 178. See also cultural sciences; *Wissenschaft*
gender, 4–5, 8, 103, 242, 247, 251, 266–267, 314n8, 315n6, 317n31
genesis, 1–2, 18, 28, 31, 48, 63, 66, 86–87, 102, 145, 152, 283n46, 289n22; active genesis, 33, 54; genesis of community, 8–9, 265, 296n12, 300n21; passive genesis, 33, 54, 310n14
genetic phenomenology, 19, 28, 33, 46, 97, 143, 283n46, 284n49, 284n50, 285n17, 291n38, 309n2; genetic psychology, 135, 143
Gilligan, Carol, 252, 266, 296n12, 314n9, 314n10, 315n9
Göttingen, 7, 20, 24, 66–67, 101, 108–109, 125, 258, 266, 280n5, 281n15, 283n47, 285n18, 287n45, 292n53, 295n8, 298n5, 299n7, 299n8, 300n20, 305n4
Greek, 19, 29, 205, 300n21; Greek logos, 224; Greek metaphysics, 20, 197, 221, 226; Greek ontology, 218; Greek thinking, 110, 208, 219, 220–225, 228, 236

habitualities, 26–28, 34, 282n31, 283n42
harmonious verification, 49, 54
Hart, James, 152, 291n37, 302n38, 305n2, 305n6, 305n7, 306n9
Heidegger, Martin, xi, 3, 8, 15, 17, 31, 66–67, 84, 93–94, 102, 170, 173–190, 194, 197–201 passim, 206–208, 212, 214–215, 219–220, 224, 240, 244, 249, 267, 282n27, 283n45, 283n48, 286n25, 292n53, 294n77, 301n28, 301n35, 305n3, 307n2, 307n3, 307n6, 307n8, 307n9, 307n10, 307n11, 307n12, 308n15, 308n17, 308n19, 208n20, 308n21, 309n9, 310n14, 310n16, 312n2
Hekman, Susan, 266, 315n6, 315n7, 315n8
Here, 7, 24, 47–48, 51–52, 55–63, 68, 81, 85, 88–90, 175, 181, 191, 294n4. See also There
hermeneutic, 32, 42, 45, 165, 174, 182186, 197, 250–251, 270, 278, 283n49, 306n1, 307n1, 307n3, 312n1, 312n2, 312n3, 313n7; hermeneutical circle, 186, 307n3
history, 26, 31–33, 63, 66, 87, 92, 103, 205, 209, 228, 236, 284n50, 310n13, 311n11, 312n3
horizon, 2, 6, 10, 22, 45, 55, 62, 86, 93, 164, 174, 186, 194, 198, 215, 217–229 passim, 239–240, 249, 276, 284n3

hospitality, 11, 195
Hume, David, 33–34, 223, 302n46
Husserl, Edmund, xi–xii, 2–3, 6–11,
  15–16, 19–97, 101–109, 112–118,
  121, 123, 127–133 passim, 136–137,
  146, 149–164 passim, 174–182
  passim, 185–210 passim, 215,
  218–219, 222, 224, 229–233, 236,
  241, 244, 247–251, 254–263 passim,
  266–267, 270–273, 275–276, 279n2,
  280n7, 280n4, 281n7, 281n9,
  281n15, 281n23, 282n27, 282n28,
  282n29, 282n30, 282n32, 282n34,
  282n36, 282n37, 282n39, 283n43,
  282m46, 283n45, 283n47, 283n48,
  283n49, 284n5, 284n49, 284n52,
  284n53, 284n54, 284n1, 284n4,
  284n5, 285n10, 285n13, 285n17,
  285n18, 286n26, 287n45, 287n1,
  287n4, 287n45, 288n5, 288n9,
  288n10, 288n12, 288n27, 288n29,
  288n29, 288n32, 289n13, 289n14,
  289n15, 289n17, 289n17, 289n19,
  289n21, 289n23, 290n24, 290n34,
  291n35, 291n36, 292n53, 293n70,
  294n3, 294n4, 295n6, 262n11,
  298n21, 299n7, 299n9, 299n10,
  301n31, 301n32, 301n34, 302n40,
  302n43, 303n52, 303n54, 304n5,
  304n11, 304n1, 305n3, 305n4,
  305n5, 307n2, 307n5, 307n9,
  310n11, 310n14, 311n17, 312n1,
  312n2
Husserliana volumes XIII, IV, XV,
  6, 16, 67, 81, 85, 89, 94–97, 136,
  279n2, 290n28, 293n70, 293n71
hypostasis, 204–205, 310n13

I-Thou, 12, 171–172, 218, 240, 244,
  268–269, 272, 303n55, 310n15,
  314n21. See also face of the other;
  tout autre; wholly other
icon, 278, 318n44

id quo, 34
idealism, 15, 19, 30–32, 35, 38, 91,
  101–102, 105–106, 109, 115–118,
  161, 248, 280n5, 282n35, 283n43,
  283n47, 285n18, 293n60, 294n3,
  295n6, 301n33, 302n39, 303n61,
  309n4
Ideas II, 6–7, 16, 65–84, 88, 91, 94,
  96–96, 102, 104, 136, 149, 248,
  284n54, 285n16, 286n28, 286n29,
  288n4, 288n5, 288n7, 288n11,
  289n13, 289n16, 289n19, 290n23m
  293n68, 294n1, 294n4, 296n11,
  297n18, 301n34, 303n51, 304n9,
  314n11
il quod, 34
il y a, 11, 204–205, 208, 310n12. See
  also alimentation
imagination, 54–56, 272, 274, 318n44;
  analogical imagination, 218,
  275–276; imaginative variation, 49,
  55, 61, 86, 164, 230, 260, 270–271,
  316n13; sympathetic imagination, 91
impossible, 190, 195, 219–222, 228,
  253, 255, 271–272
inauthenticity, 179, 184–185, 187, 244,
  249, 307n4, 307n11, 308n20
incarnation, 48, 291n36, 291n42,
  292n49, 292n52. See also body of
  the other; embodiment
induction, 21, 110
in-feeling, 3, 121, 134
infinity, 10, 18, 20, 35, 85, 196–199,
  201, 203, 207–212, 215, 2017–218,
  220, 222–232 passim, 242, 249,
  271–272, 277–278, 293n67, 309n9,
  309n10, 310n15, 311n3, 311n11;
  false infinity, 20, 35, 227–229
Ingarden, Roman, 2, 8, 91, 101,
  109, 118, 135, 189, 240, 283n47,
  286n18, 292n53, 293n60, 293n61,
  294n3, 299n8, 301n28, 303n3,
  304n6

inner experience, 77–78
inner perception, 127, 140, 142–143, 145, 159
inter-monadic community, 59. See also cultural world; public world; spiritual world; we-world; with-world
internal time consciousness, 7, 60, 230, 304. See also temporality
intersubjectivity, 1–3, 5–6, 16, 18, 37–38, 45, 55, 58–59, 63, 65–58, 83, 85–86, 89, 92–97, 103–104, 117, 126–127, 136, 147, 149, 161, 175, 194, 199, 201, 209, 240, 242, 244, 247–248, 258, 264, 273, 283n49, 284n50, 287n39, 287n46, 287n2, 291n38, 293n55, 293n70, 293n72, 296n11
intuition, 21–24, 47, 71, 73, 84, 89, 91, 110–111, 114, 143, 145, 218, 257, 281n9, 281n15, 281n22
Irigaray, Luce, 309n9

James, William, 151

Kant, Immanuel, xi, 22–23, 34–35, 38, 56, 110–112, 118, 288n9, 302n46, 307n6
Kearney, Richard, 278, 318n44
Kern, Iso, 21, 95–96, 293n70
Kierkegaard, Sören, xi, 180, 186, 253, 269, 308n19, 311n1
Kockelmans, Joseph, 193, 281n7, 281n17, 282n35, 286n19, 287n39, 287n2, 309n4
Körper, 7, 47, 52–54, 57, 69, 71, 73–74, 81, 191, 286n28, 289n15. See also body of the other; my body; physical body

Landgrebe, Ludwig, 68, 95
language, 106, 146, 150, 154, 157, 164–165, 169, 184, 195, 204–206, 209–211, 217, 219–225, 227, 228–229, 232–233, 236, 242, 249, 261, 265, 268–269, 271, 287n48, 309n22, 310n14, 311n11, 313n7, 318n37
Lauer, Quentin, 55, 60, 287n39, 287n46, 287n2, 287n3, 288n12
law of association, 31, 33, 49, 54
Lawson, Leonard, 88
Lebech, Mette, 251, 312n1, 313n6
Leibniz, Gottfried Wilhem, 28, 32282n29
Levinas, Emmanuel, 3, 6, 9–11, 15, 18, 24, 56, 63, 67, 84, 93–94, 102, 106, 170, 189–236, 244, 249–250, 253, 255, 260–267 passim, 272, 274–277, 280n4, 284n15, 285n10, 288n39, 290n24, 293n67, 297n13, 298n21, 298n1, 301n28, 305n3, 309n7, 309n10, 310n11, 310n12, 310n13, 310n14, 310n15, 310n16, 311n17, 311n6, 311n9, 311n11, 314n21, 315n11
Lieb, 54, 71, 73. See also live body; living body
lifeworld, 8, 18, 60–61, 66, 79, 87–88, 95, 97, 149, 173, 189, 258, 266, 290n34, 296n10, 296n12
Lipps, Hans, 109, 292n53, 299n8, 303n3
Lipps, Theodore, 3, 122, 125, 134–137, 140, 144, 146, 255, 257, 279n4, 290n29, 290n34, 292n53, 303n53, 304n7, 304n8
live body, 53, 81, 88, 157, 247, 253. See also *Lieb*; living body; embodiment
living body, 7, 44, 48, 53, 55, 71, 74, 79, 81, 154–159, 164, 199–200, 230, 262. See also *Lieb*; living body; embodiment
localization, 47–48, 72–74, 81
Locke, John, 162, 302n46, 306n15

Makkreel, Rudolf, 42, 97, 285n16, 293n68, 294n75, 294n76, 294n77, 294n78, 294n4, 304n9, 304n10, 314n11, 314n12, 314n13, 314n14
Marion, Jean-Luc, 206, 272, 317n28, 317n29
Marshall, Barbara, 273
Mead, George Herbert, 33
Merleau-Ponty, Maurice, 15, 94, 125, 164, 254, 281n15, 287n48, 305n3
metaphysics, 21, 180, 195, 200, 211, 217, 221, 223, 225, 227–229, 235–236, 242, 280n2, 280n4, 281n16, 281n20, 284n53, 290n33, 295n6, 301n30, 311n8, 313n3, 313n4, 315n1
Mitfühlung, 121, 304n7; with-feeling, 17, 134
Mohanty, Jintendranath, 23, 97, 118, 281n21, 281n25, 290n27, 290n34, 301n33, 302n45, 302n46
monad, 25–28, 59, 82, 88, 102, 162, 179, 226, 230–231, 262, 267, 282n29, 284n50, 284n2, 296n10; monadological, 7–9, 11, 26–28, 32, 63, 66, 78, 83, 86, 102, 105, 150, 171, 179, 187, 201, 247, 252, 255, 264, 282n34, 290n32; monadology, 48, 62, 65, 76, 117, 119, 179, 181, 248, 267, 270–271, 289n21. *See also* concrete monad
moral reasoning, 266
Moran, Dermot, 81–82, 279n2, 279n3, 280n7, 290n29, 290n30, 295n5, 297n15
Murray, Michael, 268, 271, 316n21, 317n26, 317n27
my body, 46–54 passim, 72–75 passim, 81–82, 144, 159, 190, 192, 254, 289n13, 290n26, 301n34. *See also* body of the other
mysterium tremendum, 170, 213, 241, 255, 263, 296n13. *See also* numinous

Nakhnikian, George, 24
Natanson, Maurice, 23, 39–40, 42, 87, 92, 117, 162, 279n3, 280n1, 280n3, 281n13, 281n14, 281n19, 283n44, 285n6, 285n7, 285n8, 285n9, 285n10, 285n16, 290n31, 291n43, 291n44, 291n47, 293n59, 293n66, 302n37, 306n14
nature, 2, 4, 10, 21–23, 40, 45, 48–49, 52, 58–59, 61, 63, 65, 68–72, 74–77, 86, 101, 109, 112, 118–119, 123, 133, 136, 141, 143, 149, 151, 153, 159, 175, 187, 195, 243–244, 248, 250, 253–254, 267, 276, 294, 296n10, 300n16, 301n34, 303n51, 303n51, 303n61, 303n4, 304n4, 304n7, 312n12, 315n1. *See also* animate nature, 71–72, 75
natural attitude, 87, 106, 140–142, 184, 256, 284n4, 284n5, 285n12
natural sciences, 20–21, 34, 49, 68–69, 72, 76
Noddings, Nel, 265, 314n9, 314n10, 315n2, 315n11, 316n11
noema, 20, 23, 25, 28–32, 35, 41, 45, 70, 91–93, 195–196, 199, 202, 221, 229, 283, 301n32; noematic unity, 91. See also *noemata*
noemata, 28, 30, 35, 202. See also *noema*
noesis, 25, 91–93, 196, 199, 229, 301n32
non-phenomenality, 11, 18, 170–171, 221, 225, 231, 242–243, 251, 255, 263–264, 269–270
non-primordial, 2, 18, 41, 47, 49, 103, 134, 138–139, 142, 144–146, 158, 169, 187, 258, 263, 294n4
now-point, 152, 154. *See also* duration; pure present; temporality
numinous, 210, 264, 296n13. See also *mysterium tremendum*

objectivity, 2, 23, 3–38, 45, 56, 58–62, 68–69, 73, 77–80, 83–84, 117–118, 135, 224, 247, 296n10, 312n1, 316n14
ordo amoris, 112, 117, 244, 248
Otto, Rudolf, 264, 297n13

pairing, 7, 49, 53–55, 61, 81–93 passim, 133, 136, 149, 152, 157, 164, 191, 230, 239, 241, 243, 247, 255–256, 259–261, 263, 270–272, 275–277
personalism, 113, 296n12, 305n1, 314n9, 317n24
phenomenology of empathy, xii, 1–6, 9–12, 16–17, 20, 59–60, 62, 84, 93–94, 103, 105, 135, 169–171, 191, 193, 196, 241–243, 247–248, 250, 260–264 passim, 269, 273–274, 278–279, 286n24, 290n34
philosophical attitude, 20–21
physical body, 47, 74, 158–160, 164. See also body of the other; *Körper*; my body
Plato, xi, 113, 220; platonic, 118, 153, 302
primordial 119, 121, 123, 125, 128–129, 134, 137–139, 141–146 passim, 150, 156, 158, 160, 162, 169, 172, 179, 181–183, 186–191 passim, 195, 197, 199–200, 212, 219, 224, 230, 240, 255, 256–258, 261, 263, 266, 294n4, 297n14, 301n34; primordial experience, 2, 18, 41, 52, 54, 78, 103, 119, 129, 134, 137–139, 144–146, 158, 169, 263, 301n1, 307n12, 309n23, 310n16, 315n11
principle of all principles, 21
projective empathy, 119, 122–124, 127–128
protention, 29, 35, 81, 154, 230
psychic causality, 150
psychologism, 116, 118, 135–136, 150, 247, 288n10, 301n33, 302n40, 302n43, 304n5; psychologistic, 30, 33, 35, 71, 288n10, 302n40, 304n7
public world, 17–18, 59, 63, 170, 184, 249. See also cultural world; inter-monadic community; spiritual world; we-world; with-world
pure present, 203. See also duration; now-point; temporality

quasi-transcendental, 11, 218, 270–271, 311n2

ready-to-hand, 173–176, 181, 308n13, 308n14
realism, 116, 118, 302n40, 315n1
reciprocal solidarity, 11, 265. See also *solidarity*
reciprocity, xii, 6–9, 59, 66, 78, 81, 83, 88–92, 97, 99, 105–106, 192, 210, 215, 227, 244, 247, 249, 260, 264–265, 267–268, 287n45, 295n9
reduction, 7–8, 11, 16, 19–21, 23–28 passim, 39–48, 51, 53, 59, 85–87, 95, 114, 117, 154, 161–163, 190, 202–203, 232, 236, 249, 269, 289n12, 282n34, 282n36, 282n37, 283n42, 285n5, 285n18, 291n35; reduction to the sphere of ownness, 7–8, 42–48, 51, 282n34
regional ontologies, 71
Reinach, Adolf, 2, 8, 109, 189, 283n47, 292n53, 298n5, 298n7, 299n7, 301n28, 303n3
res cogitans, 26, 204, 253
res substantia, 26
retention, 20, 35, 72, 81, 92, 152–154, 230
revelation, xii, 115, 171, 197, 202, 235, 272, 275
Ricoeur, Paul, 43–44, 52, 55, 59, 91, 118, 286n20, 286n21, 286n33, 286n34, 286n37, 286n38, 287n41,

Ricoeur, Paul *(continued)*
287n43, 287n44, 293n63, 301n29, 302n44, 312n2, 313n7
Rojcewicz, Richard, 68
Rosenzweig, Franz, 277

Sartre, Jean-Paul, 94, 188, 282n27, 286n25, 287n47, 294n77, 301n28, 301n35, 305n3, 316n13
Saturation, 205–207
Scheler, Max, 2–3, 8–9, 67, 84, 89, 93–94, 101–133 passim, 136, 139, 150–151, 159, 182, 187, 189, 191, 194, 229, 240, 244, 248–250, 254, 257, 259, 261, 264, 267, 270, 277, 280n7, 283n47, 286n18, 292n53, 293n67, 295n8, 297n14, 298n20, 298n21, 298n3, 298n5, 298n6, 299n10, 299n11, 299n12, 299n13, 300n18, 300n20, 300n22, 301n28, 302n39, 302n46, 302n48, 303n50, 303n51, 303n52, 303n54, 303n55, 303n60, 303n61, 303n3, 303n4, 304n7, 305n1, 305n3, 310n17, 313n7
Schutz, Alfred, 83, 279n3, 280n31, 290n34
secret, 35, 51, 157, 194, 198, 210, 224–226, 228–229, 271–272, 308n21. *See also* Climacus, Johannes
social ontology, 1–2, 9, 11, 15, 67, 89, 92, 92, 96, 149, 170, 209, 240–241, 244, 251, 253–254, 258–259, 262, 279n2, 279n3, 282n27, 286n25, 292n55, 294n77, 295n5m, 301n35, 306n18; ethics as social ontology, 259
solidarity, 11, 90, 105–106, 260–261, 264–266, 274, 313n3. *See also* reciprocal solidarity

solipsism, 9, 26, 32, 39–40, 43, 62, 91, 106, 121, 160–163, 248, 282n26, 283n48, 285n7
solus ipse, 17, 39, 87, 180, 291n35
sphere of ownness, 7–8, 41–53 passim, 56–62, 78, 81, 84, 91, 114, 116, 119–120, 123, 127, 130, 190, 240, 255, 282n34, 289n20, 290n26, 301n36, 305n5
spiritual world, 66, 68, 74–76, 301n34. *See also* cultural world; inter-monadic community; public world; we-world; with-world
static analysis, 32, 35, 45, 48, 62, 284n50, 285n17
Stein, Edith, xi–xii, 2, 3, 6, 8–11, 17, 20, 66–67, 84, 89–90, 93–95, 101–109, 115, 125, 133–165 passim, 174–175, 187–191, 193–194, 196–197, 229, 240, 244–278 passim, 279n1, 280n6, 280n7, 281n15, 283n47, 286n18, 287n45, 287n4, 291n48, 292n53, 294n1, 294n2, 294n3, 294n4, 295n8, 295n9, 296n10, 296n11, 296n12, 297n14, 297n16, 297n17, 297n19, 298n21, 298n4, 298n5, 298n7, 299n7, 299n8, 299n9, 299n10, 299n12, 300n20, 300n28, 301n28, 302n39, 303n51, 303n4, 304n8, 304n11, 304n12, 304n13, 302n1, 305n1, 305n4, 309n2, 310n14, 312n1, 312n2, 312n3, 313n7, 313n8, 314n8, 314n9, 314n13, 314n16, 315n1, 315n10, 315n11, 316n13, 316n20, 317n39
symmetry, 10, 60, 227, 234–235, 249, 259, 266, 271, 275; analogical symmetry, 10, 261; asymmetry, 260; dissymmetry, 231, 234, 236; ethical asymmetry, 10, 172, 234, 236, 249, 253, 261, 264, 271, 275;

ethical symmetry, 218, 236, 259, 261; transcendental symmetry, 10, 217–218, 233–234, 236
sympathy, 3, 109, 118–130 passim, 214, 244, 303n51, 303n61, 303n4, 304n4, 304n7, 310n17, 311n1; reflexive sympathy, 140

temporality, 33, 86, 105, 149, 152–154, 173, 200, 213, 283n42, 300n18, 305n2, 305n6, 306n, 306n9. *See also* duration; internal time consciousness; now-point; pure present
the they, 9, 177–178, 201, 249, 261, 264, 307n4, 307n11, 308n18, 308n19, 310n16
There, 7, 43, 49, 51–53, 55–57, 75, 81, 85, 87–88, 90–91, 119, 131, 185, 187, 190–191, 294n4; Being-there, 52, 175. *See also* Here
Theunissen, Michael, 45, 97, 282n27, 286n25, 286n30, 287n49, 294n77, 301n35
totality, 9–10, 18, 27–28, 69, 74, 83, 109–110, 151, 173–174, 180, 190, 194–195, 201, 214–224 passim, 227–231 passim, 242, 249, 305n, 309n8, 309n10, 310n15
tout autre, 217–218, 242, 277. *See also* face of the Other; I-Thou; wholly other
trace, 10, 18, 22, 170–171, 199, 210, 217–218, 220, 223–224, 227, 235, 243, 253, 264
transcendence, 1–3, 10–12, 15–21 passim, 34, 38–39, 41, 43, 45–46, 50–52, 56–57, 64, 66, 85, 96, 149, 169–172, 193–196, 199–200, 204, 208–209, 219, 221, 227–228, 230–234, 236, 239–240, 242–245, 251, 253, 255–259, 262–266, 269–270, 272, 274–278, 283n43, 284n1, 284n2, 284n5, 291n36, 291n42, 292n49, 292n52; nonappearance of transcendence, 11, 18, 171–172, 243, 257–258; transcendent transcendence, 50
transcendental ego, 7, 26–27, 30, 32, 34–39 passim, 43, 46, 62, 83–84, 97, 106, 109, 115–118, 121, 128–129, 152, 160–163, 240, 248, 258, 281n15, 284n52, 286n27, 289n14, 301n33, 301n34, 301n36. *See also* ego; alter ego
transcendental intersubjectivity, 37, 83, 93–96, 104, 117, 136, 149, 161, 247
transcendental reduction, 16, 19–20, 23, 28–35 passim, 40, 87, 154, 161–163, 283n42

understanding, 1, 3–4, 11, 19–20, 33, 39, 42, 55, 58, 61062, 66, 68–69, 80, 86, 89–90, 93–94, 97, 105, 111, 113, 118–119, 122, 124–125, 145, 150, 155–156, 169, 171, 174, 181–183, 186–187, 192, 221, 223, 240, 248, 250, 261–273 passim, 276, 279n3, 285n16, 290n26, 290n34, 293n68, 294n75, 294n78, 294n4, 296n10, 302n40, 304n9, 305n1, 306n15, 307n3, 308n19, 308n21, 309n23, 312n3, 314n11, 315n1. See also *Verstehen*
Urban, Petr, 270, 296n12, 304n1, 305n1, 314n8, 314n9, 315n10 317n24

Vetlesen, Arne Johan, 271–275, 317n33, 317n34, 317n35, 317n36, 317n37
Verstehen, 42, 257, 307n3. *See also* understanding

via negativa, 221, 263
violence, 192, 194, 196, 198, 211–236 passim, 242, 249, 274, 280n4, 284n53. *See also* arché-violence

we-world, 2, 59, 87, 90, 165, 279n3, 291n48, 306n18, 312n2. *See also* cultural world; inter-monadic community; public world; spiritual world; with-world
wholly other, 10, 18, 194–195, 199, 205, 209, 212, 217–218, 220–236 passim, 240, 249, 253, 255, 257, 264, 266, 277. *See also* face of the other; I-Thou; *tout autre*
with-world, 68, 175, 177–178, 180, 308n13. *See also* cultural world; inter-monadic community; public world; spiritual world; we-world
Wissenschaft, 117. *See also* cultural sciences; *Geist*
Wyschogrod, Edith, 223, 311n8

Zahavi, Dan, 90, 279n2, 292n48, 292n55, 293n58, 295n6, 306n18

www.ingramcontent.com/pod-product-compliance
Lightning Source LLC
Chambersburg PA
CBHW031704230426
43668CB00006B/99